ET   29625

PRINTED PROPAGANDA
UNDER LOUIS XIV

PRINTED PROPAGANDA UNDER LOUIS XIV

Absolute Monarchy and Public Opinion

BY JOSEPH KLAITS

PRINCETON UNIVERSITY PRESS

29625

063564 2

Copyright © 1976 by Princeton University Press
Published by Princeton University Press,
Princeton, New Jersey
In the United Kingdom: Princeton University Press,
Guildford, Surrey

ALL RIGHTS RESERVED

Library of Congress Cataloging in Publication Data
will be found on the last printed page of this book

Publication of this book has been aided by
The Andrew W. Mellon Foundation

Printed in the United States of America
by Princeton University Press,
Princeton, New Jersey

29625

FOR MY PARENTS

CONTENTS

CONTENTS

29625

PREFACE

THIS book seeks to integrate a pair of related themes: the political-diplomatic history of Louis XIV's reign and the role of print in the second half of the seventeenth century. My hope is to contribute to two active areas of historical scholarship. First is the renewed—or perhaps simply new—interest in the last part of the reign of Louis XIV, a concern spurred by the recent revisionist syntheses of John B. Wolf and Lionel Rothkrug, authors who, for different reasons, stress the significance of the long twilight that closed the Sun King's reign. Second is the problem of the sociology of the book, which in recent years has become a leading theme in the historiography of early modern Europe. The stimulating articles by Elizabeth L. Eisenstein and Robert Darnton and, for seventeenth-century France, the remarkable work of Robert Mandrou and Henri-Jean Martin have helped to kindle interest in such topics as censorship, clandestine pamphleteering, and the origins of the periodical press, all central themes of this monograph.

During the years this book has been in preparation, my research has been supported by generous fellowship and grant support which I am pleased to acknowledge here. A Fulbright-Hays fellowship and awards from the University of Minnesota helped subsidize fourteen eventful months of dissertation research in Paris during 1967 and 1968. A summer fellowship from Oakland University permitted a return to Paris in 1971 for research that led to significant broadening of the manuscript. Finally, a research fellowship at the Folger Shakespeare Library in 1974 enabled me to complete the writing under ideal working conditions.

No American who has written a book on French history can fail to have accumulated a long list of institutional debts

ix

on two continents. A glance at this book's bibliography will indicate the extent of my obligations to the staffs of the Archives Nationales in the Hôtel Soubise, the Archives des Affaires étrangères on the quai d'Orsay, the Archives du Ministère de Guerre at Vincennes, the Bibliothèque de l'Arsenal, and the Bibliothèque Nationale's departments of Imprimés and Manuscrits. Less obvious are debts to a number of libraries in the United States for granting access to numerous rare printed works, among them many which I could not locate in France. These are the Library of Congress, the Folger Library, the libraries of Columbia University, Princeton University, Stanford University, the University of California at Berkeley, the University of Michigan, and the University of Minnesota.

A shortened version of chapter 2 appeared in the *Proceedings of the Second Conference of the Western Society for French History* with the title "Censorship Under Louis XIV." Several paragraphs have been reproduced from my article, "Men of Letters and Political Reform in France at the End of the Reign of Louis XIV: The Founding of the Académie Politique," *Journal of Modern History*, 43:4 (1971), 577–597.

At different times many people read or listened to parts of this book and were kind enough to offer suggestions. I wish to thank in particular Paul W. Bamford, Richard M. Brace, William F. Church, Georges Dethan, Elizabeth L. Eisenstein, Ragnhild Hatton, Robert M. Kingdon, Philip A. Knachel, B. Robert Kreiser, George T. Matthews, John C. Rule and Howard M. Solomon. Thanks also to Donald Bailey, Richard Bingham and Richard Jackson, each of whom took time from his own research in Paris to check a stray source, thus sparing me the transatlantic scholar's endemic dismay over the missing citation.

With appropriate symmetry, John B. Wolf, under whose direction at the University of Minnesota this book began, also oversaw the final draft's composition in a seminar at the Folger Library. In the years between, his suggestions and encouragement continually rekindled my enthusiasm. He has my deepest thanks, as does Orest Ranum, who ever since undergraduate days has been generous with his time, with good advice, and with warm support.

I am delighted to acknowledge the singular professional help and personal concern of Marian Wilson, editorial adviser in the College of Arts and Sciences, Oakland University. Among numerous other services, she unraveled my chronically messy syntax, introduced some order into the anarchy of the footnotes, and delivered my translations from the English equivalent of *franglais* which was their original condition. As many others have discovered, producing a manuscript with her is both education and pleasure for an author.

My greatest thanks are to my wife, Barrie, who contributed her many talents at every stage. Without her this project never would have progressed to print.

Waterford, Michigan
Thanksgiving 1975

Reading proof gives me a welcome opportunity to thank the members of the seminar on popular culture of the Davis Center for Historical Studies at Princeton University for the careful criticism they gave parts of this book in February 1976. In particular, Lawrence Stone, Roger Chartier, Robert Darnton, Ralph Giesey, Robert Forster, Theodore K. Rabb and Herbert Rowen were most helpful in pinpointing problems and suggesting alternate formulations; I want to acknowledge their assistance even if most of their excellent ideas must await the occasion of another book or, more likely, the skills of another writer. Plainly these people and the others named above have contributed only to the book's strengths; the author alone is responsible for its weaknesses. Finally I would like to express my appreciation to Lewis Bateman of Princeton University Press for his exacting and sympathetic editorship.

J. K.

THE following abbreviations are employed in the notes:

AAE   Archives du Ministère des Affaires étrangères, Paris
      CP = Correspondance Politique
      MD = Mémoires et Documents
AG   Archives du Ministère de Guerre, Vincennes
AN   Archives Nationales, Paris
BA   Bibliothèque de l'Arsenal, Paris
BN   Bibliothèque Nationale, Paris
      Imp. = Département des Imprimés
      Ms. fr. = Manuscrits français
      N.a.fr. = Nouvelles acquisitions françaises

PRINTED PROPAGANDA
UNDER LOUIS XIV

CHAPTER ONE

The Nature of Early Modern Propaganda

MONARCHY AND THE ADVENT OF PRINT

PROPAGANDA is as old as rulership and as novel as twentieth-century technology. Today propaganda calls to mind the instruments of mass communication and socialization: radio, television, film, large-circulation newspapers, and compulsory public education. Without these tools the modern propagandist is unimaginable; with them, he can reach and hope to manipulate virtually every member of an advanced industrial society. Yet the lineage of propaganda can be traced back at least to the emperors of ancient Rome, whose coins, commemorative arches, and other forms of display demonstrate that in antiquity awesome magnificence was a necessary part of governance. In medieval Europe impressive ceremonial continued to be a symbolic representation of princely power, and often, as in the rite of coronation and the ritual of the king's touch, these ceremonies served to lift the monarch to the threshold of the supernatural. Ritual and display, then, are ancient elements in the psychology of authority.

To be sure, the audience for premodern propaganda was not only comparatively small by current standards, but also comprised a much more limited segment of the total population; before the advent of mass states the "political nation" was a larger or smaller elite.[1] It would nevertheless be a serious mistake to assume that the definition and character of

---

[1] See Melvin Small, "Historians Look at Public Opinion," in *Public Opinion and Historians, Interdisciplinary Perspectives*, ed. Melvin Small (Detroit, 1970), p. 14.

the "public" remained fixed from ancient times to the nineteenth century. During this long period there were important transformations in the audience for and hence in the nature and purposes of propaganda. For example, the two great church-state confrontations of the high Middle Ages—the so-called investiture controversy of the eleventh century, and the conflict two hundred years later between Pope Boniface VIII and Philip the Fair of France—each evoked a distinctive brand of polemic. The tracts of the Gregorian reform were Latin manuscripts directed at clerics and monks almost exclusively. But by the thirteenth century Philip's councillors issued a barrage of written pieces directed at a nonecclesiastical audience, perhaps as a response to growing lay literacy. For the still illiterate majority, the crown took its cue from church preachers and sent orators around France to address the populace with speeches composed by the king's ministers. A socially broadened audience for propaganda dictated a difference in tone, and so in this dispute, for the first time in the Middle Ages, the concerns of the people at large were introduced into the discussion. Significantly, Philip the Fair convened the Estates General, an assembly of notables, and a general assembly at Paris to listen to and advertise their support of the king.[2] The French Renaissance monarchy proceeded to develop the tradition of propaganda through assemblies. By carefully blending sessions of local and provincial assemblies with meetings of the Estates General, the crown cultivated a procedure that allowed it to summon the representatives of several orders to suffer flattering harangues, impressive visual displays of royal majesty, and other devices calculated to bind them to the interests of the crown. For similar reasons of propaganda as well as finance, princes all over Europe fostered their estates during the Renaissance.[3]

[2] Helene Wieruszowski, *Von Imperium zum nationalen Königtum* (Munich, 1933), pp. 114–140.

[3] J. Russell Major, *Representative Institutions in Renaissance France* (Madison, 1960), *passim*.

These predominantly aural methods of propaganda were profoundly affected by the advent of print at the end of the fifteenth century. Although the importance of printing has long been a commonplace to historians of early modern Europe, until recently remarkably little attention was devoted to defining the precise nature of its impact. We are just beginning to understand, for example, the role of print as a precondition for the ideological revolutions we call the Reformation and the Enlightenment.[4] Clearly, printing helped make rapid social change possible in early modern Europe, if only by multiplying enormously the size of a writer's potential audience. Yet the invention of printing also reinforced the cleavage between the literate and the illiterate. In the age of print the written word came to assume an ever increasing role. Since in most parts of Europe the vast majority of people remained unlettered until after the French Revolution,[5] the period from the fifteenth to the eighteenth centuries saw the emergence of two parallel cultures: a relatively small reading public, and a larger illiterate group which existed in a culture of sound. Doubtless the lines dividing these groups were often blurred and indistinct. Long after Gutenberg, literate people continued to cultivate habits of memory and oral rhetoric derived from the age of script. On the other hand, the visual world of print was

---

[4] See the excellent articles by Elizabeth L. Eisenstein, esp. "Some Conjectures About the Impact of Printing on Western Society and Thought: A Preliminary Report," *Journal of Modern History*, 40:1 (March 1968), 1–56; and "L'Avènement de l'imprimerie et la Réforme," *Annales-E.S.C.*, 26:6 (1971), 1355–1381. On the effects of printed pamphlets in the eighteenth century, see Robert Darnton, "Reading, Writing and Publishing in Eighteenth-Century France: A Case Study in the Sociology of Literature," *Daedalus*, 100:1 (Winter 1971), 214–256.

[5] Michel Fleury and Pierre Valmary, "Les Progrès de l'instruction élémentaire de Louis XIV à Napoléon III," *Population*, 12 (1957), esp. 80–91; F. Furet and W. Sachs, "La Croissance de l'alphabétisation en France XVIIIᵉ–XIXᵉ siècle," *Annales-E.S.C.*, 29 (1974), 714–737; Lawrence Stone, "Literacy and Education in England, 1640–1900," *Past and Present*, No. 42 (February 1969), pp. 69–139.

impinging even on the auditory universe of the unlettered. By the seventeenth century there had grown up an extensive printed popular literature destined for an illiterate audience through the medium of the village storyteller.[6]

This kind of crossover was particularly common in the area of propaganda. Princes who had employed the cumbersome methods of manuscript to communicate with their subjects switched quickly to print to announce declarations of war, publish battle accounts, promulgate treaties, or argue disputed points in pamphlet form. Theirs was an effort, as one authority has put it, to "win the psychological war which prepared and accompanied the military operations" of rulers.[7] In France, the content of this propaganda literature conveyed much the same sort of message as did the royal speeches to the estates, addresses which were themselves regularly circulated in print. The root idea was to evoke the notion of the *patrie* as the realm of France and to represent the king as the personification of this *patrie*.[8] In similar fashion, the English crown under Henry VIII and Thomas Cromwell made systematic use of both Parliament and press to win public support for the Reformation.[9]

For a time after the invention of printing, then, the estates and the printing press remained twin pillars of princely propaganda. But beginning in the early seventeenth century, a number of rulers and ministers—dubbed "absolutist" by

[6] Eisenstein, "Some Conjectures," pp. 30 ff.; Geneviève Bollème, *Les Almanachs populaires aux XVIIe et XVIIIe siècles* (Paris, 1969), esp. pp. 14 ff.; Natalie Zemon Davis, *Society and Culture in Early Modern France* (Stanford, 1975), pp. 189–226.

[7] Jean-Pierre Seguin, *L'Information en France de Louis XII à Henri II* (Geneva, 1961), p. 46.

[8] André Bossuat, "La Littérature de propagande au XVe siècle," *Cahiers de l'histoire*, 1 (1956), 142–146; P. S. Lewis, *Later Medieval France, the Polity* (London, 1968), pp. 7–8, 63–66, 77. See also M. Yardeni, *La Conscience nationale en France pendant les guerres de religion (1559–1598)* (Louvain, 1971).

[9] G. R. Elton, *Policy and Police, the Enforcement of the Reformation in the Age of Thomas Cromwell* (Cambridge, 1972), pp. 171–216.

later historians—began to abandon assemblies of estates. Composed of articulate and increasingly well-organized orders, the estates in many parts of Europe were becoming foci of opposition to the crown instead of tools that served princely power. In France the regency of Louis XIII saw the last meeting of the Estates General before 1789; it also saw the founding of the first royally sponsored newspaper in Europe. The replacement of the volatile assembly by the controlled weekly *Gazette* is a concurrence symptomatic of the importance Cardinal Richelieu attached to print in his state-building objectives.[10]

Richelieu well understood the significance of public opinion in the state and the role of print in forming opinion.[11] A writer sympathetic to the cardinal stated Richelieu's own assumptions about polemical writings: "Those who wish to subvert a state try by all manner of means to imprint [*imprimer*] in the minds of subjects a bad opinion of the Prince. Writings are the chief tool used in drawing this picture. They are the gate from which emerge both respect and rebellion."[12] The obvious conclusion drawn by Richelieu was that writings must be regulated to protect against rebellion as well as to promote respect. The latter, positive use of the pen was especially necessary, given the ultimate futility of effective censorship restrictions. Although the Code Michaud of 1629 made writers of illegal works on

[10] Major, *Representative Institutions*, pp. 19 ff. On Richelieu and the *Gazette*, see Howard M. Solomon, *Public Welfare, Science and Propaganda in Seventeenth Century France: The Innovations of Théophraste Renaudot* (Princeton, 1972), pp. 100–161.

[11] There is a considerable literature on Richelieu's propaganda. Three major recent works are Etienne Thuau, *Raison d'état et pensée politique à l'époque de Richelieu* (Paris, 1966), esp. pp. 169–177 and 214–226; Henri-Jean Martin, *Livre, pouvoirs et société à Paris au XVIIe siècle, 1598–1701*, 2 vols. (Geneva, 1969), esp. pp. 258–275, 433–471; and William F. Church, *Richelieu and Reason of State* (Princeton, 1972), pp. 109–115, 340–349, and *passim*.

[12] *Discours au roi touchant les libelles faits contre le gouvernement de son état*, quoted in Thuau, *Raison d'état*, p. 170.

affairs of state subject to trial for lèse majesté, Louis XIII's chief minister knew that the limited enforcement powers of the crown would never close off the flow of clandestine publications printed in France and abroad.[13] Thus, as Gabriel Naudé summarized the policy he helped to shape, the prince himself must hire "skilled pens, have them write clandestine pamphlets, manifestos, artfully composed apologies and declarations, in order to lead [his subjects] by the nose."[14] For these reasons, Richelieu not only fostered Théophraste Renaudot's *Gazette* but also employed numerous scholars, poets, and mere hacks to explain and justify royal policy and to exalt the image of Louis XIII in France and Europe. As another of Richelieu's writers put it: "Arms uphold the cause of Princes, but well-tempered books publicize their equity and orient public affections to regard them as epiphanies of justice."[15]

To censor and to sponsor—this formula summarizes Richelieu's policy on printed opinion. In applying this maxim the cardinal-minister was far from unique among seventeenth-century statesmen, although certainly he was unsurpassed in his systematic thoroughness. Richelieu communicated to his creatures and other subordinates his concept of the royal servants' duty to glorify and publicize their monarchical master. How then did Richelieu and other seventeenth-century statesmen differ from modern propagandists? Are there in fact any differences beyond those stemming from technological resources?

In answering these questions, it is important to observe that, while historians often have underestimated the novel consequences of printing in seventeenth-century Europe,

---

[13] On the mechanics of Richelieu's censorship, see Martin, *Livre*, pp. 441–466. The absence of regularized censorship under Henry IV is discussed by Alfred Soman, "The Theatre, Diplomacy and Censorship in the Reign of Henri IV," *Bibliothèque d'Humanisme et Renaissance*, 25:2 (1973), 276, 282, 284.

[14] Quoted in Thuau, *Raison d'état*, p. 172.

[15] F. de Colomby, quoted *ibid.*, pp. 170–171.

equally misleading would be any attempt to define the essential character of the age in the light of this giant technological step. Concerning all the basic conditions of life, European society in the seventeenth century remained overwhelmingly premodern. Even literacy remained a minority achievement everywhere in Europe despite the impetus of print. The innovation of printing was absorbed by a social and cultural order altogether different from our own and essentially continuous with earlier patterns of life and thought.

If we are to understand early modern propaganda without anachronism, then, we should consider the fundamental assumptions of the day about the nature of authority and human psychology. In the seventeenth century the right of established authorities to censor dangerous ideas was rarely questioned. The dominant paternalist patterns of thought held that all authorities were servants of God and bidden to shield their flocks from ungodly ideas.[16] Further, since truth was regarded as unitary and knowable, men of state and other authorities had no reason to doubt that in censoring they were acting as upholders of truth. Only with the Enlightenment did the European consciousness come to regard truth as elusive, multiple and relative. Thus, while liberal-democratic political assumptions preclude authoritarian thought control, the assumptions of absolutism made censorship a mandatory concern of authoritative government.

In France the crown fought a long and ultimately successful battle to wrest the right of censorship from the church. This outcome reinforces the conclusion that in early modern Europe the state had become the chief official arbiter of public morality. That society could not long cohere without some such arbiter was an opinion so universally held that people hardly ever bothered to formulate it. Moreover, the state was perceived not only as a referee which would prevent and penalize violations but also as an active supplier of information and tutelage. According to the political

---

[16] Church, *Richelieu*, p. 507.

9

precepts of the age, a government which failed to guide and lead citizens to a correct understanding of disputed points would have been judged unworthy of its high calling. Thus the French monarchy was duty bound not only to regulate printed opinion but also actively to direct it.[17]

Does this imply that seventeenth-century propaganda was intended to be as manipulative as our modern varieties? In their private correspondence Richelieu and his contemporaries described themselves not as falsifiers but as enlighteners, bringing the beacon of truth to people who were searching for guidance.[18] Before dismissing such appraisals as an advanced form of self-serving delusion, we might pause to consider in what ways the propaganda of absolutist France differed from the modern variety. Contemporary propaganda rests on a base of psychological assumptions which were unknown in Richelieu's day. Axiomatic for today's propagandists is the notion that men are creatures of their conditioning and can be manipulated by the application of suitable stimuli. Thus modern propaganda is intentionally contrived to exploit the mythic and irrational, attempting to undermine critical, independent thinking.[19] The concept of the malleability of man, from which modern propaganda derives, is still another Enlightenment postulate that flew in the face of the conventional wisdom of Christian

[17] Cf. Peter Fraser, *The Intelligence of Secretaries of State and Their Monopoly of Licensed News, 1660–1688* (Cambridge, 1956), p. 117; ". . . the reasons of state that justified the Secretarial monopoly of news were not considerations of the inconvenience of hostile comment so much as the belief that unofficial news would be 'false news' founded upon rumour or bad intelligence."

[18] Later, Daniel Defoe stated that the purpose of his political gazette, *The Review*, was "to open the eyes of the deluded people and set them to rights in the things in which they are imposed upon." See Marjorie Nicolson, introduction to *The Best of Defoe's Review*, ed. William L. Payne (New York, 1951), p. xvi.

[19] Unusually acute comments on modern propaganda can be found in Jacques Ellul, *Propaganda, the Formation of Men's Attitudes* (New York, 1965), pp. 6, 25–26.

Europe.[20] In the early seventeenth century man was defined not by his capacity for change (or "improvement," as Enlightenment thinkers were optimistically to put it) but by his innately unchanging nature. Man's very immutability severely limited the potential range of propaganda.

Further, in its vision of political and cultural life the seventeenth century was dominated by strong biases toward continuity and against change. Aristocracy, religion, classical learning, and monarchy itself were cults whose prestige derived from their lengthy lineage. Innovations, even radical ones, had to be justified by reference to past precedents which were often misreadings or nostalgic imaginings of historical reality. And in political confrontation the authority of the past was perceived as the best kind of weapon. That there was nothing new about this in seventeenth-century Europe is precisely the point, for the burden of the past weighed upon the age of Richelieu quite as much as and possibly more than upon Philip the Fair's.

The cult of kingship, which became the central expression of political feeling in seventeenth-century France, was built upon a long tradition of reverence for the monarchy. As a sacred being who could transmit divine cures by his touch, the ruler of France was infinitely far from the modern politician seeking legitimacy by manipulating the public with a variety of propaganda devices and techniques. Nor did the monarchy need to validate itself with an ideology built upon contract theory or concepts of social utility. Instead, the cement of the French state was a set of widely held and deeply felt traditional values about authority, shared assumptions which cast the king not as a political actor explaining his actions and seeking approval but as a quasi-divine personage whose will was the very expression of right action, truth, and justice. Thus a major theme of printed propaganda during the first half of the seventeenth century was the French king's miraculous power to bring about a

[20] Peter Gay, *The Enlightenment: An Interpretation*, 2 vols. (New York, 1967–1969), II, 511–521.

cure for scrofula by touching the diseased. Habsburg pamphleteers attempted to play down the importance of this gift; Henry IV's personal physician published an elaborate and very popular treatise upholding the divine origins and miraculous effects of the royal touch; and in Richelieu's time a supporter of the French cause in Catalonia appealed to the royal miracle as an argument conceived to win local support for the Bourbon side.[21] No instance better illustrates the principle of the continuity of royal symbolism in the new age of print.

THE SUN KING AND THE COMMUNICATIONS REVOLUTION

If the traditional propaganda of the French monarchy was expressed in a variety of symbolic images which reflected aspects of the just, pious, and brave king, the reign of Louis XIV brought this tradition to its climax. For this monarch prestige was the very substance of power. From the earliest years of his personal rule the young king's actions reflected deep concern for the psychological component of kingship. An elaborate court etiquette whose theme was service to the king's person made Louis a living embodiment of monarchical supremacy. The choice of Apollo's emblem further symbolized the centrality of the Sun King. And since every god must have his temple, the complex of Versailles was created at least partly for the purpose of impressing Frenchmen and foreigners with the grandeur of the French monarchy. All this represented an effort to make tangible the mystique of kingship that lay at the heart of absolutism, lifting the monarch above mere humanity to the plane of supernatural myth. The man who wore the crown had to

[21] Marc Bloch, *Les Rois thaumaturges. Etude sur le caractère surnaturel attribué à la puissance royale particulièrement en France et en Angleterre* (Strasbourg, 1924), pp. 342-344, 365-367; see also Roland Mousnier, *The Assassination of Henry IV*, trans. Joan Spencer (London, 1973), pp. 240-250.

play the part of a demigod, and Louis XIV fulfilled the role brilliantly. As virtuoso performer in the elaborate piece of baroque stagecraft that was his reign, he wanted Europe to believe that he also had composed the script, built the set, designed the costumes, and directed the action. By identifying himself totally with his role of monarch, Louis gave dynamic life to absolutist ideology.[22]

In the artwork of the absolutist state, French society was to be much more than a passive audience. Louis XIV's government intended that the king's subjects should participate in the ceremony of monarchy. Thus under Colbert's leadership a variety of corporate groups were founded and molded into vehicles of royal grandeur. We see this most clearly in the drive to organize science, letters, and the arts under the umbrella of royal academies. Richelieu had created the French Academy for literary men, but Colbert went much further when he introduced the principle of functional division in founding academies for music and the dance, for inscriptions and medals, for painting and sculpture, for architecture, and for the sciences. Each of these specialized academies organized a branch of learning or expression under royal control and made service to the crown its primary purpose.[23] The Academy of Music, for example, produced operas and ballets which not only glorified the idea of kingship and the person of the ruler but also took their themes from current political developments. The Academy of Inscriptions was charged with designing medals appropriately commemorating the achievements of the Sun King. Even the Academy of Sciences, it was hoped, would achieve technological advances that might find economic or military

[22] On these general themes, see John B. Wolf, *Louis XIV* (New York, 1968), pp. 269–285, 357–378.

[23] Probably the best introduction to these academies is the last chapter of Frances A. Yates, *The French Academies of the Sixteenth Century* (London, 1947). Martin, *Livre*, pp. 436–439, 667–670, 769–771, places strong emphasis on the crown's use of royal academies for propaganda purposes.

applications. The artistic academies were closely tied to the court ceremonial that so impressed visitors to Versailles. In particular, the productions of the Academy of Music were a mainstay of the ceaseless round of spectacles devised by Louis' government as the aesthetic manifestations of the Sun King's magnificence. By translating the king's actions into the symbolic language of music and poetry, the academicians performed an artistic apotheosis of politics.[24] In itself the act of apotheosis was no novelty, but what Colbert added was a set of corporate institutions through which such portrayals could be systematically, even bureaucratically, expressed.

Important as they were, these awesome academic and other spectacles could reach only that tiny fraction of the public resident at court. The enormous scale of Versailles nonetheless was dwarfed by France's twenty million inhabitants. Thus royal servants recognized the need to transmit the idea of the king's grandeur beyond the narrow orbit of the court and capital. Intendants, provincial governors, and other officials throughout France were mobilized to accomplish this purpose through techniques similar in many ways to those in use at the court. Visual and musical spectacles echoed the king's military triumphs, celebrated royal births and escorted members of the king's family to provincial cities. Fireworks, elaborate tableaux, and sumptuous feasts complete with fountains spouting wine became regular items of expenditure in every *généralité*. In these celebrations all urban dwellers might take part. Only the municipal elite and other "persons of quality" could cap the festivities with balls at the intendant's residence, but such public manifestations as cannon fire, street illuminations, and the pealing of church bells were enjoyed by the *peuple* as well.[25] Thus

[24] Robert M. Isherwood, *Music in the Service of the King* (Ithaca, 1973), esp. pp. 103–113, 150–169, 336–349; Roger Hahn, *The Anatomy of a Scientific Institution: The Paris Academy of the Sciences, 1666–1803* (Berkeley, 1971), pp. 1–83.

[25] Among many surviving accounts, see esp.: *Feu de joie tiré à Dijon le dimanche 28. Novembre 1688 pour la prise de Philisbourg*

the centralized domestic administration created by Colbert and his associates during the 1660's and 1670's provided a vehicle for systematically communicating the traditional message of monarchical grandeur.

Of all the mythic imagery enhancing the cult of monarchy, that of religion was the most fundamental. It was, for example, an ancient practice of French kings to fulfill the biblical injunction by offering thanksgiving to God for blessings bestowed. Their providential view regarded God as the source of all good fortune, and the monarchy translated this abstraction into Te Deum ceremonies that crystallized the message of divine protection for the king. After each manifestation of God's favor, Louis XIV unfailingly sent letters to the bishops and archbishops of France ordering them to arrange thanksgiving services throughout their dioceses. While each parish church carried out the king's order by holding its own Te Deum ritual, those of the cathedral churches were particularly impressive. In attendance there at the king's orders were the municipal authori-

---

(Dijon, 1688), BN, Imp., Lb³⁷.3933; *Description du feu de joie dressé devant l'Hostel de Ville pour la prise de la ville de Namur* (n.p., 1692), BN, Imp., Lb³⁷.4012; *Relation sommaire de ce qui a été fait à Toulon pendant le séjour que Nosseigneurs les Ducs de Bourgogne et de Berry y ont fait* (Paris, 1701), BN, Imp., Lb³⁷.4162; *Relation de ce qui s'est fait à Lyon, au passage de Monseigneur le Duc de Bourgogne et de Monseigneur le Duc de Berry* (Lyon, 1701), BN, Imp., Lb³⁷.4166; *Relation de ce qui s'est passé à Châlon sur Saône à l'entrée de Msgr. le Duc de Bourgogne, le 14 Avril 1701* (Lyon, 1701), BN, Imp., Lb³⁷.4168; *Relation des réjouissances faites à Caen par Monsieur Foucault, . . . Intendant de Basse-Normandie, pour la naissance de Monseigneur le Duc de Bretagne* (Caen [1704]), BN, Imp., Lb³⁷.4267; Alexandre Dubois, *Journal d'un curé de campagne au XVIIᵉ siècle,* ed. Henri Platelle (Paris, 1965), p. 141; *Journal d'un bourgeois de Caen, 1652–1733,* ed. G. Marcel (Paris, 1848), *passim.* Raymond Céleste, "Bordeaux au XVIIIᵉ siècle, le roi d'Espagne à Blaye, Bordeaux et Bazas (1700–1701)," *Revue historique de Bordeaux,* 1 (1908), 49–61, 134–149, discusses Philip V's passage through southwestern France. For a general evaluation, see Isherwood, *Music,* pp. 295–298, 313.

ties, resplendent in their robes of office. In a dozen cities of France the judges of the parlements were also required to lend their prestige by their presence. The magnificence of these occasions made Te Deum services a species of entertainment in the seventeenth century. More than this, by means of religious ritual the crown reinforced the sense of shared symbolism that bound the king and his Catholic subjects.[26]

The prelates of the Gallican church soon learned how to refine their role as servants of Louis XIV's national policies. Typically they saw to it that the king's letters ordering a Te Deum service were printed for wide circulation in the dioceses. But the clerics were more than simple agents of transmission. The bishop of Châlons-sur-Marne, for example, amplified the king's laconic order for a Te Deum upon the birth of a royal heir in 1704 into an elaborate model sermon which he printed and sent to every priest under his jurisdiction. The sermon expatiated upon the unmatched advantages of an assured succession to the French throne. Thus armed, even the least imaginative priest in the diocese should

[26] 1 Timothy 2:1–2. *Journal d'un bourgeois de Caen*, pp. 66–67, 75, 114–115, 117–118, 135–136, 139, 146–147. The Bibliothèque Nationale has dozens of royal orders for Te Deum services from this period, among them the following: *Lettre du Roy, envoyée à Monseigneur l'Archévêque de Paris, sur le sujet de la prise de la ville et Château de Tournay* (Paris, 1667), BN, Imp., Lb[37].3579; *Lettre du Roy, envoyée à Monseigneur l'Archévêque de Paris, sur la prise de la Ville de Douay et Fort Descarpel* (Paris, 1667), BN, Imp., Lb[37].3582; *Lettre du roy envoyée à Messieurs les Prevost des Marchands et Echevins de la Ville de Paris, pour assister au Te Deum, et faire faire des feux de joye, et autres réjouissances publiques, pour la prise de la Ville de Maëstrick* (Paris, 1679), BN, Imp., Lb[37].3641; *Lettre du roi écrite à Monseigneur l'Archévêque de Paris, pour faire chanter Te Deum en l'Eglise de Nôtre Dame, afin de remercier Dieu de la prise de la Ville de Philisbourg par l'armée du Roy, commandée par Msgr. le Dauphin* (Paris, 1688), BN, Imp., Lb[37]. 3930; *Lettre du Roy, écrite à Msgr. l'Archévêque de Paris pour faire chanter le Te Deum en l'Eglise Nôtre Dame, en action de grâces de la prise de Barcelonne par l'armée de Sa Majesté en Catalogne* (Paris, 1697), BN, Imp., Lb[37].4099.

have been able to deliver an oration acceptable to king and bishop. The medium of the press served here to regularize and extend throughout the realm an ancient form of propaganda.[27]

There were, however, few occasions for public celebration in the problem-ridden second half of Louis XIV's reign. The number of military victories dwindled during the exhausting War of the League of Augsburg (1688–1697) and sank nearly to zero in the catastrophic War of the Spanish Succession (1701–1714). Meanwhile famine stalked the land in 1693–1694 and, even more ferociously, in 1709–1710. The prospect of an orderly succession to the throne evaporated with a stunning series of deaths in 1711–1712, leaving only a frail infant to protect France from a constitutional crisis. There seemed no end to the tragedies and, while Louis finally came to believe that God had abandoned him, the prelates of France, long used to triumphal services, now took it upon themselves to organize public prayers and processions beseeching the return of divine favor.[28]

[27] *Lettres du Roy écrites à Monseigneur l'Evêque Comte de Châlons, Pair de France, pour faire chanter Te Deum dans l'Eglise Cathedrale, et dans toutes celles de son Diocese, en action de grâces de la Prise de la Ville de Suze par l'Armée du Roy, commandée par Monsieur le Duc de la Feuillade; Et de la naissance de Monseigneur le Duc de Bretagne. Avec le Mandement de Mondit-Seigneur* (Châlons, 1704), BN, Imp., Lb^{37}.4264.

[28] BN, Mss. fr. 23209, fols. 210, 231, 251; these are letters from Colbert de Torcy to the Bishop of Châlons-sur-Marne discussing the prayers ordered by the prelate. A satirical verse of 1704 addressed to the Virgin Mary pointed to the irony of Te Deum orders in Louis XIV's reduced circumstances (*Mercure historique et politique*, October 1704, p. 440):

> Faut-il toujours, Reine des Anges,
> Qu'au lieu de chants de joye, et de chants
>   de louanges,
> Louis jadis vainqueur, à present atterré,
> Ordonne au Cardinal, son Cousin de Noailles,
> Comme en un jour de funerailles,
> De chanter le *Miserere*.

Still the royal government continued to resort to the Te Deum service as a way of arousing patriotic fervor, blaming France's enemies for the prolonged warfare. Clearly, the king's Te Deum orders were politically motivated during the disastrous last wars; they did not abate even when Louis was reduced to seizing upon minor skirmishes as the occasion for reassuring celebrations. As one of Louis' enemies grudgingly admitted in 1690, "Whenever the king wins a battle, takes a city or subdues a province, we [i.e., Frenchmen] light bonfires, and every petty person feels elevated and associates the king's grandeur with himself; this compensates him for all his losses and consoles him in all his misery."[29] Meanwhile, Louis' printed episcopal letters took every opportunity to confide to his subjects during the War of the League of Augsburg that "if there be any thing that Flatters Me in a Conquest of this Importance, 'tis not so much the Glory that attends it, or the Enlarging my Dominions, as the hope which it gives me, that My Enemies, wearied with their Losses, will condescend at length to the Offers I have made 'em long since, for the putting an End to this War: 'Tis also this Hope, which obliges Me, to redouble My Thanksgivings to Heaven, and to protest, at the same Time, before Him that knows the very Thoughts of My Heart, that there is nothing which I more ardently Desire, then to put My Subjects into a Condition, of Glorifying Him in Peace."[30]

[29] Les Soupirs de la France esclave, qui aspire après la liberté (1690), in The Impact of Absolutism in France, trans. and ed. William F. Church (New York, 1969), p. 108. (Cf. the similar comments of Nicolas Gueudeville, publisher of the anti-Louis L'Esprit des cours de l'Europe, quoted by M. Yardeni, "Gueudeville et Louis XIV, un précurseur du socialisme, critique des structures sociales louis-quatorziennes," Revue d'histoire moderne et contemporaine, 19 [1972], 602, 606.)

[30] Lettre du Roy, écrite à Monseigneur l'Archévesque de Paris . . . pour faire chanter le Te Deum en action de grâces de la prise de la Ville de Namur (Paris, 1692), BN, Imp., Lb^{37}.4011; trans. in The Present State of Europe, July 1692, pp. 258–259.

When Louis at last "gave peace to Europe," as he put it in 1697, the king once again used the printing press to emphasize his willingness to abandon dynastic goals for the sake of his subjects:

> The happy successes with which God has favored my arms in the course of so long a war have never removed me from the sincere desire I have for peace, which was the unique purpose I aimed for in all my enterprises. Although the glorious expeditions of this campaign and the advantages they promised for me might have engaged me to uphold my interests and press my claims even further, I have abandoned them . . . and have made it my rule to consecrate the fruits of my conquests to the repose of Europe. I am sufficiently recompensed for everything that this moderation costs me by the end it makes of all the evils of war. The prompt comfort which will accrue to my people and the pleasure I receive in rendering them happy are sufficient compensation for everything I sacrifice on their behalf. And the *éclat* of the greatest triumphs is not worth the *gloire* of repaying the zeal of my subjects, who have lavishly expended their blood and their goods unceasingly and with uniform ardor.[31]

The coming of peace was an event marked by government- and church-sponsored celebrations throughout France. The inevitable Te Deum services were accompanied by drum-and-trumpet processions of municipal authorities, the magistracy, clerical officials, and platoons of soldiers. In Paris the peace was proclaimed in customary fashion at twelve separate locations, with the better part of a day taken up in formal parade from the Hôtel de Ville to the Tuileries, the Pont Neuf, the Place Royale, and so forth. At each

[31] *Lettre du Roy, écrite à Monseigneur l'Archévêque de Paris, pour faire chanter le Te Deum en l'Eglise Nôtre-Dame, en action de grâces de la Paix* (Paris, 1697), BN, Imp., Lb[37].4102.

stop a herald formally announced the peace, to the accompaniment of brass fanfares, shouts of "Vive le Roy" and other "joyful acclamations." Under the supervision of the lieutenant general of police, the participants completed their appointed rounds and disbanded at the Saint-Jean cemetery. Later there were bonfires, cannon displays and fireworks. Provincial communities celebrated on a lesser scale but with equal gusto. Near Tournai, at the extreme northern corner of France, the magistrates and the abbot of Saint-Amand staged religious processions and secular tableaux, officially proclaimed the peace in three different corners of their tiny community, made the air ring with trumpets and no less than a ton of exploding cannon powder, and finally threw a magnificent banquet for all and sundry. Even those who could not read the king's public letters could appreciate the symbolic joining of the king's peace to the nation's celebration.[32]

These rites of peace illustrate the way traditional ceremonial practices were amplified in the Sun King's reign by the application of bureaucratic regularity and the use of print. The printed word also communicated the king's verbal messages abroad, as foreign gazettes habitually published Louis' edicts and public letters verbatim. From 1660, and particularly after 1680, the political periodical, one of the seventeenth century's most lasting innovations, grew rapidly in circulation. More than a dozen French-language gazettes were published in Holland in the second half of Louis XIV's reign, most of them edited by Huguenot émigrés escaping the Sun King's persecutions. The non-renewal of the licensing act in 1695 permitted a similar explosion of journals in England. Thus the maritime enemies

---

[32] Ceremonies were often the occasion for bitter disputes over precedence, as at the coming of peace in 1678; see Andrew P. Trout, "The Proclamation of the Peace of Nijmegen," *French Historical Sudies*, 5:4 (Fall 1968), 477–481. On the celebrations at Saint-Amand, see Dubois, *Journal*, pp. 118–119.

of Louis XIV harbored a flourishing group of periodicals that provided a rich and regular source of information and opinion. Appearing at intervals varying from semi-weekly to bimonthly, these gazettes soon became a permanent feature of western European life. We are dealing here with a new phenomenon whose social implications, though hard to measure with exactitude, were profoundly important.[33] The democratizing communications revolution that stemmed from the birth of the periodical press certainly contributed to a breakdown in cultural isolation and helped produce a more sophisticated, cosmopolitan culture in which provincial and even national boundaries were blurred. This was particularly true of the French-language Dutch gazettes, whose messages were directed as much at readers outside

[33] Short titles of major French-language gazettes published outside France before 1715, with founding dates: *Gazette de Bruxelles* (1649), *Gazette de Leyde* (1680), *Gazette de Rotterdam* (1683), *Mercure historique et politique* (The Hague, 1686), *Gazette d'Amsterdam* (1688), *Gazette de Berne* (1689), *Gazette de La Haye* (1690), *Lettres historiques* (The Hague & Amsterdam, 1692), *La Quintessence des nouvelles* (The Hague & Amsterdam, 1697), *L'Esprit des cours de l'Europe* (The Hague & Amsterdam, 1699), *Gazette d'Utrecht* (1710); see Gabriel Bonno, "Liste chronologique des périodiques de langue française du XVIIIᵉ siècle," *Modern Language Notes*, 5 (1944), 3–7. Bonno is now superseded by J. Sgard, "Table chronologique des périodiques de langue française publiés avant la Révolution," in M. Couperus, *L'Etude des périodiques anciens: Colloque d'Utrecht* (Utrecht, 1970), pp. 172–211. On these publications, see E. Hatin, *Les Gazettes de Hollande et la presse clandestine au XVIIᵉ et XVIIIᵉ siècles* (Paris, 1865), *passim*. For a bibliography of English and continental gazettes published between 1660 and 1688, see Fraser, *Intelligence*, pp. 167–169. Pierre Bayle (quoted by Louis Trenard, in C. Bellanger *et al.*, *Histoire générale de la presse française* [Paris, 1969], I, 159) remarked shortly after 1700 that "le nombre des gazettes qui se publient par toute l'Europe est prodigieux" and proposed a historical analysis of the phenomenon. Nearly three centuries later his call remains unanswered, although M. Yardeni, "Journalisme et histoire contemporaine à l'époque de Bayle," *History and Theory*, 12:2 (1973), 208–229, has recently attacked one side of the problem.

Holland as within. In their editorial commentary the Dutch journals helped to shape the remarkably uniform ideology of opposition to Louis XIV that underlay the anti-French coalitions of the later wars.

This was an ideology first formulated in pamphlet literature directed against the Sun King which had developed by the middle of Louis' reign. These anonymously published *libelles* and *lardons* contained both personal and political attacks. Indeed, given the still largely personal nature of politics in the seventeenth century, any criticism of the monarch's character was at least implicitly a political attack, and, conversely, competent political critics always took account of Louis XIV's personality in making their assessments. Some pamphlets were more personal than others, however, especially those composed of scurrilous attacks upon the sexual and other private proclivities of the king, his family and close associates. The pornographic fantasies of seventeenth-century Europeans often cast monarchs and other *grands* as leading characters, perhaps representing a sublimation of repressed hostility that could not be directly expressed.[34] Less escapist were the books and pamphlets that directly attacked Louis XIV's policies. As early as the 1660's there had appeared detailed and effective criticisms of the Sun King's belligerent posture and outsized pretensions. François de Lisola, the zealous Franc-Comtois servant of Emperor Leopold I, was only the most famous of many writers who protested not only against specific French actions from the War of Devolution onward but also argued that Louis XIV's ultimate goal was nothing less than univer-

[34] The fertility of this literary harvest can be gauged by listing a few titles imported from the United Provinces in 1698: *Bâtard de Navarre, Ancien bâtard protecteur de nouveau, Tombeau des amours de Louis XIV*; see BN, Clairambault 492, fol. 220. Certainly the most famous work of this type was R. de Bussy-Rabutin, *Histoire amoureuse des gaules*. On this literature in general, see P.J.W. Malssen, *Louis XIV d'après les pamphlets répandus en Hollande* (Amsterdam, 1936); and H. Gillot, *Le Règne de Louis XIV et l'opinion publique en Allemagne* (Paris, 1913), pp. 21–27.

sal monarchy.[35] As Louis' reign progressed, the fear of universal monarchy under the Bourbons became the touchstone of anti-French propaganda. Since at the same time the Sun King's wars became increasingly unpopular with many of his own subjects, we find replicated in the writings of Louis' domestic critics much the same picture of the king as is conveyed by the works of his foreign enemies.[36] In this way the king's wars created a French market for printed criticism, and the smuggled pamphlets in turn nurtured the hostile image of the king in France. Meanwhile the picture of Louis XIV as a rapacious aggressor bent on universal monarchy, which had originated with Lisola and his pamphleteering allies, was disseminated in Europe primarily through the work of French-speaking journalists in Holland, who rammed home the message month after month for more than thirty years.

Clearly, by the first years of the eighteenth century, the available sources of political information and opinion had multiplied all over western Europe. One measure of this surge in printed news and comment was the sudden and dramatic proliferation of periodicals, but non-serial pamphlet works also increased in rate of publication around 1700. Although precise figures are hard to find for most parts of Europe, a study of Swiss library holdings indicates that the average annual output of political pamphlets increased from just over twenty in the years 1661–1698 to about forty for the period 1699–1710. Of 1500 separate titles known to have been published during Louis XIV's personal reign, just over six hundred, or about forty percent, appeared after 1698.[37] Plainly, the complex legal and political ques-

[35] On Lisola, see Alfred F. Pribram, *Franz Paul, Freiherr von Lisola, 1613–1674, und die Politik seiner Zeit* (Leipzig, 1894).

[36] Even today, the historical image of Louis XIV is still conditioned by the propaganda of his own time; see Ragnhild M. Hatton, "Louis XIV: Recent Gains in Historical Knowledge," *Journal of Modern History*, 45:2 (June 1973), 277–279.

[37] Derived from R. Meyer, *Die Flugschriften der Epoche Ludwigs XIV* (Basel, 1955), pp. 12–13.

tions of the Spanish succession and the continent-wide, even global warfare of these years fanned an avid interest in the affairs of states.[38] While the enormous scale of military action in the War of the Spanish Succession required unprecedented numbers of men and heretofore unknown levels of governmental expenditure, public involvement in political and military events also reached a scale impossible to attain before the age of the printed pamphlet and the periodical.

This development was well understood by the most important royal councillor of Louis XIV's last years, secretary of state for foreign affairs Colbert de Torcy, who coordinated the French propaganda examined in this book. There is overwhelming evidence in Torcy's official correspondence of his concern with propaganda, and nearly all of his attention was devoted to the printed varieties: books, pamphlets, and serial publications. The obvious reason for this bias is that Torcy was concerned with influencing the views of foreigners who were physically removed and psychologically resistant to the symbolisms of French nonverbal propaganda. The ceremonies and practices associated with the Bourbon cult of kingship inevitably suffered a loss of potency when exported. But more than this, new cultural patterns gaining influence in the United Provinces and England late in the seventeenth century made the cult of kingship seem to many intellectually empty, morally odious, and emotionally repulsive. In these places a political frame of reference founded on principles of empirically derived utility was making rapid headway. Fundamental reorientations of western values would soon result from the successful intellectual challenge of a rational constitutionalism to traditional notions of legitimacy which rested upon inheritance, divine right, and sacred attributes. Then too, in these Protestant lands monarchy had been shorn of legend and

[38] G. A. Cranfield, *The Development of the Provincial Newspaper, 1700–1760* (Oxford, 1962), pp. 70 ff., discusses the heavy emphasis given to foreign and especially war news in the English press of the early eighteenth century.

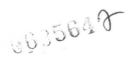

miracle, thanks in large part to the influence of anti-magical Calvinist theology. The cult of monarchy, as understood in France, was in an important sense incompatible with the leading reformed sects in the homelands of Louis XIV's most bitter enemies.

No total immunity to these changes existed even in France, where the medieval, humanist, and classical foundations of reverence for the crown proved difficult to displace. The *frondeurs* of the mid-seventeenth century had challenged aspects of the cult of kingship in their thousands of printed *Mazarinade* pamphlets,[39] but the symbolism of divine monarchy received its widest expression during the next thirty years. Panegyric, ritual, and display effectively muffled subversive forms of expression. Louis XIV, down to the last year of his reign, continued to touch thousands of the scrofulous. But while popular practice followed traditional patterns, the criticisms that came after 1690 from Fénelon, Vauban, Boisguillebert, and Boulainvilliers, among others, were at base an attack upon the cult of absolute monarchy, though not upon the institution of the crown itself. Meanwhile, the defenders of sacred monarchy maintained an ominous silence on the miracle of the royal touch. All this was a reflection of similar, more thoroughgoing manifestations of a *crise de conscience* affecting Europe during the second half of Louis XIV's reign, and they foreshadowed the full-scale domestic critique of French absolutism that came in the next generation, Montesquieu's generation, when Usbek would write, "Ce roi est un grand magicien."[40]

[39] Philip A. Knachel, *England and the Fronde* (Ithaca, 1967), *passim*.

[40] On Fénelon, Vauban, and other articulate critics, see Lionel Rothkrug, *Opposition to Louis XIV: The Political and Social Origins of the French Enlightenment* (Princeton, 1965); Roland Mousnier, "Les Idées politiques de Fénelon," *XVIIᵉ siècle*, Nos. 12–14 (1951–1952), pp. 190–206; Sébastien Le Prestre, Maréchal de Vauban, *Projet d'une dixme royale*, ed. E. Coornaert (Paris, 1933); and Werner Gembruch, "Reformforderungen in Frankreich um die Wende von

29625

What gave the views of Louis XIV's critics special pointedness was the backdrop of the War of the Spanish Succession. Unprecedentedly long, costly beyond all example, and clearly dynastic in its origins, the war seemed to many well-informed subjects of the Sun King an unmitigated disaster for France. In this way, fears abroad of a Bourbon universal monarchy merged with the dawning French sentiment that the king's interests might diverge from those of the nation. This combination of objections, formulated in books, pamphlets, and periodicals, comprised a critique impossible to answer in visual imagery, by religious ritual or with panegyrics. If the critics were to be refuted, it would have to be on their own field of argument and, externally at least, on their own terms. Thus Torcy's propaganda response also came in printed form, and books, pamphlets, and serial publications became the dominant vehicle of propaganda as formulated during the last phase of Louis XIV's reign.

MINISTER-PROPAGANDIST

Between the propaganda of Richelieu and Louis XIV's total propaganda, the crucial mediating figure was Colbert. In-

---

17. zum 18. Jahrhunderts," *Historische Zeitschrift*, 209 (October 1969), 265–317. (Although Fénelon's private comments were highly critical of Louis XIV in 1709, the public sermons of the archbishop of Cambrai remained conventionally orthodox. He concluded one order for public prayers supplicating God "pour la prosperité des armes du Roi, afin qu'il nous procure, selon ses desseins, un repos qui console l'Eglise aussi bien que les peuples, et qui soit sur la terre une image du repos céleste." *La Clef du cabinet des princes de l'Europe*, June 1709, p. 376.) Huguenot and other French critics are discussed in the neglected work of Friedrich Kleyser, *Der Flugschriftenkampf gegen Ludwig XIV. zur Zeit des pfälzischen Krieges* (Berlin, 1935). Much evidence on popular opposition can be found in A. de Boislisle, "Le Grand Hiver et la disette de 1709," *Revue des questions historiques*, 73 (1903), 442–509; 74 (1904), 486–542. On popular and learned attitudes to the royal touch, see Bloch, *Les Rois thaumaturges*, pp. 356, 363, in which the line from *The Persian Letters* became a famous epigraph.

heritor of the legacy, if not the titles, of the cardinal-ministers in whose image he was trained, Colbert vastly expanded the scope of crown propaganda. In so doing, Colbert forged a chain that joined the great crown servants of the early seventeenth century with the most important minister of Louis XIV's last years: his nephew, Colbert de Torcy. The Colbert dynasty represented not only a family tie but a continuity of tradition that helped lend a degree of consistency to absolutist principles of statecraft throughout the century. Colbert de Torcy was ever conscious of his great predecessors and intentionally modeled himself upon them.

Jean-Baptiste Colbert, Marquis de Torcy, secretary of state for foreign affairs and royal minister from 1699 to the Sun King's death in 1715, was a second-generation minister. His father, Charles Colbert de Croissy, who preceded Torcy as foreign minister, had named this, his first son, for the brother and patron who founded the ministerial clan of Colbert. The choice of name expressed hope as well as respect and gratitude, for young Jean-Baptiste was raised as heir apparent to his father's offices. Colbert de Croissy sent his son to the Collège de La Marche in Paris, where he was trained in philosophy and law, becoming an *avocat* in 1683 at age eighteen. This was three years after Louis chose Colbert de Croissy as secretary of state for foreign affairs, replacing the discredited Simon Arnauld de Pomponne. In 1684 Torcy began an educational tour of European capitals that was to occupy him for the next five years. He visited Lisbon and Madrid, London and Rome, as well as parts of Scandinavia and Germany. At every stop there was some small official duty to perform; for example, he conveyed Louis XIV's greeting to the king of Portugal upon his accession to the throne. These missions provided an excuse for the young man to write reports to the king in which he displayed a precocious grasp of the diversity of European politics and considerable insight into the character of the people he met.[41]

[41] On Torcy's early career, see the family portrait written by his

Croissy's careful presentation of his son to Louis bore fruit when the king granted Torcy the *survivance* of his father's office of secretary of state for foreign affairs. During the War of the League of Augsburg, father and son worked at the administration of the growing and increasingly complex bureau of foreign affairs. The young man accompanied the king on the campaigns of 1691 and 1692 and carried out the duties of secretary of state while Croissy remained at Versailles. Torcy's intelligence, ability, and charm impressed Louis, but when Croissy died in 1695 he would not entrust the delicate peace negotiations under way to so young and untested a secretary. Fortunately, an experienced hand was available, for Louis had meanwhile recalled Arnauld de Pomponne to his council. At Croissy's death, Torcy was confirmed in his father's office of secretary of state for foreign affairs, while Pomponne stayed on as minister and member of the king's council. The ministerial revolution was capped by the symbolic reconciliation of the Colberts and their rivals: at Louis' command, Torcy married Pomponne's daughter, Catherine-Félicité. From all accounts, it was a happy match, and it appears that the same was true of the relationship between Pomponne and Torcy from 1696 to 1699. Pomponne supervised the negotiations for the Treaty of Ryswick and set the policy of handling the question of the Spanish succession through partition treaties, but with his death Torcy became a full-fledged minister. He had already been sitting in on council meetings for more than a year. At thirty-four years of age, he was the product of more careful training for ministerial office

---

daughter, the Marquise d'Ancezune, BN, Mss. fr. 10668. This has been printed in J. Marchand, "La Vie du Marquis de Torcy," *Revue d'histoire diplomatique*, 46 (1932), 310–343; 47 (1933), 51–76, 189–214. Some of Torcy's memoirs appear in J. Marchand, *La Mission extraordinaire du Marquis de Torcy et son voyage en Danemark-Norvège et en Suède, 1685* (Paris, 1951). For Croissy's letters to his son during this period, see L. Delavaud, "L'Éducation d'un ministre," *Revue de Paris* (1910), pp. 331–368.

than any of Louis' "second-generation" advisers, with the possible exception of Colbert's son, Seignelay. Torcy's career shows that the practice of ministerial dynasticism could produce well-prepared, experienced officials.[42]

Torcy's tenure as foreign minister was dominated by the burdens of a catastrophic war. From 1702 to 1708 Louis' armies lost all the important battles. In 1709 France was paralyzed by the coldest winter and worst crop failure in living memory. Famine followed. At the same time, the Sun King's enemies erected impossible peace terms and long-sought peace negotiations broke down. In these years a foreign minister did well simply to survive. Castigated by the impatient, the ambitious, and the merely long-suffering, a victim of the frustrated Louis' outbursts against his advisers,[43] Torcy managed to retain his self-assurance. Other ministers, notably Michel Chamillart, who was controller-general of finance and led the war department until 1709, were defeated by misfortune. But Torcy was sustained in part by his belief in providence as the arbiter of events, especially in its guise as the god of battle. Like Louis XIV, Torcy concluded that God had abandoned France and was punishing her, but unlike his king the minister never lost his faith that one day France's enemies would suffer divine retribution for their greed and shortsightedness.[44]

[42] On Torcy's family life, see L. Delavaud, "Une Grande Dame du XVIIIe siècle: Marguérite-Thérèse Colbert de Croissy, Duchesse de Saint-Pierre," *Revue du XVIIIe siècle*, 1 (1913); L. Delavaud, "Scènes de la vie diplomatique au XVIIIe siècle," *ibid.*, 2 (1914). On Pomponne and Torcy, see Pomponne to Louis, 3 March 1697, AAE, MD, France 305, fols. 81–82. For a discussion of Torcy's family and finances, see William Roth, "Jean-Baptiste Colbert, Marquis de Torcy," in Roland Mousnier, *Le Conseil du roi de Louis XIII à la Révolution* (Paris, 1970), pp. 175–203.

[43] *Journal inédit de Jean-Baptiste Colbert, Marquis de Torcy*, ed. F. Masson (Paris, 1884), p. 125.

[44] Among many examples, here is one passage from Torcy's *Journal*, p. 282, dated 30–31 August 1710: "Lorsque Dieu nous regardera en pitié, que le temps de punir l'orgueil de nos ennemis sera venu, pour lors, il les aveuglera à leur tour; le voile dont il a couvert nos yeux

When the opportunity for peace presented itself in 1711, Torcy made the most of it. His private negotiations with the English at Versailles and Fontainebleau produced far more of the Treaty of Utrecht than did the galaxy of princes and plenipotentiaries gathered in Holland. Then Torcy and Marshal Villars negotiated peace with the emperor in 1714. The king, very old and very tired, slipped back into the shadows in these years, but Torcy was by no means done when the war was. The last year of the reign saw the beginnings of a policy of rapprochement with the house of Austria meant to insure that the peace should not be soon disturbed, as well as an attempt to install the Stuart pretender in England. After 1710 Torcy was something like a chief minister, first among his colleagues and holding the full confidence of his old and broken master.[45]

Torcy's diplomatic initiatives in the unfavorable political atmosphere of his period of tenure were accompanied by a series of far-reaching, imaginative administrative reforms. Under his leadership an archive of diplomatic dispatches and memoranda was collected, organized and established in permanent quarters. Attempts were made to establish a pool of professional, trained diplomatic secretaries to provide stability in the practice of foreign affairs, and closely

---

depuis tant d'années se dissipera. Nous rougirons et nous profiterons de nos fautes que nous ne voulons pas encore avouer, et cet aveu sera le premier miracle qu'il opérera en notre faveur, comme il en a fait tant d'autres depuis six ans pour nous humilier."

[45] Torcy is occasionally referred to as "le premier ministre" from 1710; see La Blinière to Pecquet, Gertruydenberg, 17 June 1710, AAE, CP, Hollande 225, fol. 86. Matthew Prior and other foreign observers thought of Torcy as Louis' "chiefest minister," and so he was for foreign affairs; but we should remember that the other ministers of this period—Pontchartrain, Voysin, Desmarets, and Beauvillier— were all strong and competent men. In no sense was Torcy's position comparable to Richelieu and Mazarin, true chief ministers to whom other councillors were subservient in a patron-creature relationship. Cf. John C. Rule, "King and Minister, Louis XIV and Colbert de Torcy," in *William III and Louis XIV*, ed. R. Hatton and J. S. Bromley (Liverpool, 1968), pp. 213–236.

tied to this effort was the founding of the Académie politique as a school for prospective members of the foreign service. Historians are now becoming aware of a "second reform period" late in Louis XIV's reign, the features of
which in many ways parallel the innovations of the 1660's.
Thus, Colbert de Torcy's lineage may be taken as symbolic
of the continuity of ministerial reform connecting the early
and late stages of Louis XIV's reign.[46]

Nonetheless, this powerful minister of a state historians
call absolutist had to be constantly wary of opposition. During the peace negotiations, Henry St. John, Viscount Bolingbroke, the English secretary of state, remarked on "the
nature of our government and the character of our people,
how many precautions we have to take, how many opinions
we must reconcile [*esprits à ménager*]." Torcy's answer
reveals that he, unlike many historians, was well aware of
the power of public opinion in Louis XIV's state: "One of
[the faults of] the French Nation is to be eager and impatient, and when the responses on as important an affair
as the peace come too slowly for the taste of the public,
innumerable voices are raised against those the public holds
responsible. Sometimes, too, private interest contributes to
the public's censure, and I assure you that there are moments
when even the most accomplished Stoic would be pained
to maintain his tranquility. Finally, my lord, if we are not
obliged here to reconcile opinions [*ménager les esprits*], we
at least find and we experience every day that despite national differences men are very much alike in their way of
thinking."[47]

[46]A. Baschet, *Histoire du dépôt des archives des affaires étrangères*
(Paris, 1875), pp. 101–116; Joseph Klaits, "Men of Letters and Politi-
cal Reform in France at the End of the Reign of Louis XIV: The
Founding of the Académie Politique," *Journal of Modern History*,
43:4 (December 1971), 577–597; Maurice Keens-Soper, "The French
Political Academy, 1712: A School for Ambassadors," *European
Studies Review*, 2 (October 1972), 329–355; Hatton, "Louis XIV:
Recent Gains," pp. 285–288.
[47]Bolingbroke to Torcy, 21 November/2 December 1712, AAE,

The "national differences" of political organization between absolutist France and constitutional Britain did not immunize Torcy from effective criticism. Many powerful and articulate Frenchmen did not believe that peace would ensue from the talks with England. In his correspondence with Bolingbroke, Torcy called these skeptics "infidels," people of no faith. With each concession to the allies he suffered renewed vilification. After Louis and Torcy gave up their long struggle to regain Tournai at the bargaining table, the minister wrote to Bolingbroke of "what I personally am suffering from this change of position; the infidels are victorious and I receive reproaches that other services will never efface."[48] And Matthew Prior, Bolingbroke's man at the French court, vouched for Torcy's discomfort: "I supped last night *pro more* with the family [Torcy's], and we were all merry, except Monsieur de Torcy, who is really a good deal concerned, and faith! with reason; he has more enemies than I thought, and has reason to apprehend every shock in our affairs."[49] In his *Mémoires* Torcy remarked that the prime mover in one of the cabals against him was none other than the leader of the French negotiating team at Utrecht, Marshal d'Huxelles.[50] Piqued perhaps by jealousy of the foreign minister, who was doing the real bargaining for peace while the great show of a peace conference went

---

CP, Angleterre 240, fols. 204–206. Torcy to Bolingbroke, Versailles, 10 December 1712 (copy), AAE, CP, Angleterre 242, fol. 202. The latter has been printed in *Letters and Correspondence Public and Private of the Right Honourable Henry St. John, Lord Viscount Bolingbroke*, ed. G. Parke (London, 1798), III, 213.

[48] Torcy to Bolingbroke, Versailles, 26 October 1712, Parke, *Letters . . . Bolingbroke*, III, 166.

[49] Prior to Bolingbroke, Fontainebleau, 2/13 September 1712, *ibid.*, III, 60.

[50] *Mémoires du Marquis de Torcy*, in *Nouvelle collection des mémoires pour servir à l'histoire de France*, ed. Michaud and Poujoulat, ser. 3, VIII (Paris, 1839), 636–661.

through its paces in Holland, d'Huxelles wrote to his friends at court, intimating that Torcy's negotiating strategy would prove unsuccessful. The marshal's criticisms were not original. All over France, people were speaking out against the slow pace of the talks, as Torcy himself admitted in his memoirs. "Their impatience for peace increased every day; they expressed themselves concerning it in a scandalous manner; they charged the king with want of solicitude to conclude it, and found fault with this pretended neglect. People of all ranks would have had him bend to the Dutch and their allies. In proportion as the negotiation advanced, the apprehension of missing the critical minute increased, and made a deeper impression even on those who were particularly informed of its present state."[51]

Dissatisfaction was so intense that no decision could silence the critics: "So long as his majesty insisted upon that restitution [of Tournai], they murmured in France at his firmness; and a great many people, wise in their own imaginations, looked upon it as a foolish obstinacy, to persist in demanding a town, which they were sure that France would never recover by treaty. What comparison, said they, between Tournay and peace; and is it not much better to relinquish a town, than to lose the opportunity of concluding a treaty so necessary to the safety of the kingdom? After he had given up Tournay, those very politicians grew louder in their complaints, stiling it weakness in the king, to leave the enemy in possession of a town so necessary for the security of his frontier." The conclusion Torcy drew in retrospect is that "Affairs of state would be very ill-administered, if the sovereign was to be guided by the public talk, or to consider it as the rule of his conduct. He ought frequently to stop his ears, if he would avoid the perilous shelves of political navigation. He should never lose sight of his point, but pursue constantly the same course, without

---

[51] *Ibid.*, p. 722a, as translated in *The Memoirs of Jean-Baptiste Colbert, Marquis de Torcy*, 2 vols. (London, 1757), II, 332–333.

suffering himself to be lulled to sleep by warbling syrens, or yielding to the complaints of mariners."[52]

Thus Torcy the memoirist, long after the event. Yet while the war was on, the foreign minister could not afford such Olympian detachment. Grumblings meant danger, and if there was opposition in 1712, with Torcy near the height of his influence, his status should have been far more precarious in previous years. By his own testimony we know of the criticism after the abortive peace talks of 1709. Torcy told a correspondent in Holland that he found himself "alone in maintaining, against the general opinion, that there is no way to arrive at a peace other than the route we have followed and [I have] no proof at hand for supporting my opinion."[53] Yet the minister knew how to combat his critics and opponents: he calculatingly exposed his burdens to Matthew Prior in 1712 and to the Dutch in 1709 in order to convince the foreign negotiators that he had gone as far as he could toward a peace compromise. For Torcy, then, wartime diplomatic conditions made foreign and French domestic opinion two sides of a single ministerial problem. And so, as we shall find, when negotiation was impossible or fruitless, he attempted to manipulate opinion both at home and throughout Europe by censorship, planted news and comment, royal pronouncements and commissioned political tracts.

[52] Torcy, *Mémoires*, in Michaud and Poujoulat, *Nouvelle collection*, p. 733, as translated in Torcy, *Memoirs* (London ed.), ii, 371–372.

[53] Torcy to Petkum, Marly, 21 October 1709 (minute), AAE, CP, Hollande 220, fol. 21.

CHAPTER TWO

Censorship

THE royal ministers of seventeenth-century France had a special horror of public, uncontrolled political discussion. Along with that other forbidden subject, religion, rulership was regarded as a mystery, and its practice was reserved to a few select initiates holding the confidence of the monarch. Even the official learned academies which the government patronized were specifically prohibited from prying into matters of state. Anyone who dared invade the sacred precincts with printed criticism was likely to be confronted with the fury and contempt of crown servants. The word they used to describe critical writings, *libelles*, accurately connotes the lavish disdain with which the government regarded these efforts. Seventeenth-century antiquarians found ample proof that Roman jurisprudence had meted out capital punishment to authors of defamatory writings, and by making this crime a species of treason the formulators of French absolutism attempted to emulate the imperial age they so admired.[1]

We have already seen that a theory of censorship was fundamental to absolutism, but the effort to translate this theory into reality is a subject that needs discussion. The printing press, because it had become a primary means of

[1] A. Aubery, *Histoire du Cardinal de Richelieu* (Paris, 1660), pp. 212–213; Martin, *Livre*, pp. 441–466. On the academies, see Yates, *French Academies*, p. 304*n*, quoting Fontenelle, and Charles Perrault's letter to Colbert, in *Lettres, instructions et mémoires de Colbert*, ed. Pierre Clément, 8 vols. (Paris, 1862–1882), v, 512–513. Even Théophraste Renaudot, an intimate of Richelieu, steered clear of politics in his Bureau d'Adresse conferences; see Solomon, *Public Welfare*, p. 88.

disseminating information, affected the crown's censorship efforts in two opposite ways. First, by greatly multiplying the potential number of copies that could be made of a given item, print made restricting the *distribution* of already-published materials a nearly unattainable goal. On the other hand, however, the cumbersomeness of the process by which printed works were manufactured meant that the *production* of publications might plausibly be controlled. Accordingly, under the leadership of Colbert and, later, that of Chancellor Pontchartrain, Louis XIV's government introduced systematic regulation of the production side of the publishing industry. The intent was to impose a network of interlocking authorities over the manufacturing process so as to allow surveillance of each and every printing press.[2]

The Parisian printers were at the center of the crown's plans. Already the publishing capital of France, Paris was systematically favored by administrative policies of regulation through centralization. Working with Nicolas de La Reynie and his successor, Marc-René Voyer d'Argenson, the crown-appointed lieutenants general of police in Paris, and through the municipal assembly of booksellers and printers, Colbert and Pontchartrain drastically reduced the number of presses in Paris by driving the smaller houses out of business and barring additional guild members. The remaining large houses were given preferential privileges, allowing

[2] The following discussion is based on David T. Pottinger, *The French Book Trade in the Ancien Régime, 1500–1791* (Cambridge, Mass., 1958), pp. 54–81; Martin, *Livre*, pp. 662–772; Madeleine Ventre, *L'Imprimerie et la librairie en Languedoc au dernier siècle de l'Ancien Régime (1700–1789)* (Paris & The Hague, 1958), pp. 75–215; Jean Quéniart, *L'Imprimerie et la librairie à Rouen au XVIIIᵉ siècle* (Paris, 1970), esp. pp. 172–178; Raymond Birn, "The Profits of Ideas, *Privilèges en librairie* in Eighteenth-Century France," *Eighteenth-Century Studies*, 4:2 (Winter 1970), 132–134; and Paul Chauvet, *Les Ouvriers du livre en France des origines à la Révolution de 1789* (Paris, 1959), pp. 205–209, 211–212, 490–492. Much of this literature is ably summarized by R. Mandrou, *Louis XIV en son temps, 1661–1715* (Paris, 1973), pp. 161–168.

them to ruin or reduce to dependency printers in such formerly thriving provincial centers as Lyon, Rouen, and Bordeaux. Corporate exclusivism and the interests of the crown were here combined. This centralization permitted a vigilant direction of the remaining Paris presses and also made it less likely that a Paris publisher would risk his reputation by printing forbidden works. By applying the same principles of rigorous control to the paper industry, the crown attempted to limit the supply of raw materials and hence oversee the printers' output. These measures were joined with royal censorship of individual books by a system of prior restraint. As regularized under Pontchartrain, the chancellor's office, upon request from the lieutenant of police, appointed an examiner for each manuscript proposed for publication in Paris. Only after receiving assurance from the examiner that submitted works were free of danger to religion and public morals did the government authorize publication.

Before making even a preliminary judgment about the effectiveness of the royal censorship apparatus, it is essential to distinguish between the controls imposed on book production and those attempted on circulation. The remarkable aspect of the crown's management of book manufacturing, as opposed to distribution, was not the occasional lapses from which it suffered but its general effectiveness throughout the reign, at least in Paris. Taking into account the limitations imposed upon absolutist government by the undeveloped administrative technology of the age, the organization of book production under Louis XIV was fairly well contrived to serve the crown's needs.[3]

Where the censorship apparatus proved inadequate was not in managing production but in overseeing circulation. It was impossible to organize effective checks upon the vast

[3] Martin, *Livre*, pp. 757–772; Birn, "Profits," p. 134. Anne Sauvy, *Livres saisis à Paris entre 1678 et 1710* (The Hague, 1972), p. 5, apparently finds a decline in rigorous enforcement of production controls after 1700, but offers no evidence for this chronology.

numbers of French-language writings manufactured abroad and imported into France, especially from the United Provinces. Private commercial contracts provided for the marketing of books from Holland, and, since the Dutch had become the leaders of the European publishing industry, crown efforts to tamper with these arrangements met with resistance from French booksellers and their customers, even in wartime. Although it was of course possible to ban specific imported works, such edicts were always difficult to enforce. Smuggling a batch of prohibited works hidden in a bulky commercial shipment remained a common practice, and bribery of customs officials often succeeded where concealment did not. The large number of entry points for books into France, including both port cities and frontier towns, increased the likelihood that at least some consignments of banned works would slip through. Once inside the country, control was theoretically possible through surveillance of the bookdealers' stocks, but despite regular inspections by the lieutenant general's office in Paris many illegal books found their way to buyers in the capital. In the provinces controls were much looser, and the suffering, dependent bookdealers of such cities as Rouen and Lyon had little prudential inhibition against trading in prohibited works from abroad. Free of the careful supervision under which Parisian printers operated, provincial publishers even produced many forbidden works for sale all over France.[4]

The relative freedom of circulation enjoyed by writings from abroad considerably diminished the effectiveness of the government's campaign to control the reading matter of Frenchmen. Especially after the revocation of the Edict of Nantes in 1685, the works of French writers published abroad grew dramatically in volume and significance. The revocation prompted a mass migration of skilled Huguenots to various countries of refuge in Protestant Europe. Hugue-

[4] Martin, *Livre*, pp. 591–596, 739–753, and esp. 758–759; *Archives de la Bastille*, ed. F. Ravaisson-Mollien (Paris, 1882), XIII, 27–31; Quéniart, *L'Imprimerie*, pp. 22–23; *Lettres . . . de Colbert*, VI, 28n.

not writers tended to gravitate to Holland, where thought and the publishing industry enjoyed relative freedom. Smaller groups could also be found in England, Switzerland and Germany. Many of these authors produced unexceptionable scholarly works which the French government had no interest in prohibiting. Colbert de Torcy himself took advantage of a negotiating trip to The Hague in 1709 to open an account with a prominent local dealer who specialized in French-language books.[5] Other writers, however, as we have already observed, applied their hatred of Louis XIV in a variety of literary formats, including gazettes, pamphlets, and book-length tracts.

Each issue of a typical gazette consisted of articles datelined from the various courts and capitals of Europe. In publishing their correspondents' contributions, the editors gave mass circulation to material that was initially written for distribution via manuscript newsletters. For although the printed periodical had become a permanent institution by the end of the seventeenth century, the newsletter trade continued to thrive. In France, where censorship restrictions limited the availability of printed news, these *nouvelles à la main* or *gazettes à la main*, as they were variously called, remained the single most important source of information on war and diplomacy. Inconspicuously composed and copied by Grub Street writers all over Europe and easily distributed via the mails, the manuscript newsletters were passed from hand to hand in personal correspondence. It was a universally observed courtesy to include a one- or two-page manuscript news summary in letters, so in this way ordinary social and business correspondence provided the vehicle for news circulation. The newsletters also came to be sold more or less openly on city streets. The *nouvellistes* who composed these manuscripts not only provided material for the printed gazettes but also copied and circulated news they found in the journals. As simultaneous source and

[5] Torcy to Moetjens, Marly, 15 November 1709 (minute), AAE, CP, Hollande 220, fol. 150.

39

agent of dissemination for printed news, the newsletters were a response to the pressures of censorship that continued to restrict the influence of print.[6]

In analyzing the reaction of the French government to the threat posed by free circulation of gazettes, pamphlets, and manuscript newsletters, we are hampered by the absence of the most important documentary sources. Of the relevant archives, those of the chancellor, the crown official responsible for preventive censorship, and of the lieutenant of police, who dealt with censorship violations in Paris, survive only in fragments. Given these gaps in the sources, we will never have a complete picture of censorship procedures under Louis XIV. But because of the important role taken by Colbert de Torcy in censorship matters between 1700 and 1715, the records of the foreign ministry, combined with the archives of the Bastille, supply enough material for at least a rough sketch of the government's methods.

Torcy's participation in literary censorship stemmed partly from principles of government organization and partly from personal circumstance. Often under the *ancien régime* jurisdictions overlapped or were fragmented, and censorship was a case in point. The secretary of state for foreign affairs was given censorship authority over all literary material concerning diplomacy and foreign relations. Like so much else in Louis XIV's government—and perhaps in any government—this was an elastic authority that could be stretched or shrunk, depending on the inclinations of the person who occupied the office. During Torcy's tenure the foreign minister wielded his administrative control over censorship regularly and systematically. His growing influ-

---

[6] See F. Funck-Brentano, *Figaro et ses devanciers* (Paris, 1909). Examples of *nouvelles à la main* for 1701–1704 are in AN, M. 757, No. 4, and 766. They were written by Père Léonard; see AN, M. 766, No. 6. Cf. J.-B. Vanel, *Une Nouvelliste lyonnaise à la fin du règne de Louis XIV* (Lyon, 1903), p. 25; see also Bellanger, *Histoire*, I, 177. On the survival of newsletters in the age of print, see Fraser, *Intelligence*, p. 43.

ence in general governmental affairs probably contributed to his control of this special area, but more important was the close working relationship Torcy developed with d'Argenson, the capable lieutenant of police for Paris after 1697. In the challenging last years of Louis XIV, d'Argenson succeeded in maintaining the traditions of administrative strength he inherited from his predecessor, La Reynie. He kept in close touch with Torcy, via both correspondence and face to face conversations during the foreign minister's many visits to Paris. Over the years Torcy and d'Argenson became friends and close colleagues, so much so that the lieutenant intended one of his two subsequently much-celebrated sons for a diplomatic career under Torcy's patronage.[7]

There were also family precedents for Torcy's concern with Paris. His father, Colbert de Croissy, was at one time intendant of Paris and retained both his contacts and concern with the city after his elevation to the foreign ministry. During the War of the Spanish Succession, d'Argenson was required by Torcy to refer to Versailles all requests for the printing or sale of literary material which concerned foreign affairs. The foreign minister and his *commis* carefully evaluated each request, and the lieutenant of police passed on the minister's orders to the offices of the assembly of booksellers and printers in Paris. In general, the guild itself enforced the ministerial decisions, supervising its own members. Thus Torcy could rely on the energetic d'Argenson to bring to his attention any manuscript on war and diplomacy which had been presented for the censor's approval in Paris, as well as many similar books and pamphlets printed abroad and sent to Paris for sale. Throughout the war we find the foreign minister acting to prohibit the printing or sale of books, pamphlets and engravings whose contents were embarrassing to the government or disrespectful of the monarch.[8] He also issued permits for the publication and

[7] See the list of students enrolled in Torcy's short-lived Académie politique, AAE, MD, France 221, fol. 72.

[8] Torcy to d'Argenson, 18 February 1704, AAE, MD, France 1129,

distribution of works presented for approval when they favored the government's cause.[9]

These measures kept Parisian book production in hand, but they dealt not at all with the rest of the kingdom. Rouen remained a particularly notorious center for the printing of prohibited works, despite the best efforts of Chancellor Pontchartrain to exert his authority over the book trade there. Between 1700 and 1710 Pontchartrain lamented that "printing of bad books goes on at Rouen with greater liberty than ever," that "there is no place in the kingdom where prohibited *libelles* are printed with more license than in Rouen," and, worst of all, that "Paris is often flooded with these editions." His protests to the intendant and parlement at Rouen were ineffective, once again demonstrating that by alienating provincial publishers the policy of controlling book production through centralization in Paris was in part self-defeating.[10]

---

fol. 10; d'Argenson to Torcy, Paris, 6 August 1706, AAE, CP, Suisse 174, fol. 334; Torcy to d'Argenson, Versailles, 7 August 1706, AAE, CP, Suisse 174, fol. 345; Torcy to d'Argenson, 26 December 1712, AAE, CP, Hongrie 16, fol. 353; Torcy to d'Argenson, Versailles, 1 April 1713 (minute), AAE, CP, Angleterre 248, fol. 324; d'Argenson's reply, *ibid.*, fol. 324. An exception is noted in d'Argenson to Torcy, Paris, 10 October 1703, AAE, MD, France 1118, fols. 156–157, where d'Argenson apologizes for having let slip into print a critique of one of Torcy's propaganda tracts. "Je ne souffriray plus que l'on imprime de mon authorité aucun ouvrage ou la politique ait la moindre part. C'est bien assez que la liberté françoise se repande en discours inconsiderez sur ce sujet sans qu'elle passe jusqu'aux Escrits." For the collaboration of the predecessors of Torcy and d'Argenson, see Croissy to Renaudot, Versailles, 17 April 1692, BN, N.a. fr. 7492, fol. 198; also d'Argenson to Delamare, BN, Mss. fr. 21745, fol. 55. The ministerial tutelage of the Paris lieutenants general of police is discussed by Orest Ranum, *Paris in the Age of Absolutism* (New York, 1968), pp. 272–292.

[9] D'Argenson to Torcy, Paris, 11 June 1702, AAE, CP, Cologne 54, fols. 273–274. Bourgeois du Chastenet to Torcy, Paris, 14 September 1711, AAE, CP, Cologne 60, fol. 65.

[10] Quéniart, *L'Imprimerie*, pp. 22–23. Other provincial cities were also centers for prohibited books; see G. Parguez, "Essai sur l'origine

Despite governmental impotence in the provinces, Torcy and d'Argenson moved consistently and vigorously against the *ad hominem*, slanderous *lardons* published abroad, confiscating them whenever they were discovered in Paris and taking reprisals against those implicated in their distribution. Toward the foreign gazettes and pamphlets less personal in tone, the authorities adopted a more flexible attitude. The censors tried to make certain that they were not reprinted in France and that the Parisian peddlers did not hawk them to the *peuple* in the streets. In general, however, they gave the literate and politically conscious tacit permission to purchase the gazettes at the several Parisian "news bureaus" where well-bred people gathered. Offensive gazettes and tracts were seized when discovered, but the authorities knew—it was already a truism at the end of the seventeenth century—that the notoriety of censorship tended to make a book more desirable, so that from the government's viewpoint some writings might better be left in uncensored obscurity.[11]

---

lyonnaise d'éditions clandestines de la fin du XVIIᵉ siècle," in *Nouvelles études lyonnaises* (Geneva, 1969); and A. Lottin, *Vie et mentalité d'un lillois sous Louis XIV* (Lille, 1968), pp. 178–180.

[11] D'Argenson to Torcy, Paris, 28 May 1702 (and minute of Torcy's reply), AAE, CP, Hollande 198, fol. 266; Torcy to d'Argenson, Versailles, 26 February 1704 (minute), AAE, MD, France 1129, fol. 18; d'Argenson to Torcy, 11 October 1704, AAE, CP, Angleterre 216, fol. 205; Torcy to d'Argenson, Fontainebleau, 15 October 1704, AAE, MD, France 1129, fol. 181; Torcy to d'Argenson, Fontainebleau, 2 August 1712 (minute), AAE, MD, France 1187, fol. 14; Torcy to d'Argenson, 9 September 1712 (minute), AAE, MD, France 1187, fol. 69; *Notes de René d'Argenson*, ed. L. Lanchey and E. Mabille (Paris, 1866), p. 74. D'Argenson to Torcy, Paris, 3 August 1709: "Il me semble que ce livre se decrie par luy mesme malgré le goust que la deffens donne ordinairement pour les ouvrages les plus mediocres" (AAE, CP, Hollande 221, fol. 304). Sauvy, *Livres saisis*, pp. 12–14, counts 122 confiscations (83 works) of books on political themes between 1678 and 1701 in Paris; surely this was only a small fraction of the total number of prohibited volumes circulating there. Among the most frequently seized works during this period were the

Torcy had more direct ways of coping with the inflammatory literature from abroad. He went to the source of the infection and pressed foreign governments to exercise self-censorship over their writers by banning the gazettes, tracts, and *lardons*. Thus, in April of 1701, while French and Dutch ministers traded charges of designs for war, d'Avaux, Louis' envoy to the United Provinces, protested against the Amsterdam monthly, *L'Esprit des cours de l'Europe*, for its defamation of the king and its accusations of French plans for aggression. The envoy told Torcy: "I am conducting myself in conformity with what your father formerly prescribed to me in similar situations, that is, to ignore these things, to despise them and above all not to bring complaints about them before the Estates-General until I am assured that they will make a judicial example. . . . I will find means to have this *libelle* brought to the attention of the Estates-General without making an appearance there and without committing the king."[12]

Within a month d'Avaux was able to report that "the Pensionary [Heinsius] had sent word that we will not see *L'Esprit des cours* any more and that the author has been absolutely forbidden to write in the future; this was accomplished without compromising the King's name in the affair."[13] Unfortunately for d'Avaux, he did not notice that the disappearance of *L'Esprit des cours* was mostly titular.

---

calumnious *Vie de Turenne* by Courtilz de Sandras (see B. M. Woodbridge, *Gatien de Courtilz, Sieur du Verger* [Baltimore, 1925]) and the supposed *Testament politique de Louvois*—works which insulted the crown by misrepresenting two of its foremost servants. For a discussion of "permissions tacites" after 1715, see François Furet, "La 'librairie' du royaume de France au 18ᵉ siècle," in Geneviève Bollème et al., *Livre et société dans la France du XVIIIᵉ siècle* (Paris & The Hague, 1965), pp. 3–32.

[12] D'Avaux to Torcy, La Haye, 14 April 1701, AAE, CP, Hollande 193, fol. 192. The precedents alluded to by d'Avaux are summarized in Hatin, *Gazettes*, pp. 93–97.

[13] D'Avaux to Torcy, La Haye, 12 May 1701, AAE, CP, Hollande 194, fol. 48.

Its editor, Nicolas Gueudeville, arranged for an associate to go on publishing the journal under a new name, *Nouvelles des cours de l'Europe*. The gazette did not so much as miss an issue, and after d'Avaux left Holland its original title and author were resumed.[14]

It was easier to regulate the press of the neutral Swiss cantons. Basel, a center of Huguenot activity on the French border, was particularly susceptible to influence, as this letter from Torcy to Puyzieulx, Louis' ambassador to Switzerland, makes clear:

The King has always despised this type of publication and His Majesty never has wanted his ministers to make complaints in his name. But it is so difficult for an ambassador to suffer a breach of the respect due to his master, and especially to a master like His Majesty, that if you ask my counsel I will tell you, Monsieur, that I would have the magistrates of Basel warned to pay more attention to what is printed in their city. If they should answer that they do not have the authority to prevent it, liberty being complete in that city, I would have the authors of these works threatened with the punishment their insolence deserves, to be received even in Basel itself. Threats of this kind will probably suffice to contain them, but if they are not any more well behaved [*plus sage*], I believe it will not be difficult to find ways of correcting them harshly. I draw your attention to the city of Basel, Monsieur, because it is so close to

[14] Bayle to Marais, 6 March 1702, quoted in Hatin, *Gazettes*, p. 190. Guillaume de Lamberty, Gueudeville's replacement, gave his version of the affair in his *Mémoires pour servir à l'histoire du XVIIIᵉ siècle* (Amsterdam, 1735), I, 391. Torcy also claimed some influence over this Dutch gazette during wartime; see his letter to La Chapelle, Versailles, 26 February 1706 (minute), AAE, CP, Suisse 173, fols. 144–145. For a discussion of *L'Esprit des cours de l'Europe*, see Yardeni, "Gueudeville," pp. 598–620. On a similar, not very fruitful effort to control the Dutch press in 1670, see Pomponne to Lionne, La Haye, 3 July 1670, AAE, CP, Hollande 90, fols. 258–259.

Huningue [of which Puyzieulx was royal governor] that you would have greater facility in carrying out whatever you might find suitable. And when you have restored these writers to duty, be it by authority of the magistrates, which is the better way, or by other means, I am persuaded that you will find the other Protestant cities better behaved; without, however, involving the authority of the King in a matter entirely indifferent to His Majesty, but which cannot be so regarded by his subjects.[15]

This passage reveals much about Torcy's assumptions regarding censorship. Its tone of bombastic, arrogant paternalism was a reflection of the crown's renewed self-confidence immediately after the Bourbon succession in Spain. Yet, although in all other governmental matters the king's servants sought to identify their actions with the personal will of the monarch, Torcy and the royal ambassadors here specifically dissociated their protests from the king's person. To preserve the dignity of the king and of the king's reputation, ministers and diplomats made it a consistent principle to deal with offensive printed attacks on their own initiative. As a subject and crown servant, Torcy took vigorous action to defend the reputation of the monarch from printed attacks. For to allow or seem to allow the Sun King direct contact with such despised, contaminated literature would have been to destroy the very reputation of royal grandeur Torcy hoped to preserve. In the field of censorship, then, the king's ministers had to be their own masters, guarding Louis XIV from a menace that his sense of the monarchical role forbade him even to acknowledge.

Once during the War of the Spanish Succession Torcy

[15] Torcy to Puyzieulx, Fontainebleau, 10 October 1701, AAE, CP, Suisse 132, fols. 150–151; Puyzieulx to Torcy, Soleure, 1 November 1701, AAE, CP, Suisse 129, fols. 161–161ᵛ. Cf. Meyer, *Flugschriften*, p. 22n. The *Gazette de Berne* had a readership in eastern France; see Puyzieulx to Bernage, Soleure, 21 November 1703, AAE, MD, France 1580, fols. 251–252.

and d'Argenson succeeded in permanently silencing an un-
friendly foreign journal. This was the misleadingly titled
Journal littéraire de Soleure, published during 1705 in the
duke of Lorraine's capital of Nancy. Its editor, the Pre-
monstratensian Father Charles-Louis Hugo, filled the seven
issues of his short-lived bimonthly with *ad hominem* attacks
upon the authors of competing gazettes and pamphlets. Unfortunately for Hugo, some of the works he criticized had
been commissioned by Torcy. As soon as the foreign minister and the lieutenant of police saw the first issues of the
Journal littéraire they banned its distribution in France, even
though the publication was being transported to Paris in
the packets sent by no less a personage than the duchess of
Lorraine to her mother, Madame, Louis XIV's sister-in-law.
The ban in France meant commercial ruin for the Nancy
journal, and it ceased publication at the end of 1705.[16]

As the war dragged on, Torcy grew increasingly resent-
ful of the contents of the Dutch gazettes and political tracts.
From 1709 to 1712 he protested vehemently to his contacts
in Holland that the government of the United Provinces
should take steps against the offending authors. His stated objections were twofold—that the journals were printing what
should have been deemed secret news of the peace negotiations, and that the wild slander of the tracts only served to
"embitter hearts which one should be seeking to reconcile."[17] One of the considerations that led Torcy to abandon

[16] On the authorship and circulation of this journal, see Delamare's
notes in BN, Mss. fr. 21741, fol. 180; BN, coll. Lorraine 269, fol. 43;
and A. Barbier, *Dictionnaire des ouvrages anonymes*, 4 vols. (Paris,
1872–1879), II, 1035. Reviews of tracts commissioned by Torcy appeared in *Journal littéraire de Soleure*, January 1705, p. 77 (*Manifeste
de l'Electeur de Bavière*); and April-May 1705, pp. 236 ff. (*Lettres
d'un suisse*). Hugo also publicized the anti-French tracts of Casimir
Freschot in his issues of April-May 1705, pp. 225–227; June-July 1705,
pp. 395–400; and October-November 1705, pp. 484 ff. On the actions
taken by Torcy and d'Argenson against this journal, see BN, Mss. fr.
21741. fol. 181; and Père Léonard's notes in AN, M. 758, No. 6[18].
[17] Torcy to Basnage, 14 January 1712 (copy), AAE, CP, Hollande
242, fol. 10.

all hope of working with the Dutch to negotiate a general peace after the disappointments of 1709 and 1710 was what he regarded as the faithlessness exhibited by the leaders of the United Provinces, first in leaking news of the secret bargaining, then in misrepresenting the positions taken, and in impugning the sincerity of the French at The Hague and Gertruydenberg negotiations.[18] One could have no confidence in and hence no dealings with enemies who broke the rules of diplomacy, Torcy complained. Also, the Dutch authorities appeared to be unaware of the "respect due to crowned heads," a respect singularly lacking in tracts published under their jurisdiction.[19] As soon as Torcy gained a modicum of leverage through his negotiations with the English Tories, he laid it down almost as a precondition of the assembly of Utrecht that the offensive gazettes and other tracts from Holland be censored.[20]

[18] Torcy accused the Dutch of bad faith in 1709 (*Mémoires*, p. 570). And he maintained that they stirred up people's suspicions "à leur persuader que l'unique but de la France étoit de les tromper" in 1710 (pp. 640–641). "Le public en étoit si persuadé [that the Gertruydenberg conferences would fail] qu'on offroit communement à La Haye le pari de trois contre un sur l'inutilité des conférences" (p. 641). The leaders of the alliance "ne cessoient de répandre qu'il falloit se défier continuellement de ses artifices [France's] et n'oublièrent rien pour empêcher que la sincerité des intentions du Roi ne fut connue et ne fit sur les peuples une impression trop vive" (p. 642).

[19] Torcy to Petkum, Versailles, 4 April 1709 (minute): "Je ne puis m'empescher de vous dire à cette occasion que je suis toujours surpris de voir jusqu'à quel point de licence on permet à quelques autheurs de ces écrits publics de s'emporter contre le respect deub aux testes couronnées" (AAE, CP, Hollande 217, fols. 242–242^v).

[20] Torcy to Basnage, 14 January 1712 (copy), AAE, CP, Hollande 242, fol. 10: "Mais il faudroit en le [the peace negotiations; "ce grand ouvrage" is the antecedent] commenceant bannir cette foule d'Escrits impertinens dont la plus grande partie ne contient que des repetitions fades et ennuyeuses, des reflexions insipides que plusieurs mauvais Ecrivains repandent depuis un grand nombre d'années." But Torcy was careful to add this request of his learned Huguenot correspondent: "Vous me ferez cependant plaisir Monsieur lorsqu'il paroit quelqu'un de ces Ecrits de me les envoyer et je vous prie en

Torcy had an additional, private objection to the Dutch gazettes of 1709 and 1710: they printed news from France, and the news they printed was almost all bad. In his *Mémoires* he wrote repeatedly of the damage done to the royal bargaining position by the conviction, held as an article of faith by the allies, that France was near collapse and that Louis would be compelled to accept any terms his enemies might suggest in order to save king and kingdom from total ruin.[21] At times Torcy himelf was not far from accepting this desperate counsel, and certainly there was a peace-at-any-price faction led by powerful spokesmen within Louis' council, but the foreign minister consistently argued that if the French hoped to negotiate from strength they must first disabuse the allies of their exaggerated notions of impotence and defeatism in France.[22]

Events showed that the allies miscalculated in placing their demands so high at The Hague and Gertruydenberg. One explanation for their errors is the extravagant conception they had of France's straitened condition. Their information

---

mesme temps d'y adjouster un mémoire de la dépense qu'il faut necessairement faire pour les avoir." Significantly, Torcy never protested against the *Lettres historiques* of Basnage de Beauval or the *Bibliothèque universelle et historique* of Jean Leclerc, publications which avoided slander and *ad hominem* argumentation. Cf. Yardeni, "Journalisme," pp. 219, 225.

[21] See, for example, this passage on 1709: "Les discours étoient aussi tristes que les sujets de raisonnemens: on enchérissoit encore sur les mauvais état du royaume; et ce que chacun disoit, vrai ou faux, passoit dans les pays étrangers. . . . Les nouvelles que les étrangers en recevoient persuadoient sans peine qu'elles [the provinces of France] étoient épuisées d'hommes et d'argent" (Torcy, *Mémoires*, p. 583).

[22] The allies were suffering too, but "l'idée qu'on a en Hollande de notre mauvais état fait d'étranges effets, et ceux que la guerre fait souffrir dans ce pays oublient leur peines, dans l'espérance qu'ils ont d'accabler la France" (Torcy to Beauvillier, La Haye, 14 May 1709, in Torcy, *Mémoires*, pp. 599–600; also cf. p. 654). For the opinions of Prince Eugene and Van der Dussen of France's need for peace, see Winston S. Churchill, *Marlborough*, 6 vols. (New York, 1933–1938), VI, 68–69.

on this matter was drawn largely from their own gazettes, and the gazettes' sources were the manuscript newsletters of the day which private correspondents throughout France enclosed in their letters to relatives, friends, and associates. While it might have been in the crown's interest to do so, it was an impossible task to eliminate these newsletters by censorship. Contemporaries frequently remarked on the passion of the fashionable Parisian public's taste for newsletters. The recently established coffeehouses had become an upper-class meeting place and the main exchange point for manuscript gazettes.[23] Thus, when Puyzieulx reported from Switzerland that "there are in Strasbourg dangerous writers who are not only recounting the events of Alsace all over this country and sending reports to Freiburg-im-Breisgau, but who also add their own explanations and private opinions," Torcy was not optimistic about curbing them. He knew that many in Strasbourg were not fond of the king's rule, so even after the foreign minister sent royal orders to La Houssaye, the intendant of Alsace, suppressing these newsletters, Torcy had to conclude that "it will be difficult to do so."[24]

Instead of attempting the impossible, the foreign minister made use of the same tactic that he relied on for the published gazettes by going to the source of the newsletter-writers' information. The hard news of politics, war, and diplomacy was exchanged only among the participants, but this exchange usually went through the post, the weak link in the chain of governmental as well as private secrecy.

[23] Bellanger, *Histoire*, I, 173; Martin, *Livre*, pp. 757–758; F. Funck-Brentano, *Les Nouvellistes* (Paris, 1905), p. 246. Cf. Ravaisson-Mollien, *Archives de la Bastille*, XI, 19–21; and *Lettres . . . de Colbert*, VI, 28 and 401.

[24] Puyzieulx to Torcy, Soleure, 19 March 1704, AAE, CP, Suisse 148, fols. 274–274ᵛ. Torcy to Puyzieulx, Versailles, 27 March 1704, AAE, CP, Suisse 147, fol. 278. Also cf. G.-B. Depping, *Correspondance administrative sous Louis XIV* (Paris, 1851), II, 787. On anti-French pamphlets in Strasbourg, see Georges Livet, *L'Intendance d'Alsace sous Louis XIV* (Paris, 1956), pp. 801–803.

Through the hands of the postal clerks passed diplomatic dispatches, letters from officers in the king's armies, and complaints on all manner of subjects. Torcy, who in addition to his other offices was superintendent of the post, maintained a *cabinet noir*, a specialized postal bureau whose function was systematically to open, read, summarize and re-expedite the correspondence of certain crucial figures in France.[25] The *commis* assigned this task had access to more news of France than anyone outside the government and most people within it. Clerks placed in other bureaus of the post office also had considerable opportunity to open dispatches that passed their way, and chronically low salaries made many of them open to corruption, either as writers or suppliers of news. It was on these purveyors of secret, incriminating information that Torcy chose to clamp down.[26]

First, an ordinance of June 1705 prohibited the writing and distribution of newsletters, but this was rigorously enforced only in Paris and not for long even there.[27] By the following June and July it was necessary to forbid this activity once more "by an express order of the King given

[25] See E. Vaillé, *Le Cabinet noir* (Paris, 1950), pp. 111–126. Vaillé believed complaints of Marshal Villars on interference with his mail were genuine, despite the unreliability of the source Vaillé used. His hunch was right; the original exchange of letters is Villars to Torcy, Denain, 27 July 1709, AAE, MD, France 1166, fols. 146–148; Torcy to Villars, 2 August 1709, *ibid.*, fols. 166–166ᵛ. The charge of superintendent of the post surely gave Torcy great advantages over his fellow ministers, generals and other men of state. For an impressive account of how Torcy used the post to retain a strategic place in diplomacy from 1715 to 1718, after his removal from his other offices, see E. Bourgeois, "La Collaboration de Saint-Simon et de Torcy," *Revue historique* (1905), 251–277.

[26] Some postal clerks cleared 12,000 livres annually from this moonlighting; AAE, MD, France 1145, fols. 251–254ᵛ. Postal clerks at frontier towns were also active in smuggling prohibited printed works into France, and Torcy had one such clerk arrested in 1712; Ravaisson-Mollien, *Archives de la Bastille*, XIII, 27–31.

[27] Funck-Brentano, *Figaro*, pp. 116–122.

[Parisians] by the Marquis de Torcy."[28] Again the writing abated for a time, then resumed at full strength. Now d'Argenson acted, arresting several *nouvellistes*.[29] Under interrogation the writers implicated many postal clerks as their suppliers, and late in October 1706 thirty *commis* of the Paris post office were arrested.[30] The news mills immediately ground to a halt. From the depositions of the arrested we learn that nearly all the clerks of the Paris post had worked with the newsletters before the prohibition of this practice, that many were still doing so, either as writers or contributors, that there was a well-developed network for the exchange of news among the newsletter-composing postal clerks of Lyon and Paris, and that many prominent people were on the address lists for the postal clerks' newsletters, among them the bishops of Orléans and Bayonne and even the royal intendants at Orléans and Brest.[31] At least three of the arrested *commis* served two-month sentences in the Bastille at the end of 1706.[32]

The orders against manuscript newsletters were promulgated anew in 1707, and a few writers were singled out for punishment. Torcy had, nevertheless, a special reason to press for strict enforcement early in 1708:

> The license of writers of *gazettes à la main* [wrote Torcy to d'Argenson] is becoming so great . . . that the security of the public's letters is suffering considerably. As these people are in liaison with several *commis* of the post, from time to time letters are found to have been opened for the purpose of extracting the news necessary to make a profit from the traffic in gazettes. Within the last few days, the nuncio has complained that the letters he wrote to Rome had been opened, as

28 AAE, MD, France 1145, fols. 261–265ᵛ.

29 *Ibid.*, fols. 233–240, 242–246.

30 Funck-Brentano, *Figaro*, p. 12.

31 AAE, MD, France 1145, fols. 251–254ᵛ, 261–265ᵛ, 267–272ᵛ.

32 BA, Ms. 10571. Cf. Funck-Brentano, *Figaro*, pp. 121–122; but Funck-Brentano's source citation is incorrect.

well as those which were sent him in the same mail. As the interest of the King and that of the public are joined on this occasion with His Majesty's desire to accord proper satisfaction to this minister, he has commanded me to send you his orders for the arrest and imprisonment in the Bastille of two *commis* suspected of this crime.[33]

The by now familiar routine of arrest, temporary suspension of the Parisian newsletters, and their gradual reappearance was played out again. By August 1708 another dragnet was necessary. This one turned up six *nouvellistes*, some of them authors and the rest only salaried copyists. The celebrity of the recipients of the gazettes had not diminished since 1706: the *premier président* of the Parlement of Dijon, the bishop of Montpellier, the abbé d'Estrades at his abbey near Rouen, the lieutenant general of Valogne, and the intendant of Burgundy were all regular readers.[34] Newsletter subscriptions were expensive because of their high per-copy production cost, and it is clear that only the rich could afford them. One of the interrogations revealed that an author was receiving news about Germany from a certain "Jourdan" of Bar-le-Duc (a man we will meet again), and that news of Flanders could be learned simply by going to the "news bureaus" at the Tuileries.[35] All the arrested denied having connections in the ministries or in the post office, "which," commented d'Argenson, "appears almost unbelievable, since their news is well founded and accurately datelined." The lieutenant of police recommended that the offenders be shut up in the Hôpital as "vagrants . . . who subsist only by criminal means," except for one who, as a

[33] Ravaisson-Mollien, *Archives de la Bastille*, XI, 429.

[34] AAE, MD, France 1160, fol. 129. Cf. F. Weil, "Les Nouvellistes," in *La Régence* (Paris, 1970), pp. 75–76, 79–80.

[35] AAE, MD, France 1160, fols. 152–156. On the news bureaus, see Funck-Brentano, *Les Nouvellistes*. A printed spoof of the news bureaus is in BN, Mss. fr. 24477, fols. 70–73ᵛ. For Claude Jordan, see below, chap. 3, n. 44.

gentleman, should receive a punishment "more suitable to his family"—exile to his ancestral home in the Auvergne, far from Paris.[36]

As one might guess, this example was not a permanent deterrent to the postal clerks. In 1710 Torcy warned d'Huxelles and Polignac, the Gertruydenberg negotiators, of "an Estienne Caillant who has been active for a long time in passing news of France to Holland."[37] And in 1711 this alarming news came from d'Iberville to Torcy:

> A *gazette à la main* named *Mansuent* is being composed at Lyon and distributed rather widely in Switzerland, Germany, Italy and in the provinces of the Rhône around the Lyonnais. This gazette is written with such frivolousness and imprudence that on divers occasions it does harm to the King's reputation and his affairs abroad. . . . The intendants of Lyon have been warned of this disorder from time to time. They have brought some remedy in forbidding the author of these letters from continuing to circulate them. But this prohibition has only resulted in a suspension of several issues, for the *commis* of the post at Lyon favor this gazette (it is said) because they receive a share of the author's profits. The partisans of the allies do not fail to bring these things up, to write about them in England, Holland and elsewhere. . . . Englishmen attached to the new government have vouchsafed to me their surprise that while peace is desired and even pursued by France, people there tolerate or close their eyes to things so likely to create obstacles in England.[38]

[36] AAE, MD, France 1160, fols. 152–156.

[37] Torcy to d'Huxelles and Polignac, Versailles, 15 April 1710 (minute), AAE, CP, Hollande 224, fol. 57; cited in Funck-Brentano, *Figaro*, p. 86.

[38] Memorandum by Cambiagues to d'Iberville, and d'Iberville to Torcy, Paris, 18 November 1711, AAE, CP, Angleterre 234, fols. 108–110. On the ineffectiveness of censorship at Lyon, see Depping, *Correspondance administrative*, II, 704, 705–706, 781–782.

As we have seen, this was not the only occasion of interference in the course of foreign affairs by authors of the newsletters. But whereas Torcy's partnership with d'Argenson gave him some effective power in Paris, there was little the minister could do about the inaction of the authorities at Lyon. Such were the limits of absolutist centralization.

As the very sensitive negotiations with the allies continued in 1712, Torcy took measures to avert damage to the peace talks from indiscretions circulating *à la main*. He ordered the jailing of Girod, "the first *nouvelliste* of the war of the Camisards" and the Paris correspondent of "the allied gazetteer in Switzerland."[39] The foreign minister again wrote to d'Argenson that "you cannot pay too much attention to the harmful talk of the *nouvellistes*."[40] Finally, in November 1712, Torcy was able to report: "The writers on political affairs are keeping silent here because it appears that these works do nothing but embitter people, and this is not suitable at a time when one should seek out all possible means to reconcile them. If the response that Prior [the English negotiator] is bringing leaves something to be desired, these pens, idle for so long, will be permitted to practice once more."[41] By then Torcy had learned to use the newsletters as a bargaining tool, to be applied and removed according to circumstance. Torcy was exploiting public news sources here much as the Dutch leaders had in 1709 and 1710. At that point the French foreign minister complained strenuously about these tactics, but in 1712 times had indeed changed. The relative negotiating strength of the combatants was now altogether different, and by the primary canon of diplomatic morality this necessitated an alteration of principle.

[39] Ravaisson-Mollien, *Archives de la Bastille*, XIII, 33.

[40] Torcy to d'Argenson, Fontainebleau, 2 August 1712, AAE, MD, France 1187, fol. 14.

[41] Torcy to Gaultier, Versailles, 2 November 1712, AAE, CP, Angleterre 240, fol. 85.

From this discussion two conclusions can be drawn. First, the public appetite for news and political comment was much too great to be stifled by the crown's relatively meager resources. This was an appetite that cut across cultural boundaries, embracing even the increasingly news-conscious almanacs of the barely literate; it can also be measured in the growing numbers of "news bulletins" printed as the seventeenth century wore on.[42] A second conclusion is that the foreign minister, far from becoming indifferent or giving up in the face of overwhelming public hunger for uncensored sources of opinion, vigorously coordinated a mixed policy of regulation and calculated, tacit acquiescence. In Paris, at least, this policy achieved some success, especially in controlling the production of printed works. The exception that demonstrates the flexibility of his strategy is Torcy's occasional shrewd tolerance of an unfettered debate in print. In some circumstances, he knew, a wide range of literary discussion might serve the government's purposes. This was the case in 1711, after the death of Emperor Joseph I. The French government's policy on the question of the imperial succession was to prevent his brother Charles's election, either by the choice of a non-Habsburg emperor or by a simple postponement of the election pending a general peace. The issue was complicated by a dispute over the legality of any decisions taken by the rump electoral council sitting without its banned, French-allied members, the electors of Cologne and Bavaria. Then there was the question of how the princes might squeeze concessions of authority from the imperial candidates. All this was more than enough to set pens to work, and Torcy cannily allowed tracts to run wild on these complicated questions. In the five months between Joseph's death and Charles's election, numerous works on the imperial succession appeared in

42 Bollème, *Almanachs*, pp. 98–101, 108–109, 117; Louis Desgraves, "Les 'Bulletins d'Information' imprimés à Bordeaux au XVIIe siècle," *Bulletin de la Société des Bibliophiles de Guyenne*, No. 79 (1964), pp. 17, 46–54.

Paris. The simultaneous publication in France of so many books on a single political subject was a unique event for the entire war period.[43] It resulted from the foreign minister's exercise of his censorship powers in reverse, suspending censorship for his own ends. The crown-controlled *Journal des savans* summarized the situation with studied naïveté: "There have perhaps never appeared so many books at one time on the Constitutions of the Empire as have been published since the death of Joseph of Austria, the last Emperor. . . . The bookdealers have hastened to serve their own interests by printing new editions of the treatises on this subject. And authors, moved by a natural enough desire to match their observations with others', have also taken the opportunity to make political arguments, in accordance with their conception of the status of the peoples concerned."[44] The writer might well have added the government to the list of those benefiting from the debate over the imperial election.

We have seen that Torcy used his powers of censorship to manipulate the sources of opinion for the king's advantage, but the foreign minister went considerably beyond simple reaction to the initiative of others. Torcy's prohibitions of gazettes, newsletters, and the like were only a complement of the positive steps he took to mold opinion. It is these measures we propose to examine in the remaining chapters of this book.

[43] The uniqueness of 1711 can be confirmed by a perusal of new books reviewed in *Journal des savans* and *Journal de Trévoux*. For these periodicals during the war years, see below, chap. 3.

[44] *Journal des savans*, 23 November 1711, p. 621. That Torcy did not lift the lid on censorship entirely is demonstrated in this passage from a review in the next issue of *Journal des savans*, 30 November 1711, p. 636: "Cet Ouvrage est d'impression étrangère; les affiches apprendront où il se debitera à Paris, *s'il s'y debite*. . . . l'auteur prouve que l'Empire étoit héréditaire du temps de Charlemagne . . ." (emphasis added). See also below, chap. 8, at n. 69.

CHAPTER THREE

The French Periodical Press

FRENCHMEN of 1700 turned to foreign sources for political
news and opinion because they provided more information,
greater variety of format, and livelier commentary than was
available in domestic publications. Whether one's taste ran
to public law and textual criticism, military reports and
political narrative, satire or slander, there were suitable
works published abroad. The monthly output of the Dutch
presses alone often ran to sixty different gazettes, journals,
and political pamphlets.[1] In comparison with this flood of
literature from the lowlands, French production amounted
to little more than a trickle during Louis XIV's reign.

The contrast is particularly striking with respect to political periodicals. While the newly invented gazette served
to democratize access to political information, to the leaders
of absolutist France this was dubious progress at best. Thus,
although a dozen new French-language gazettes had mushroomed abroad after 1685, at the beginning of the War of
the Spanish Succession only one news journal was permitted
to publish in France. This was the ancient *Gazette*, founded
in 1631 by Théophraste Renaudot under the protection of
Richelieu. The *Gazette* appeared weekly in Paris throughout Louis XIV's personal reign, and in the years since its
founding its format of eight or twelve octavo pages changed
hardly at all. Neither had its relationship to the crown, for

[1] [Jean Donneau de Visé], *Recueil de diverses pièces touchant les
préliminaires de paix proposez par les Alliez, et rejettez par le Roy*
(Paris, 1709), p. 151. In 1709 there were at least eighteen newspapers
in England, comprising a total of fifty-five issues per week. W. B.
Ewald, Jr., *The Newsmen of Queen Anne* (Oxford, 1956), p. 7. Cf.
above, chap. 1, n. 33.

the Renaudot family continued to hold an exclusive license or "privilege" to put out a political journal.[2]

The notion of privilege was crucial in limiting the number of periodicals published in France. To censoring authorities suspicious of any open political discussion, the contractual privilege granted by the crown was a way of controlling printed information. To the privilege holder, on the other hand, it was a protective guarantee of exclusive, monopolistic rights. In old-regime France, where press freedom and copyrighting were unknown, the interests of the government and of licensed publishers combined to restrict the legal sources of news.[3]

From 1679 the holder of the *Gazette*'s exclusive license was Eusèbe II Renaudot, grandson of the journal's founder. Eusèbe was an adviser of Colbert de Croissy, and he remained close to the foreign ministry during Torcy's tenure, especially during the young man's first years in office. But Abbé Eusèbe, unlike his amazing grandfather, found it difficult to combine the interests of an *érudit* with the task of editing a weekly newspaper. While busy making his scholarly reputation as an orientalist, Renaudot delegated the management of the *Gazette* to secretaries. Often away from Paris on research trips, the abbé was only titular publisher of the *Gazette*.[4]

Frequently during Louis XIV's reign, the crown used the *Gazette* as the vehicle for planted stories. For example,

[2] On the *Gazette* under Théophraste Renaudot and his descendants, see Solomon, *Public Welfare*, pp. 100–161, 216–217.

[3] Cf. Funck-Brentano, *Nouvellistes*, pp. 3–8.

[4] F.-A. Duffo, *Correspondance inédite d'Eusèbe Renaudot avec le Cardinal François-Marie de Médicis, 1703–1704* (Paris, 1926), demonstrates that Torcy and Renaudot met frequently in these years. Duffo, *Un abbé diplomate* (Paris, 1928), prints Renaudot's letters to Torcy of January-July 1701, when Renaudot was in Rome. See also A. Villiers, *L'Abbé Eusèbe Renaudot* (Paris, 1904), pp. 40 ff., 86–87; and Bruno Neveu, "La Vie érudite à la fin du XVIIe siècle d'après les papiers du P. Léonard de Sainte-Catherine (1695–1706)," *Bibliothèque de l'Ecole des Chartes*, 124 (1966), 464.

Louvois, the great war minister, is said to have virtually dictated the content of the *Gazette* from his bureau between 1689 and his death in 1691.[5] So too did Colbert de Torcy at the outset of the War of the Spanish Succession, when the *Gazette* summarized d'Avaux's three memoirs to the Dutch Estates General of February and March 1701. In all three issues, the articles reveal the drift of royal policy when they add that the general belief in Holland was that war was near, that the Dutch had forbidden the removal of horses from their provinces, and that they were continuing to arm their ships.[6] These judgments surely were also meant to lend credence to the war taxation Louis was preparing to institute during these months. Also in 1701, the *Gazette* served Torcy as the vehicle for a concocted story meant to protect one of Louis' allies in Italy, the duke of Mantua. Duke Ferdinand Charles had promised to allow French troops to occupy his territory by a treaty with Louis of February 1701. But in order to keep this agreement secret, Tessé, one of the French commanders on the scene, reported the duke's wish that an item in the Paris *Gazette* tell of the pressure brought upon him by French and Spanish troops to surrender his capital city. Torcy solicited a draft from Tessé which purported to show that Ferdinand had no choice but to yield. This item, in Tessé's words "half fig and half grape," appeared, slightly edited by Torcy, in the *Gazette* of 16 April.[7]

The *Gazette*'s privilege, in addition to allowing weekly publication in Paris, also authorized the weekly printing of provincial editions exactly duplicating the Paris version in Lyon, Toulouse, Rouen, Troyes, and Besançon. Printers in Montpellier and Châlons also published annual editions of the *Gazette* in book form. Despite the geographical extent of

[5] C. Rousset, *Histoire de Louvois et de son administration politique et militaire* (Paris, 1861–1863), IV, 376 ff.

[6] *Gazette*, 26 February 1701, pp. 94–95; 5 March 1701, pp. 104–106; 19 March 1701, pp. 128–129.

[7] Tessé to Torcy, Mantoue, 6 April 1701, AAE, CP, Mantoue 32, fols. 115–116. *Gazette*, 16 April 1701, p. 150.

its distribution, however, the circulation of the *Gazette* was not great even by the relatively modest standards of the time. Although figures on the press run of French periodicals are almost entirely absent until after 1715, indirect evidence can provide some rough guidelines to the audience for these publications. The price of a single issue apparently dropped from a peak of four sous during the Fronde to one sou in the 1680's, with the purchasing power of four sous roughly equivalent to that of one franc in modern currency. But even if its lowered price put it within reach of many urban dwellers, the *Gazette*'s limited press run, which we know did not exceed two hundred copies weekly in Troyes, indicates that this journal did not reach an especially large readership.[8]

In fact, the tone of the *Gazette* was not at all suitable for a popular audience. At least as important as its role as reporter of military and diplomatic news was that of providing a social calendar for the court. The articles from Paris gave much space to descriptions of royal *fêtes* and diligently recorded news of promotions and honors bestowed by the king upon *les grands*. The notion of the *Gazette* as a sort of honor roll or official aristocratic newsletter seems to have been so deeply entrenched that when Molière wanted to ridicule the dilution of honor he used the *Gazette* as a symbol of aristocratic exclusivity:

> Eh! madame, l'on loue aujourd'hui tout le monde,
> Et le siècle par là n'a rien qu'on ne confonde;
> Tout est d'un grand mérite également doué,
> Ce n'est plus un honneur que de se voir loué;

[8] Claude Lanette-Claverie, "La Librairie française en 1700," *Revue française d'histoire du livre*, n.s., 2:3 (1972), 24. Marie-Thérèse Blanc-Roquette, *La Presse et l'information à Toulouse des origines à 1789* (Toulouse, 1967), pp. 59, 92 ff.; M.-N. Grand-Mesnil, *Mazarin, la Fronde et la presse, 1647–1649* (Paris, 1967), pp. 36–37. After 1685 the *Gazette* was also reprinted at Avignon; see René Moulinas, "Les Journaux publiés à Avignon et leur diffusion en France jusqu'en 1768," *Provence historique*, 18 (1968), 122, 128, 130; also see below, chap. 5, n. 98.

D'éloges on regorge, à la tête on les jette,
Et mon valet de chambre est mis dans la gazette.[9]

Often the *Gazette*'s accounts of military actions were couched in terms of panegyrics, indicating that their primary purpose was not to convey information but to laud valorous deeds. In this respect, the Paris *Gazette* was very different from its confreres published in Holland. Many of the latter not only disdained aristocratic values but openly ridiculed the pretensions of royalty. The Paris *Gazette*, however, was intended to be a record of contemporary history and, as such, it conformed to the canons of good historical writing in seventeenth-century France, one of which was to chronicle the greatness of the nobility.

In content as well as tone the *Gazette* was set apart from the foreign press. Even when it reported news of politics the *Gazette*'s accounts were usually brief, bald, and devoid of interpretive commentary. For the greater part of Louis XIV's reign the *Gazette* consistently neglected detailed discussion of sensitive political news, especially domestic news. As one diplomat observed in 1711, "The desire for news of France, on which the authorized *Gazette de Paris* is so restrained, gives [foreign gazettes and manuscript newsletters] a large market" around Lyon.[10] In general, official surveillance strictly limited the depth of domestic coverage in the European press of the day; this was the main impetus for readers everywhere to seek out foreign newspapers. Censorship was stricter in France than elsewhere; hence the

[9] *Le Misanthrope*, III.vii.

> "Madam, everyone's the object of praise nowadays,
> And therefore are all things confused in this age;
> When all with the highest merit are endowed,
> It's no great honor to find oneself renowned.
> On praise we've a glut, there's no stop in sight yet,
> And even my lackey's written up in the Gazette"
> (Author's translation).

[10] D'Iberville to Torcy, Paris, 18 November 1711, AAE, CP, Angleterre 234, fols. 108–110.

notorious weakness of the *Gazette*'s Paris and Versailles articles. To choose two examples of this neglect from the period of the War of the Spanish Succession, we find that during the famine of 1709 the articles from abroad reported on hardship in the lands of Louis' enemies but uttered not a word on the situation in France. The same ostrichlike behavior was characteristic of the journal's treatment of the defeats at Blenheim, Ramillies, and Oudenarde in simple *relations*, with only passing and halfhearted efforts to place them in some sort of redeeming explanatory perspective.[11] While the foreign gazettes were perennial vehicles for virulent anti-French propaganda, the *Gazette* throughout Louis' reign typically made little attempt at rebuttal, prompting Pierre Bayle to remark: "If one compares the *Gazette de Paris* with those of other nations, it will be seen that we are incomparably more modest and reserved than our neighbors. We do not threaten the King's enemies; we do not compute the King's forces or his armaments; we do not provide an almanac of the campaign; we do not startle anyone with predictions. In a word, the Paris article . . . gives not the slightest hint that France is currently at war. As for the other gazetteers, they have a different method. They speak openly of leagues and grand schemes. Their threats go so far as to say that the conquest of France will be merely a practice round for her enemies' avant-garde."[12]

Royal servants conscious of public opinion were deeply disturbed by the *Gazette*'s inadequacies in these areas. Vauban was one such, and before Louvois began to exploit the *Gazette* the master engineer chastised him for his neglect: "A sober, impersonal journal denying itself all discussion and commentary is of no service at all abroad. . . . It is not impermissible in gazettes to embellish good news or soften bad. I would like to find someone who could skillfully ridicule the gazettes of Holland and Brussels for the

---

[11] Boislisle, "Le grand hiver," pp. 445, 465 and n. *Gazette*, 1704, pp. 416–417, 428–429; 1706, pp. 272–275; 1708, pp. 345–348, 359–360, 371–372.
[12] Quoted in Hatin, *Gazettes*, p. 18.

infinity of hyperbole they put out. For it is most shameful to us that all Europe considers French better spoken in foreign lands than in France itself. I know you consider the *Gazette* a bagatelle, but abroad they do not regard it so, and I think they are right. For after all, the *Gazette* has the power to mold opinion, and that is the only way those who do not personally witness events can evaluate our actions."[13]

Why did Torcy, who showed himself so sensitive to the importance of public opinion in other respects, fail to heed critics like Vauban? The *Gazette* of 1700–1715 reads very much like the issues of previous years, in which propaganda purposes were served only irregularly in brief aberrations from a norm of laconic blandness. Typical of the journal's reserve was its complete silence on Torcy's negotiating mission to The Hague in 1709. The discussions were never mentioned in the *Gazette*, even when they became common knowledge from foreign sources. But it is important to see that the explanation for this particular omission is a key to Torcy's general treatment of the *Gazette*. He and the Dutch negotiators had agreed beforehand to keep the talks secret, and Torcy lived up to his part of the bargain even while he castigated his negotiating partners for leaking the news to Dutch journalists.[14] This incident was representative of Torcy's perennial dilemma: how to use the *Gazette* as an effective propaganda organ without offending foreign gov-

---

[13] *Vauban, ses oisivités et sa correspondance*, ed. Rochas d'Aiglun (Paris, 1910), II, 110. Although the social and literary status of gazette editors was generally low, by 1700 the genre was gaining the respect of many critics. Thus Vigneul-Marville (pseudonym of Noël-Bonaventure d'Argonne) remarked: "The gazette, which most people consider a trifle, is in my view one of the most difficult literary creations. . . . It requires great skill with language, the ability to narrate precisely and concisely. It requires knowledge of warfare on land and sea, of geography, history, politics, the interests of princes, the secrets of courts, the *moeurs* and customs of every nation in the world" (*Mélanges d'histoire et de littérature* [Rouen, 1700], II, 60–62; quoted by Yardeni, "Journalisme," pp. 215–216).

[14] See above, chap. 2, n. 18; below, n. 33; and below, chap. 7, n. 34.

ernments who well knew that this was an official crown-controlled journal.

The difficulty was that the *Gazette* was much more and much less than a newspaper. As a recognized organ of the king's government, it was a potential negotiating tool for the foreign minister. And as such, the journal had to operate within a tight perimeter of permissible news beyond which lay a vast, untouchable area of potential incrimination. For the king's gazette violently to attack the foe in print might be good for domestic morale, but it could only exacerbate the problems of wartime foreign relations.[15] This tension between the opposed requirements of public propaganda and private diplomacy can be illustrated by considering the role of the *Gazette* in the Anglo-French peace negotiations of 1711–1713. In these years the journal's articles were manipulated by Torcy and Gaultier, the French agent in London, to influence the opinion of a very small, select readership—the queen of England and her ministers. Earlier in the war the *Gazette* followed Louis' policy on the illegitimate status of Queen Anne by consistently styling her the "Princess who reigns in England." A personal affront of this sort was a major obstacle in the French campaign to win the trust and confidence of English leaders. For this reason, Torcy saw to it that Anne was granted her title of "Queen of Great Britain" in the *Gazette*'s issues of 1712.[16] Gaultier reported the effect of the change in this way: "Each time

[15] See, for example, Gaultier to Torcy, Londres, 7 November 1710, AAE, CP, Angleterre 230, fol. 362: "Les reflexions continuelles que l'Autheur de la Gazette de Paris fait dans les articles de la Haye et de Londres sur les divisions qui regnent presentement parmy nous paroissoient icy a bien de gens hors de saison et faites à contretems parcequ'il n'est pas encore tems de chanter victoire et qu'il faut voir auparavant quel parti prendra le prochain Parlement, ou celuy de la paix ou celuy de la guerre." This deviation ceased immediately, and the *Gazette*'s articles resumed their usual blandness.

[16] Gaultier to Torcy, Londres, 24 December 1711 (O.S.), AAE, CP, Angleterre 234, fol. 229; Torcy to Gaultier, Versailles, 16 December 1711 (minute), *ibid.*, fol. 247.

the post arrives here from Holland, the Queen never fails to ask if there is a *Gazette de Paris*, and she is delighted to read the London article. This is why our friends ask you to order that from now on there will be nothing in it that might displease this Princess." And Torcy assured Gaultier that "we will pay more attention to this matter in the light of the report you have given me."[17] Thus, long before the Treaty of Utrecht gave Louis' formal recognition to Anne's throne, the journal that she regarded as his official spokesman had conceded this point and underscored French willingness to smooth the path to peace.

The other side of the medal of royal recognition was for Louis to deny it to James II's son. This was a more delicate matter, for Louis could not appear to be abandoning the unfortunate Pretender. However, it was possible for the *Gazette* to ignore young James Edward. Whereas earlier in the war the Paris journal had devoted diligent attention to the doings at the court of Saint-Germain, all mention of the Stuarts in France disappeared from the issues of 1711 and after. When it was conveniently arranged for James to leave France early in 1713, Torcy carefully planted the story elsewhere but noted that "if it is inserted in the *Gazette de France* . . . it will appear unnatural, for that gazette long ago ceased to refer to [James] in any manner whatsoever."[18] Even when it was essential for the French to deny reports in the Dutch gazettes of a new title—duke of Gloucester—

[17] Gaultier to Torcy, Londres, 27 January 1712, AAE, CP, Angleterre 237, fol. 33ᵛ; Torcy to Gaultier, Versailles, 8 February 1712 (copy), *ibid.*, fol. 52ᵛ. The "Preliminaries of October," 1711, signed by Mesnager and St. John, committed Louis to recognize Anne as the rightful monarch.

[18] Torcy to Gaultier, Versailles, 24 March 1713 (copy), AAE, CP, Angleterre 248, fol. 298. Similarly, in 1708 the crown altered the *Gazette*'s usage on Prince Rákóczi, elevating the French-supported Hungarians from "Mécontents" to "Confédérés" (B. Köpeczi, *La France et la Hongrie au début du XVIIIᵉ siècle* [Budapest, 1971], p. 381; see pp. 391–431 for the *Gazette*'s reporting of the Hungarian rebellion).

taken by the Pretender, Torcy sought to rebut this "malicious and false news" by obtaining retractions from the foreign gazettes themselves, not through a denial in the official *Gazette* which, as Torcy wrote, had to "maintain a profound silence" on James.[19] Thus, in the case of the Paris *Gazette*, the king's patronage and the exclusive privilege inherited by Eusèbe Renaudot severely narrowed the range of its usefulness as propaganda. For the most part, Torcy was compelled to sacrifice the potential of the journal as an instrument of foreign propaganda and domestic *ralliement* so as to serve the government's diplomatic interests abroad, interests that might be defeated by patriotic passions in print.

If the *Gazette* was of only limited use in royal propaganda, France's sole privileged literary magazine, *Le Mercure galant*, was even less helpful to Torcy. The *Mercure* was founded in 1672 by Jean Donneau de Visé and continued under his editorship until his death in 1710. Now Visé's privilege had specified that the monthly magazine would make no mention of politics, and in the preface to his first issue the *Mercure*'s editor advised his readers that he would not discuss news of foreign affairs or matters of state.[20] Instead, Visé proposed a journal of song, poetry, and literary criticism with which to charm and please his largely female audience. Composed in the style of an intimate letter to a fashionable lady, the *Mercure* became a great success. While sensitive literati decried Visé's style as, in La Bruyère's phrase, "a step below zero," the *Mercure*'s wide influence made it an important arbiter of taste for two generations. It helped set the uniform standards of thought and behavior which provided a cultural cement for the diverse leisured groups of urban French society. Torcy's mother, who pre-

[19] Torcy to Gaultier, Versailles, 28 September 1712 (minute), AAE, CP, Angleterre 239, fols. 331ʳ–332.

[20] AN, Minutier Central, Donneau de Visé, p. 163; Roger Duchêne, "Lettres et gazettes du XVIIIᵉ siècle," *Revue d'histoire moderne et contemporaine*, 18 (1971), 489.

sided over a sparkling Paris salon, was a subscriber and avid reader.[21]

Her son, however, remained less enthusiastic about Visé's work. Almost from the start, the *Mercure* had begun to trespass into the political sector. First, arguing accurately enough that the *Gazette* was too vague and general, Visé began to offer news of important marriages and deaths, rewards provided by the king for his servants, and "fine actions of those exhibiting notable valor in the armies."[22] Like the *Gazette*, the *Mercure* was providing its readers with a record of aristocratic accomplishments. By the 1680's Visé had expanded his military coverage to include reprinting accounts of military engagements. Such *relations* of battles, sieges and so on were published in vast profusion all over Louis XIV's France. A few were carried in the *Gazette*, but Visé printed many more and even brought out supplementary volumes of the *Mercure* recording the full course of various army campaigns. With his businessman's interest in warfare, the editor capitalized on the hunger of his readership for military information. During the war of 1688–1697, Visé published a regular series of supplements to the *Mercure*, but by 1700 his health was failing and the military supplements of the War of the Spanish Succession appeared only occasionally, twice in 1702 and 1707 and once in 1704. In 1705 he issued a "history" of Louis' reign since 1697, composed entirely of extracts from the *Mercure* and published in no less than ten volumes, but with such huge type and spacious margins that the whole could easily have been condensed to a single slim volume of more normal design.[23] These supplements were published as money-mak-

21 D.-F. Camusat, *Histoire critique des journaux* (Amsterdam, 1734), II, 200. Michel Gilot, "Quelques sortes de lettres de lecteurs," in Couperus, *L'Etude*, p. 86. In Toulouse, the reprinted *Mercure* sold for 8 to 10 sous per issue between 1700 and 1710 (Blanc-Roquette, *Presse*, pp. 115, 117). See also Visé to Torcy, Paris, 18 April 1704, AAE, MD, France 1129, fol. 56.

22 *Mercure galant*, 1672, unpaginated preface to first issue.

23 P. Mélèse, *Un homme de lettres au temps de Louis XIV, Donneau*

ing enterprises, but Visé, well aware of Torcy's convictions on the subject of propaganda, justified his ventures to the foreign minister in terms broader than profit: "I brought out a similar work during the last war, and its success was so great that the public wished another, even asked for it with some fervor. I need not tell Your Greatness of the good effects that this type of work produces in foreign countries, since Your Greatness knows this better than anyone and often takes pains to have such works written and distributed abroad for the good of the state."[24] Finally, Visé began to offer explicit rebuttals of anti-French gazettes and pamphlets.[25]

The trouble was that Visé's ability as a political propagandist was meager at best. Bayle found his refutations of foreign gazettes clumsy and his postured threats embarrassingly foolish. Jean-Baptiste Racine, the playwright's son who undertook several diplomatic missions under Croissy and Torcy, blamed Visé for disfiguring French victories, and when victories became scarce after 1700 Bayle accused Visé of compounding the problem in his patently overoptimistic discussions of Blenheim and Ramillies.[26] The heedless Visé also created diplomatic problems for Torcy, as for example in 1706 when, after the foreign minister had explicitly prohibited the publication in Paris of a sensitive address by

---

de Visé, fondateur du Mercure galant (Paris, 1936), pp. 227–239. On relations in general, see Blanc-Roquette, Presse, pp. 31 ff. On the reprinting of the Mercure and its supplements in Toulouse, see ibid., p. 118.

[24] Visé to Torcy, Paris, 18 April 1704, AAE, MD, France 1129, fols. 56–57.

[25] Mélèse, Homme de lettres, pp. 227–228, 236; Hatin, Gazettes, p. 115.

[26] Hatin, Gazettes, p. 116; Charles Ledré, Histoire de la presse (Paris, 1958), p. 39n; Pierre Bayle, Réponse aux questions d'un provincial (Rotterdam, 1705–1707), I, 151; Bayle to Dubos, Rotterdam, 6 August 1705, in Pierre Bayle, Oeuvres diverses (La Haye, 1727–1730), IV, 856–857. See also A. Lombard, L'Abbé du Bos (Paris, 1913), p. 114; and Journal des savans (Amsterdam ed.), January 1708, pp. 113–124.

Puyzieulx to the Swiss diet, Visé went ahead and printed it anyway. The result was a minor sensation in Holland, forcing Torcy to deny that Puyzieulx had given the speech in the first place.[27]

Although they were infuriated by the *Mercure*'s indiscretions, Torcy and d'Argenson could do little to control its author. Visé's privilege made him almost immune from censorship. At last, however, in 1709 the lieutenant of police and the foreign minister were handed an opportunity to bring to heel the unpredictable *Mercure*. D'Argenson told Torcy that "for several years this writer has appeared to be in need of an examiner and an inspector; I hope this incident will serve to advertise this necessity and put an end to the vexing independence which has so often brought him well-taken reproof."[28] The incident in question was Visé's publication of still another supplement to his magazine. This one appeared in July 1709, immediately after the collapse of peace talks with the Dutch. Instead of recounting a military campaign, it described another kind of battle, under the title *Recueil de diverses pièces touchant les prélimi-*

[27] *Mercure galant*, July 1706, pp. 287–291; d'Argenson to Torcy, Paris, 5 August 1706, AAE, CP, Suisse 174, fol. 334; Torcy to d'Argenson, Versailles, 7 August 1706, *ibid.*, fol. 345; Bayle to Dubos, Rotterdam, 7 November 1706, in *Choix de la correspondance inédite de P. Bayle*, ed. E. Gigas (Copenhagen & Paris, 1890), p. 116. See also *Mercure galant*, March 1704, pp. 75 ff. This speech and the reasons for Torcy's embarrassment are discussed below, chap. 5, at n. 26.

Some of Visé's supplements were translated and published abroad; e.g., his *Diary of the Siege of Luxembourg by the French King's Forces Under the Command of the Mareschal de Crequi* (London, 1684); and *A History of the Siege of Toulon* (London, 1708). In the latter work's dedication Visé accused the anti-Bourbon monarchs of maintaining the war effort "for their private Interests only," and in order to make their subjects "more Submissive, by rendering them Miserable." The translator had to warn his readers of the author's "Notorious Partiality" and "False Representations," attributing them to his "Malice or Ignorance." Insults of this sort only exacerbated the French foreign minister's difficulties.

[28] D'Argenson to Torcy, Paris, 5 July 1709, AAE, CP, Hollande 221, fol. 284.

naires de paix proposez par les alliez et rejettez par le Roy.[29] The book comprised five items: an introduction describing Torcy's return from his negotiating trip to The Hague and the king's decision to continue the war; two purported letters by Parisians commenting on the political situation; Louis' famous open letter of 12 June 1709 reporting on the peace talks; and excerpts, with editorial remarks by Visé, from supposed Dutch letters on the news of the day.

When Torcy saw this book, he exploded. At once he issued an order in the king's name for d'Argenson to seize and confiscate all the copies at the Paris printer's shop. The lieutenant general appeared there in person to make certain that this mandate was carried out.[30] Then Torcy had d'Argenson send secret agents to printers, binders and booksellers throughout France, as well as to Visé's office, to discover whether the forbidden book was still being sold. These measures apparently succeeded; very few copies survived, and the book is extremely rare today.[31] At the same time, Torcy disowned the *Recueil* in letters to his foreign contacts. The minister's Dutch correspondents, who foreshadowed the tendency of later historians to overrate the power of the French government, had leaped to the conclusion that Visé's book was somehow inspired by the court and expressed royal policy. Foreigners assumed that the privileged status of the *Mercure*, like that of the *Gazette*, made it to some degree an instrument of the government. In response, Torcy insisted that the book was published without permission and went on to tell of its suppression by the king's order. He urged the Dutch to note that the style of the "nasty pamphlet" should suffice to prove that it was purely Visé's invention, concluding ruefully that "a foolish

[29] Published as a supplement to *Mercure galant*, June 1709; also published separately (Paris, 1709).

[30] D'Argenson to Torcy, Paris, 5 July 1709, AAE, CP, Hollande 221, fol. 283.

[31] D'Argenson to Torcy, Paris, 3 August 1709, AAE, CP, Hollande 221, fols. 303–304. Louis G. Michaud, *Biographie universelle*, XLIII, 641–642.

writer does more harm to those he intends to praise than a man of wit does to his enemies by attacking them with the pen."[32]

Why was Torcy so disturbed by Visé's *Recueil*? As we know, the foreign minister had promised not to publicize the peace talks of 1709. Only a fortnight before he was undercut by the appearance of Visé's "nasty pamphlet," Torcy was upbraiding the allied negotiators in Holland for printing the peace preliminaries and publicly claiming that he had signed them.[33] Now the foreign minister could only deny official responsibility for the *Recueil* and hope that he would be believed.[34] Visé's book embarrassed Torcy not because he disagreed with its substance but because he did not think it fitting that all one's convictions be made public. For example, the *Recueil* harped on the theme of the selfishness of allied leaders: Marlborough, Eugene, Heinsius, the emperor, "the princess who governs in England" on "a throne that does not belong to her"—all were said to want continued war in order to perpetuate their personal power. Torcy was convinced that much of this was true, but to admit it in print was publicly to challenge the good will of his negotiating partners.[35] This was not beneficial to a government beset by crisis. Furthermore, it was necessary in Torcy's view somehow to make the allies believe that Louis was now ready to deal faithfully with them and that the arrogant king they remembered was no more. But here is Visé's description of Louis' attitude in June 1709: "Although

---

[32] Torcy to Petkum, Versailles, 18 July 1709, AAE, CP, Hollande 219, fol. 132ᵛ; the quotation is from Torcy to Basnage, Versailles, 15 August 1709, Hollande 219, fols. 193–194.

[33] Torcy to Petkum, 20 June 1709 (minute), AAE, CP, Hollande 219, fol. 62.

[34] Torcy began his explanation to Petkum with the phrase, "Vous ne me croirez peut estre pas." AAE, CP, Hollande 219, fol. 132ᵛ.

[35] *Recueil de diverses pièces*, pp. 24–25, 30–31, 36, 143, 146. "Marlborough, sachant que sa perte était attachée à la paix, employait tous ses efforts, tout son crédit, pour l'éloigner" (Torcy, *Journal*, 29 June 1710, p. 214). Also see Torcy, *Mémoires*, p. 650a.

the King found the propositions of the Allies of a nature not only not to be heard, but also to be rejected with contempt, His Majesty, with his usual courtesy, ordered Monsieur de Torcy to report his refusal of the propositions in terms demonstrating that the King maintains his self-possession and self-control at all times. Therefore nothing in what this minister wrote communicated the proper contempt with which the preliminaries were regarded by the Council. . . . Everyone found it very strange that the Allies had dared to make propositions that a monarch less discreet than the King could not have heard without exhibiting strong indignation, without giving these propositions the name they deserve."[36] There were some items in Visé's book that Torcy might have approved had they been set in another context: a description of the enthusiastic reaction of Parisians to the king's public letter; note of the sad state of the economy in Holland and England; an attack on the disrespectful political tracts issued in Holland; a reminder to Frenchmen that their monarch still had untapped resources for war; a refutation of the allies' claim that Torcy had agreed to the peace terms but had been overruled.[37] All of these points would have pleased a foreign minister anxious to exploit public opinion, and most of them found their way into the propaganda tracts we will examine in later chapters. As was true of the *Gazette*, however, the reputation that the *Mercure galant* carried abroad as a vehicle for French policy was enough to make it unusable as a tool of royal propaganda, even had it been possible to control its editor. Visé was dead by 1710, and his successor as holder of the *Mercure*'s privilege carefully steered clear of politics for the duration of the war. Once again, the danger to the conduct of foreign affairs that lay in the indiscretions of a patronized magazine outweighed, in Torcy's eyes, the benefits that might accrue to the king's cause from news intended to inspire Frenchmen.

[36] *Recueil de diverses pièces*, pp. 5–7, 9.
[37] *Ibid.*, pp. 10–11, 82–83, 95 ff., 151 ff.

Torcy had better success with the two scholarly periodicals published in France during the War of the Spanish Succession, the *Journal des savans* and the *Mémoires pour l'histoire des sciences et des beaux-arts*, popularly known as the *Mémoires de Trévoux*. These ancestors of the modern learned journal mixed reviews of serious books with articles on scientific subjects and had readers everywhere in Europe. Most of these readers surely did not suspect that the political comments of the scholarly editors often mirrored the views of Louis XIV's foreign minister.

From its founding in 1665 the *Journal des savans* was bound to the French crown through ties of patronage. Established under Colbert's auspices partly in order to publicize the achievements of the new royal academies, editorship of the *Journal* was reorganized in 1701 and placed under the official control of Chancellor Pontchartrain, who conferred responsibility for the actual management of the *Journal* upon his scholarly nephew, Jean-Paul Bignon. By this time the *Journal des savans* had become one of the two or three most respected scientific publications in Europe. Its weekly Paris issue was reprinted in Amsterdam even during wartime, reflecting the psychological separation of politics and learning that was typical of an age without nation-states or doctrines of total war. This publication served as a forum for detached discussion, and its uncommitted stance represented what one modern student has called "a kind of revolution in the world of letters and science."[38] Yet throughout the War of the Spanish Succession the *Journal des savans* served as a secret vehicle for royal propaganda. Six or seven propaganda pieces commissioned by Torcy were reviewed in the

[38] Harcourt Brown, "History and the Learned Journal," *Journal of the History of Ideas*, 33 (1972), 377. See also Raymond Birn, "Le *Journal des Savants* sous l'Ancien Régime," *Journal des savants*, No. 1 (1965), pp. 15–28; and J. Ehrard and J. Roger, "Deux périodiques français au XVIIIᵉ siècle: le 'Journal des Savants' et les 'Mémoires de Trévoux,'" in Bollème, *Livre*, pp. 33–59. The *Journal des savans* was also reprinted in Toulouse; see Blanc-Roquette, *Presse*, p. 97.

Journal. These works included manifestos by princes allied to Louis, collections of propaganda pamphlets, and full-length books. Each received a lengthy and sympathetic summary by the *Journal's* editors.[39]

The stance of the *Mémoires de Trévoux* was even more partisan than that of its senior confrere. The Jesuit editors of the *Mémoires* were chiefly motivated by a desire to rebut the anti-Catholic, anti-French periodicals published in England and Holland. They summarized their credo in their first issue, published early in 1701: "In the disputes that often arise among men of letters about scientific matters, the editors of the *Mémoires* will take no part whatever. . . . They will observe the same neutrality in all else, save with regard to religion, morality and the state, in which matters it is never permitted to be neutral."[40] The *Mémoires de Trévoux* were published under the official patronage of the duc de Maine, one of the king's illegitimate sons. (Trévoux was the chief town of the principality of Dombes, theoretically an independent enclave within France, in which the duke was sovereign.) Although the homage which the editors repeatedly paid to their patron for his alleged love of learning was probably mere conventional rhetoric, Maine did have a

---

[39] The works reviewed were [Charles Davenant], *Essays upon the Ballance of Power* (London, 1701), *Journal des savans*, 9 January 1702; [Johann Karg], *Manifeste en forme de lettre pour S.A.S.E. de Cologne* (Paris, 1702), *ibid.*, 5 June 1702; [Ulrich Obrecht], *Excerpta historica et juridica de natura successionis in monarchiam hispaniae* (n.p., 1701), *ibid.*, 26 June 1702; [Jean de la Chapelle], *Lettres, mémoires et actes concernant la guerre présente* (Basel, 1703), *ibid.*, 12 February 1703; [Jean-Baptiste Dubos], *Les interests de l'Angleterre malentendus dans la guerre présente* (Amsterdam, 1704), *ibid.*, 5 May 1704; [Jean-Baptiste Dubos and Johann Karg], *Manifeste de l'Electeur de Bavière, avec les additions* (n.p., 1705), *ibid.*, 8 June 1705; [Jean-Baptiste Dubos], *Histoire de la ligue faite à Cambray* (Amsterdam, 1709), *ibid.*, 16 September 1709. All of these works will be discussed in subsequent chapters. On the political content of this journal, see Jacqueline de La Harpe, *Le Journal des Savants et l'Angleterre, 1702–1789* (Berkeley, 1941), pp. 302–303.

[40] *Journal de Trévoux*, January-February 1701, preface.

sense of the importance of public opinion. In 1709 he declared to Madame de Maintenon, "The King must restore the love of Frenchmen for their masters. . . . [I] hold it as an unshakable principle that a prince is lost as soon as he has lost the confidence of his subjects."[41]

Under this sort of aggressive patronage and management, the *Mémoires de Trévoux* enthusiastically reviewed ten propaganda pieces issued by Torcy between 1701 and 1713, many of which were also simultaneously reviewed in the *Journal des savans*. In accord with their stated disdain of neutrality in affairs of state, treatment of these works in the *Mémoires* was in general less restrained and more committed in tone than were the reviews in the *Journal des savans*. Phrases like "this excellent book" and "truths which merit the attention of the public" are scattered through the reviews of propaganda works in the *Mémoires*.[42] Thus the *Mémoires de Trévoux*, like the *Journal des savans*, supplemented Torcy's propaganda campaigns by lending the prestige of learned journals to the efforts of the crown's hired pens.

[41] Letter of 3 June 1709, quoted in *Mémoires de Saint-Simon*, ed. A. de Boislisle, XVII, 599–600. See Alfred R. Desautels, *Les Mémoires de Trévoux et le mouvement des idées au XVIII⁵ siècle, 1701–1734* (Rome, 1956), p. vii; cf. John N. Pappas, *Berthier's Journal de Trévoux and the Philosophes* (Geneva, 1957), pp. 15–16.

[42] The works reviewed, all of which will be discussed in subsequent chapters, are: [Ulrich Obrecht], *Excerpta historica et juridica de natura successionis in monarchiam hispaniae* (n.p., 1701), Part 1, March–April 1701, pp. 90–99; Part 2, May–June 1701, pp. 194–207; [Jean de la Chapelle], *Lettres, mémoires et actes concernant la guerre présente* (Basel, 1703–1704), Part 1, March 1703, pp. 417–428; Part 2, October 1703, pp. 1785–1789; Part 3, April 1704, pp. 575–583; *Manifeste du duc de Mantoue* (n.p., 1703), August 1704, pp. 1389–1399; [Jean-Baptiste Dubos], *Les Interests de l'Angleterre malentendus dans la guerre présente* (Amsterdam, 1704), October 1704, pp. 1682–1688; [Jean-Baptiste Dubos], *Histoire de la ligue faite à Cambray* (Amsterdam, 1709), December 1709, pp. 2049–2079; [Jean de la Chapelle], *Lettres d'un suisse à un français* (Basel, 1709), June 1710, p. 1085; [H. Bourgeois du Chastenet], *Les Interests des princes de l'Allemagne* (Paris, 1712), March 1713, p. 551.

The propaganda role of the scholarly journals, while important, was nevertheless narrowly confined by several built-in limitations. First, the format of these publications precluded any propaganda format but the book review. Second, their international reputation among savants inhibited unrestrained partisanship; even the editors of the *Mémoires, engagés* as they were, argued defensively that their interest in contemporary political events emerged from a respectable scholarly concern with history and jurisprudence.[43] Above all, neither scholarly periodical was in any sense comparable to the foreign gazettes as a vehicle for news. Hence neither answered Torcy's need for a publication that would effectively offset the anti-French bias of existing foreign newspapers. We have seen that the *Gazette* was useless for this purpose because of complications ensuing from its privileged status, and that the *Mercure* remained beyond Torcy's control. What was lacking in 1700 was a political journal that would follow the government's lead without appearing to be an organ of state. This requirement was met at last by *La Clef du cabinet des Princes de l'Europe*, a monthly gazette which began publishing in July 1704 at Luxembourg, occupied at the time by French troops. By the end of 1706 the *Clef du cabinet* had acquired a royal privilege permitting its sale throughout France and had added an edition published at Verdun to its ongoing Luxembourg operation. The substantially identical new edition, bearing the more formal title of *Journal historique sur les matières du tems*, provided the name by which this gazette was colloquially known throughout the eighteenth century: *Journal de Verdun*. During the second half of the War of the Spanish Succession, this periodical often disseminated French propaganda to a regular readership.

Torcy does not seem to have played any part in founding

---

[43] *Journal de Trévoux*, March-April 1701, p. 86: "l'affaire qui tient maintenant toute l'Europe en suspens, est du ressort de la République des Lettres, puisqu'elle roule sur plusieurs points d'Histoire et de Jurisprudence."

this new gazette. He sent some money to its publisher, Claude Jordan, early in 1704, but Jordan was never on Torcy's payroll.[44] Yet the foreign minister subscribed to every issue of the journal from the start,[45] and this careful monitoring led to his first attempt to control the new publication. The circumstance was that in the fifth number, dated November 1704, Jordan had printed a *Lettre escrite de Suisse le 15. Octobre 1704 au sujet d'un projet de Paix générale.* The anonymous letter writer argued for partition of the Spanish empire, leaving Spain and the Indies to Philip V but transferring Naples, Sicily, and Milan to Charles, ceding the Spanish Netherlands to Max Emmanuel of Bavaria, and suitably compensating England and the duke of Savoy.[46] Coming as it did only three months after the disaster of Blenheim, this piece could not but heighten the fears of Philip and Max that their interests were about to be betrayed by Louis. Torcy, for his part, hastened to reassure the worried princes that Louis had nothing to do with the *Lettre escrite de Suisse* and that his devotion to their cause was undiminished.[47]

[44] Torcy to d'Audiffret, Versailles, 24 February 1704, AAE, CP, Lorraine 55, fol. 155; cf. ms. note, purportedly by Jordan, in *Clef du cabinet*, 1, BN, Imp., Lc².59. (For consistency, all references to this journal will appear under the title *Clef du cabinet*, except when the *Journal historique* [Verdun ed.] contains material not appearing in the *Clef*.) On the authorship of this journal, see E. Hatin, *Histoire de la presse en France* (Paris, 1859), II, 277–286; see also Alphonse Sprunck, "La Première 'gazette' du duché de Luxembourg," *Annales de l'Institut archéologique de Luxembourg, Arlon*, 92 (1961), 139. On the periodical's circulation, see Gilot, "Lettres de lecteurs," p. 86.

[45] Torcy to Rouillé, Versailles, 23 December 1704, AAE, CP, Bavière 51, fol. 43.

[46] *Clef du cabinet*, November 1704, pp. 353–360. This *Lettre* was also printed separately in Holland or Geneva: Louis to Rouillé, Versailles 22 December 1704 (minute), AAE, CP, Bavière 49, fol. 195; Torcy to Rouillé, Versailles, 23 December 1704, Bavière 51, fol. 43.

[47] Rouillé to Torcy, Bruxelles, 18 December 1704, AAE, CP, Bavière 49, fol. 186; Rouillé to Torcy, Bruxelles, 20 December 1704, *ibid.*, fols. 191–192; Louis to Rouillé, Versailles, 22 December 1704

The *Lettre escrite de Suisse* was neither a French trial balloon nor a news leak, and it might not have caused such a furor were it not for the coincidence of its title. At this time Torcy was subsidizing Jean de la Chapelle to produce a series of propaganda pamphlets which appeared under the title *Lettres d'un suisse*. To buttress the king's denial of responsibility for the *Lettre escrite de Suisse*, the next *Lettre d'un suisse* contained a specific disclaimer of French authorship. La Chapelle took the occasion to append, no doubt with Torcy's approval, an attack upon the *Clef du cabinet des Princes*: "It does not require much ability to make a bare compilation of everything published in the gazettes during the preceding month. . . . I don't know what opinion people in other countries have of that pompously titled *Chamber Key of the Princes*, but here [in Switzerland] it is said that this key doesn't unlock a thing, and that the princes' chamber is very badly furnished."[48]

Torcy's vigorous response demonstrates that the *Clef* had already become a widely read journal of considerable influence. Its first few issues established a format that remained intact for the rest of the war—printed *relations*, political items from manuscript newsletters and anonymous polemics interspersed with poems and songs. The mixture of the political and the literary surely broadened the appeal of the new monthly, and in combining the two subjects Jordan was following the formula—although reversing the proportions—originated by Donneau de Visé in the *Mercure galant*.[49]

Shortly after La Chapelle's attack upon Jordan's gazette, Torcy began to see that he might use the *Clef* for the crown's purposes. Perhaps what inspired the foreign minister

---

(minute), *ibid.*, fol. 194; "Mémoire en forme d'instruction pour Rouillé," 4 March 1704, Bavière 50, fols. 167–171; Torcy's memorandum on his interview with Monasterol, *ibid.*, fols. 172–174.

[48] [Jean de la Chapelle], *Vingt-huitième lettre d'un suisse*, December 1704.

[49] See the comments of the Abbé Prévost, as quoted in Hatin, *Histoire*, II, 289–290.

was that, beginning with the first issue of 1705, the *Clef du cabinet* reprinted a number of recently published propaganda pamphlets commissioned by Torcy. The *Manifeste de l'Electeur de Bavière* appeared in January and two of La Chapelle's *Lettres d'un suisse* were published in March and May.[50] Soon the Dutch *L'Esprit des cours de l'Europe* was warning its readers about the *Clef*'s "monarcholatry" and Bourbon sympathies. In July 1705 Jordan acknowledged that some Dutch journalists "use speech very different from mine with regard to France"; but he maintained that his own "moderation" and "respect for sovereigns" did not cause him to "do damage to historical truth."[51] We do not know whether Torcy or his propagandists took any initiative in publishing the French propaganda tracts in the *Clef* early in 1705, but the absence of evidence suggests that they did not play an active role. Jordan probably just reprinted these tracts when they happened to fall into his hands. Certainly Torcy could have taken steps to ban this practice had he so desired, but instead we find that as 1705 wore on, Jordan developed a regular habit of reprinting the *Lettres d'un suisse* as they appeared. The journal lent credibility to these inspired tracts, as when Jordan vouched for the origins of a straw man, pro-Dutch pamphlet which was printed and then rebutted by Torcy's mythical Swiss.[52]

Within a few months Torcy decided that the *Clef* could serve as a permanent auxiliary in his propaganda arsenal. Up to this time, Jordan had no authorization to send his publication to Paris for distribution. But in September 1705 the foreign minister proposed tacit permission to d'Argenson: "I think," wrote Torcy, "that we can tolerate this journal without giving it an explicit permit, provided that the author continues in the same vein in which he has begun. But as I

[50] *Clef du cabinet*, December 1704, p. 440; January 1705, pp. 7–44; March 1705, pp. 185–201; May 1705, pp. 344–357.

[51] *L'Esprit des cours*, March 1705, p. 256; *Clef du cabinet*, III, *avertissement*.

[52] *Clef du cabinet*, May 1705, p. 388; June 1705, pp. 443–462; August 1705, pp. 99–111.

do not know whether the distribution of this journal will prejudice the works of some individuals who may have privileges for similar books, I would be happy to hear your opinion."

Interestingly, d'Argenson's reaction was not favorable. He pointed out that some of the earlier issues were anti-French, and added, not very consistently, that "the author ought to be rewarded in some other way than by exposing him to the political reflections of our first-rank *nouvellistes* who are only too anxious to penetrate into the secrets of the ministries and to criticize the decisions taken there." The lieutenant of police had other objections:

> This book will do much less for the King's interests abroad once it is known that its circulation is being tolerated here. . . . Tolerances of this kind do not remain hidden for long. The bookdealers who know the secret will be the first to divulge it. This will make our Parisian critics say that it is a work composed by order of the court and provides an opportunity for foreign writers to publish the same thing in the *libelles* with which they have diverted the public for so long. It is also certain that this book, with its rather elegant and highly concise style, will do considerable prejudice to the *Mercure galant* and that it is imitating the scheme of the *Lettres d'un suisse.* . . . For the rest, if you decide that the arguments for toleration should prevail, I consider myself obliged to inform you that the inspection of each issue can only be carried out in your offices and under your supervision, because only there can one judge what can be said and what must be suppressed.

Torcy, who had commissioned the *Lettres d'un suisse* and had no affection for the *Mercure*, was ready to run these risks and meet these conditions; so, with the issue of October 1705, *La Clef du cabinet des Princes* was removed from the list of books prohibited in Paris.[53]

[53] Torcy to d'Argenson, Marly, 22 September 1705, AAE, MD,

Meanwhile, Jordan continued to publish French propaganda tracts. A rebuttal of a response to the *Manifeste de l'Electeur de Bavière* appeared, along with summaries and lengthy excerpts from seven of the nine *Lettres d'un suisse* published between March 1705 and September 1706. In the early part of 1707, Jordan harped on the unreliability of the Dutch gazettes and punctured stories from Holland that purported to prove Louis' disinclination toward peace.[54] By this time, the *Journal de Verdun* had become a privileged publication. The registers of the guild of booksellers and printers note mysteriously that "le Sieur***" was granted a permit to distribute his gazette in Paris at the end of November 1706.[55] No longer merely "tolerated," Jordan had arrived. We must note, however, that despite its privileged status the gazette's authorship remained anonymous. Torcy and d'Argenson no doubt conspired to keep Jordan's identity secret, and the subterfuge should have helped confuse the Parisian critics who worried the lieutenant of police. At the same time, from its centrally located presses at Luxembourg and Verdun, the journal continued to be distributed and to attract an extensive readership outside France.

For the remainder of the war, the *Journal de Verdun* served Torcy's interest by placing news reports in favorable perspective and by reprinting selected speeches, letters and propaganda tracts. To choose a few examples, the gazette disputed allied accounts of Oudenarde's catastrophic results, admitted France's widespread misery in 1709 but warned against exaggerating its impact on the king's war-making

---

France 1137, fol. 250; d'Argenson to Torcy, Paris, 23 September 1705, AAE, MD, France 307, fols. 48–51. BN, Mss. fr. 21743, fols. 73–74.

54 *Clef du cabinet*, November 1705, pp. 331–342. See above, nn. 47 and 50, for *Lettres d'un suisse* in issues of March through August 1705. *Clef du cabinet*, September 1705, pp. 180–193; October 1705, pp. 258–268; April 1706, pp. 242–268; May 1706, pp. 332–344; June 1706, pp. 413–420; September 1706, pp. 170–186. *Clef du cabinet*, May 1707, p. 364; June 1707, pp. 431 ff.

55 BN, Mss. fr. 21949, p. 146, dated 29 November 1706.

power, published running accounts of the negotiations of
The Hague (which, it will be recalled, could not appear in
the *Gazette*), and reproduced official French statements explaining the breakdown of the renewed peace talks of 1710.[56]
The journal also followed Torcy's line on the negotiations
with England by first denying reports of secret contacts and
then summarizing the pro-French Tory propaganda tracts.[57]
In 1708 Jordan summarized a French-concocted *Testament
politique* meant to reveal the supposedly universal ambitions
of the house of Austria, and later argued for its genuineness.
He then went on to call attention to the controversy over
the liberties of Italy and the legality of the emperor's inva-
sion in this characteristic passage: "I will not undertake to
summarize the arguments of the two sides. . . . All I can say
about it in general is that those of the Emperor appear to
me better supported than those of the Italian princes. The
latter have nothing to base their independence on except
some old parchments, treaties, cessions, donations, concor-
dats, and the words of some orators. But the claims of the
Emperor are founded on the rights that Charlemagne and
his successors down to Charles V held in Italy. They are
supported by two armies which have entered the ecclesiastical state and which now occupy the greater part of it,
even though there has not yet been any declaration of war
between the Pope and the Emperor."[58] Throughout, Jordan
attempted to avoid the *ad hominem* tactics of many Dutch
gazettes. Limiting himself to what he termed "historical
facts," he rejected invective and slander,[59] thereby reflecting

[56] *Clef du cabinet*, September 1708, pp. 221–222; February 1709, pp.
92–93; March 1709, p. 165; June 1709, pp. 411–412; July 1709, pp. 21–
22, 53–60, 84–87; August 1709, pp. 89–92, 112–116; April 1710, pp.
232, 271–273; May 1710, pp. 349–350; June 1710, pp. 413–414; July 1710,
pp. 40–43; August 1710, pp. 108–109; September 1710, pp. 196–208.

[57] *Clef du cabinet*, December 1711, pp. 431–433; May 1712, pp. 363–
374.

[58] *Clef du cabinet*, March 1709, pp. 182–183.

[59] *Journal historique sur les matières du tems*, January 1707,
avertissement.

Torcy's heartfelt loathing for personal discourtesy in propaganda, no matter what the source. Yet because the *Journal de Verdun* had only a shadowy relationship with the French government, it could argue for example that Prince Eugene and the duke of Marlborough were perpetuating the war for their personal gain, which Torcy believed but certainly would not state in the *Gazette* and had to censor in the *Mercure*.[60] Similarly, Torcy also planted news in the *Journal de Verdun*: an item on James Edward's stay with the duke of Lorraine and his forthcoming travels outside France, a story which Torcy did not want in the *Gazette*, was inserted in Jordan's monthly. When Jordan had acquired a privilege in 1706, he was also assigned a censor, the intendant of Metz, Saint-Contest. The censor reviewed each issue of the journal after publication, in search of damaging information. Occasionally he found something serious enough to notify Torcy about, as in 1712 when Jordan published a false report concerning the Stuart Pretender. Saint-Contest checked with Torcy to see if the story were true and then followed the minister's order to obtain a retraction.[61]

From 1705, then, Torcy used the *Journal de Verdun* to influence opinion at home and abroad. He was nonetheless careful to keep his distance from Jordan's publication. It was printed at Verdun and Luxembourg, far from the court. The foreign minister avoided admitting that he knew the editor's name and made disparaging references to the periodical in his letters. The overwhelming bulk of the items in the journal were not placed by Torcy. But there can be

[60] *Clef du cabinet*, May 1713, pp. 334–335. Köpeczi, *La France et la Hongrie*, pp. 454–455, 468–469, 478–480, 494–495, 505–506, summarizes the treatment of the Rákóczi rebellion in the *Clef*.

[61] Torcy to Saint-Contest, 1 September 1712 (minute), AAE, CP, Angleterre 242, fol. 49; Saint-Contest to Torcy, Metz, 19 October 1712, *ibid.*, fol. 149. Cf. "Extrait du Journal historique," *ibid.*, fol. 163, with *Clef du cabinet*, November 1712, p. 323. Also cf. *ibid.*, May 1713, pp. 334–335; and Torcy to Gaultier, Versailles, 24 March 1713 (copy): "Je le [James] prieray d'en faire mettre la nouvelle dans un mauvais journal qui s'imprime à Verdun" (AAE, CP, Angleterre 248, fol. 298).

no doubt that the *Journal de Verdun* regularly performed as an instrument of French propaganda. The *Gazette* and the *Mercure* were tied in the popular mind to the French government, but the new and mysterious publication remained a puzzle to most readers. Torcy spun out the mystery to the end of the war. He struck a balance between leaving the gazette independent and reducing it to an organ of the crown. To choose either extreme would have been to abandon the journal as a credible, effective propaganda medium.

In sum, Torcy's use of the *Gazette*, the *Journal des savans*, the *Mémoires de Trévoux*, and the *Journal de Verdun* was geared to each publication's special character and audience. In this, as well as in his ultimate silencing of the *Mercure galant*'s counterproductive political commentary, the foreign minister often found ways to rebut the attacks of foreign gazettes. More, he tried to offset the illicit manuscript newsletters by commissioning newsletters of his own that would offer the government's view of affairs. Eusèbe Renaudot wrote one set of newsletters to a correspondent in Italy, and probably to many others all over Europe.[62] At the same time, the foreign minister encouraged the publication of pro-French gazettes abroad when he subsidized Puyzieulx's printing of a weekly newsletter at the French embassy in Soleure for circulation in Switzerland, Germany, Italy, and eastern France.[63] This last point suggests that Louis' ambassadors themselves acted as propagandists, and in the next chapter we will see how this was so.

[62] Duffo, *Correspondance . . . d'Eusèbe Renaudot: 1703–1704; 1705–1707* (Paris, 1915); *1708–1712* (Paris, 1927). These letters are really weekly *nouvelles à la main*; they are an excellent source for the politics of the period.

[63] See the correspondence of Puyzieulx and Bernage from 1703 to 1706 in AAE, MD, France 1580, fols. 251–254, 257, 262, 264, 270, 272, 273, 280, 293, 299, 303; AAE, MD, France 1581, fols. 4, 6ᵛ, 9, 12ᵛ–13, 15ᵛ, 21, 48ᵛ; also Puyzieulx's statement of expenses, AAE, CP, Suisse 152, fol. 418.

CHAPTER FOUR

Colbert de Torcy and the Tradition of French Pamphlet Propaganda

SCHOLARLY opinion has been divided on the role of government-sponsored pamphlet propaganda under the Sun King, some historians holding that Louis XIV disdained printed polemical warfare, others maintaining that the monarch often showed an intuitive understanding of its importance.[1] Close examination reveals that both views are partly correct, for sponsorship of paid pamphlet propaganda was indeed a feature, although not a consistent one, of Louis XIV's personal reign. In fact, the crown's policies passed through at least three distinct phases from 1661 to 1715. The first extended to the end of the 1660's and was characterized by wide-ranging efforts supervised by Colbert to recruit and pension many French and foreign writers. In a second period, stretching from the collapse of this campaign in the early 1670's to the end of the War of the League of Augsburg in 1697, the crown virtually abandoned the sponsorship of pamphlet propaganda. The final phase, beginning in the late 1690's and continuing to the close of the reign, saw Colbert de Torcy attempt a revival, though on a more modest scale, of his uncle's recruitment and publication drive.

[1] Representative views may be found in E. Bourgeois and L. André, *Les Sources de l'histoire de France: le XVIIᵉ siècle*, vol. IV: *Journaux et pamphlets* (Paris, 1924), introduction; C.-G. Picavet, *La Diplomatie française au temps de Louis XIV (1661–1715)* (Paris, 1930), pp. 210–221; Georges Livet, "Louis XIV et l'Allemagne," *XVIIᵉ siècle*, Nos. 46–47 (1960), pp. 46–50; and G. Zeller, "French Diplomacy and Foreign Policy in Their European Setting," *New Cambridge Modern History*, vol. V: *The Ascendancy of France, 1648–1688*, ed. F. L. Carsten (Cambridge, 1961), 208.

These wide-ranging disparities over the sixty-year reign tend to indicate that the key to the crown's concern with pamphlet propaganda lies in the changing attitudes of the various royal ministers, not in the convictions of the king himself.

While it has rarely been viewed in the perspective of the entire reign, the initial, Colbert-directed phase is relatively well known and needs only cursory review here. Continuing and expanding practices established under Richelieu and Mazarin, the royal treasury distributed an average of over 100,000 livres annually to artists, scientists and writers between 1664 and 1672.[2] Outlays of this magnitude could only be justified by an ideology of rulership that cast men of letters as servants of the state, publicizing the monarch's generosity as a patron of culture, and thus embellishing his *gloire*. The publication of pamphlet propaganda was only one part of the many-faceted campaign directed at harnessing scholarship to the Sun King's apollonian chariot, but to judge from Colbert's concentration on this element in his correspondence, defending the king's actions in print became one of his major concerns. Particularly in the years around the War of Devolution, Colbert worked continually to oversee the production of convincing tracts arguing Louis' case. Employing the aged poet Jean Chapelain as liaison with the republic of letters, Colbert distributed large quantities of money and encouragement to dozens of men of letters within France and abroad, particularly in Holland and Germany.[3]

The return on this investment of cash and confidence was disappointingly meager. No amount of money could buttress the rather dubious legal foundations of French

[2] Clément, *Lettres . . . de Colbert*, v, 466–498.

[3] *Ibid.*, p. 622; *Lettres de Jean Chapelain*, ed. P. Tamizey de Larroque, 2 vols. (Paris, 1883), II, 462–464, 469, 472, 494, 501–503, 509, 517, 522, 528–529, 532, 536–538, 543–546, 590n, 606n, 659, 782, 786, 795–796, 818; J. Collas, *Jean Chapelain* (Paris, 1912), pp. 349–425, and esp. 426–443.

justifications for the king's attack upon the Spanish Netherlands, and enemy pamphlets had little difficulty in disposing
of Louis' labored rationales. Then, with the appearance of
Lisola's enormously influential *Le Bouclier d'état et de justice* in 1668, the king came to be seen in Germany and the
United Provinces as a bellicose, insatiable despot intent on
reducing Europe to universal monarchy under French domination.[4] In those places a growing anti-French reaction made
it dangerous to soften the firm lines of this unflattering portrait, even by means of anonymous pamphlets. Few of the
tracts commissioned by Colbert were written, fewer still
printed, and none had significant impact.[5] By 1672—the first
year of the Dutch war—Chapelain was dead, Colbert had
allowed his German contacts to wither, and no other royal

[4] Paul Schmidt, "Deutsche Publizistik in den Jahren 1667–1671,"
Mitteilungen der Institut für österreichischen Geschichte, XXVIII
(1907) 577–630; Johannes Haller, *Die deutsche Publizistik in den
Jahren 1668–1674* (Heidelberg, 1892); E. Longin, *François de Lisola*
(Dole, 1900), esp. pp. 102–109; Hans von Zwiedineck-Südenhorst,
Die öffentliche Meinung in Deutschland, 1650–1700 (Stuttgart, 1888),
pp. 77–117. Gillot, *L'Opinion publique*, is an excellent analytical
treatment of this pamphlet literature.

[5] The Sun King did print a manifesto outlining his claims to the
Spanish Netherlands; see *Louis XIV: Mémoires for the Instruction
of the Dauphin*, ed. and trans. Paul Sonnino (New York, 1970), pp.
129–131. This manifesto, probably composed by Antoine Bilain, was
published in 1667 under the title *Traité des droits de la reine très-
chrétienne sur les divers états de la monarchie d'Espagne*. Ironically,
its influence was far less than that of a simultaneously published
French treatise issued illegally and against Colbert's wishes. This latter
piece was Antoine Aubery's *Des justes prétentions du Roi sur l'Empire* (Paris, 1666), whose exorbitant claims embarrassed the government and landed its author in the Bastille. Nevertheless, it was received outside France as an authoritative governmental statement
(Schmidt, pp. 587–596). William F. Church, "Louis XIV and Reason
of State," in John C. Rule, ed., *Louis XIV and the Craft of Kingship*
(Columbus, Ohio, 1969), pp. 383–386, places the French propaganda
of this period in the context of the Sun King's general theory of
foreign policy.

minister attempted their resuscitation. After 1673 royal *gratifications* to foreigners ceased completely.[6]

Thus, when Louis attacked the United Provinces, concern with pamphlet propaganda was virtually nonexistent in the central government of France. While his enemies produced almost daily polemics vilifying the Sun King, no systematic effort was made to explain the king's offensive to an astonished and fearful European public.[7] Not all crown servants were content to forsake the propaganda battlefield, but absence of interest on the part of the royal ministers frustrated any plans for a comprehensive French counterattack. Most instructive in this regard is the experience of Louis Verjus, who occupied several diplomatic posts in Germany during and after the Dutch war.[8] Verjus had been a literary figure of some note and was elected to the French Academy before launching his diplomatic career. Sensitized by background to the role of print in the formation of opinion and aware that the diffuse, decentralized nature of German political organization necessitated communication with a relatively

[6] Mandrou, *Louis XIV*, p. 177. The decline of French popularity and propaganda in Germany is reflected in the career of Johann Frischmann, an Alsatian who wrote for Mazarin and Colbert but who found himself increasingly isolated both from Paris and Germany after the 1660's. See Paul Wentzcke, *Johann Frischmann, ein Publizist des 17. Jahrhunderts* (Strasbourg, 1904), pp. 88, 93, 112, 113n, 123, 129–130, 135–136.

[7] "The Dutch war . . . was one instance in which Louis XIV embarked on an aggressive war quite without benefit of any legal or moral justification" (Church, "Louis XIV and Reason of State," p. 386). The Sun King's declaration of war in 1672 was a pro forma document which did not attempt the presentation of a rationale. Meanwhile, at least 177 separate political pamphlets appeared from 1672 through 1674, nearly all of them anti-French (Meyer, *Flugschriften*, pp. 13, 156, and *passim*).

[8] For a profile of Louis Verjus and a discussion of his relationship with foreign minister Arnauld de Pomponne, see B. Auerbach, *La France et le Saint Empire Germanique depuis la paix de Westphalie jusqu'à la Révolution française* (Paris, 1912), pp. 194–200.

large number of influential people, Verjus quickly began a unilateral effort to rebut what he deemed the half-truths of anti-Louis propaganda. Recruiting his cleric brother, Antoine, as diplomatic secretary and literary collaborator, between 1672 and 1675 Verjus wrote, printed, and circulated nearly a dozen French, Latin and German tracts in defense of royal policies.[9] One measure of their impact was the appearance in 1674 of a work by Lisola with the punning title *La Sauce au Verjus*, in which the Habsburg diplomat strove to rebut the French verbal counteroffensive. Louis Verjus, rightly flattered and encouraged by this enemy attestation to his influence, argued to his superiors in France that this response should be interpreted as proof of the value of pro-French pamphlet propaganda in Germany.[10]

The propaganda campaign of the two brothers met with curious indifference in the king's council, however. Simon Arnauld de Pomponne, foreign minister from 1672, nur-

[9] I cannot identify all the Verjus tracts by title, but the diplomatic dispatches plainly refer to eight or nine different pamphlets by the brothers printed in 1673 and 1674. *Pamphlet A*: A. Verjus to Pomponne, Neuhaus, 30 May 1673, AAE, CP, Munster 3, fol. 128; A. Verjus to Pomponne (June 1673), *ibid.*, fol. 103; A. Verjus to L. Verjus, 20 June 1673, *ibid.*, fol. 88; L. Verjus to Pomponne (June 1673), AAE, CP, Prusse 9, fol. 132. *Pamphlet B*: L. Verjus to Pomponne, Cologne, 27 June 1673, AAE, CP, Cologne 11, fol. 110; L. Verjus to Pomponne, Cologne, 29 June 1673, *ibid.*, fol. 121; L. Verjus to Pomponne, Berlin, 6 August 1673, AAE, CP, Prusse 9, fol. 194. *Pamphlet C*: L. Verjus to Pomponne, Berlin, 6 August 1673, AAE, CP, Prusse 9, fol. 194. *Pamphlets D, E, F, G, H*(?): L. Verjus to Pomponne, Berlin, 26 September 1673, AAE, CP, Prusse 10, fol. 79[v]. *Pamphlet I*: L. Verjus to Courtin, 28 March 1674, AAE, CP, Cologne 12, fol. 164; L. Verjus to Pomponne, Berlin, 4 April 1674, AAE, CP, Prusse 11, fols. 322[v]-323; L. Verjus to Pomponne, Berlin, 11 August 1674, *ibid.*, fol. 344; Pomponne to L. Verjus, camp near Besançon, 6-8 May 1674, *ibid.*, fols. 403[v]-404; L. Verjus to Pomponne, Berlin, 16 May 1674, *ibid.*, fol. 465; L. Verjus to Pomponne, Berlin, 29 May 1674, *ibid.*, fols. 490[v]-491.

[10] L. Verjus to Pomponne, Berlin, 14 February 1674, AAE, CP, Prusse 11, fol. 133[v]; L. Verjus to Pomponne, Berlin, 28 February 1674, *ibid.*, fol. 192.

tured a personal dislike for Louis Verjus and deep convictions about the uselessness of French propaganda in Germany and Holland. This combination of sentiments made it inevitable that in issuing their pamphlets the Verjus brothers had to overcome not only the hostility of Louis XIV's enemies but also the lukewarm response of the king's close adviser. The French pamphleteers were crippled by a chronic shortage of funds for printing and distributing tracts. They were ordered to have their manuscripts sent to Paris for printing, and the inevitable delays and difficulties of transport drastically diminished the circulation and timeliness of the pamphlets. Louis Verjus' repeated requests in 1673 and 1674 for money to establish a French-controlled printing press in Germany went unfulfilled by Pomponne, prompting the diplomat to observe resignedly that "in France it does not seem to be considered of much consequence to influence public opinion [*toucher les esprits*], even though . . . it is certain that doing so would increase by half the force of the cannon and armies employed."[11]

Pomponne's continued apathy toward propaganda confirmed Verjus' assessment. In 1674 the envoy repeatedly called attention to the impact of popular francophobia on princely policy in Germany. "Germans," he noted with wry bitterness, "are surely not preserved from such hatred by the million screaming tracts they read, study and trust as Scripture, while—the *Bouclier d'état* remaining unanswered—Lisola's six or seven sophisms disguised in a thousand ways and circulated through a good part of Europe have aroused everyone against us." Verjus reminded Pom-

---

[11] L. Verjus to Pomponne, 27 November 1673, AAE, CP, Prusse 10, fol. 160. At first, the Verjus pamphlets were printed on the press of the friendly Bishop of Paderborn, but the growing German opposition to France ended this practice. A. Verjus to Pomponne, Neuhaus, 29 May 1673, AAE, CP, Munster 3, fol. 128; A. Verjus to Pomponne (June 1673), *ibid.*, fol. 103; L. Verjus to Pomponne, Berlin, 26 September 1673, AAE, CP, Prusse 10, fol. 79ᵛ; L. Verjus to Pomponne, Berlin, 29 May 1674, AAE, CP, Prusse 11, fol. 490ᵛ; Pomponne to L. Verjus, 19 June 1674 (minute), AAE, CP, Prusse 11, fol. 494ᵛ.

ponne of the good effect of French propaganda in Riche-lieu's day and mused on "how much, for good and for bad, manuscript and printed pamphlets count among the Germans and how much could sometimes be saved in subsidies and in troops by taking advantage of the passions and prejudices of peoples and thus influencing their attitudes." But since royal policy gave little weight to such considerations, he continued, even the most transparent enemy pamphlets "are reprinted here, read by everyone and remain persuasive in the absence of a contrary opinion."[12]

Still Pomponne continued to brush aside Verjus' request for money to subsidize a German printing operation, responding that while "it is true that *libelles* have some effect among the Germans and it could be advantageous to defend ourselves from our enemies by the same means, . . . they have the advantages of a public predisposed in their favor and a general state of mind unsympathetic to us."[13] This sort of passive fatalism amounted in Verjus' eyes to a self-fulfilling prophecy: "It is true [he wrote back to Pomponne] that the general state of public opinion is entirely predisposed against us, . . . but it must nevertheless be declared that our enemies owe this advantage principally to their writings and to our silence. The whole empire would have roused itself against the declaration of war presented by the emperor to the diet of Regensburg . . . if only its basis and consequences had been disclosed there. . . . This declaration,

---

[12] L. Verjus to Pomponne, Berlin, 30 March 1674, quoted in Hans Prutz, *Aus den Grossen Kurfürsten letzten Jahren* (Berlin, 1897), p. 338; L. Verjus to Pomponne, Berlin, 10 April 1674, AAE, CP, Prusse 11, fols. 338ᵛ–339. Cf. Picavet, *Diplomatie française*, pp. 210–211.

[13] Pomponne to Verjus, camp near Besançon, 6–8 May 1674 (minute), AAE, CP, Prusse 11, fol. 404. Pomponne's reputation for conciliation and compromise is not in evidence in his correspondence with Verjus; on this important minister, see the works of Herbert H. Rowen, "Arnauld de Pomponne: Louis XIV's Moderate Minister," *American Historical Review*, 61:3 (1956), 531–549; and *The Ambassador Prepares for War: The Dutch Embassy of Arnauld de Pomponne* (The Hague, 1957).

the *Bouclier* and several other miserable papers of the sort left unanswered make and will long make more enemies for us in Germany than all the money in France could ever make us friends."[14] Even as he penned these blunt lines Verjus knew that too much time had been lost; for in the same dispatch he informed Pomponne that he would not find "a single man who for 10,000 écus would print ten lines favorable to France in any language whatsoever." Soon the Verjus brothers stopped writing pamphlets which gained them nothing at court.

The perspective expressed by Pomponne in his letters to Verjus typifies ministerial attitudes toward pamphlet propaganda in the second phase of Louis XIV's reign. Relying on aggressive intimidation and cash subsidies to princely allies, the ministers of the 1670's and 1680's saw little need to cajole, convince, or attempt to affect the intellect in any way. Few if any of the political pamphlets of this period can be identified as crown-sponsored publications,[15] and when Louis did deign to address Europeans in print, as for instance in his manifesto of September 1688 defending French attacks in Germany, his messages sounded tones of truculent paternalism that made his enemies regard them as insulting ultimata.[16] In the arrogant and bellicose French policies of these decades the appeal to reason and sympathy found little place.

[14] L. Verjus to Pomponne, Berlin, 29 May 1674, AAE, CP, Prusse 11, fols. 490ᵛ-491. Cf. Picavet, *Diplomatie française*, p. 211.

[15] For instance, despite an avalance of documentation, Jean Orcibal, *Louis XIV contre Innocent XI* (Paris, 1949), pp. 32-47, found only circumstantial evidence connecting government ministers with the pamphlets espousing Louis' objections to the policies of Pope Innocent.

[16] See V.-L. Tapié, "Quelques aspects généraux de la politique étrangère de Louis XIV," *XVIIᵉ siècle*, Nos. 46-47 (1960), p. 22; Richard Place, "The Self-Deception of the Strong: France on the Eve of the War of the League of Augsburg," *French Historical Studies*, 6:4 (1970), 459-473; and Orcibal, *Louis XIV contre Innocent XI*, pp. 25-27.

There is some evidence that during the War of the League of Augsburg several of Louis XIV's councillors hesitantly began to reintroduce the weapon of the pen. Louvois, his son and successor Barbézieux, and Colbert de Croissy probably sponsored a few scattered manuscript and printed pamphlets as part of their attempt to split the anti-French coalition, particularly in Germany.[17] Crucial in the nascent campaign to win back Germans alienated by Louis' belligerence was the role of Ulrich Obrecht, *prêteur royal* at Strasbourg from 1685. A respected scholar in the German world of letters, professor of imperial and public law at the University of Strasbourg since 1672, Obrecht became a member of the Alsatian city's new governing elite after its incorporation into Louis XIV's kingdom. As a prize convert to Catholicism, he was officially instructed in the faith by no less a personage than Bossuet, and soon found himself recruited by the royal ministers as an influential consultant on matters of German law and politics, subjects on which French ignorance seems to have been almost unlimited.[18]

Inevitably for a man of his background, Obrecht was soon drawn into a role of responsibility for censorship in Strasbourg. As *prêteur royal* he vigilantly banned subversive works, demonstrating that the crown was now controlling publication in the guise of protector of religion and morality. As ministerial consultant he collected, summarized, and forwarded to Versailles the many anti-French pamphlets which filtered over the Rhine from Germany. At the end of the War of the League of Augsburg, Obrecht composed rebuttals to these pamphlets, although his responses were perhaps never distributed in printed form. The assiduous

[17] M. Vanhuffel, *Documents inédits concernant l'histoire de France et particulièrement l'Alsace et son gouvernement sous Louis XIV* (Paris, 1840), p. 160. Rousset, *Louvois*, IV, 395–396.

[18] On Obrecht, see the *éloge* in *Journal de Trévoux*, November-December 1701, pp. 216–236; H. Bresslau's article in *Allgemeine deutsche Biographie*, XXIV, 119–121; and Livet, *L'Intendance*, esp. pp. 386–387, 416–417, 457, 637–638, 651–652, 669, 909.

attention he paid to French censorship interests very likely reflects sentiments of bitter vengeance directed against the former leadership of his city; for in 1672 Obrecht's father, George, had been publicly executed after publishing a pamphlet critical of the municipal authorities.[19]

Then, between 1697 and 1700 Obrecht undertook a series of diplomatic missions in Germany and convinced the newly installed Torcy that the foreign ministry ought to cultivate German public opinion in a systematic, regular manner. To Obrecht this meant attendance by French representatives at meetings of deputies of the German imperial circles, especially those of Franconia, Swabia, and the Upper Rhine. These bodies had formed a major organizing and financing administration for the empire's military operations during the war of 1689–1697, and now French diplomats, at Obrecht's insistence, began to use their gatherings as an occasion for convincing the delegates of their master's good will and just pretensions.[20]

Argumentation of this sort became essential in November 1700, when Louis announced his acceptance of Charles II's testament bestowing the Spanish succession upon the Sun King's grandson, Philip. Predictably, francophobe pamphleteers throughout Europe at once raised the old cry of universal monarchy against the Bourbons.[21] More important,

[19] Livet, *L'Intendance*, pp. 797–803; Georges Livet, "Problèmes rhénanes du XVII⁰ siècle. Libelles et pamphlets à la fin du XVII⁰ siècle. Strasbourg entre la France et l'Empire," *Cahiers de l'Association interuniversitaire de l'Est* (Strasbourg), No. 6 (1964), pp. 23–31.

[20] Auerbach, *France et le Saint Empire*, pp. 242–243, 255. Also Torcy to Obrecht, Marly, 18 July 1698, AAE, CP, Allemagne 335, fol. 305.

[21] Carl Ringhoffer, *Die Flugschriften-Literatur zu Beginn des spanisches Erbfolgekrieges* (Berlin, 1881), *passim*. Franklin Ford observed that the events of the 1680's and after "touched off a storm of anti-French indignation among the literate classes of the Empire. The output of hostile pamphlet literature reached a new high. Admittedly, such expressions could influence French-subsidized princes and ministers only if and when patriotism began to look profitable."

Emperor Leopold I immediately embarked on a war to assert Habsburg claims over the Spanish empire. By way of assisting French diplomatic efforts in Germany to justify Louis' acceptance of the testament, Obrecht, who was serving in Frankfurt-am-Main at the time, promptly asked Torcy's permission to publish a monthly compilation of juridical opinion favorable to the French position. To a royal government still dominated by suspicious caution about pamphlet propaganda, Obrecht suggested brochures consisting "exclusively of extracts faithfully copied and drawn from the fundamental laws of Spanish history and jurisprudence." He explained that "if one were to issue something in tract form it would only serve to stimulate contrasting writings which would be evaluated according to individual prejudice, while the sort of memoirs proposed, consisting as they do entirely of passages from disinterested authors, cannot be attacked without directly attacking authors who carry more weight in the public's judgment than any pamphlet opposing them."[22] This proposal quickly won Torcy's approval, and between December 1700 and March 1701 there appeared four monthly brochures published in Latin, French, and Spanish excerpting the works of such authorities as Grotius, Molina, and Mariana. Also printed were such relevant documents as the texts of the testaments of Emperor Charles V and Philip II. Each monthly issue was held to a slim fifteen or twenty-five pages, and this brief, periodical-like format was intended, Obrecht told Torcy, to facilitate their broad distribution, to make their content more palatable, and continually to present new ideas to the reader.[23] Only Obrecht's

---

Not that the wrath of the publicists was necessarily an expression of public opinion in any present-day sense of the term; but the views of a wide variety of German-speaking individuals might under certain circumstances awaken significant echoes in the chancelleries." *Strasbourg in Transition, 1648–1789* (Cambridge, Mass., 1958), p. 60.

[22] Obrecht to Louis, Frankfort a/M, 21 December 1700 (copy), BA, ms. 6516, fols. 351–352ᵛ.

[23] *Ibid.* The pamphlets bore the title *Excerpta historica et juridica*

failing health prevented extension of the series beyond March 1701.

The *prêteur royal* died at Strasbourg in August, but even in his last weeks he remained actively involved in the French diplomatic and propaganda campaign to avoid a general war over the Spanish succession. In his final letters to Louis and Torcy, one of Obrecht's concerns was the outline of a projected full-scale legal treatise rebutting the imperial claims to Spain.[24] The young foreign minister also solicited and followed to the letter Obrecht's advice on a major diplomatic problem of the moment: the proper mode of response to the recent imperial citation of the French-allied duke of Mantua as a contumacious vassal. This citation and its accompanying imperial ban deprived Duke Ferdinand Charles of the legal title to his offices and prepared the way for a military campaign against Mantua by Emperor Leopold's forces. A "placard war," organized by the opposing generals, Catinat and Eugene of Savoy, was already under way in Mantua and neighboring towns to convince the local populace of the justice and benefits inhering in their respective causes. Obrecht, however, was primarily concerned with German opinion, hoping that Leopold's harsh treatment of an Italian prince might be viewed in Germany as a worrisome omen of his plans for other princes who followed policies independent of the emperor. Thus Obrecht advised, and Torcy relayed the message to the French envoy in Mantua, that Ferdinand write to each imperial elector and to the Regensburg diet protesting Leopold's actions. To

---

de natura successionis in monarchiam Hispaniae and are catalogued as BN, Imp., O^c 565. Their authorship is established by the *Journal de Trévoux*, November-December 1701, pp. 226–227. For reviews, see above, chap. 3, nn. 39 and 42.

[24] Letter to Obrecht, 31 January 1701, BA, ms. 6516, fol. 387; Louis to Obrecht, Marly, 21 July 1701 (minute), AAE, CP, Allemagne 343, fol. 252; Obrecht to Louis, Strasbourg, 26 July 1701, *ibid.*, fol. 93; summary of Obrecht to Louis, Frankfort, 18 June 1701, AAE, MD, Allemagne 49, fol. 224.

these public documents Obrecht wished to add a manifesto issued under the duke's name as the key barrage in a multi-faceted propaganda offensive.[25] But the Alsatian's death and Ferdinand's reluctance to act decisively in his own defense combined to abort this campaign. Although the duke wrote perfunctory letters of protest to the imperial electors, he feared antagonizing Leopold still further with a public manifesto. Louis' envoy in Mantua supervised the drafting of such a manifesto, but Ferdinand kept postponing its appearance. When finally published in 1703, it was uselessly obsolete.[26]

Despite Obrecht's death, the concern for propaganda that he had impressed upon the young Torcy became a central feature of the new foreign minister's approach to diplomacy in Germany. For a full year before the imperial diet formally declared war on France in mid-1702, Torcy continually urged Louis Rousseau de Chamoy,[27] French ambassador at the imperial diet, to compose and circulate manifestos and pamphlets making known the French contention that

[25] Obrecht to Louis, Strasbourg, 8 July 1701, BN. N.a. fr. 7488, fols. 106-108ᵛ; Louis to d'Audiffret, Marly, 21 July 1701, AAE, CP, Mantoue 31, fol. 164; d'Audiffret to Louis, 23 July 1701, Mantoue 31, fol. 268; Louis to d'Audiffret, 9 August 1701, *ibid.*, fols. 226-228; letter of Catinat and Vaudemont, *ibid.*, fol. 203 (cf. AN, K. 1304, No. 10). A copy of the treaty between Louis and Ferdinand is in AAE, CP, Mantoue 32, fols. 50-55. On Italian reaction to the Mantua affair, see Dubos to Thoynard, Rome, 17 April 1701, in Paul Denis, *Lettres autographes de la collection de Troussures* (Beauvais, 1912), p. 114.

[26] D'Audiffret to Louis, 7 October 1701, AAE, CP, Mantoue 31, fols. 335-336. The manifesto appeared, in French and Latin, as *Exposition des droits du ... Duc de Mantoue, ... contre deux prétendus decrets impériaux ...* (Mantua, 1703). For a review, see above, chap. 3, n. 42. On the *Gazette*'s handling of the Mantua affair, see above, chap. 3, n. 7.

[27] On Rousseau, see Auerbach, *France et le Saint Empire*, pp. 240-242, 256-257. Rousseau wrote an interesting manual on diplomacy, *De l'art de négocier*, ed. L. Delavaud (Paris, 1912). His son was a member of Torcy's Académie politique; see Klaits, "Men of Letters," p. 583n.

"the emperor is profiting . . . from the weakness of the German princes by establishing his absolute authority in the empire. His daily maneuvers against these princes should be enough to convince them that they have no other genuine enemy than the emperor and that it is against his power that they ought to take the proper precautions, not to let themselves be blinded by the fear of an imaginary peril inspired in them by the house of Austria."[28] Torcy did not expect printed polemics to change the opinions of those moved by "passion or private interest." "But," he insisted to Rousseau, "it still is worthwhile to distribute them even if they only serve to persuade those who are not prejudiced."[29] These urgings, so different from Pomponne's attitude thirty years earlier, led Rousseau to compose and print three pamphlets during 1701 and 1702 and to distribute two others written by Baron Karg von Bebenburg, chief minister of the French-allied Elector Joseph Clement of Cologne.[30]

[28] Louis to Rousseau, 13 April 1702, AAE, CP, Allemagne 344, fols. 172–173.

[29] Louis to Rousseau, 30 March 1702 (minute), *ibid.*, fol. 151.

[30] The five pamphlets are: (1) [Louis Rousseau de Chamoy], *Traduction de la réponse d'un gentilhomme italien à une lettre d'un de ses amis sur la prétendue proscription du duc de Mantoue* (n.p., n.d.). For editions and attribution, see appendix.

(2) [Louis Rousseau de Chamoy], *Lettre de M***** escrite à M*** Envoyé Extraordinaire de *** à la Haye contenant diverses reflexions sur le traitté conclu entre l'Empereur, le Roy d'Angleterre et les Estats-Généraux des Provinces Unies le 7 septembre 1701* (Frankfurt, 1701). For editions and attribution, see appendix.

(3) [Louis Rousseau de Chamoy], *Réponse de Mr. de . . . Envoyé de Mr. le Duc . . . à Mr. de . . . aussi Envoyé du mesme Prince à . . . contenant diverses reflexions sur les mandements de l'Empereur contre Mr. l'Electeur de Cologne* (Frankfurt, 1702). For editions and attribution, see appendix.

(4) [J.F.I. Karg von Bebenburg(?)], *Réflections sur les mandemens impériaux contre M. l'Electeur de Cologne* (Frankfurt, 1702), AAE, CP, Cologne 51, fols. 147–172. Manuscript copy, AAE, CP, Cologne 52, fols. 149–152^v. Des Alleurs to Torcy, Bonn, 16 February 1702, AAE, CP, Cologne 52, fol. 147: "Je vous envoye Monseigneur des réflections que l'on a fait icy sur les Mandemens imperiales. M. le

The pamphlet barrage of 1701–1702 signaled the ascendance of a new attitude toward pamphlet propaganda in the French government, an attitude which assumed that subsidies and armed might were no longer sufficient to carry out the Sun King's objectives.

The five pamphlets of 1701–1702 all sought to illustrate the dangers of German princely reliance on the Habsburgs. Louis and his councillors well knew that accepting the Spanish testament inevitably meant war with Leopold, but they hoped to limit the conflict by depriving the emperor of help from the imperial princes. While Torcy understood that the open wounds produced by thirty years of French aggression precluded a credible return to the propaganda of Richelieu and Mazarin casting France as the protector of German liberties, the foreign minister still hoped that most of the princes and the imperial circles would at least regard it as in their interest to remain neutral in the dispute between Louis and Leopold. Thus French pamphlets, echoing the royal diplomatic dispatches, harped incessantly on the irrelevance of the Spanish succession to German interests.[31] "The emperor," wrote Rousseau, "is not waging war in Italy in his imperial capacity but in his quality of Archduke of Austria and for domestic claims unrelated to the empire."[32] Leopold's real aim in dragging the empire into the

---

Chancelier Karg ayant trouvé à propos de les rendre publiques excepté l'article qui est marqué; j'en ay aussy envoyé une copie à M. le M^{al} de Boufflers pour les faire imprimer à Bruxelles."

(5) [J.F.I. Karg von Bebenburg], *Manifeste en forme de lettre pour S.A.S.E. de Cologne, dont les moyens sont tiré de la lettre latine qu'Elle a écrite à l'Empereur le 19 mars 1702* (Paris, 1702). Many copies comprising several editions in BN, Imp.; see under Karg in *Catalogue des Auteurs*. On this tract, see Des Alleurs to Torcy, Bonn, 25 February 1702, AAE, Cologne 54, fol. 115.

31 There are striking parallels, even as to wording, between these pamphlets and the confidential diplomatic letters. Compare, for example, Rousseau's *Traduction de la réponse d'un gentilhomme italien* with Louis to Rousseau, 6 July 1701 (minute), AAE, CP, Allemagne 341, fol. 275.

32 *Traduction de la réponse d'un gentilhomme italien*, p. 6.

conflict was "aggrandizement and the self-ascription of a despotic power in Germany."[33]

The emperor's banning of Ferdinand, and his similar move against Elector Joseph Clement of Cologne after that prince-archbishop aligned himself with Louis, gave Rousseau and Karg opportunities to protest against Leopold's violations of the imperial constitution. Characterizing Leopold's failure to consult the Regensburg diet on these issues as an "unprecedented irregularity," one French pamphlet went on to ask rhetorically, "Doesn't this manner of treating the Estates . . . clearly show the contempt in which the court of Vienna holds the Diet?" The moral was plain: Leopold's government "is musing on how to establish precedents of this kind for the purpose of acceding to that supreme, monarchical authority in the empire which it has envisaged for so long."[34] The treatment of Joseph Clement was particularly flagrant, for the elector's "liberty, once violated, will bring about imperceptibly the total ruin of the German Nation."[35] By asking the elector's subjects to renounce their oaths of allegiance to him, Leopold was said to be reducing the princes to the status of private persons, one step toward his goal of abolishing the Golden Bull and all the laws and constitutions of the empire.[36] The imperial court "simply wants to engage the states of the empire in a war which it finds desirable, and it cannot bear that those who fear their country will become a theater of action do not answer to its desires; this is the whole crime of the elector of Cologne."[37] As Karg put it in Joseph Clement's ghostwritten manifesto protesting his ban, "It is only to my lack of devotion to the private purposes of Your Most Serene House's aggrandizement that I owe the intensity of my persecution. I perceive very clearly that my crime consists . . . only in that I could not

[33] *Réponse de Mr. de . . .* , p. 20.
[34] *Traduction de la réponse d'un gentilhomme italien*, pp. 7–8.
[35] *Manifeste . . . pour S.A.S.E. de Cologne*, p. 4.
[36] *Réflections sur les mandemens impériaux*, last paragraph.
[37] *Réponse de Mr. de . . .* , p. 13.

sacrifice my states and the rights of the empire to Your Sacred Imperial Majesty's interests."[38]

For the sake of the emperor's private interests, French propaganda argued, Germany was being drawn into a war of which, were it to become generalized, "neither we nor our sons will perhaps see the end."[39] While imperial pamphleteers maintained that war was necessary to save Europe from Louis' universal monarchy, the irony noted by Rousseau was that this very war would infinitely increase the power of the house of Austria. Indeed, "it is none other than the Most Christian King [Louis] who is working to preserve the balance of which so much has been said, for the Spanish monarchy cannot possibly be dismembered without leaving France superior."[40] "The so-called union of these two monarchies had to be established in the minds of the public," declared Rousseau, "and there has been a great effort to make this the basis of all the *libelles* and other publications which have been circulated, to steep the world in this idea and to profit from its credulity."[41] Since Louis and Philip have promised that France and Spain shall never be united and that their commerce will remain separate, the threat of universal monarchy is a "phantom of which the court of Vienna is making good use for the purpose of blinding men's minds to its own intentions."[42]

All five of the tracts of 1701–1702 owed their origin to the orders and suggestions of Colbert de Torcy, relayed over Louis' signature in dispatches to Rousseau and Karg. In these two writers, the young foreign minister found men capable of continuing Obrecht's tradition. In fact, Baron Karg's services almost mirrored those once performed by the Alsatian. Beginning in the latter half of 1701, Torcy came to rely increasingly on Karg for expert advice about German political and historical matters. Long ministerial

---

[38] *Manifeste . . . pour S.A.S.E. de Cologne*, p. 26.
[39] *Réponse de Mr. de . . .* , p. 19.
[40] *Ibid.*, p. 20. [41] *Lettre de M******, p. 9.
[42] *Réponse de Mr. de . . .* , p. 20.

experience in both the Bavaria and Cologne branches of the Wittelsbach dynastic service made Karg a master of the mysteries of German constitutional law. Karg was the individual most responsible for arranging the secret treaty tying the Cologne electorate to France. Then, initiating a voluminous correspondence with Louis' diplomats all over Germany, Joseph Clement's ministers sent them anonymous tracts defending the Bourbon succession in Spain even before he used these contacts to circulate his own and Rousseau's pamphlets. Soon Karg became the recipient of an annual royal *gratification* and property in France that compensated him for the emperor's vindictive seizure of his domains.[43]

Acting on Torcy's initiative, French diplomats, military men, and agents in several European states arranged for the distribution of the Rousseau-Karg literature. Since censorship barred their publication in Germany, the pamphlets were variously printed in Holland, Brussels, and Paris, and then were sent back to Germany in French diplomatic packets for dissemination at the courts and assemblies. All five were printed in French, and one also appeared in a Latin edition. The absence of German-language editions does not seem crucial, given the limited audience of minis-

[43] On Karg's career in general, see Max Braubach, *Kurköln, Gestalten und Ereignisse aus zwei Jahrhunderten rheinischen Geschichte* (Münster, 1948), pp. 181–199. Torcy's relationship with Karg moved from suspicion in early 1701 (*Recueil des instructions données aux ambassadeurs et ministres de France*, Vol. 28:2: *Etats allemands— Cologne*, ed. G. Livet [Paris, 1963], p. 118) to warmth (*ibid.*, p. 121) and close collaboration (des Alleurs to Torcy, Bonn, 30 June 1701, AAE, CP, Cologne 50, fols. 126–217ᵛ; des Alleurs to Torcy, Bonn, 13 September 1701, AAE, CP, Cologne 51, fol. 31ᵛ; Louis to des Alleurs, Versailles, 19 September 1701 [minute], *ibid.*, fol. 33; Louis to Karg, Versailles, 8 December 1701, *ibid.*, fol. 348; Louis to des Alleurs, Versailles, 29 December 1701 [minute], *ibid.*, fol. 394ᵛ; Blainville to Torcy, Kaiserwerth, 28 January 1702, AAE, CP, Cologne 52, fol. 107ᵛ). Samples of Karg's correspondence with French diplomats are Karg to d'Iberville, Bonn, 2 January 1701, AAE, CP, Cologne 50, fol. 6; d'Iberville to Karg, Mayence, 5 January 1701, *ibid.*, fol. 9.

ters, diplomats, delegates, and princes to whom they were addressed.[44]

What was the impact of these pamphlets on the German scene? Of course, gauging the precise effect of a pamphlet or group of pamphlets is virtually impossible in the absence of any measuring device capable of isolating this one element from the many variables involved in forming opinion. To be sure, Rousseau believed that pamphlet propaganda was an effective way of getting across a diplomatic point, possibly even superior to direct, oral contact. He told Versailles that delegates to the Regensburg diet might neglect to report a conversation in their dispatches to their superiors, but they never failed to enclose copies of printed matter. It was no less clear to Rousseau, however, that most German leaders were either creatures of the imperial court or too cowed to protest against Leopold's maneuvers.[45] Then too, circulation of the Rousseau and Karg tracts was severely hampered by wartime conditions of transport and by cen-

[44] Rousseau to Torcy, Ratisbon, 1 September 1701, AAE, CP, Allemagne 342, fol. 116; Rousseau to Torcy, Ratisbon, 5 September 1701, *ibid.*, fol. 120. Rousseau to Torcy, 12 January 1702, AAE, CP, Allemagne 344, fol. 35. Des Alleurs to Torcy, Bonn, 16 February 1702, AAE, CP, Cologne 52, fol. 147; des Alleurs to Louis, Bonn, 4 March 1702, *ibid.*, fol. 243^v; des Alleurs to Torcy, 15 April 1702, *ibid.*, fol. 271; des Alleurs to Boufflers (copy), Bonn, 20 March 1702, AAE, CP, Cologne 54, fol. 115; Boufflers to Chamillart, Bruxelles, 7 February 1702, AG, A1. 1560, pièce 47; Boufflers to Karg, 19 April 1702, printed in L. Ennen, *Der spanische Erbfolgekrieg und der Kurfürst Joseph Clemens von Köln* (Jena, 1854), pp. xviii–xix; Rousseau to Torcy, Ratisbon, 13 March 1702, AAE, CP, Allemagne 344, fol. 134^v; Rousseau to Louis, Ratisbon, 13 March 1702, *ibid.*, fol. 138^v; Rousseau to Torcy, Ratisbon, 16 March 1702, *ibid.*, fol. 147; Louis to Rousseau, Marly, 30 March 1702 (minute), *ibid.*, fol. 151; Rousseau to Torcy, Ratisbon, 17 April 1702, *ibid.*, fol. 186. On the Paris editions, see Torcy to d'Argenson, Versailles, 23 April 1702, AAE, CP, Cologne 54, fol. 243; d'Argenson to Torcy, Paris, 26 April 1702, *ibid.*, fol. 244.

[45] Rousseau to Louis, Ratisbon, 13 March 1702, AAE, CP, Allemagne 344, fol. 138^v; Rousseau to Louis, Ratisbon, 15 August 1701, AAE, CP, Allemagne 342, fol. 77^v.

sorship of pro-French works in Holland and Germany. With the exception of the manifesto written under Elector Joseph Clement's name, none of these works appears to have been mentioned in contemporary periodicals or reprinted in subsequent editions.

In any case, Louis XIV's wildly imprudent political acts in·1701 spoke far louder than his diplomats' pamphlet propaganda. By September French occupation of the barrier forts in the Spanish Netherlands, the acquisition by French merchants of monopoly rights to the immensely valuable Spanish slave trade, and Louis' edict declaring Philip still eligible for succession to the French throne helped solidify a Grand Alliance of Habsburg Austria, England, and the United Provinces. The Sun King's recognition of James II's son as rightful heir to the English throne made the allies' accusations of universal monarchy and Bourbon hegemony in Europe all the more credible. During March 1702 the German imperial circles, whose neutrality had been eagerly sought and optimistically anticipated in France, joined the anti-Bourbon coalition, and three months later Rousseau was expelled from the empire. In all Germany only the Wittelsbach electors of Cologne and Bavaria joined Louis and Philip against the powerful anti-Bourbon alliance.

None of these setbacks to French diplomacy caused Torcy to doubt the importance of continued pamphlet propaganda. Indeed, with Louis' diplomats barred from enemy courts, the printed word became the most effective if not the only available way to influence opinion. But without help from the now preoccupied and overworked Karg, and deprived of an extensive network of resident diplomats to compose, print and circulate pamphlets, new authors and techniques had to be found. Thus, as soon as the anti-Bourbon alliance took form, Torcy began to assemble a group of paid pamphleteers to continue the work of propagandizing Europe.

His first attentions were directed toward England. From the moment Louis accepted the Spanish testament, the crown's dispatches to London had shown a keen awareness of the importance of propaganda in English politics. In announcing Philip's accession, the Sun King ordered his envoy, Marshal Tallard,

> to let the public know that the King's sole aim is to maintain peace, that England and Holland have nothing to fear from His Majesty's plans as long as they follow their true interest in seeing to it that war is not renewed on any pretext whatever, that the accession of a Prince of France to the Spanish throne will not mean any change in the status of that monarchy. It would be good to have these ideas disseminated in London and in the Provinces, so that the members of the next Parliament can be confirmed in their current opinion that this event will cause no prejudice at all to the ordinary commerce of the Nation, that it is up to them to peacefully reap the profits that they have always found in their dealings with Spain and that the English can only lose if they lightly follow actions that they are being inspired to undertake contrary to their true interests.[46]

Tallard accordingly had the king's messages to the Dutch Estates General translated and circulated in England,[47] but by the end of January 1701 Louis was convinced that the

[46] *Recueil des instructions données aux ambassadeurs et ministres de France*, vol. 25, 2: *Angleterre 3, 1698–1791*, ed. P. Vaucher (Paris, 1965), pp. 60–65. On the role of printed propaganda in England around 1700, see Lawrence Hanson, *Government and the Press, 1695–1763* (Oxford, 1936); Douglas Coombs, *The Conduct of the Dutch: British Opinion and the Dutch Alliance during the War of the Spanish Succession* (The Hague, 1958); James O. Richards, *Party Propaganda Under Queen Anne: The General Elections of 1702–1713* (Athens, Ga., 1972); and E. S. de Beer, "The English Newspaper from 1695 to 1702," in *William III and Louis XIV: Essays 1680–1720 by and for Mark A. Thomson*, ed. R. Hatton and J. S. Bromley (Liverpool, 1968), pp. 117–129.

[47] Tallard to Louis, London, 22 December 1700, AAE, CP, Angleterre 190, fol. 37ᵛ; Tallard to Louis, 27 December 1700, *ibid.*, fol. 48.

English "Nation, aroused by the speeches and various pamphlets which the King of England is having distributed, has commenced to consider the war necessary to its security." Still Tallard continued to disseminate Louis' public statements to the Dutch.[48]

He also began negotiations aimed at recruiting the well-known Sir Charles Davenant as a French pamphleteer. Davenant was a member of Parliament, an erstwhile commissioner of the excise, and a founder of the new science of "political arithmetic." In his economic writings of the 1690's he had attempted to apply the techniques of quantification not only to commercial matters but to affairs of high politics, contending that it was possible and desirable to define the interests of states by computational means. These analytical works were also highly polemical; as one of his critics put it, Davenant's writing on commerce was frequently "interlarded with some untoward Insinuations against the Government." Indeed, Davenant had written forcefully of what he saw as England's subservience to a new "moneyed interest" of monopolists and war profiteers who dominated William III's Whig administration. Convinced as he was that heavy English involvement in the War of the League of Augsburg had been a commercial disaster for the "landed interest," Davenant was an author whose viewpoint was highly compatible with the French desire to limit England's role in the Spanish succession war.[49] Shorn

---

[48] Louis to Harcourt, 27 January 1701, in C. Hippeau, *L'Avènement des Bourbons au trône d'Espagne* (Paris, 1875), II, 443–444; Tallard to Louis, 15 February 1701, AAE, CP, Angleterre 190, fol. 118ᵛ; Tallard to Louis, 12 February 1701, *ibid.*, fol. 185.

[49] Davenant's critic was the anonymous author of *Animadversions on a Late Factious Book* (London, 1701), p. 5. Davenant's relevant writings are collected in *The Political and Commercial Works of Sir Charles Davenant*, ed. Sir Charles Whitworth, 5 vols. (London, 1771). For a bibliographical list and the dating of Davenant's works, see David Waddell, "The Writings of Charles Davenant (1665–1714)," *The Library*, ser. 5, 11:3 (September 1956), esp. 207–208. On Davenant's career and contributions to economic thought, see G. N. Clark,

of crown office after the Glorious Revolution and short of funds to support his large family, Davenant did not discourage French overtures for a subsidy in the first months of 1701, though he delayed making a firm commitment in hope of drawing a higher price.[50]

After Tallard's recall in April, the Davenant negotiations were taken over by Nicolas Poussin, accredited by Louis as resident at the court of William III. To indicate his good faith, Davenant submitted to Poussin the draft of a pamphlet called *The True Picture of a Modern Whig* and at the resident's request excised several passages unfavorable to France before the published version appeared in August 1701. To judge this tract in perspective, however, we ought first to examine Davenant's twin pamphlets of March 1701, *An Essay upon the Balance of Power* and *An Essay upon Universal Monarchy*. The monarchy of the title was that

---

English Commercial Statistics, 1696–1782 (London, 1938), pp. 12–19. For opinions about Davenant's position in the political spectrum of his day, see the differing views of J.G.A. Pocock, "Machiavelli, Harrington and English Political Ideologies in the Eighteenth Century," *William and Mary Quarterly*, 3rd ser., 22:4 (October 1965), 577–578; Isaac Kramnick, *Bolingbroke and His Circle: The Politics of Nostalgia in the Age of Walpole* (Cambridge, Mass., 1968), pp. 237–243, 309; and J.A.W. Gunn, *Politics and the Public Interest in the Seventeenth Century* (Toronto, 1969), pp. 241–243. Part of the confusion about interpreting Davenant's constantly shifting positions stems from the failure to see his works as propaganda, not political theory.

[50] On Davenant's relations with the French, see, for parts of the story, G. M. Trevelyan, *England in the Reign of Queen Anne*, 3 vols. (London, 1930–1934), I, 141, 154, 443; Stephen B. Baxter, *William III* (London, 1966), p. 379; and F. Salomon, *Geschichte des letzten Ministeriums Königin Annas von England, 1710–1714* (Gotha, 1894), p. 50*n*. These accounts must be supplemented by the following diplomatic dispatches: Poussin to Torcy, London, 11 August 1701, AAE, CP, Angleterre 210, fols. 307ᵛ–309; Poussin to Torcy, London, 5 September 1701, *ibid.*, fols. 363ᵛ–364; Poussin to Torcy, London, 8 September 1701, *ibid.*, fols. 370–372; Torcy to Poussin, Marly, 15 September 1701, *ibid.*, fol. 375.

of the Bourbons, and this work is a vigorous attack on Louis
XIV. Davenant portrayed the Sun King as a prince who
had turned France into a garrison state. The house of Bourbon, now comprising Spain as well as France, he deemed a
threat to the world. Emphasizing France's great strength
despite recent famine and plague, Davenant conjured up the
possibility of a united Bourbon empire. "Such a monarchy
would be so strong, that all the rest of Christendom would
be utterly unable to resist it. This sad prospect has occa-
sioned these papers. And it is to be hoped, all good Englishmen will bend their principal thoughts, and exert their utmost strength, both now and in future times, to prevent the
growth of such a power which may be interrupted in its
first settlement."[51] This seems clear enough, but Davenant's
simultaneously published *Essay upon the Balance of Power*
is a far more ambivalent piece. Here, while he reinforced
his conviction that the solution by testament upsets the
European power balance, the author was nonetheless sharp-
ly critical of William's ministers. These men, he wrote, grew
rich in conducting the previous war and sought vainly to
forestall Bourbon aggrandizement through vague and mis-
guided partition treaties. Davenant concluded by advocating
war—a war which in his view was likely to be long and
hard—in order to expel French garrisons from Spanish territory in the Netherlands and assure an independent Spain
uninfluenced by French advice, but not to dethrone Philip.
At the same time, however, he stressed the need to protect
English liberties and professed to fear, based on the experience of the past decade, that war under the old ministers
would hasten the drift from freedom. Thus, the total effect
of Davenant's essays of March 1701 is ambiguous. He waves
the flag, no doubt, but his patriotism opposes the government of England quite as much as that of France.[52]

[51] Davenant, *Works*, IV, 25–28.

[52] *Ibid.*, III, 297–360, esp. 326, 338–340, 351. Also published with
these essays of March 1701 was Davenant's *The Right of Making*

Davenant's pamphlet of August 1701, *The True Picture of a Modern Whig*, differs from its antecedents less in argument than in emphasis. This was the work which Davenant edited at Poussin's request. Here the author paid only passing attention to the French menace, except for a passage in which, to defend himself from Whig charges that he had taken French money, he harked back to his strong support of war in the March tracts. Having thus covered himself and assured his credibility, Davenant refrained from attacking France and instead reaffirmed at great length and with passion his mistrust of the perfidious motives of the Whigs. The Whig in Davenant's dialogue sets forth the party's strategy in the preceding session of Parliament: to stampede the nation into a Whig-managed war. Had Parliament refused, "we would have made Jacobite and French Pensioner, so ring through the whole kingdom, that a dissolution would have been unavoidable." Davenant allowed that William was a defender of English liberties, but he held that the Whigs proposed to milk the landed classes of their wealth through taxation, to destroy Parliament and to pave the way for absolute rule.[53]

So pleased was Torcy with *The True Picture of a Modern Whig* that he promised Davenant a diamond ring as the French crown's initial payment to its new pamphleteer. But the day after this commitment was dispatched to Poussin saw the death of James II at Saint-Germain and Louis' announced recognition of the Stuart heir as rightful ruler of

---

War, Peace and Alliances, an effort to show by means of a catalogue of precedents that the English constitution prohibited the monarch from embarking on foreign adventures without prior consultation and authorization.

[53] *Ibid.*, IV, 132–133, 177–178. According to Richards, *Party Propaganda*, p. 38n, Robert Harley, the future Tory minister of Queen Anne's last years, helped Davenant with the writing of this tract, as he assuredly did by providing records for the March 1701 tracts (Angus McInnes, *Robert Harley* [London, 1970], p. 60). However, there is no evidence directly linking Harley with Torcy at this point.

England. Having already concluded the Grand Alliance, William III did not hesitate to order Poussin expelled from his kingdom as soon as news of Louis' insult crossed the channel. A courier who was immediately dispatched to locate Poussin and serve him with his exit orders found the French diplomat dining out in London with none other than a highly embarrassed Charles Davenant. Not only did Poussin's departure deprive Versailles of its only convenient contact with Davenant, but public confirmation of the writer's already suspected association with Louis' representative destroyed his reputation. Hounded as a "Poussineer," Davenant lost his Commons seat in the election of late 1701. But from the forum he retained in Grub Street he struck back at his enemies in a pamphlet called *Tom Double Return'd Out of the Country*, published in January 1702. Davenant branded the Whig exposé a fraud: Poussin was a stranger to him, introduced only that evening and supped with for under an hour. Davenant described the "slander" of his honor as a typical act of Whig treachery; were not the Whigs, after all, leading the nation to war, not out of principle but for profit, so as to "over-balance the land interest"?[54]

Falsification of his dealings with Poussin proved an insufficient safeguard for Davenant. Summoned before the House of Lords in 1702 for writing "scandalous and seditious libel," he soon accomplished a prudent about-face and in 1704 brought out a new pamphlet advocating *Peace at Home and the War Abroad*. Any further contact with the French crown would have been suicidal for Davenant, while for his part Torcy must have known that the Englishman's useful-

[54] Davenant, *Works*, IV, 214–215, 222–223, 263–264. See also *A Vindication of Dr. Charles Davenant* . . . (London, 1702). Insinuations of Davenant's venal relationship with the French crown are in *Animadversions on a Late Factious Book*, pp. 5, 60, 64a; and *The Tories Great Doubts and Difficulties Fully Resolv'd, by More Important Doubts and Difficulties. With Some Queries about Monsieur Poussin Paying his Foy to three Members of the H——— of C———s* (London, 1701), p. 2.

ness ended with the Poussin dinner party. In the words of a contemporary pamphleteer bitterly opposed to Davenant, war "unites Factions, and silences even Libellers of the Publick, by directing all stirring Spirits against a common Enemy."[55] Yet Davenant's association with French propaganda has an epilogue, for later in the war French writers in Torcy's employ tried to appropriate his techniques of political arithmetic in their propaganda works. More broadly, the Davenant episode, like the German efforts of Obrecht, Rousseau and Karg, demonstrates Torcy's energetic concern with pamphlet propaganda. With the coming of general war, hiring enemy subjects as writers became impractical; instead, as we shall see in subsequent chapters, Torcy turned to homegrown authors for both domestic and foreign propaganda.

[55] *Animadversions on a Late Factious Book*, p. 64. Torcy's secret agents in England kept him informed of Davenant's judicial difficulties and subsequent recantations. See AAE, CP, Angleterre 212, fol. 143, and AAE, CP, Angleterre 213, fol. 254ᵛ.

CHAPTER FIVE

Jean de la Chapelle and the
Lettres d'un suisse

OBJECTIVES

THE revived French sponsorship of pamphlet polemic stimulated by Torcy in 1701 and 1702 was a response to public demand and reflected the ever-growing need for diplomats to concern themselves with printed propaganda. Yet however energetic was the French pamphlet offensive in the first two years of the War of the Spanish Succession, its effectiveness is very questionable. Davenant's works apparently achieved more influence than did the Rousseau and Karg tracts, but the appeal of the Englishman's pamphlets was limited to his countrymen both by language and content. As Torcy's ambitious and wide-ranging wartime diplomacy embraced many parts of Europe, what the minister required was an equally universal propaganda forum, one which also would address itself to a French audience.

The *Lettres d'un suisse à un françois* were to supply this forum. Forty-eight anonymous pamphlets appeared under this title between June 1702 and January 1709, ranging in length from about twenty to forty duodecimo pages. In the thirty-six months from September 1702 to September 1705 thirty-six *Lettres* were published, and while thereafter the pamphlets appeared with less regularity, back numbers continued to be reprinted and collected in various formats. The *Lettres* were transformed into *Briefe*, *Epistolae*, *Letterae*, *Cartas*, and *Letters* as they were published in half a dozen languages for a Europe-wide audience.[1] They evoked

---

[1] Unless otherwise specified, citations of *Lettres d'un suisse* below follow the form *LS* 1, 1:4, where *LS* represents the series, the arabic

bitter criticism in Holland-based periodicals, were credited
with diplomatic victories by French representatives, espe-

---

number following represents the number of the letter in the series,
and the roman-arabic combination refers to volume and page in the
six-letter collections published 1703–1709 (BN, Imp., Lb^{37}.4341).
Individually published pamphlets in this series generally bear the
simple title *Lettre d'un suisse à un françois*. In the collected editions
the title was sometimes extended to read *Lettres d'un suisse à un
françois où l'on voit les veritables interests des Princes et des Nations
de l'Europe qui sont en guerre et divers mémoires et actes pour servir
de preuves à ces lettres*; other collected editions, however, bear the
title *Lettres, mémoires et actes concernant la guerre presente*. The
provenance is invariably given as Basel in the collected editions and,
with exceptions to be noted below, is the same in the single-letter
editions. The BN *Catalogue des auteurs*, in its entry for Jean de la
Chapelle, may be consulted for a detailed bibliographical list. To
this list should be added, however, G. 6311, comprising quarto editions
of single *Lettres* 1, 6, 7, 8, 9, 10 and 11 bound together, editions
identical to the quarto additions listed under La Chapelle in the
Catalogue des auteurs; and G. 17144, a duodecimo edition of Nos.
1–6 in the series unlike all other BN copies, under the title *Lettres,
mémoires et actes, où l'on voit que l'Empereur et le feu Roi Guillaume sont comme l'âme de la guerre presente, et tout ce que les
Ambassadeurs de S.M.I. ont fait en Italie, en Allemagne, en Angleterre, en Portugal, en Hollande et en Suisse est pour tâcher de faire
soûlever les Peuples contre leurs légitimes Souverains, et pour par-
venir à l'execution de ses vastes desseins* (Basel, 1703). The Library
of Congress has an octavo edition of the first twenty-one *Lettres
d'un suisse* unlike all BN copies: *Lettres d'un suisse qui demeure en
France, à un françois, qui s'est retiré en suisse, touchant l'estat present
des affaires en Europe* (n.p., 1704). Sometimes shortened reprints of
certain *Lettres d'un suisse* appeared in *Clef du cabinet*, as follows:
LS 28 (March 1705, pp. 184–201); LS 30 (May 1705, pp. 344–357);
LS 31 (June 1705, pp. 443–461; see also May 1705, p. 388); LS 33
(September 1705, pp. 180–193); LS 34 (October 1705, pp. 258–268);
LS 37 (April 1706, pp. 242–268); LS 38 (May 1706, pp. 332–344, and
June 1706, pp. 413–420); LS 39 (September 1706, pp. 170–186). A
Latin translation of the thirteenth *Lettre*, evidently part of a series
edition, is bound in AAE, CP, Suisse 140, fols. 201–210^v as *Helvetii
ad Gallum Epistolae, Epistola Decima-Tertia* (n.p., n.d.). An Italian
translation, *Diciottesima lettera scritta da uno svizzero a uno franzese
suo amico*, is in BN, Imp., 4° M. 641 and AAE, CP, Suisse 151, fols.
368–375^v. No German, Spanish or English translations have come to
light, but for evidence that they existed, see below, nn. 88–94.

cially in Switzerland, and their author, Jean de la Chapelle, became a close counselor to Torcy as the two men collaborated in producing the pamphlets. The *Lettres d'un suisse* joined the advantages of a periodical to those of the occasional pamphlet. Their regular appearance in numbered issues lent continuity to the venture, allowing references back to previously published numbers and the development of important themes over a series of issues. As Pierre Bayle remarked in an essay on the *Lettres d'un suisse*, even the repetition of key arguments in issue after issue was a virtue in propaganda: "It is of extreme importance that people's hopes continually be kept up. These hopes require constant fueling, for they are like lamps which consume their oil and go out if they are not refilled with care. . . . [*Nouvellistes*] are the purveyors, the public distributors of this oil."[2]

While imitating the periodicity of the gazettes, La Chapelle's adoption of the genre of the *lettre* permitted greater latitude of style and content than was appropriate to a news journal. The purported Swiss struck the tone of an intimate, freewheeling, and informal social correspondent. Unconstrained by the news periodical's need to provide a universal account of events, the *Lettres d'un suisse* were a hybrid composed of one part informational report, one part political polemic, one part learned disquisition, and one part witty epistle. Their appeal, as contemporary readers remarked, stemmed from their combination of serious political argument with lively prose.[3]

[2] Bayle, *Réponse aux questions d'un provincial*, part 3, chap. v.

[3] See, for example, the account by the Marquis de Puyzieulx of Swiss reaction to the early *Lettres*: "On les y loue, et on les y approuve fort. Elles detrompent de beaucoup de fausses impressions, qu'on prend sur les nouvelles débitées par nos ennemis, et elles instruisent de beaucoup de choses qu'il est bon de mettre au jour, et que ces mesmes ennemis veulent tenir cachées. Il y a dans ces lettres un feu d'une vivacité surprenante, et ce qui est rare en un mesme esprit, c'est que ce feu est accompagné de beaucoup de delicatesse, et de politesse." Puyzieulx to Torcy, AAE, CP, Suisse 135, fol. 186. Cf. Duchêne, "Lettres et gazettes," pp. 498–500, on the gap

The political content of the *Lettres* reflected the close supervision of Torcy and the contributions of other French diplomats, but their literary style was the exclusive creation of Jean de la Chapelle.[4] Son of an ennobled professor of law at the University of Bourges, by 1702 the forty-seven-year-old La Chapelle had already achieved distinction in the disparate worlds of letters and finance. After studies in classical literature at Bourges, La Chapelle was attached to the princely house of Conti in the late 1670's; meanwhile his father purchased for him the charge of *receveur des finances* at La Rochelle. With the Contis, La Chapelle held the office of *secrétaire des commandements* for the far-flung holdings of the two youthful princes, Louis-Armand and François-Louis. But the Contis found something more than a financial manager in La Chapelle. Under their patronage he wrote four tragedies on classical themes, dramas which were staged at Paris with moderate success between 1680 and 1684. One was performed before the king at Saint-Germain, and a fifth play provided the curtain-raiser for *Bérénice* in the very first performance of the Comédie Française.[5] When the Conti brothers tired of the imaginary

---

between news journals and personal correspondence; this was the gap bridged by the *Lettres d'un suisse*.

[4] Biographical sources for La Chapelle are BN, Dossiers bleus 168, pièce 2 (No. 4455); AN, M. 758, No. 6[18]; *ibid.*, MM 824, fol. 34 (Léonard papers); and the materials used in the only two modern studies of La Chapelle: Hanns Zipper, *Jean de la Chapelle* (Weilburg-Lahn, 1920); and René Roux, "Les Missions politiques de Jean de la Chapelle, de l'Académie française (1655–1723)," *Revue d'histoire diplomatique*, 40 (1926), 241–248. The account by d'Alembert, *Histoire des membres de l'Académie françoise* (Paris, 1787), IV, 113–130, is unreliable, as is much of the information in J. de Boislisle, *Les suisses et le marquis de Puyzieulx* (Paris, 1906), pp. xxvii, lvi, lxxv. Except for tangential comments by Roux, a brief discussion by Zipper (pp. 108–111) and a paragraph or two in Richard Feller, *Die Schweiz und das Ausland im spanischen Erbfolgekrieg* (Bern, 1912), pp. 83–85, the *Lettres d'un suisse* have escaped historical investigation.

[5] For La Chapelle's place in the literary life of his day, see Zipper, *La Chapelle, passim*; P. Mélèse, *Répertoire analytique des documents*

romance of their world at Chantilly and in 1685 secretly fled France for Hungary to take up arms in the crusade against the Turks (from which the Most Christian King had remained carefully aloof), they took with them not only the future Prince Eugene of Savoy but also their adviser and cohort, Jean de la Chapelle. Back in France three years later, the princes rewarded La Chapelle for his services by supporting him in a successful campaign for election to the French Academy. Soon afterward, La Chapelle took up service under the royal intendant of finance, Caumartin, and in the 1690's he cut a grand figure in Paris with his big house, fine furnishings, and lavish table.

A heritage in law, humanist studies, experience in public finance, success as a playwright, some direct knowledge of Europe beyond the Rhine: La Chapelle brought a richly varied background to the first of his *Lettres d'un suisse*. By writing for Torcy he hoped to demonstrate his talents in diplomacy, eventually take up a foreign post, and thus add another facet to his many-sided career. In 1700 Racine's

---

contemporains d'information et de critique concernant le théâtre à Paris sous Louis XIV, 1659-1715 (Paris, 1934), pp. 171-178; John Lough, *Paris Theatre Audiences in the Seventeenth Century* (London, 1957), pp. 53-54; and P. Mélèse, *Le Théâtre et le public à Paris sous Louis XIV, 1659-1715* (Paris, 1934), pp. 137-138, where the famous epigram about La Chapelle is quoted:

> "J'approuve que chez vous, Messieurs,
> on examine
> Qui du pompeux Corneille et du tendre
> Racine
> Excita dans Paris plus d'applaudissemens:
> Mais je voudrois qu'on cherchât tout
> d'un tems
> (La question n'est pas moins belle)
> Qui du fade Boyer ou du sec La Chapelle
> Excita plus de sifflemens."

Zipper, pp. 169-172, shows that La Chapelle's tragedies were outdistanced in frequency of performance *only* by those of Corneille and Racine during this period, surely not an entirely disgraceful record.

son seemed to be commencing a career in the king's service abroad; should La Chapelle, who had delivered a double-edged eulogy to his great fellow tragedian before the Academy, aspire to any less?[6] La Chapelle's personal letters to the Marquis de Puyzieulx, French ambassador to Switzerland, make it clear that authorship of the *Lettres d'un suisse* was intended as the stepping-stone to a diplomatic career. Until 1704 La Chapelle hoped to become the royal representative at the court of the French-allied Elector Max Emmanuel of Bavaria, but after the catastrophe of Blenheim and the elector's exile from his homeland, the creator of the pamphlet Swiss turned his aspirations to Switzerland itself, where he hoped to assist and eventually succeed his aging friend, Puyzieulx.[7] When Torcy sent him to the French

[6] Maurice Henriet, "Discours de M. de la Chapelle sur Racine à l'Académie française (1699)," *Annales de la Société historique et archéologique de Château-Thierry* (1902), pp. 53–67.

[7] La Chapelle's correspondence with Puyzieulx amply documents his diplomatic ambitions. Toward the end of 1703 panegyrics to Max began to appear in the *Lettres d'un suisse*, and the ambassador agreed to recommend their author to the elector. *LS* 18, III:226–228; La Chapelle to Puyzieulx, Paris, 11 October 1703, AAE, CP, Suisse 144, fols. 246–247; La Chapelle to Puyzieulx, Paris, 25 November 1703, *ibid.*, fols. 411–413ᵛ; La Chapelle to Puyzieulx, Paris, 29 November 1703, *ibid.*, fols. 421–422; La Chapelle to Puyzieulx, 3 December 1703, *ibid.*, fol. 426; La Chapelle to Puyzieulx, 7(?) January 1704, *ibid.*, fol. 635; La Chapelle to Puyzieulx, Paris, 29 August 1704, AAE, CP, Suisse 152, fols. 183–184; Puyzieulx to Max, 19 December 1703, AAE, CP, Bavière 47, fol. 396 (unsigned copy in Puyzieulx's hand). All through 1705 La Chapelle urged Puyzieulx to ask that Torcy send him to Switzerland: La Chapelle to Marquise de Tibergau [December 1704], AAE, CP, Suisse 161, fols. 280–281ᵛ; La Chapelle to Puyzieulx, Paris, 13 March 1705, AAE, CP, Suisse 151, fol. 299. Puyzieulx, in ill health, was growing progressively more restive with the trials of his assignment. La Chapelle had to implore him to consider the careers of his friend and of his son—an officer in the king's army—and not retire while they still needed support for advancement: Puyzieulx to Torcy, Soleure, 20 November 1703, AAE, CP, Suisse 142, fols. 101ᵛ–102; Puyzieulx to Torcy, 15 December 1703, *ibid.*, fol. 179; La Chapelle to Puyzieulx, 18 March 1704, AAE, CP, Suisse 151, fols. 326–329ᵛ. The old man was presented in La Chapelle's

embassy at Soleure early in 1706, these goals seemed on the verge of fulfillment;[8] but after eighteen successful months as Puyzieulx's right-hand man and surrogate, La Chapelle's chances were shattered by the disputed award of the succession to the county of Neuchâtel upon King Frederick I of Prussia. Several of the unsuccessful French claimants to Neuchâtel appear to have convinced Louis XIV that La Chapelle had used his influence to support his erstwhile patron, Conti, who also had been a contestant.[9] That these

letters with the vision of bringing peace to Europe by enlisting the Swiss as mediators between the warring coalitions; and an early peace, La Chapelle and Puyzieulx were convinced, was essential for France. See La Chapelle to Puyzieulx, 7 August 1705, AAE, CP, Suisse 162, fols. 303–304: "Nos affaires sont toujours pitié. Bon citoyen comme vous estes, si vous estiés icy, si vous voyiés de pres tout qu'on voit, vous pleureriés des larmes de sang. Je vous asseure que la poire est plus meure que ne pensent nos ennemis. En verité il l'en fault bien peu que nous ne soyions à l'extremité. Donnés nous la paix si vous aimés votre patrie."

[8] So optimistic was La Chapelle that he even sold his charge before departing France. Puyzieulx to Torcy, 27 May 1705, AAE, CP, Suisse 158, fols. 137–138ᵛ; La Chapelle to Puyzieulx, 3 June 1705, AAE, CP, Suisse 162, fols. 138–139; La Chapelle to Puyzieulx, 10 October 1705, AAE, CP, Suisse 162, fols. 99–100; La Chapelle to Puyzieulx, 27 October 1705, *ibid.*, fols. 103–104; Puyzieulx to Torcy, 16 November 1705, AAE, CP, Suisse 160, fols. 90–93; Torcy to Puyzieulx, Marly, 16 December 1705, AAE, CP, Suisse 166, fol. 122; La Chapelle to Puyzieulx, Paris, 17 December 1705, AAE, CP, Suisse 163, fol. 299; Puyzieulx to Torcy, 30 December 1705, AAE, CP, Suisse 160, fol. 204.

[9] On the Neuchâtel affair, see E. Bourgeois, *Neuchâtel et la politique prussienne en Franche-Comté, 1702-1713* (Paris, 1887). Minister of War Chamillart was convinced that anyone "dependant de Monsieur de Torcy" must have been partial to Conti (Matignon to Chamillart, Neuchâtel, 22 August 1707, AG, A1, 2036, pièce 49). Meanwhile Chamillart did not hesitate to make clear to French diplomats that he favored the candidacy of Matignon (Chamillart to La Closure, Fontainebleau, 19 September 1707 [minute], AG, A1, 2036, pièce 69). For his part La Chapelle maintained the strictest neutrality, indicating to Torcy that "Un de mes amys [Conti] ne se conduit pas comme il devroit pour ses propres Interets, mais je me donneray bien de gard de luy rien escrire" (La Chapelle to Torcy, Soleure, 10

accusations were entirely groundless was irrelevant, for, as Torcy told La Chapelle at the time, "You would have to be an angel to avoid the suspicions . . . [of those] who blame the impartial for all the difficulties they are encountering."[10] La Chapelle's propaganda writing continued on a reduced scale after 1707, but his career as a diplomat was permanently throttled.

In the first instance, then, the *Lettres d'un suisse* were the product of their author's personal ambitions. Yet very quickly Torcy recognized the worth of the pamphlets and proceeded to take a direct role in their composition and circulation. After the letters had become a well-established success, Torcy admitted to Puyzieulx that the initiative in their creation was entirely La Chapelle's and that at first the foreign minister had been skeptical of their value. Only after showing the manuscript of the initial *Lettre* to several respected advisers and anonymously distributing the early numbers to French diplomats and other foreign contacts did Torcy declare the experiment a success, urge La Chapelle to continue writing, and bestow upon him a royal pension.[11]

March 1706, AAE, CP, Suisse 169, fol. 88ᵛ). Bourgeois, *Neuchâtel*, pp. 183-193, prints many of La Chapelle's letters to Torcy on this subject. For other aspects of La Chapelle's diplomacy in Switzerland, see Roux, "Missions politiques"; and Braubach, *Geschichte und Abenteuer*, pp. 175-176, 205-206.

[10] Torcy to La Chapelle, Marly, 26 May 1707 (minute), AAE, CP, Suisse 179, fol. 27ᵛ. See also Torcy to Puyzieulx, 26 May 1707, AAE, CP, Suisse 185, fol. 22 ("On le soupconne tellement d'etre attaché aux interêts de M. le Pᶜᵉ de Conty et de travailler pour luy que quelque indifference qu'il puisse faire paroistre rien ne sera oublié pour le decrier auprez du Roy"); Torcy to Puyzieulx, Versailles, 15 June 1707, *ibid.*, fol. 36ᵛ; Torcy to Puyzieulx, 23 June 1707, *ibid.*, fol. 39.

[11] Puyzieulx to Torcy, Soleure, 5 November 1702, AAE, CP, Suisse 135, fols. 128-129; Torcy to Puyzieulx, Versailles, 13 November 1702, AAE, CP, Suisse 132, fols. 370ᵛ-371; note by Léonard, AN, M. 758, pièce 6¹⁹. La Chapelle's annual pension of 2000 livres (increased to 3000 livres in 1714) commenced at the end of 1703 (AAE,

Torcy's early doubts about the *Lettres* reflect the traditional caution of Louis XIV's ministers in handling printed propaganda. La Chapelle, unlike Verjus and Rousseau de Chamoy, was not an experienced diplomat; neither was he a learned jurist in the mold of Obrecht, Karg and their predecessors of the Colbert period. The foreign minister's professionalism, one aspect of which was his disdain for amateur gazette writers, lent a restraining hand to the range of the official propaganda pen in France. Thus La Chapelle's literary background was by no means an automatic virtue in Torcy's estimation. The satirical dialogues of the skilled Grub-Street pamphleteer Eustache Le Noble, which appeared in France at intervals from 1689 to 1709 and to which are often ascribed government backing, were regarded as pleasantries by Louis' diplomats, harmless perhaps but without much political value.[12] Very different in Torcy's opinion was La Chapelle's ability not only to produce stylistically distinguished pamphlets but also to draw out significant propaganda themes from "a few memoranda and a bit of instruction."[13]

MD, France 1118, fol. 200; AAE, MD, France 307, fols. 45[v], 111[v], 193[v], 281[v], 308[v]; AAE, MD, France 308, fol. 61; AAE, MD, France 309, fol. 92; AAE, MD, France 310, fol. 367). La Chapelle considered the amount so low that it hardly merited the term pension: "On m'a fait une espece de gratification, elle n'est que deux mille francs, on la baptize pension" (La Chapelle to Puyzieulx, 14 December 1703, AAE, CP, Suisse 144, fol. 50).

[12] Eustache Le Noble, *Le Cibisme* (1690); *La pierre de touche politique* (1691-1692); *Les travaux d'Hercule* (1693-1694); *Les nouveaux entretiens politiques* (1702-1709). There is no firm evidence of the crown's patronage of Le Noble; see Hatin, *Gazettes*, pp. 119-124; H.-J. Martin, "Un polemiste sous Louis XIV: Eustache Le Noble (1643-1711)," *Positions des thèses de l'Ecole nationale des Chartes* (1947), pp. 85-91. His political pamphlets were suspended in 1692 because of protests to Croissy by the Portuguese ambassador. Yet Martin, *Livre*, pp. 669-670 and 899-900, claims that Le Noble's work was directed by the government in an effort to turn "leurs propres armes contre ses ennemis."

[13] Torcy to Puyzieulx, Versailles, 13 November 1702, AAE, CP, Suisse 132, fol. 370.

The instruction was provided by Torcy in person at Versailles and by letter when the writer was in Switzerland. The minister's written suggestions were very full, sometimes providing a completely articulated skeleton of a pamphlet. Torcy examined each proposed *Lettre* in draft form, regularly inserted changes, occasionally rejected whole manuscripts outright, and on at least three occasions scrapped approved pamphlets which had been made suddenly obsolete by events. Comparison of these memoranda with the printed *Lettres* makes it clear that La Chapelle was not engaged in mere sycophancy when he wrote that the minister guided his pen.[14] La Chapelle also received suggestions from other diplomats, most prominently from his old confidant Puyzieulx, who had hailed the pamphlets' effectiveness even before he discovered their author's identity. From his strategic diplomatic location at Soleure, Puyzieulx, like Torcy, constantly fed documentary material to the propagandist and proposed the subject matter of new tracts.[15] In this way a triangular collaboration developed

[14] La Chapelle to Puyzieulx, Paris, 12 February 1703, AAE, CP, Suisse 143, fols. 117-118; La Chapelle to Puyzieulx, Paris, 31 August 1703, AAE, CP, Suisse 144, fols. 162-163; La Chapelle to Puyzieulx, Paris, 25 November 1703, *ibid.*, fols. 411-413; La Chapelle to Puyzieulx, 21 December 1703, *ibid.*, fol. 538; La Chapelle to Puyzieulx, 3 April 1704, AAE, CP, Suisse 152, fol. 130; Puyzieulx to Torcy, Paris, 3 April 1705, AAE, CP, Suisse 161, fol. 75ᵛ; La Chapelle to Puyzieulx, Paris, 10 October 1705, AAE, CP, Suisse 163, fols. 99-100; La Chapelle to Puyzieulx, Paris, 19 October 1705, *ibid.*, fols. 101-102; Torcy to La Chapelle, Marly, 20 May 1706 (minute), AAE, CP, Suisse 170, fols. 65-66ᵛ; La Chapelle to Torcy, 9 July 1706, *ibid.*, fol. 212; Torcy to La Chapelle, Versailles, 25 November 1706, AAE, CP, Suisse 172, fols. 41-44; Torcy to La Chapelle, Versailles, 1 December 1706 (minute), *ibid.*, fols. 52-53; La Chapelle to Puyzieulx, Soleure, 1 December 1706, AAE, CP, Suisse 175 (cf. *LS* 40), fol. 292.

[15] Among many letters attesting to this collaboration, see esp. La Chapelle to Puyzieulx, 13 August 1703, AAE, CP, Suisse 144, fols. 168-169, where the writer asked for comments on a just-published *Lettre* "qui estoit toutte entiere sur les matieres de Suisse, sur lesquelles j'esperois, ou que vous me releveriez de mes fautes ou que par des nouvelles lumieres vous m'encourageriez à parler encore aux

that allowed the *Lettres d'un suisse* to echo with accuracy the leitmotifs of French diplomacy.

But the pamphlets of the Swiss did more than reflect French policy. On many occasions they amplified and deepened diplomatic campaigns, supplying a perspective that could not be achieved by more conventional methods. Thus Torcy hid behind the mask of the anonymous Swiss to argue publicly in ways which Louis XIV forbade to his diplomats. This was especially true in Switzerland, where the habits of politics demanded constant attention to public opinion. The influential *Gazette de Berne* was an organ of pro-Habsburg opinion which Puyzieulx countered by a weekly gazette for circulation throughout the cantons and neighboring regions of France. Speeches of foreign representatives at the frequent diets of the Catholic and Protestant cantons and at the semi-annual general diet of the full Helvetic union were printed and widely distributed. Moreover, the representatives of France's enemies often wrote public letters to the leaders of the cantons; these too were often published. The imperial ambassador, Count von Trautmannsdorff, was especially partial to printed communication with the cantons, and from the Austrian's arrival in 1701 we find Puyzieulx busy with replies to his sallies.[16]

Suisses. . . . Je recommence à travailler sur une autre lettre, dont le sujet est la capitulation de l'empereur et les violations qu'il y a faites; n'y a-t-il rien qui soit bon à dire aux Suisses sur ce sujet?" See also La Chapelle to Puyzieulx, 12 January 1703, AAE, CP, Suisse 143, fol. 11; La Chapelle to Puyzieulx, Paris, 12 February 1703, AAE, CP, Suisse 143, fol. 118; La Chapelle to Puyzieulx, 7 January 1704, AAE, CP, Suisse 144, fol. 635; La Chapelle to Puyzieulx, Paris, 13 February 1704, AAE, CP, Suisse 151, fol. 145. Puyzieulx's letters to La Chapelle have not survived.

[16] On Puyzieulx's gazette, see the ambassador's discussion of the need for this sort of publication in his letter to Louis, Soleure, 12 November 1701, AAE, CP, Suisse 129, fol. 185^v. Puyzieulx remarks here that his predecessor, Amelot, issued a similar gazette during the War of the League of Augsburg. See also the embassy's expense statements, AAE, CP, Suisse 152, fol. 418, and AAE, CP, Suisse 161,

There were occasions, however, when it was unacceptable for Puyzieulx to reply openly to Trautmannsdorff. Early in 1702, Besenval, a leader of the canton of Lucerne and a veteran of Louis' army, wrote an anonymous *mémoire* in answer to one of Trautmannsdorff's efforts; Puyzieulx had it published with Torcy's hearty approval.[17] Meanwhile, Trautmannsdorff's style was becoming so offensive to Puyzieulx, so filled with "insults that would shame even les Halles," that Louis' ambassador sometimes hesitated to transmit a copy of his attacks to Torcy.[18] French diplomats were overcome with professional disgust at this conduct. La Closure, France's resident in Geneva, said apropos of Trautmannsdorff: "There are enemies for whom one still retains some friendship and some esteem, but it would be truly difficult to imagine such a thing for this type of person."[19]

---

[17] fol. 77. On its circulation in France, see Puyzieulx to Bernage (draft), 21 November 1703, AAE, MD, France 1580, fols. 251–252: "J'ay esté obligé, Monsieur, de faire imprimer toutes les semaines une gazette dans cette ville pour detruire les mauvaises impressions que la Gazette de Berne et les faux bruits des Emissaires de l'Empereur faisoient dans la Suisse; comme j'apprens que l'on a un grand goût dans le comté de Bourgogne pour cette Gazette de Berne ne jugeriez-vous pas à propos que j'eusse l'honneur de vous envoyer regulierement une douzaine d'exemplaires de notre gazette afin que vous eussiez la bonté de les faire repandre? J'ay crû que cela ne laisseroit produire un bon effet pour le service du Roy." Bernage's weekly acknowledgments of receipt of twelve copies of the gazette are in AAE, MD, France 1580, fols. 253, 257, 262, 264, 270, 272, 273, 280, 293, 299, 303ᵛ. On Puyzieulx and Trautmannsdorff, these citations from 1701, AAE, CP, Suisse 128, can be duplicated for subsequent years: Puyzieulx to Louis, 11 June 1701, fol. 286ᵛ; Puyzieulx to Torcy, 12 July 1701, fol. 329; Puyzieulx to Louis, 9 July 1701, fol. 332; Puyzieulx to Louis, 23 July 1701, fol. 370; Puyzieulx to Louis, 30 July 1701, fol. 380ᵛ.

[17] Puyzieulx to Louis, 31 May 1702, AAE, CP, Suisse 133, fol. 419; Louis to Puyzieulx, 6 June 1702, AAE, CP, Suisse 132, fol. 269ᵛ; Louis to Puyzieulx, 27 July 1702, *ibid.*, fol. 300.

[18] Puyzieulx to Torcy, Soleure, 17 February 1703, AAE, CP, Suisse 139, fol. 161ᵛ.

[19] La Closure to Puyzieulx, 10 April 1703, AAE, CP, Genève 23, fol. 304.

In May 1703 Puyzieulx thought it his duty to respond to an attack by Trautmannsdorff on the grounds for the Bourbon successsion in Spain, but even though the ambassador carefully limited himself to matters concerning Swiss affairs, the draft of his reply was vetoed at Versailles, with this explanation from the king:

> Although it contains very strong and forceful arguments for proving the injustice of the emperor's claims and that of the war he has undertaken, it is not suitable for you to write this letter to the cantons [because] this would establish them somehow as judges of matters which they cannot decide [i.e., the question of the Spanish succession]. You should only write to them in your office of my ambassador on matters that concern them uniquely. Further, this would be to engage in a literary dispute with Count von Trautmannsdorff and to give him occasion to converse with the public by means of the libels the emperor should long ago have forbidden him to publish.[20]

Puyzieulx confined himself to verbal and private rebuttal of Trautmannsdorff's arguments, as Louis had suggested. The ambassador noted, however, that "in this country when a pamphlet goes unanswered, people are persuaded that it is a sign that one agrees with what is contained therein," and Torcy accepted this observation as a maxim for relations with the Swiss.[21]

In view of Louis' reluctance to involve his ambassador in public arguments, another technique had to be found, and the anonymous *Lettres d'un suisse* were an ideal solution.

[20] Louis to Puyzieulx, Versailles, 15 May 1703, AAE, CP, Suisse 147, fol. 84.

[21] Puyzieulx to Louis, Soleure, 25 May 1703, AAE, CP, Suisse 140, fol. 88ᵛ. Cf. La Chapelle to Torcy, Soleure, 10 February 1706, AAE, CP, Suisse 168, fol. 49: "Icy plus qu'ailleurs on se repaist de nouvelles et d'escrits. Un ministre qui voudroit ne point donner de memoires et de harangues au public y seroit fort meprisé."

"M. de Trautmannsdorff," wrote Torcy, "will give their author occasion to exercise his talent."[22] Thus Trautmannsdorff's challenge to the Bourbon succession in Spain was answered in a *Lettre d'un suisse* that had Obrecht as its source for refuting the Habsburg claims.[23] Again, when Trautmannsdorff attempted to show that the French despised the Swiss by claiming that they were always made objects of ridicule in French comedies, neither Louis nor Puyzieulx would condescend to respond. The anonymous Swiss, however used his first-hand knowledge of the theater to make mincemeat of the argument and then mocked the ambassador for introducing so frivolous a point.[24] Trautmannsdorff's conceits provided such good material for La Chapelle's rebuttals that at the ambassador's recall to Vienna in 1705, Torcy was moved to lamentation and told Puyzieulx, "I do not believe that anyone could better serve His Majesty than he has."[25]

On one occasion while La Chapelle was in Switzerland, he let his pamphleteer's tone of openness creep into an oration composed for delivery by Puyzieulx at the Swiss general diet of July 1706, eliciting an abrupt reminder from Torcy of the difference between the roles of royal ambassador and anonymous propagandist. Puyzieulx had begun his speech to the delegates by making a clean breast of French military setbacks at Ramillies and in Spain:

> Every time that I have come into this Illustrious Assembly, I have endeavoured to give you new Marks of the King my Master's Friendship. I have had frequent Opportunities of doing it, in acquainting you with his Victories, and in sharing with you the Joy occasioned by our happy Success. Fortune at present has favoured our Enemies; and I am now come to give you Expres-

[22] Torcy to Puyzieulx, Versailles, 15 March 1703, AAE, CP, Suisse 147, fol. 51.
[23] *LS* 10, II:110–114.   [24] *LS* 7, II:30–32.
[25] Torcy to Puyzieulx, Marly, 23 April 1705, AAE, CP, Suisse 166, fol. 5.

sions of the same Friendship and Confidence, without concealing from you the Affront she has put upon us.

It is not usual for Ministers of my Character themselves to declare the Misfortunes of their Sovereigns: But the King, my Master, is unacquainted with those mean Politicks to deceive his Allies and his People by false Reports. His Arms have been unsuccessful in Catalonia, and in Flanders. He himself has commanded me to tell you so. On one side the Fury of the Rebels has mistaken and repulsed their Lawful King, who has come to free his Faithful Subjects from the Oppression of a Foreign Power: On the other, the Courage of the French has hurried them with too great Eagerness into the midst of Enemies, of whose Strength they were misinformed, and whose Numbers have triumphed over their Valour. A vast Country abandoned, and lofty Towns brought under Consternation, have proved the Reward of the Conquerors.

It is not to seek from you, my Lords, the Comfort that is found in the midst of one's Misfortunes, by relating them to sincere Friends, that I recal to mind so melancholy a Thought: It is rather to comfort and encourage you. The King, my Master, is persuaded of your Affection for his Sacred Person, and of the Share you take in all that happens to him: . . .[26]

La Chapelle reported to Torcy on the "good effect" of this speech: "It has silenced the King's enemies who were getting ready to exult and jeer; it enchanted the Swiss and has obliged them to seek out on their own everything that can lessen the sense of our adversity."[27] Yet although the text of this oration was printed in Switzerland and carried far and wide by Dutch gazettes, Torcy moved to prohibit its publi-

[26] Quoted from *The Present State of Europe*, July 1706, p. 280. Printed copies of this speech are in AAE, CP, Suisse 174, fols. 292–293ᵛ; and Lamberty, *Mémoires*, IV, 180–181.

[27] La Chapelle to Torcy, Soleure, 9 August 1706, AAE, CP, Suisse 171, fols. 30ᵛ–31.

cation in Paris,[28] explaining to La Chapelle: "I found [the speech] very good, but I will assure you confidentially and, if you please, for you alone that I was afraid it would not be to the King's taste. While one cannot conceal public disgraces, it seems that an avowal made by an ambassador has revived them."[29] In the next *Lettre d'un suisse*, however, La Chapelle was permitted to expand at length upon the theme of Puyzieulx's oration.[30]

In summary, then, an ambassador in Switzerland had to enact the parts of polemicist and confidant, but since these were roles that Louis XIV denied to his diplomats the *Lettres d'un suisse* took on these tasks instead.

CONTENT

Examination of the content of the *Lettres d'un suisse* demonstrates the composers' resourcefulness in discovering varied applications for this diplomatic tool. The substance of the Swiss's message shifted in accord with the changing emphases of French diplomacy. In this section our aim is to consider the amplification given French diplomatic theses by La Chapelle's pamphlets.

In 1702, when Torcy still nurtured hope of limiting British participation in the war effort, six of the first eight issues were contrived for an English audience and expanded upon Charles Davenant's themes.[31] England, the Swiss held, was being enticed into a war which served only the interests of Emperor Leopold and the Dutch. As we have seen, this was a major thesis of French diplomacy from the day Louis accepted the Spanish testament. To argue this key point

[28] D'Argenson to Torcy, 5 August 1706, AAE, CP, Suisse 174, fol. 334; Torcy to d'Argenson, Versailles, 7 August 1706, *ibid.*, fol. 335. This speech was also printed by Visé in *Mercure galant*, August 1706 (see above, chap. 3, n. 27). For the reaction in Holland, see Bayle to Dubos, Rotterdam, 7 November 1706, Gigas, *Correspondance*, p. 116.

[29] Torcy to La Chapelle, Marly, 27 July 1706, AAE, CP, Suisse 170, fols. 234ᵛ-235.

[30] *LS* 40, VII:203 ff.   [31] *LS* 1, 4, 5, 6, 7, 8.

with the flexibility appropriate to the broad spectrum of English political opinion, La Chapelle resorted to the invention of two additional letter writers, an English Presbyterian living in Holland and an Anglican from Canterbury, both friends of the supposed Swiss through whom the Englishmen's views are transmitted. Both the Presbyterian and the Anglican profess themselves inspired by love of their *patrie*, and both think the good of their country will be served by an early peace or by withdrawal from the continental war. The Presbyterian sees England's welfare—political, commercial, and religious—tied to that of the Dutch. He eulogizes the deceased King William and urges the immediate accession of the elector of Hanover. Aiming to re-establish his sect as the dominant religion of his homeland, he is obsessed with fear of entangling alliances with the heretic emperor. The war seems to the Presbyterian a dangerous distraction, and he takes pains to show by a comparison of English and French resources that the much richer France will never be subdued. Scoffing at what he regards as England's illusory wealth of public funds, "bills of the Exchequer" and the stocks of various trading companies, he holds that the value of these resources subsists only in men's opinions and hence are inherently unsettled. Thus, claims the Presbyterian, English finances are built on a weak foundation, while those of France are solidly based on greater population and material wealth. He concludes that England, already overburdened with taxation, should withdraw from a foolhardy war and stick to trade.[32]

The Anglican follows a different route to a similar conclusion. The Presbyterian, he maintains, "is only English by birth, for his soul is Dutch; he is a greater enemy to us than the Papists." "For myself, . . . I am neither Jacobite nor Williamist, neither Tory nor Whig: I am an Englishman. I belong to no cabal, I am for my country." England, in this version, has been dragged into war in a plot concocted by William to make Holland, his adored homeland, the

[32] *LS* 4, 1:50–89.

ruler of the universe. We can almost hear Tallard's dispatches as the Anglican describes William's emissaries circulating through the country, stirring up the peaceful English and electing a bellicose Parliament. William, while feigning a desire for peace, signed treaties and formed alliances for war: "He had the art of appearing driven and compelled to do it by his peoples." But now that William is dead, argues the Anglican, we should trust in our glorious queen, whose policy òught to be that of the arbiter giving peace to Europe.[33]

Torcy's informants told him of the many powerful Englishmen who were half-hearted about the war, and La Chapelle skillfully exploited the conflicting motives for this sentiment. Yet Torcy had his propagandist adopt the popular French view that all Englishmen were united in concern for their commerce, so the Swiss spoke in his own guise in another early letter on the war's potential damage to the English wool trade. "Woolens are the base and foundation of England's commerce and thus the source of all her wealth." But Spanish wool was essential to this trade, since the coarse English wool had to be combined in the weave with the finer product of merino stock. In peacetime, five hundred Spanish ships visited England each year, according to the Swiss. Then will not the war bring disaster to England's trade? "Commerce is like a river, which, if once diverted from its accustomed path, whether by a dike of fallen trees or rocks, goes off to water other land and soon digs itself a new bed, from which it is often difficult to redirect it to the original." Should England continue the war, even if Archduke Charles gains the Spanish crown, English commerce will have lost. In La Chapelle's analysis, then, the hatred of the Spaniards for the English, aroused by the wartime destruction of their trade, would long outlast the war.[34]

The pattern of French diplomacy in Germany charted

[33] *LS* 6, I: 136–162, esp. 138–146. [34] *LS* 7, II: 1–36, esp. 2, 6.

La Chapelle's course in the Swiss's many letters on imperial affairs. Until Blenheim, Louis' ministers looked forward to the empire's early removal from the war; even after 1704 Torcy continued his diplomatic efforts to induce a reduction in the military expenditures of the imperial circles. Toward this end, twenty of La Chapelle's *Lettres* developed the anti-Habsburg themes which had been central in the earlier writings of Obrecht, Rousseau, and Karg.[35] Framing his argument in a defense of the German *patria*, the Swiss drew explicitly on a long tradition of German constitutional jurisprudence to show that the empire was not a monarchy but a species of republic whose *chef*, the emperor, had few of the prerogatives of an absolute ruler. This had been the position of the important public law theorist of the mid-seventeenth century, Bogislav von Chemnitz, who wrote under the pen name of Hippolithus a Lapide.[36] While the Swiss prudently refrained from total acceptance of this radical view, his letters follow Chemnitz in holding that German liberties were in imminent danger of being swept away by the machinations of the house of Austria. As Chemnitz's work had not yet been published in any language but Latin, the Swiss's presentation of his thought, drawn from a French manuscript translation in La Chapelle's possession, undoubtedly introduced fresh ideas to the bulk of his audi-

[35] *LS* 1, 5, 11, 12, 13, 16, 17, 18, 24, 26, 27, 28, 30, 33, 34, 35, 42, 44, 46, 47. Cf. La Chapelle to Puyzieulx, Paris, 31 July 1705, AAE, CP, Suisse 162, fol. 298: "Vous recevrés avec cette lettre le pacquet à l'ordinaire de la derniere lettre du Suisse. . . . Elle traite encore d'autres choses bien convenables à l'assemblé des cercles. On croit icy qu'il seroit bien important que vous l'y fassies passer le plustost que vous pouvés." This refers to *LS* 34.

[36] On Chemnitz, see F. Weber, "Hippolithus à Lapide," *Historische Zeitschrift*, 29 (1873), 254–306; *Recueil des instructions données aux ambassadeurs et ministres de France depuis les traités de Westphalie jusqu'à la Révolution française*, Vol. 18: *Diète germanique*, ed. B. Auerbach (Paris, 1912), xi–xiii; and Hanns Gross, *Empire and Sovereignty. A History of Public Law Literature in the Holy Roman Empire, 1559-1804* (Chicago, 1973), pp. 235–250.

ence.[37] With evidence culled from an anti-monarchical reading of the imperial capitulations and other constitutional documents, the Swiss could take his cue, as Pierre Bayle observed, from the rich literature of Protestant constitutional thought published in Germany from the Peace of Augsburg to the treaties of Westphalia.[38]

One step beyond these writers was the Swiss's contention that the house of Austria aspired to universal monarchy. Early in his epistolary career, La Chapelle had countered German fears of Bourbon ambitions by dismissing universal monarchy as a state imaginary as Plato's republic.[39] Later, however, he turned the accusation against its very authors, and, by pointing to the Habsburgs' treatment of Bohemia and Hungary, their plots to make the imperial dignity hereditary in their house, their efforts to establish despotic sovereignty in Germany, and their attempts to destroy the French monarchy, La Chapelle's Swiss presented an articulate case for reversing the traditional charge against Louis XIV.

Among the republican features of the empire, in the Swiss's view, was the right of princes to depose their elected leader. But far from taking this to heart, the Swiss lamented, the empire was allowing Leopold to use the war as a cloak for the destruction of German liberties. In this connection it is notable that several letters of the Swiss are devoted to a defense of the cause of the Hungarians in their struggle for

---

[37] For the Swiss's use of Hippolithus a Lapide, see esp. *LS* 12, 13. La Chapelle's knowledge of this writer was derived from a French translation of Chemnitz's *Dissertatio de ratione status in imperium romano-germanico* (1647), by Bourgeois du Chastenet. The manuscript of this translation was submitted for Torcy's approval in 1703, and the foreign minister turned it over to La Chapelle, from whom it had to be retrieved eight years later. See Bourgeois du Chastenet to Torcy, Paris, 14 September 1711, AAE, CP, Cologne 60, fol. 65. The translation finally appeared as *Interêts des princes d'Allemagne*, 2 vols. (Paris, 1712). No German translation was published until later in the eighteenth century.

[38] Bayle, *Réponse*, part 3, chap. vi.

[39] *LS* 5, I:126–128.

independence from Habsburg rule. Louis was supporting Prince Rákóczi with secret subsidies when these tracts were published, and, like his master, La Chapelle exhibited a certain prudent fastidiousness in trafficking with the insurgents. The Swiss took pains to point out that most rebels were nothing but seditious troublemakers with only false grounds for their grievances. The Hungarians, however, stood apart from these unworthies, for their nation retained the constitutional right to depose its king. Coercive tactics used at the Pressburg congress of 1687, at which the crown of St. Stephen was declared hereditary in the house of Austria, not only made its decisions illegal but also might serve as a warning to the German princes on the fate in store for their freedoms.[40] The Hungarian situation was also illustrative for the Swiss of another favorite device in the Habsburg

[40] *LS* 21, IV:101–106; *LS* 24, IV:275–276; *LS* 44, VIII:38–65. Cf. Louis' instructions to des Alleurs, Versailles, 1 April 1704 (draft), AAE, CP, Hongrie 10, fols. 35–36: "Il ne s'agit pas en cette occasion de soustenir des sujets rebelles à leur Prince legitime, quelque utilité que le Roy pust en retirer dans la conjoncture presente. Sa Majesté auroit peine à s'y resoudre. L'exemple de l'Empereur ne l'y determineroit pas, on ne verroit pas les ministres de France employés à former des conspirations en Hongrie aussy que les ministres de l'Empereur ont travaillé depuis la guerre à susciter des revoltes dans les Royaumes de Naples, de Sicile et dans celuy d'Espagne. [The next sentence is crossed out in this draft:] Sa Majesté bien eloignée de soutenir une nation contre son souverain a longtemps hezité à donner aux Hongrois les assurances qu'ils luy ont demandés de sa protection. Mais le juste éloignement de Sa Majesté à secourir une nation soulevée contre son souverain ne peut regarder le Prince Ragotzy ny les Hongrois . . . [because] les loix les plus anciennes du Royaume d'Hongrie les auctorisent à prendre les armes lorsque leur Roy contrevient à son Serment." The dispatch then goes on to show how the Hungarian rebels can be justified legally. On the juridical basis of Louis XIV's support for these rebels, see Köpeczi, *La France et la Hongrie*, pp. 52–57; cf. pp. 444–447, 460, 471, 477, 489–490, for a full discussion of the Hungarian rebels in the *Lettres d'un suisse*. On Louis XIV's general concern for legitimacy, see Andrew Lossky, "Some Problems in Tracing the Intellectual Development of Louis XIV from 1661 to 1715," in Rule, *Louis XIV*, pp. 337–338.

tradition: the dangling of the Turkish menace before Germany as a pretext for dissolving diets and trampling on German liberties while Christendom was transfixed by the specter of the infidel. Resplendent in his cloak of defender of the faith, the emperor, in the Swiss's pamphlets, nevertheless allied with the infidel king of Morocco in the battle for Spain, while his other allies, the English, helped to smuggle rich Jews out of Portugal.[41]

Not least in the Swiss's catalogue of accusations against the house of Austria was that they turned the formerly friendly Germans into implacable enemies of France. This transformation was accomplished by blaming the Bourbons for every misfortune in Europe. France replaced the Ottoman as the demon in Habsburg mythology, wrote the Swiss, and the chimerical ideal of the balance of power substituted for that shopworn cliché, the defense of Christendom. So well did the Habsburgs succeed that everything France undertook was viewed in the empire as an attack on Germany, whether it was the "re-establishment of a Catholic King dethroned by a heretic usurper" (that is, James of England dethroned by William), or "the defense of the rights of a prince unanimously named by the peoples to the succession of a monarchy belonging to him" (Philip V of Spain). Not a war or rebellion occurred in Europe without being attributed by the house of Austria to the agitation of France: "There is scarcely a village beyond the Rhine, where some miserable little jurisconsult in the pay of the emperor doesn't mount the podium to harangue the people night and day, depicting the French as monsters unleashed against Germany. . . . This fantasy has been presented to the people so often, decked out in so many different and carefully contrived guises to seduce and fascinate, that finally it gained credence and has passed for truth. The people have drunk it in [*s'en est imbu*] and have become mad. . . . The error of the people has affected the court of the princes. . . . They have delivered themselves up blindly to the em-

[41] *LS* 11, II:172.

peror. . . . They do not see behind them their true [enemy], who is raising his arm to crush them."[42]

Where declamations failed, the Swiss continued, the pro-Habsburg German gazettes succeeded in misleading not only the "simple German woman" who reads them but even "most of those who govern the imperial circles [who] learn of European affairs only from these gazettes."[43] Accusing Habsburg propaganda of big-lie techniques, the Swiss explained how the myth of the French menace had become entrenched: "This perseverance in repeating the same refuted and dispelled arguments is one of the principles of Austrian politics. The house of Austria hopes that the impatience, the flightiness, the hastiness of the French spirit will tire of always responding to the same things, to the same things over and over. But that house will never tire, it will never retire from tiresome repetition. The house of Austria will rehash them all over again eternally, flattering itself that the vote and approval of men will be for whoever has last spoken and received no response. The world will accustom itself to take for truth that which is no longer contradicted. Then the house of Austria will triumph, its rights will be made incontestable and the reasoning stand without reply."[44] And why had not France rebutted these Austrian charges? The Swiss had a ready answer:

I have thought about this for some time and I am more confirmed than ever in my opinion. France, having relied overmuch on the goodness of her cause and perhaps presuming too much on the force of her arms, has neglected to write and to inform all peoples of the justice of her claims and of her designs. Her enemies, made more haughty by her patience and more strong by her silence than by the truth and equity of their rights, have published, with a hundred thousand trumpets, throughout the universe, monstrous calumnies against

[42] *LS* 16, III:126 ff.   [43] *Ibid.*, p. 123; *LS* 13, III:12.
[44] *LS* 22, IV:128–129.

her and against her King. The falsifying libels and the hateful pictures have been scattered to the four quarters of the world. No Frenchman has contradicted them; the silence was taken for a conviction. Hatred of the name of the French was engraved unconsciously in the hearts of simple, deceived people. France had only sometimes to treat them as judges and to instruct them. They would not then have been enemies so often.[45]

Here behind the veil of the Swiss's rhetoric is still another indication of the conscious break with past policies which Torcy was undertaking.

Already we have seen why letters supposedly written by a Swiss had to concern themselves with the politics of the Helvetic confederation. La Chapelle's disguise as an expatriate Swiss Catholic living in Paris was probably the most serviceable foreign mask for a French propagandist because of the sympathy many Swiss Catholics had for Louis' policies, quite apart from the usefulness of this ruse in furthering French diplomatic objectives in Switzerland.[46] And while La Chapelle was in residence at Soleure during 1706 and 1707, the *Lettres d'un suisse* became adjuncts to the relatively narrow purposes of the French embassy there.[47] Even

[45] *LS* 12, II:182–183. Cf. the Swiss's discussion of French propaganda connected with the War of Devolution, *LS* 41, VII:234.

[46] Cf. Bayle, *Réponse*, part 3, chap. vi.

[47] The four *Lettres d'un suisse* published while La Chapelle was at Soleure (*LS* 37–40) were all first printed in Switzerland under separate titles and were included only later as numbered *Lettres* in the series. See La Chapelle to Torcy, Soleure, 10 January [read February] 1706, AAE, CP, Suisse 168, fol. 46: "Je vous prie, Monsieur, de trouver bon que l'escrit que je vous envoye [*Réflexions sur le renouvellement du Capitulat de Milan* (1706), AAE, CP, Suisse 193, fols. 378–389ᵛ] soit compté pour une lettre du Suisse [*LS* 37]. J'ay fait un preambule qu'on n'a point imprimé icy, et que je prends la liberté de le joindre à l'imprimé, affin que si vous l'approuvez l'imprimer en forme d'une lettre, de mesme qu'ont esté beaucoup d'autres dans lesquelles j'ay inseré des escrits sous quelque nom supposé." Torcy approved this plan, and the next three *Lettres d'un suisse* had a similar genesis.

earlier, though, La Chapelle's pamphlets sought to further Torcy's diplomatic objectives in Switzerland, the most important of which were to acquire for Philip V the Swiss troops promised by treaty to the king of Spain (a goal not achieved until 1706) and to prevent active military involvement in the anti-French coalition by any of the cantons. Thus many of the anti-Habsburg arguments employed in the *Lettres d'un suisse* about Germany were adapted by La Chapelle to Swiss circumstances, often using the pamphleteer's favorite target, Count von Trautmannsdorff, as a point of departure.[48] Taking advantage of his ostensible Swiss origin to advertise the intensity of his Helvetic patriotism, the pamphleteer characterized his reaction to one of Trautmannsdorff's outbursts: "I have been persuaded, like some ancient philosophers, that the *patrie* of an *honnête homme* is wherever he is content or wherever he finds good people. I used to think that love of country was a rather noble conception more apt to inspire mental reflections than the sentiments of the heart. But today my personal experience dissuades me of this opinion. Rumors of events in Switzerland are causing me intense uneasiness and agitation which are not the result of reflective meditation. I feel, I acknowledge that this passion which has prompted the expression and execution of so many great things is less a light of reason, if one may put it so, than an instinct of nature."[49] The classicist-turned-Swiss then described his feelings at the spectacle of the emperor, "this new Philip of Macedon," who would deprive the Swiss of their liberty; he could hardly restrain himself from rushing off to join his compatriots in defense of their freedom. In a literary sense he did not restrain himself, for subsequent *Lettres d'un suisse* outline the nature of the threat to the Swiss. The house of Austria, it is argued, whose cradle is in the mountains of Switzerland, has never reconciled itself to the loss of its original homeland; im-

[48] The following pamphlets are concerned wholly or in part with Swiss affairs: LS 3, 7, 9, 10, 25, 29, 30, 37, 38, 39, 40, 42.

[49] LS 9, II:70.

perial ministers, plotting to re-establish their rule, seek to split the Swiss confederation and thus pave the way for the destruction of its liberty.

Having established the genuineness of his patriotic credentials, the literary Swiss proceeds to warn of the emperor's tactics. Through its ambassador, the egregious Trautmannsdorff, the Viennese court wishes to turn Swiss Protestant against Swiss Catholic. The war, in Trautmannsdorff's proclamations to the Protestant cantons, was portrayed as a religious struggle against that persecutor of Protestants, Louis XIV. La Chapelle, disguised as a Swiss Catholic, replied that this was nonsense, and for further credibility he inserted the same opinion in the mouth of the Frenchman in Switzerland to whom the *Lettres d'un suisse à un françois* were addressed, a Huguenot who purportedly left France for religious reasons. The war, "they" wrote, was political, not religious; else how can one explain the alliance of Catholic Habsburgs and Protestant Dutch and English? And surely the emperor, that persecutor of the Hungarian Calvinists, was hardly in a position to deliver accusations to Louis![50]

On the other hand, La Chapelle was not averse to the suggestion that the Dutch were fighting to achieve a Protestant hegemony in Europe. This thought surely would unsettle the Swiss Catholics. As for Swiss Protestants, whom one would not wish to antagonize by wild accusations against their co-religionists, La Chapelle ingeniously contrived to place the notion of Dutch religious motives in the mouth of a fictitious Dutchman, and then had the Swiss bitterly refute the Dutchman's contention, arguing once again his consistent thesis that this was a political, not a religious, war. Thus the Swiss Protestants would be placated, while seeds of doubt might hopefully be sown among the Catholics.[51] Trautmannsdorff's real motive in raising the religious issue,

[50] *LS* 3, I:34 ff.; *LS* 10, II:125. Cf. *LS* 41, VII:234–239, where the Swiss defends Louis' revocation of the Edict of Nantes.
[51] *LS* 31; *LS* 32.

according to the Swiss, was to arouse the mutual hatred of Catholics and Protestants so as to shatter Swiss unity. In a triumphant conclusion the Swiss maintained that this unity, their primary bulwark against destruction, could be preserved best by friendship with the house of France, whose kings wished to uphold Switzerland as a barrier against the Habsburgs and as a source of military manpower.[52]

The theme of Habsburg ambition was also applied to other parts of Europe in the *Lettres d'un suisse*. Two numbers near the end of the series adapted this thesis to the circumstances of Italy in 1708. Bourbon forces had been driven out of Italy two years earlier, but Torcy hoped to reopen hostilities so as to reduce the pressure on Louis and Philip in the Netherlands and Spain. The Swiss pamphlets were meant to be one facet of this quickly abandoned campaign, an indication of the importance the foreign minister now attached to printed propaganda.[53] Spain was a target aimed at more consistently than Italy by the Swiss. There the issue of Habsburg domination was obviously the fundamental question during the succession war. In the eight pamphlets which concern Spain especially, La Chapelle gave much space to refuting imperial manifestos directed at an Iberian audience and to demonstrating why Spain and Portugal would not profit from the accession of the Austrian Archduke Charles to the disputed Spanish throne. This inevitably led the Swiss into the murky quagmire of Philip's legal rights to the Spanish succession, but as this was a territory previously charted by Obrecht the Swiss was content to achieve

[52] *LS* 14, III:74 ff.
[53] *LS* 46; *LS* 47. Torcy to d'Iberville, Versailles, 15 November 1708 (draft), AAE, CP, Gênes 47, fol. 210; Torcy to Dupré, Versailles, 15 November 1708, AAE, CP, Toscane 43, fol. 203. On Torcy's Italian scheme, see the royal instructions to Tessé, dated 31 August 1708, in *Recueil des instructions données aux ambassadeurs et ministres de France depuis la paix de Westphalie jusqu'à la Révolution*, Vol. 17: *Rome*, ed. G. Hanotaux (Paris, 1911), 403 ff.; and *Mémoires et Lettres du Maréchal de Tessé*, ed. R. de Troullai (Paris, 1886), II, 276–294.

a safe passage by following the learned Alsatian's guide and even introduced him by name as a universally respected scholar. For the Catholic audience of Spain the Swiss emphasized once again the Habsburg alliances with heretics and infidels and lamented in melodramatic fashion the sacrileges perpetrated by English troops in Spain.[54]

The treatment of the Dutch in the *Lettres d'un suisse* is a study in ambivalence. On the one hand, the Dutch are depicted as victims of suicidal war policies; on the other, they are blamed for leading other states down the path to ruin. The Swiss advised the Dutch that their own best interests would be served by a quick end to the war. The history of the Dutch and other republics, he insisted, demonstrated the danger of war to states so constituted. Republics are particularly endangered by war because their psychological foundations are far weaker than those of monarchies: "Each individual, in a popular state the equal of every other, thinks himself sovereign. . . . Soldiers in camp forget that they had been free citizens. The discipline of the army accustoms them to monarchy and inspires a love for it. The more victorious the army, the more its general is adored. Thus the last Prince of Orange, as the Dutch will remember, only acceded to that almost despotic authority which he exercised over the Estates General by the affection of the soldiers, who overawed the people."[55]

In another letter the Swiss invoked the sage counsel of the pensionary Oldenbarneveldt, who held that the Dutch dependence on commerce necessitated a policy of peace; wartime restrictions could not fail to injure their trade.[56] Particularly self-defeating in this connection, according to the Swiss, was the Dutch-inspired ban on commerce and correspondence between France and the allies, to which the English government reluctantly agreed for a one-year term in 1703. The Swiss warned the Dutch that they were inviting

[54] *LS* 2, 8, 15, 19, 20, 22, 23, 30, 45. Obrecht is mentioned in *LS* 10, II: 110–112.

[55] *LS* 26, v:63–65.　　　　　　　　[56] *LS* 25, v:13–14.

the indignation of all Europe by this ban, for the prohibition of correspondence was "unheard-of barbarity, without precedent among civilized peoples." Rulers who make public wars for private reasons should, if they understand the interests of their states, "prevent a nation, even while it is armed to slaughter another, from allowing itself to be carried away to a relentless rage which will be transferred to the soul of each private person and succeed from generation to generation, never to be extinguished." Times change, princes die or are reconciled, but "peoples are immortal and rarely pardon one another."[57] This is especially applicable to republics; while kings reign and pass away, republics are eternal. A republic should therefore exercise unusual caution, for once her neighbors begin to mistrust her, they will do so forever.[58]

As the course of the war continued in its downward spiral, a degree of bitterness toward the Dutch crept into La Chapelle's tracts. The Dutch are accused of trying to rule the world by perpetuating their commercial hegemony and their central diplomatic position, and they are charged with self-serving intervention in the private affairs of Germany and Switzerland. The Swiss held them responsible for nearly every major war in the previous two hundred years. Significantly, the Dutch were designated the one nation for whom an appeal to *patrie* was meaningless, as these travelers were said to love only the place that enriched them. Still, in discussing the Dutch, La Chapelle often distinguished between the average citizen who was being hurt by the war and the very few rich merchants who profited from wartime shortages while self-serving leaders perpetuated the war for their own advantage.[59] Similarly, though Count von Trautmannsdorff held that the French were without both law and faith, La Chapelle did not condemn the whole German people. Disgusted with a writer who denigrated an entire nation, the Swiss had nothing but praise for Traut-

[57] *LS* 14, III:52–54.   [58] *LS* 25, V:5–8.
[59] *LS* 24, *passim.*

mannsdorff's people, only wishing "that a nation so coura-
geous and otherwise sagacious and enlightened would devote
itself to understanding her true interests."[60]

La Chapelle's efforts to distinguish between the leaders
of the Grand Alliance and the peoples of Europe was good
politics. His reasoned appeals to the Dutch, Germans, and
others for peace in their own best interests were well calculated to play upon the domestic divisions that weakened
the anti-French coalition. But in these passages we can also
perceive the self-imposed limitations of La Chapelle's appeal
to patriotism. The call to country, even while emotional in
origin and motive, was rational in precept and positive in
application. A fundamental tenet was that devotion to
liberties, unity, and monarchy should not be allowed to lead
to passionate hatred of the enemy. Patriotism has no need
of foreign devils to be effective; neither should the public
quarrels of rulers be transformed into ideological conflicts.[61]
Torcy's propaganda spoke for the professional diplomat in
an aristocratic age of dynastic wars fought for limited ends
and concluded through the compromise of a realistic peace
treaty. The spectacle of the allied leaders stirring up passions to boiling hatred of the French people inspired Torcy
to influence Frenchmen and foreigners, but not by returning hate for hate.[62]

This brief survey of the messages conveyed by the *Lettres
d'un suisse* to and about various European states and peoples

[60] *LS* 7, II: 24–25.

[61] See, on this point, *LS* 32, VI: 88.

[62] The constant presence of the concept of *patrie* in La Chapelle's
propaganda constitutes an obvious challenge to the view expressed by
R. R. Palmer and Jacques Godechot, among others, that before 1750
the modern usage of this term was not widely known. R. R. Palmer,
"The National Idea in France Before the Revolution," *Journal of the
History of Ideas*, I (1940), esp. 98–100; J. Godechot, "Nation, Patrie,
Nationalisme et Patriotisme en France au XVIIIᵉ siècle," *Annales
historiques de la Révolution française*, 43 (1971), 483–501. Cf. G. Dupont-Ferrier, "Le Sens des mots 'patria' et 'patrie' en France au moyen
âge et jusqu'au début du XVIIᵉ siècle," *Revue historique*, 188 (1940),
89–104.

should be sufficient to demonstrate the comprehensive range of the pamphlets. This all-embracing quality was both a source of weakness and strength, for, as La Chapelle remarked to Puyzieulx, letters which were suitable for one country might be disastrous in another. The author's ingenuity was hard pressed to discover the "universal remedy" in political pamphleteering, an object which he eventually concluded was as illusory as the philosopher's stone.[63] Compounding his problem was that Torcy also intended the *Lettres d'un suisse* for a domestic audience in France.[64] Thus we find the analogue of Torcy's appeals to Swiss and German patriotism when La Chapelle speaks to Frenchmen. Whereas German patriotism lay in traditional liberties and Swiss love of country was intimately bound to the concept of Helvetic union, when the Swiss described French patriotism he stressed love of the tradition of the monarchy. In a pamphlet meant to strengthen French resolve in the wake of Blenheim, the Swiss wrote this to his ostensible French correspondent: "I did not think a Frenchman had need of a foreigner to remind him of the immense resources of a powerful monarchy, one which will not be exhausted by even greater disasters. Have you forgotten the spirit of your

[63] La Chapelle to Puyzieulx, 13 February 1704, AAE, CP, Suisse 151, fol. 145. Cf. La Chapelle to Puyzieulx, Paris, 3 January 1704, AAE, CP, Suisse 144, fol. 595: "La 20ᵉ lettre qu'on imprime actuelment vous paroistra aussy propre pour la Suisse que l'autre l'estoit peu. Nous avons à parler pour plus d'un peuple, et l'Espagne et le Portugal aiment les discours contre l'heretic; il faut bien quelquefois Monsieur leur donner ce qu'il leur plaist."

[64] La Chapelle to Puyzieulx, 13 February 1704, AAE, CP, Suisse 151, fol. 145: "Ainsy nos lettres qui sont bonnes pour l'Espagne et pour la France sont mauvaises pour la Suisse." The pamphlet in question here is LS 19. Cf. La Chapelle to Chamillart (minute), 24 November 1706, AAE, CP, Suisse 172, fol. 51: "J'ay eu dessein d'inspirer aux françois et aux espagnols cette resolution, et ce courage . . . ," written apropos of a pamphlet draft. LS 15, III:95–96, laments the diminished regard for the *Lettres* that suspicion of their author's French identity has caused in France; the French praise things foreign, but "ils méprisent, et ils blasment tout ce que produit la France."

nation, as quick to recover as to become depressed? The loss in Bavaria astonishes France, but it does not overpower or discourage her. Your *patrie*, inflamed with a new zeal, says, like the Roman orator, I have seen other tempests and I have dissipated them, *alios ego ridi ventos.*" The suggested example of "another tempest" refers to the civil wars, and the hero is Henry IV.[65] "Truly," intoned the Swiss, "the French have in their affection for their kings a resource unknown to other nations."[66] Faced with the "fanatics of Languedoc" and other constant reminders of France's urgent need for peace, Torcy wanted to insure that this alleged resource was made known to Frenchmen.

After forty years of anti-Louis propaganda from abroad, Frenchmen had as much need as foreigners to hear that the king did not seek universal monarchy, that the Bourbon succession in Spain was justified, and that war had been forced on the Sun King by his enemies.[67] We shall see in succeeding chapters how these ideas were developed in Torcy's domestic propaganda during the later years of the war.

CIRCULATION, AUDIENCE, IMPACT

How were the *Lettres d'un suisse* distributed, what was the extent of their circulation and the social range of their audience, and how great was their impact? Fairly complete answers to these questions can be reconstructed from the rich correspondence in the foreign ministry archives. Whereas for many other works of Torcy's propaganda one must settle for fragmentary references or have recourse to exclusively internal evidence of the tracts, the letters of La Chapelle, Puyzieulx, Torcy, and other diplomats provide

---

[65] *LS* 26, v:50.   [66] *LS* 15, III:49–53.

[67] See esp. *LS* 41, VII:234–239, where the Swiss blames Louis' enemies for launching four wars against France. Torcy praised this pamphlet as one of La Chapelle's best efforts. Torcy to La Chapelle, Marly, 1 June 1707 (minute), AAE, CP, Suisse 179, fol. 71.

a relatively firm outline of propaganda mechanics. These men, as we shall see, took considerable pains to assure the widest possible influence for the *Lettres*.

The original, French-language *Lettres d'un suisse* usually proclaimed Basel as their place of publication on the title page. Yet the dispatches make it clear that the pamphlets were actually printed at Paris. The selection of a Paris printer was supervised by Torcy in coordination with d'Argenson, and by the end of 1703 the Delaulne presses on the rue Saint-Jacques were turning out not only individual *Lettres d'un suisse* each month but also collected editions of half a dozen batches in at least two type sizes and formats.[68] After the series ended Delaulne brought out a new definitive edition on fine paper and with mistakes corrected.[69] These collected editions also contained appendices of supplementary documents as *pièces justificatives* for the pamphlets.[70]

[68] Torcy to d'Argenson, Versailles, 3 December 1702 (minute), AAE, MD, France 1106, fol. 145: "Je remarque qu'il y a toujours un grand nombre de fautes dans l'impression des lettres du suisse et je croy qu'il seroit à propos de luy donner un imprimeur plus exact. Il ira concerter ce changement avec vous." La Chapelle informed Puyzieulx that Delaulne had taken over the printing; see his letter from Paris of 12 January 1703, AAE, CP, Suisse 143, fols. 10–11. On the various Paris editions of single *LS*, see La Chapelle to Puyzieulx, 7 January 1704, AAE, CP, Suisse 144, fol. 636; and La Chapelle to Puyzieulx, Paris, 20 January 1704, AAE, CP, Suisse 151, fol. 32. See also the publisher's announcement, *Livres imprimez à Paris chez Florentin Delaulne* [1705 or 1706], BN, Mss. fr. 32585, fol. 102: "*Lettres d'un Suisse à un François* . . . in 12.5 vol. Imprimées à Basle. Chaque volume se distribue separément, et contient six lettres. Les memes *Lettres* en un ou deux volumes in 12. de petite lettre. On distribue aussi ces *Lettres* en grand in 4 et on en reçoit une nouvelle tous les mois." The Paris editions continued to be published while La Chapelle was in Soleure, under the supervision of his wife and Blondel, one of Torcy's *commis*; see La Chapelle to Torcy, Soleure, 10 January [read February] 1706, AAE, CP, Suisse 168, fol. 47; and La Chapelle to Torcy, Soleure, 9 June 1706, AAE, CP, Suisse 170, fol. 134[v].

[69] See Delaulne's list of *Livres nouveaux*, *1711*, BN, Mss. fr. 32585, fol. 104[v].

[70] These included enemy statements, usually those rebutted in the

Although outside France the *Lettres* were often given away and their cost subsidized by the crown, the Delaulne editions were offered for sale on the domestic market. This was notwithstanding the annual appearance of the *Lettres d'un suisse* on the government's list of prohibited works,[71] no doubt representing a ministerial effort to give the impression that the pamphlets were without official auspices. The Delaulne price sheet listed the high-quality, eight-volume duodecimo edition of 1710 at sixteen livres complete.[72] Dividing this sum by forty-eight, the separate tracts should have sold for about seven sous, or somewhat less than a single issue of the *Mercure galant*.[73] But in reality the cost of individual pamphlets at first publication was almost certainly less than this because they lacked hard covers, were printed on cheaper paper, and usually omitted the supplementary memoirs of the collected editions. We know that one of La Chapelle's pamphlets sold in Holland for three sous,[74] and so it appears likely that La Chapelle's pamphlets were competitive in price with the pasquinades of Eustache Le Noble, which resembled the Swiss letters in length and format and sold for four sous apiece. As Le Noble's works reputedly achieved wide readership and then-enormous press runs of up to six thousand,[75] it can be deduced that the *Lettres d'un suisse* were priced within the reach of a *grand public* even if we cannot be certain of the precise extent of their circulation in France.

Of the pamphlets' circulation abroad we can be somewhat more certain. The archival correspondence shows that the intended audience of the *Lettres* was small in 1702 but

---

Lettres d'un suisse, as well as declarations by the Bourbons, their representatives and their allies.

[71] BN, Mss. fr. 21743, fols. 74ᵛ, 87.

[72] BN, Mss. fr. 32585, fol. 104ᵛ.

[73] Blanc-Roquette, *Presse*, pp. 115, 117, gives the price of the *Mercure*'s Toulouse reprint as 8 sous to 1703 and 10 sous thereafter.

[74] *Clef du cabinet des Princes*, June 1705, p. 443.

[75] Blanc-Roquette, *Presse*, p. 107; Martin, *Livre*, p. 900.

grew rapidly thereafter. At the outset the Swiss's letters were aimed primarily at a select, almost hand-picked audience, not necessarily for any sort of mass distribution. Thus we find that English translations of the early *Lettres d'un suisse* were sent by Torcy's secret agents in England to every member of Parliament and even to the queen herself via the penny post; Anne and certain peers were reported to be much impressed with these letters.[76] Similarly, when Puyzieulx obtained a few copies of the first numbers he distributed them personally to friends such as the leaders of pro-French cantons, friendly diplomats and several Genevan scholars.[77] These, he wrote Torcy, were the sort of people who could understand the tracts—a reference to the content, not the language. Soon, however, the ambassador began to be besieged by requests for additional copies of the much-admired pamphlets, a demand far greater than could be satisfied by the dozen or so copies of the Paris edition enclosed in Torcy's diplomatic pouch as each new number appeared.[78] The solution was to reprint the *Lettres d'un suisse* in Switzerland at crown expense, and from mid-1703 this became the standard procedure.[79] During La Chapelle's

[76] De la Touche to Torcy, London, 10 November 1702, AAE, CP, Angleterre 213, fol. 50; AAE, CP, Angleterre 215, fol. 330ᵛ.

[77] Among the scholars was Bayle's mentor, Jean-Robert Chouet; see La Closure's 1703 letters to Puyzieulx from Geneva, AAE, CP, Genève 23, fols. 239, 242ᵛ, 257, 278ᵛ, 338, 382ᵛ, 385. Puyzieulx's letters to Louis and to Torcy of 3 March 1703 (AAE, CP, Suisse 139, fols. 196, 198ᵛ) report that Besenval and Dürler, leaders of Lucerne and Soleure respectively, were among the recipients he chose for the early pamphlets, as was the papal nuncio Piazza.

[78] Puyzieulx to Torcy, Soleure, 5 November 1702 and 15 December 1702, AAE, CP, Suisse 135, fols. 128ᵛ, 239; Puyzieulx to Torcy, Soleure, 20 January 1703, AAE, CP, Suisse 139, fol. 83. Puyzieulx to Louis, Soleure, 14 April 1703, AAE, CP, Suisse 139, fol. 294: "On me demande des exemplaires de ces deux dernieres lettres [*LS* 9; *LS* 10] avec des instances incroyables."

[79] Torcy to Puyzieulx, Versailles, 4 April 1703, AAE, CP, Suisse 147, fol. 63; Torcy to Puyzieulx, undated (early April 1703), *ibid.*, fol. 58.

stay at Soleure, in fact, the pamphlets were printed first in Switzerland and only later in France. La Chapelle, Torcy, and Puyzieulx soon recognized that the appeal of the *Lettres d'un suisse* extended to an audience far greater than they had imagined at the outset. Without any change in the tone or content of the tracts, the pamphlets of 1703 and after were targeted not only at "eminent persons" but at "all sorts of people." One letter is said to express the opinions of "a good and plain Swiss."[80] Another purports to show that the "plain, ordinary person" of Swabia is very much aware of the emperor's violations of the German constitution.[81] And everyone could appreciate the satiric mockery directed at the "long and irrelevant speeches" of Count von Trautmannsdorff. As Torcy told Puyzieulx, the pamphlets must have a wide audience, for "I believe [enemy pamphlets] capable of impressing people who have only a superficial understanding of affairs."[82] And La Chapelle acknowledged that his pamphleteer's rhetoric was directed at a socially varied audience: "If the Swiss . . . is writing for all peoples and for all nations, having undertaken to make known to them their true interests, he cannot employ too much art or eloquence. Simple and delicate charms do not affect ordinary folk [*le vulgaire des hommes*]. One needs some rougher bursts of eloquence to make one's point to them. The unadorned truth is pondered only by sages. It needs ornamentation before plain people will pay it heed."[83]

It is in this connection that we ought to consider some special features of the Swiss's rhetoric. La Chapelle's literary imagery was typically classical, and his pamphlets abound with references to Tacitus and Horace. But modern readers

[80] *LS* 38, VII:69. [81] *LS* 28, V:125 ff.

[82] *LS* 9; *LS* 10; Torcy to Puyzieulx, Versailles, 27 March 1704, AAE, CP, Suisse 147, fol. 278ᵛ.

[83] *LS* 31, VI:6. On the audience for contemporary gazettes in England, see Cranfield, *Development of the Provincial Newspaper*, pp. 184–189; and Marjorie Nicolson, introduction to Payne, *The Best of Defoe's Review*, p. xvi.

can easily be misled by these apparently arcane allusions into judging them seemingly erudite works suitable only for an elite audience of scholars. In point of fact, classical references were a component of every stratum in seventeenth-century literary expression, and the popular literature of the day is replete with quotations from the ancients; indeed, much of the subject matter of popular fiction was filtered out of the classical corpus of history and mythology.[84] If anything, then, the Swiss's interminable classicist embellishment would appear to have broadened his appeal.

The most frequently invoked classical figure in the *Lettres d'un suisse* was Philip of Macedon. As the model of the imperialist, usurping outlander, Philip was paired repeatedly with various Habsburg rulers in denunciations of Austrian claims.[85] Moreover, the analogy was double-edged, for by 1700 the image of Louis XIV as a rapacious Alexander the Great was firmly impressed upon the European consciousness. In the hands of his enemies, the French depiction of Louis as a monarch worthy of Alexander's grandeur had been given an ironic twist: Alexander's aggressive conquests became an apt precedent for Louis' depredations.[86] Thus La Chapelle's use of Alexander's father was meant to demonstrate that Louis XIV's stone-casting enemies were far from blameless. Habitual reference to Philip is one of the best internal proofs of the broad cultural net thrown out by the Swiss in his pamphlets, for the Alexandrine image of Louis, in both positive and negative connotations, was a constant of political representation in seventeenth-century works intended for erudite scholars as well as those aimed at the barely literate. In the general histories of France published at the time, the line moderns draw between the higher learning and popular culture was blurred, sometimes to the point of invisibility, so that the same themes crop up at both ends

---

[84] Bollème, *Almanachs*, pp. 31–32, 108–109.
[85] *LS* 3, 1:41; *LS* 9, 11:71, among others.
[86] Gillot, *L'Opinion publique*, pp. 20, 71–72, 271.

of the cultural spectrum.[87] The special virtue of La Chapelle's pamphlets was that they combined in the self-same
work features that appealed to readers of diverse levels of
culture.

With the Swiss's tracts aimed at "all nations," translations
were of course essential, and from the first numbers we
find this matter a major concern of La Chapelle and the
diplomats. The English translations and reprintings mentioned above were accomplished in England and continued
until mid-1703, when the authorities caught up with the
only London printer willing to take on so dangerous a job.
Afterward, any *Lettres d'un suisse* that crossed the channel
went via Geneva and apparently remained untranslated.[88]
But as the English market withered, new and larger ones
emerged. Torcy ordered La Chapelle to send some of his
pamphlets to the French ambassador at Madrid for translation and republication in Spain. The pamphleteer also was

[87] Michel Tyvaert, "L'Image du Roi: légitimité et moralité royales
dans les histoires de France au XVIIe siècle," *Revue d'histoire moderne et contemporaine*, 21 (1974), 521–546; Orest Ranum, *Artisans
of Glory* (forthcoming); Bollème, *Almanachs*, pp. 117–118.

[88] De la Touche to Torcy, London, 10 November 1702, AAE, CP,
Angleterre 213, fol. 50: "Il paroît icy depuis peu un ecrit en françois
qui a pour titre *Lettre d'un Suisse à un François*. Nous en avons eu 3.
qui ont même esté traduittes et imprimées en Anglois." "Coppie d'une
Lettre escrite de Londres au Sr Davila," 23 November/2 December
1702, AAE, CP, Angleterre 214, fol. 333; agent to Torcy, 27 Novem-
ber/8 December 1702, AAE, CP, Angleterre 213, fol. 61; "Coppie de
la lettre escritte à Londres le 16 dezembre 1702," AAE, CP, Angleterre 214, fol. 360; "Coppie d'autre lettre du 12/25 January 1703
escritte au Sr Davila," AAE, CP, Angleterre 215, fol. 19^v; "Coppie
d'une lettre escritte de Londres le 22 May 1703," AAE, CP, Angleterre 215, fol. 111^v. See also La Chapelle to Puyzieulx, Paris, 4 December 1702, AAE, CP, Suisse 137, fol. 317: "Si vous estes curieux de
voir les lettres suisses traduites en Anglois je vous les envoyeray, car
à Londres on a la bonté de les faire parler anglois. On les imprime
et on nous en envoye des copies à mesure qu'elles paroissent." La
Chapelle to Puyzieulx, Paris, 8 January 1703, AAE, CP, Suisse 137,
fol. 410: "Je vous envoye les trois premieres en anglois traduites,
imprimées et repandues grandement à Londres."

required to correspond with Louis' ambassador at Rome, who received not only the French *Lettres* but also their printed Latin and Italian translations.[89] The Latin versions were at first La Chapelle's own work, but soon he turned the task over to the Jesuit Etienne Souciet, a member of the editorial board of the *Mémoires de Trévoux*. Even then La Chapelle continued to fuss with the translations, amending the syntax and fuming at the scruples of the Jesuit, who, he told Puyzieulx, had to be watched carefully lest he "eviscerate" some of the stronger passages.[90]

Puyzieulx also received copies of the Latin-translated pamphlets via the ministerial packet and multiplied them by reprinting in Switzerland.[91] At least as significant for the circulation of the *Lettres* were the German translations he supervised at the Soleure embassy. Baron, the secretary-interpreter assigned to Puyzieulx by the crown, was commissioned to render all the pamphlets into German. Once translated, they were printed under the auspices of French-allied officials in Zug by the same printer who did the Latin and French versions, an individual described by Puyzieulx as "*honnête homme*, discreet and loyal, rather extraordinary

[89] La Chapelle to Puyzieulx, 8 January 1703, AAE, CP, Suisse 137, fol. 409: "On travaille à l'italien. Quelques lettres ont esté traduites en espagnol mesme. Nous laissons faire les espagnols." La Chapelle to Puyzieulx, 12 January 1703, AAE, CP, Suisse 143, fol. 10.

[90] La Chapelle to Puyzieulx, Paris, 4 December 1702, AAE, CP, Suisse 137, fol. 317; La Chapelle to Puyzieulx, Paris, 12 January 1703, AAE, CP, Suisse 143, fol. 11; La Chapelle to Puyzieulx, 12 February 1703, AAE, CP, Suisse 143, fol. 118; AN, M. 758, No. 6¹⁹; "Eloge historique du P. Etienne Souciet," *Mémoires de Trévoux*, April 1744, p. 752.

[91] In addition to La Chapelle's letters cited in the preceding note, see La Chapelle to Puyzieulx, Paris, 8 January 1703, AAE, CP, Suisse 137, fol. 410; La Chapelle to Puyzieulx, 3 March 1703, AAE, CP, Suisse 143, fol. 195; Puyzieulx to Torcy, Soleure, 24 March 1703, AAE, CP, Suisse 139, fol. 237; Torcy to Puyzieulx, 22 March 1703(?), AAE, CP, Suisse 147, fol. 58; La Chapelle to Puyzieulx, 13 August 1703, AAE, CP, Suisse 144, fol. 169; La Chapelle to Puyzieulx, Paris, 29 July 1704, AAE, CP, Suisse 152, fol. 376.

qualities in a man of this profession." Copies of the tracts in all three languages were dispatched into the empire by way of contacts in Zurich and Basel. Thus the French embassy at Soleure became the center of a pamphlet distribution network stretching across Switzerland, Germany, and eastern France.[92]

By the end of 1703, then, La Chapelle's work had been published in six languages. The Latin version had at least two separate editions, the French at least four. What quantity of copies resulted from this explosion of editions? Hints of circulation figures are few and far between in the docu-

[92] La Chapelle to Puyzieulx, Paris, 4 December 1702, AAE, CP, Suisse 137, fol. 317: "Nous le ferons imprimer en latin, et on taschera de les bombarder en Allemagne, mais elles seroient bien plus fortes si elles parloient allemand." Puyzieulx's characterization of the Swiss printer is in his letter to Torcy of 24 March 1703, AAE, CP, Suisse 139, fol. 237. On Baron's role in the translations, see Puyzieulx to Louis, Soleure, 16 November 1702, AAE, CP, Suisse 135, fol. 177; La Chapelle to Puyzieulx, Paris, 4 December 1702, AAE, CP, Suisse 137, fol. 317; Puyzieulx to Torcy, Soleure, 15 December 1702, AAE, CP, Suisse 135, fol. 240. Torcy and La Chapelle checked Baron's work with German scholars in Paris: "M. de Torcy . . . exhortera M. Baron de continuer sa traduction allemande. . . . Il m'asseure qu'il est content de la traduction, apparemment il l'a fait voir à quelque docte allemande, car il n'entend point l'allemand non plus que moy" (La Chapelle to Puyzieulx, Paris, 8 January 1703, AAE, CP, Suisse 137, fol. 409); see also La Chapelle to Puyzieulx, 25 November 1703, AAE, CP, Suisse 144, fol. 411. Torcy authorized the German printing in Switzerland in his dispatch to Puyzieulx of 4 April 1703, AAE, CP, Suisse 147, fol. 63. German printing could not be carried out in Paris because of the unavailability of Gothic type (La Chapelle to Puyzieulx, 12 February 1703, AAE, CP, Suisse 143, fol. 117[v]; cf. Lanette-Claverie, "Librairie française," pp. 14–15). The cost of the German translation, printing and circulation, like that of the Latin and French reprintings in Switzerland, was underwritten by Torcy in special subsidies to Puyzieulx's embassy; see the expense lists in AAE, CP, Suisse 144, fols. 600–602[v]; AAE, CP, Suisse 152, fols. 418–422; AAE, CP, Suisse 161, fol. 77; and La Chapelle to Torcy, Soleure, 29 October 1706, AAE, CP, Suisse 171, fol. 218. The first of these expense lists identifies Zurich and Basel as the distribution points for empire-bound translated pamphlets.

ments, but Puyzieulx once remarked proudly that in the period of a fortnight Switzerland had been blanketed with over one thousand French copies of a particularly important *Lettre d'un suisse*;[93] the maximum distribution for a single edition, then, would seem to be in this range. Puyzieulx thought 200 to 300 pamphlets in each of three languages a "good quantity" for normal export into Germany.[94] Using 250 copies as a median and assuming, as seems reasonable, that the ambassador would require at least as many copies for internal Swiss consumption, we can deduce that the normal press run for each of three editions published in Switzerland was approximately 500. To these totals must be added the run of one Latin and three concurrently appearing French-language editions printed in Paris. We have no figures on press runs for these editions, but each was probably produced in quantities at least as great as appeared in Switzerland. The result is a grand total of about 3,500 as the estimated press run for the Latin, French and German versions of a typical *Lettre d'un suisse* in the period within six months of its initial publication. This sum does not include unknown quantities of translated English, Spanish, and Italian *Lettres* and occasional reprints of single back numbers still in demand. Moreover, the definitive edition of 1710 probably had a press run of about 1,000 if it was at all rep-

[93] Puyzieulx to Louis, Soleure, 16 June 1706, AAE, CP, Suisse 170, fol. 141ᵛ.
[94] Puyzieulx to Torcy, Soleure, 7 April 1703, AAE, CP, Suisse 139, fol. 284, informs the minister of a shipment of 200–300 Latin copies of *Lettres* 1–6 to the empire. Cf. the following dispatches: Puyzieulx to Louis, 14 April 1703, AAE, CP, Suisse 139, fol. 294: "Je les [*LS* 9; *LS* 10] fais imprimer en françois et en allemand le plus diligemment qu'il m'est possible pour contenter tout le monde. On m'écrit de tous les côtés le petit nombre que j'en ay pû faire passer jusques à present en Allemagne, les y fait rechercher avec un extreme soin, j'auray celuy d'y en faire passer une bonne quantité." Puyzieulx to Torcy, Soleure, 21 April 1703, AAE, CP, Suisse 139, fol. 311: "Comme je les fais imprimer dans les langues latine, françoise et allemande je pourray satisfaire chacun et en faire passer un bon nombre dans l'empire dans les trois langues."

resentative of contemporary publishing practices in Paris. Nor does the estimate of 3,500 include counterfeitings such as the reprints in the *Clef du cabinet des Princes*, the monthly journal that reprinted many of the Swiss's letters in 1705 and 1706.[95] Well might La Chapelle have marveled, when he arrived at Soleure in 1706, at the large quantities of *Lettres d'un suisse* he found circulating outside France.[96]

If these estimates are at all accurate, they indicate that the monthly *Lettres d'un suisse* had a per-issue circulation far greater than that of the majority of contemporary English gazettes, which operated under as favorable circumstances of literacy and freedom from censorship as were known anywhere in Europe during this period.[97] Comparative circulation statistics for French-language political periodicals are

[95] On reprinting single back issues, see La Chapelle to Torcy, Soleure, 12 March 1706, AAE, CP, Suisse 169, fol. 101ᵛ. For listing of reprints in *Clef du cabinet*, see above, n. 3; on the relatively large circulation of this publication, see Michel Gilot, "Quelques sortes de lettres de lecteurs," in Couperus, *L'Etude*, p. 86. See Martin, *Livre*, pp. 377–379, for press runs of seventeenth-century Parisian editions; average press runs did not greatly increase in the eighteenth century (Quéniart, *L'imprimerie*, pp. 98–100; and M.-A. Merland, "Tirage et vente de livres à la fin du XVIIIᵉ siècle: des documents chiffrés," *Revue française d'histoire du livre*, N.S., III:5 [1973], 92–98).

[96] La Chapelle to Torcy, Soleure, 10 March 1706, AAE, CP, Suisse 169, fol. 87. The press run of the *Lettres d'un suisse* was magnified while La Chapelle was at Soleure by the appearance of a Lyon edition; see La Chapelle to Torcy, 8 December 1706, AAE, CP, Suisse 172, fol. 93ᵛ; and La Chapelle to Torcy, Soleure, 8 June 1707, AAE, CP, Suisse 179, fol. 97. Circulation of the Swiss editions also increased during this period: see La Chapelle to Torcy, Soleure, 29 October 1706, AAE, CP, Suisse 171, fol. 218. Counterfeit editions also added to the circulation of the *Lettres*: *Clef du cabinet*, June 1705, pp. 461–462, discusses editions of *LS* 31 printed at The Hague, Amsterdam, Rotterdam, "et quelques autres Villes de Hollande."

[97] On the circulation of English newspapers, see Ewald, *Newsmen of Queen Anne*, pp. 6–8; J. M. Price, "A Note on the Circulation of the London Press, 1704–1714," *Bulletin of the Institute of Historical Research*, 31 (1958), 215–224; and Cranfield, *Development of the Provincial Newspaper*, pp. 169–175.

nonexistent before 1715 and remain fragmentary until the latter half of the century, but we know that Holland-published weeklies of the 1720's and 1730's often survived with a circulation as low as 400 and only extraordinarily reached a run of several thousand for a single issue.[98] The evidence thus points to the conclusion that the *Lettres d'un suisse* comprised one of the most well-circulated serially issued publications of the day. If we are to credit the rough rule of twenty readers per copy that is applied to the English press, we would derive a readership of up to 80,000 for the average *Lettre d'un suisse*. While this is undoubtedly far too high an estimate, if only because La Chapelle's pamphlets were subject to confiscation in many places, it should be clear that these pamphlets, which never before have been the object of historical analysis and do not even appear in scholars' lists of periodicals,[99] had an enormously wide impact during the War of the Spanish Succession.

The tools available to measure this impact, however, are not equipped with even the gross calibration of modern survey techniques. Clearly, some credence should be given to the surviving opinions of French diplomats in England, Germany, Switzerland, and Italy who praised the *Lettres* and testified to their influence. In the same vein are the endorsements of numerous foreign leaders named by Puyzieulx and other diplomats as admirers of the pamphlets. Surely Torcy's financially strapped ministry would not have subsidized the *Lettres d'un suisse* to the tune of more than

[98] See Couperus, *L'Etude*, pp. 73–74; and Moulinas, "Les Journaux publiés à Avignon," pp. 128, 130. Jean-Daniel Candaux, "Inventaire provisoire des périodiques littéraires et scientifiques de langue française publiés en Suisse de 1693 à 1795," in Couperus, *L'Etude*, pp. 128–129, finds no circulation figures whatever for such publications before 1781.

[99] Bonno, "Liste," does not include the analogous works of Eustache Le Noble either, but the recent inventory by J. Sgard, "Table chronologique," in Couperus, *L'Etude*, does, thus making the latter's omission of the *Lettres d'un suisse* even more inconsistent.

9,000 livres for 1703 and 1704[100] had the foreign minister not agreed with La Chapelle's declaration of the value of propaganda: "The issuance of pamphlets and newssheets is well repaid. The worst *mémoire* passes for truth as soon as it goes unanswered. Silence is taken as evidence of the accused party's guilt and acquiescence."[101] Further evidence of the Swiss's impact is the series of review notices which called attention to the *Lettres d'un suisse* in the privileged *Mémoires de Trévoux*—one of whose editors, it will be recalled, also acted as translator of the pamphlets—and in the crown-administered *Journal des savans*.[102] While these manifestations of a controlled press do not represent detached judgments of merit, the quality and extent of these learned journals' readership meant that any book they summarized would not fail to have its reputation enhanced and its contents given scholarly consideration. Reprinting of the pamphlets in the monthly *Clef du cabinet des Princes* served the same purpose even more directly. Further, the bitter *ad hominem* criticism of La Chapelle in Gueudeville's Holland-based *L'Esprit des cours de l'Europe* gives us a hint of the raw nerve the *Lettres d'un suisse* touched among Louis' enemies;[103] and, as La Chapelle knew, even hostile comment was good publicity. When the instinctively censorial Torcy offered to silence Gueudeville, La Chapelle urged him to refrain from stifling "foolishness that perhaps will give me

[100] La Chapelle's pension—2000 livres/year (see above, n. 13); Blondel's *gratification* for the German translations—900 livres/year; printing and distribution costs—3985 livres total for 1703-1704 (see expense lists cited above, n. 94). Costs of printing and distribution of other editions are lacking. La Chapelle's cover letter to Torcy for the expense account of the *Lettres d'un suisse* in Switzerland during 1706 (AAE, CP, Suisse 171, fol. 218) shows that expenses for that year exceeded those of any previous year.

[101] La Chapelle to Torcy, Soleure, 30 March 1706, AAE, CP, Suisse 169, fol. 158.

[102] See above, chap. 3, nn. 39, 42.

[103] *L'Esprit des cours de l'Europe*, August 1705, pp. 167–170; November 1705, pp. 552–568.

occasion to make some good replies." Such replies were attempted in two *Lettres d'un suisse* explicitly rebutting the Dutch journal.[104]

A ruse often employed by the Swiss of Paris to lend credibility to his work and thus enhance its impact was the invention of other writers as supposed authors of the pamphlets. In addition to the masks we have encountered already, La Chapelle introduced a Protestant Swiss, a Huguenot, and a "savant danois" into the *Lettres* as spokesmen for points of view not well suited to his normal disguise.[105] Occasionally, too, the Swiss was given an opportunity to refute straw-man arguments ostensibly issued from Dutch and Swabian pens.[106] To the circulation of these doubly disguised tracts La Chapelle devoted special care, dispatching untraceable manuscript copies and, in the case of a supposed Dutch pamphlet,[107] meticulously imitating the printing conventions of Holland on a Lyon press.[108] Only months after its initial publication was this last pamphlet reprinted as a *Lettre d'un suisse*.[109] Another of La Chapelle's occasional pieces never appeared in the series at all, apparently because it might have implied an overly close association of the much pitied elector of Bavaria with the still resented Louis XIV.[110] These masks were meant not only to deceive the general public but could even succeed with as sophisticated a reader as the papal nuncio in Brussels, who hastened to alert the

[104] La Chapelle to Torcy, Soleure, 10 March 1706, AAE, CP, Suisse 169, fol. 87. Cf. *LS* 36, *LS* 38.

[105] *LS* 40.   [106] *LS* 28, *LS* 29, *LS* 31, *LS* 32.

[107] The pamphlet is *LS* 31. The original title of this tract was *Lettre d'un suisse servant en Hollande à un de ses amis en Suisse*.

[108] *Clef du cabinet*, June 1705, p. 443. La Chapelle to Torcy, Soleure, 8 December 1706, AAE, CP, Suisse 172, fol. 93ᵛ.

[109] *LS* 40.

[110] *Lettre d'un gentilhomme bavarois refugié en Suisse*, in *Clef du cabinet*, November 1705, pp. 331–342. Attribution of this pamphlet to La Chapelle is based on stylistic evidence and the fact that no *Lettre d'un suisse* appeared between September 1705 and January 1706.

pope to a Protestant plot revealed by one of La Chapelle's putative Dutchmen.[111]

The impact of at least one of the Swiss's writings had a very specific and measurable effect contributing to a direct alteration in the course of events and a French diplomatic triumph. The occasion arose during 1706, while La Chapelle was assisting Puyzieulx at Soleure. Somehow the French embassy acquired an intercepted diplomatic dispatch addressed to the duke of Savoy by Mellarède, his ambassador to Switzerland. This explosive document revealed Duke Victor Amadeus' plans to destroy the Swiss confederation with the assistance of the powerful Protestant and Habsburg-oriented canton of Bern. La Chapelle composed comments making explicit the consequences of Mellarède's dispatch, Puyzieulx circulated manuscript copies among Swiss leaders to test the wind,[112] and then the ambassador published text and annotations in parallel columns under the title *Mémoire du Sieur de Mellarède Envoyé du Duc de Savoye en Suisse, avec les Reflexions sur ce Mémoire.*[113] This was the crucial *Lettre d'un suisse* of which one thousand copies were quickly printed in French and an additional quantity in German for circulation throughout the cantons.[114] Soon thereafter, the Swiss general diet convened and, although the Bernese issued a blistering protest against violation of the sanctity of the diplomatic pouch, many other cantons displayed an unwonted friendliness toward France; whereupon Puyzieulx very plausibly hailed La Chapelle's commentary as responsible for the destruction of six years of imperial plotting in Switzerland.[115]

[111] La Chapelle to Puyzieulx, Paris, 6 May 1705, AAE, CP, Suisse 162, fol. 69.

[112] Puyzieulx to Louis, Soleure, 9 June 1706, AAE, CP, Suisse 170, fol. 111.

[113] A printed copy is bound in AAE, CP, Suisse 170, fols. 113–128. It was subsequently published as *LS* 39; see La Chapelle to Torcy, Soleure, 9 June 1706, AAE, CP, Suisse 170, fol. 134[v].

[114] Puyzieulx to Louis, 16 June 1706, AAE, CP, Suisse 170, fol. 141.

[115] Puyzieulx to Louis, Bade, 9 July 1706, Suisse 170, fols. 202[v]–203[v];

TESTAMENT POLITIQUE

Despite mild efforts by French diplomats to hide the real identity of the letter-writing Swiss, inevitably the origin of the pamphlets soon became an open secret. By 1705 the very effective correspondence grapevine of the republic of letters had carried the news of La Chapelle's authorship to the scholarly and literary world.[116] Gueudeville's attacks upon the *Lettres d'un suisse* punned broadly on the name La Chapelle,[117] but even this, as we have seen, did not provoke the French pamphleteer's anger. There may well have been a built-in contradiction between La Chapelle's personal aspirations for careerist advancement and his consequent desire for public approbation on the one hand and the intrinsically veiled nature of anonymous propaganda on the other. In any case, even uninitiated readers surely did not require inside information to conclude that the partisan, knowledgeable *Lettres* likely had the official sanction of the French government. Despite the Swiss's frequent vehement denials that he was writing in the pay of France, Torcy and La Chapelle seemed to accept the fact that it was impossible to devise foolproof methods of disguise for the origin and even the authorship of most of the tracts.[118]

Puyzieulx to Louis, Bade, 16 July 1706, *ibid.*, fol. 221. The protest of Bern is printed in Lamberty, *Mémoires*, IV, 181–184.

[116] Pierre Bayle was informed of the Swiss's identity by Dubos. See Bayle to Dubos, Rotterdam, 16 April 1705, in Denis, *Lettres*, pp. 184–185; Dubos to Bayle, 25 July 1705, in Gigas, *Correspondance*, pp. 306–307; and Bayle to Dubos, Rotterdam, 6 August 1705, in Bayle, *Oeuvres diverses*, IV, 857–858; Père Léonard first attributed the *Lettres* to Le Noble but soon corrected himself (AN, M. 758, No. 6[19]).

[117] *L'Esprit des cours de l'Europe*, November 1705, p. 568.

[118] The Swiss's denials of French identity are in LS 4, I:50–52; LS 12, II:179–180; LS 16, III:121–122; LS 36, VI:206–207. Cf. La Chapelle to Puyzieulx, 12 February 1703, AAE, CP, Suisse 143, fol. 117ᵛ: "Apres tout il [Torcy] dit qu'on se vit bien que cette marchandise vient de France"; and Torcy to La Chapelle, Versailles, 25 November 1706 (minute), AAE, CP, Suisse 172, fol. 44: "Quelque nom que

Yet these men succeeded in inventing so effective a camouflage for one of La Chapelle's writings that it mystified not only the contemporary audience but modern-day historians as well. The work was a so-called *Testament politique ou derniers conseils d'un ministre de l'Empereur Léopold*, and it purported to be the final counsel of a dying Habsburg adviser. The origin and authenticity of this work have not been definitely established up to now, but we can be certain, thanks to the documentary evidence of the Quai d'Orsay archives, that it was composed by La Chapelle. This diplomatic correspondence reveals that La Chapelle drafted the falsified testament in Paris at the end of 1705, that the draft was modified and approved by Torcy, that minister and writer took elaborate pains to disguise the first Lyon edition of 1706 so as to make credible the Rotterdam provenance of the title page, that Latin, Italian, and possibly German editions appeared within the next two years, and that La Chapelle and Torcy carefully circulated these versions via both diplomatic pouches and anonymous distribution channels.[119]

La Chapelle's fraudulent political testament soon took its place as part of a genre that had mushroomed since the publication in 1688 of the testament ascribed to Richelieu. Men of state competed in drawing up manuals of maxims, hoping thereby to "add a second volume to Cardinal Richelieu's *Testament*."[120] Men of letters also competed in fabricating testaments attributed to such leaders as Mazarin, Colbert, Louvois, Vauban, and Charles V of Lorraine, all of whom had works of this type ascribed to them between 1690 and 1715.[121] These editions aroused much controversy

---

vous mettiez à la reponse à M. de Trautmannsdorff il faut que vous attende que l'autheur en sera bientost connu."

[119] See appendix.

[120] Louville to Torcy, Milan, 14 October 1702, AAE, CP, Espagne 113, fol. 145. The work referred to was by Harcourt.

[121] See *Recueil des Testaments politiques*, 4 vols. (Amsterdam-Paris, 1749), BN, Imp., La²⁸.11.

at the time, and even modern scholarship has not yet unraveled all the mysteries. While it is established that the Richelieu testament possesses a degree of authenticity, and that the testaments attributed to Louis XIV's servants are false,[122] Duke Charles's testament has been plausibly ascribed to several authors in addition to the duke himself. One theory holds that it was inspired by the French court during the Ryswick negotiations, and this is highly credible because of the similarity of the 1695 Lorraine testament to La Chapelle's 1706 falsification.[123]

The historiographical controversy over this *Testament politique ou derniers conseils d'un ministre de l'Empereur Léopold* has been carried out by scholars who had no reason to connect it with the *Lettres d'un suisse* and hence could only argue the testament's veracity on the basis of internal evidence. The debate began in 1880, when Johann Gustav Droysen found a German manuscript copy of the testament in Munich's Geheime Staatsarchiv and a published French version in the 1706 edition of Casimir Freschot's *Mémoires de la Cour de Vienne*. Droysen reprinted the French text as an appendix to the fourth volume of his *Geschichte der preussischen Politik* and argued for the authenticity of the work.[124] He found nothing curious in the testament's key

[122] On Richelieu, see L. André's introduction to his edition of the *Testament politique* (Paris, 1947). The works attributed to Louvois and Mazarin came from the pen of Courtilz de Sandras, and the Colbert testament may have had the same origin (Woodbridge, *Gatien de Courtilz*, p. 207). The work published under the title *Testament politique de M. de Vauban* (1707) was in fact Pierre Le Pesant de Boisguilbert, *Le Détail de la France*.

[123] R. Koser, "Das Politische Testament Karls V. von Lothringen von 1687," *Historische Zeitschrift*, 48 (1882), 85–88, printed excerpts from Charles's testament and from the *Testament politique* dated 1705 (of whose authorship he was unaware) in parallel columns to demonstrate their similarity. Koser follows A. de Montaiglon (ed., *Testament politique du duc Charles de Lorraine* [Paris, 1866]) in attributing this work to the Abbé de Chèvremont.

[124] J. G. Droysen, *Geschichte der preussischen Politik*, 14 vols. (Berlin, 1855–1866), part IV:4, 239–249, introduction and critical analysis; 249–270, text.

recommendation that the object of Habsburg policy ought to be "to stretch from orient to occident and make one monarchy of the two reunited empires."[125] We know of course that this was a recapitulation and extension of the aims attributed to Leopold in the *Lettres d'un suisse*, but Droysen saw no reason to search for the testament's origin in propaganda. As La Chapelle had calculatingly allowed the reader to deduce from internal evidence that the testament should have been written sometime between Blenheim and the opening of the 1705 campaign, Droysen was able to credit Count Harrach, who died during this period, with authorship of the work. The vast imperial ambitions described in the testament were anything but a surprise to the Prussian historian, and he concluded that "the testament not only contains a full professional knowledge of events up to that time, but it provides a list of suggestions which in fact would be carried out sooner or later, presenting a system of Austrian politics which in the next three decades the Viennese cabinet, in its constant sinuosity, devoted itself to realizing."[126]

What was for Droysen a "full professional knowledge of events" manifested itself in the testament in the following passages addressed to Emperor Leopold:

> The secrets of God are impenetrable. That *gloire* of Louis XIV, of which you were so rightfully envious, is one of the happy circumstances that God . . . has planned to have you reign over all the thrones of Europe. . . . The heretics have forgotten the hatred that you still maintain toward them and the proper harshness which you exercised in order to reunite them with the Church. They have considered your house their protector and the house of Bourbon their sole, implacable enemy.
>
> . . . The blindness first spread among the heretics of

125 *Testament politique*, p. 6.
126 Droysen, *Geschichte*, part IV:4, p. 243.

our Germany. Incensed by the talk of the French fugitives who claimed that the French monarchy's power was greatly diminished by the desertion of the Huguenots and who held out a vision of heretics and exiles easily reestablished by force of arms, the Germans breathed only hatred and vengeance toward their former ally and defender.[127]

The minister proceeds to counsel his master on his primary duty, which is nothing less than the extermination of these Protestant heretics. The Hungarian rebels, he declares, should not be tolerated.[128] As for Germany, "If you do not entirely destroy the influence and power of the heretics in the Empire, you will never accomplish anything truly great. Never will you render the Empire perfectly hereditary in your house." This is so because "the republican spirit possesses" the Protestants.

Observe, Sacred Majesty, that most of the German authors who have had the effrontery and the obstinacy to write against imperial authority and have contended that the Empire is a kind of republic in which you are only primary member and chief, subordinate to the entire body, have been Lutherans or Calvinists.
. . . Keep in mind the example of France. As long as La Rochelle and the Huguenots existed, royal authority was weak and subordinate to the tutelage of subjects. . . . It was to assure his successors an independence of authority and to prevent his subjects from reviving their so-called rights, that Louis XIV wanted to purge his kingdom of all sectarians, a plague as dangerous to the state as it is deadly to the Religion.[129]

Fortunately, continues the minister's testament, the princes of the empire believe that they have no common interests; hence they are divided, and each looks out only

[127] *Testament politique*, pp. 8–9. [128] *Ibid.*, p. 26.
[129] *Ibid.*, pp. 12–13.

163

for himself. The princes no longer come to the diets, but send subordinate ministers who undertake no initiatives. To reinforce this princely tendency toward disunity, the councillor would have Leopold encourage the electors of Brandenburg and Saxony in their claims for recognition as kings. These *rois de théâtre* are to be neutralized by feeding their ambitions and making imperial creatures of their servants.[130] The same policy is recommended for the elector of Hanover; his designs upon England should be fostered so as to distract him from German affairs.[131] The minister forecasts that the implementation of this advice would result in the abolition of the imperial election and the resumption of the revenues and domains of the empire.[132]

In the current war, the minister advises "the ruin of France, or at least such a total and certain weakening of that monarchy that she will no longer be in a state to succor the Germans."[133] The Spanish empire itself takes second place to the campaign against France, so much so that the minister even would accept a cession of some part of the Spanish empire to Philip, provided France were disabled; for the territorial loss could always be retrieved in some later war. He expects an early peace, and the emperor should bring this about by arranging a peace independent of his allies.[134] At the peace conference the Protestants should be allowed no important role. Especially dangerous would be the mediation of Sweden, that other traditional protector of German liberties.[135]

The war, in the imperial minister's view, offered a superb opportunity for reasserting the rights of the emperor in Italy. Not only should he occupy the duchy of Milan and the kingdom of Naples as possessions of the king of Spain, but Savoy, Ferrara, Mantua, Lucca, Siena, and Florence, and the *terra firma* of Venice all form part of the imperial patrimony. To assert his rights over these areas, the emperor

[130] *Ibid.*, p. 16.   [131] *Ibid.*, p. 18.
[132] *Ibid.*, p. 27.   [133] *Ibid.*, p. 22.
[134] *Ibid.*, p. 23.   [135] *Ibid.*, p. 11.

should break completely and openly with the pope. Otherwise Clement XI might unite all the Italian states against the house of Austria.[136] And, concludes the testament, no emperor should overlook Switzerland, "your *patrie*, the cradle of your Sacred House." Imperial policy there should be to stir up hatred between Catholics and Protestants and to make creatures of the Swiss by caresses and intrigue. Finally, La Chapelle could not resist inserting in the testament a condemnation of Trautmannsdorff for going beyond his orders and threatening the Swiss with violence when more gentle measures would have been more effective.[137]

Few historians were convinced by Droysen's ascription of these thoughts to an authentic Habsburg source, but not until Oswald Redlich addressed himself to the problem in 1928 did a full-scale refutation of Droysen's analysis appear.[138] The Austrian historian doubted that a genuine testament of this kind could ever find its way into print. But his rejection of the testament, like its acceptance by the Prussian, is based on a preconceived analysis of Habsburg policy. After a full summary of the work, Redlich exclaims: "These then are the last counsels of a minister of Kaiser Leopold! . . . Is it possible? . . . No, it is unthinkable."[139] He believed the testament was a falsification put out by one of Leopold's enemies, probably France or Bavaria. And bringing to bear the similarity of this testament's argument with that of Charles of Lorraine's testament of 1695, he decided that they had a similar political origin. Leaving aside the still-puzzling question of the Lorraine testament and its relationship to La Chapelle's, we can verify Redlich's deductions from solid manuscript evidence. The *Testament politique* indeed may have articulated imperial policies, as Droysen argued, but its origin was French.

[136] *Ibid.*, pp. 34–36.   [137] *Ibid.*, pp. 42–44.
[138] "Das angebliche Politische Testament eines Ministers Kaiser Leopolds I," in *Aus Politik und Geschichte. Gedächtnisschriften für Georg von Below* (Berlin, 1928), pp. 156–166. Redlich reviews the literature, p. 157.
[139] *Ibid.*, p. 162.

Although La Chapelle thought very highly of this fabricated work, calling it his "favorite child" and confiding to Torcy that he regarded it as his best effort up to that point,[140] the first editions of 1706 apparently did not inspire as much discussion as the Frenchmen had hoped. The work had been reprinted by Freschot and summarized in the *Clef du cabinet des Princes* of June 1706. Still, in a *Lettre d'un suisse* published during the latter part of 1707 the Swiss risked an open advertisement of the testament, suggesting that much of its advice seemed relevant to current Habsburg actions. "It is not a fictitious work, as people have attempted to argue, and . . . most of the advice given there has been carried out to the letter."[141] The Swiss listed his examples: Bavaria, where the ban issued by Emperor Joseph, Leopold's successor, conformed exactly to the testament's advice of "giving a tone of legality to the oppression of the Bavarians"; Hungary, where the emperor refused to make peace despite good opportunities; and above all, the abortive Swiss effort of 1706 to achieve mediation by Charles XII of Sweden, sabotaged by the house of Austria in accord with the testament's admonition to "prevent the king of Sweden from entering into the peace negotiations and to reject his mediation unconditionally."[142] As La Chapelle had explained to one of Torcy's *commis* just after the testament's first publication: "It is no misfortune that there are points in the Testament which can be objected to and argued. I will pretend to have the Swiss write on such matters, and these reflections will put in their proper light anything that had not been so in the Testament."[143]

A year later two more *Lettres d'un suisse* again reminded their readers of the testament and singled out imperial policies in Italy for special discussion. Indeed, a June 1708 mani-

---

[140] La Chapelle to Torcy, Soleure, 10 March 1706, AAE, CP, Suisse 169, fol. 85ᵛ.

[141] *LS* 42, VIII:251–282, esp. 254.   [142] *Ibid.*, pp. 262, 269, 282.

[143] La Chapelle to Pecquet, Soleure, 7 April 1706, AAE, CP, Suisse 174, fol. 26.

festo to the Italians issued by Emperor Joseph had seemed to mirror the recommendations of the supposed minister.[144] "The world," said the Swiss, "had given renewed attention to this work since the aims of the emperor have begun to be unmasked. . . . I am not alone in rereading the *Testament politique* of the Austrian minister. I know many people who are studying it diligently, many people who, after the Italian catastrophe, are searching in it the fate of other countries."[145] The Swiss quoted a tract printed at Lucca in July 1708 that speculated on which imperial minister was the author of the testament and reported that no one in the tiny republic "considers this testament a fictitious work anymore, now that we have seen its maxims in use, its instructions followed and its advice executed."[146]

The *Testament politique* and the two complementary *Lettres d'un suisse* of 1708 were dispatched by Torcy for French diplomats in Italy, where the tracts were meant to assist Torcy's efforts in rousing the Italian states against the house of Austria. Torcy specified to Louis' men in Genoa and Florence that these works, and especially the testament, should be distributed anonymously so as to avoid exciting suspicions about their origins. If the recipients were well chosen, he wrote, they themselves would distribute the tract even more widely.[147]

[144] Droysen, *Geschichte*, p. 247. See Louis' instructions to Tessé, in Hanotaux, *Recueil des instructions*, vol. 17: *Rome*, 394: "Il n'y a pas un moment à perdre pour s'opposer à une usurpation méditée, comme il le faut voir lui-meme dans son manifeste, depuis le règne de l'Empereur Charles-Quint. . . ."

[145] *LS* 46, VIII: 118–152, esp. 118.   [146] *LS* 47, VIII: 156–184, esp. 157.

[147] These copies were in Latin; the 1706 Italian edition published in Milan was not reprinted. D'Iberville to Torcy, Genoa, 4 November 1708, AAE, CP, Gênes 47, fol. 209; Torcy to d'Iberville, Versailles, 15 November 1708 (draft in Torcy's hand), AAE, CP, Gênes, 47, fol. 210; d'Iberville to Torcy, Gênes, 24 November 1708, AAE, CP, Gênes 46, fol. 188ᵛ; d'Iberville to Torcy, Gênes, 12 December 1708, AAE, CP, Gênes 46, fol. 220ᵛ; Torcy to Dupré (draft in Torcy's hand), Versailles, 15 November 1708, AAE, CP, Toscane 43, fol. 203. The *Testament politique* also received renewed discussion in *Clef du*

The testament and its accompanying pamphlets marked the last major campaign of the *Lettres d'un suisse*. From La Chapelle's return from Switzerland in mid-1707 to the last *Lettre* of January 1709 only seven sporadically published pamphlets appeared. Although the 1710 collected edition of all the *Lettres d'un suisse* surely was read throughout the rest of the war, and although La Chapelle penned occasional pamphlets later in the war and continued to receive an annual pension,[148] his most productive period as a political propagandist was at an end.

For this termination there were reasons both personal and political. The academician-turned-propagandist realized by 1709 that the unmerited disgrace he acquired at court after Neuchâtel was not about to be dissipated. No longer could he hope for a diplomatic post, and so faded his private purpose in writing *en suisse*.[149] At this time too, his old collaborator, Puyzieulx, suffered a complete demoralization. Now terribly old and tired, blamed too and equally unreasonably for the Neuchâtel fiasco, deprived of his only son (dead on a Spanish battlefield), and shorn of the pamphleteer whose companionship had helped make bearable the severe climate and depressingly rocky terrain of which

---

cabinet, March 1709, pp. 171–182: "On ne regarde plus le Testament politique comme un Ouvrage supposé; les Curieux qui en ont conservé des copies le lisent presentement avec attention, et examinent combien ses maximes sont conformés à ce qui se passe en Italie" (p. 171).

[148] See above, n. 11. La Chapelle also received a *gratification* of 5400 livres for his service in Switzerland (Torcy to La Chapelle, Marly, 26 May 1707, AAE, CP, Suisse 179, fol. 27).

[149] Only gradually did the permanence of his disgrace dawn on La Chapelle. Before leaving Switzerland in 1707, he could still write cheerily to Torcy: "Pour l'avenir qui me regarde je n'en ay aucune inquietude. Il est entre vos mains et je suis assés hardy pour compter sur vos bontés" (La Chapelle to Torcy, Soleure, 4 June 1707, AAE, CP, Suisse 179, fol. 91ᵛ). Torcy had raised La Chapelle's hopes by observing to Puyzieulx that "il faut pour le bien meme du service, le conserver pour d'autres occasions" (Torcy to Puyzieulx, Marly, 26 May 1707, AAE, CP, Suisse 185, fol. 22). See above, notes 9 and 10.

Frenchmen in Switzerland were forever complaining—
Puyzieulx was at last relieved of his duties and returned to
Paris in 1708.[150] Moreover, the private discontents of La
Chapelle and Puyzieulx coincided with the nadir of French
fortunes during the reign of Louis XIV. After another disastrous defeat at Oudenarde and the fall of Lille, the road
to Paris lay open. Meanwhile a terrible harvest and an even
more terrible freeze brought death by exposure and starva-
tion to vast numbers of Louis XIV's subjects. In February
1709 premature death took La Chapelle's earliest friend,
François Louis de Bourbon, prince de Conti, one of the most
fabulously wealthy men in France. Surely all this was ample
evidence, even for the king himself, that God had abandoned
him in punishment for past excesses of grandeur. Torcy
knew well that little good could come now from continued
publication of *Lettres d'un suisse*. As he told Louis' resident
at Genoa: "I would very much like to be able to soothe
[your pains] with some good news, but unfortunately the
greater part of what our enemies are circulating is true, and
when one cannot refute them, one passes some bad moments
in foreign lands." But, the foreign minister continued, one
sure solution yet remained: "Peace would be the best of all
remedies, and it is to be wished that God would inspire the
spirit of peace in men before the armies take the field once
more."[151] The peace talks which began in the early months

[150] Puyzieulx to Torcy, Bade, 27 July 1707, printed in Boislisle,
Puyzieulx, p. 162: "Je prévois que toutes les parties se plaindront
de moi." Puyzieulx to Pontchartrain, Soleure, 30 September 1707,
ibid., pp. 171 ff.: "J'ai prévu des les commencements de cette affaire,
tout ce qui est arrivé jusqu'à présent." On Puyzieulx's reactions to his
son's death, see La Chapelle to Torcy, Soleure, 18 May 1707, AAE,
CP, Suisse 179, fol. 50ᵛ. Citing this blow and the rigors of the Swiss
climate, Puyzieulx asked to be relieved of his duties only four months
later. Puyzieulx to Torcy, Soleure, 28 September 1707, AAE, CP,
Suisse 181, fols. 166–167. (On the negative connotations of Swiss
geography in this period, see Richard Feller, "Die Schweiz des 17.
Jahrhunderts in den Berichter des Auslandes," *Schweizer Beiträge
zur allgemeinen Geschichte*, 1 [1943], 68.)

[151] Torcy to d'Iberville, 10 January 1709, AAE, CP, Gênes 46,
fol. 242.

of 1709 opened a new phase of wartime diplomacy for the foreign minister; this fact along with the catastrophic condition of France moved Torcy to alter his approach to propaganda. The anonymous Swiss of Paris was to be replaced by Louis XIV himself.

CHAPTER SIX

Jean-Baptiste Dubos and the Propaganda
of the Book

THE pamphlet series was a propaganda format whose many advantages were exploited resourcefully by La Chapelle and Torcy. Yet even the most ingenious and erudite pamphlets could not match the literary prestige of full-length books. One reason the *Lettres d'un suisse* were collected in book form was to acquire for them the qualities of permanence and seriousness that hard covers bestowed. Only after escaping the ephemeral pamphlet format with its implications of Grub Street shoddiness were these works reviewed in the learned journals and did they receive the prestigious attention of the republic of letters. In this way the utility of the pamphlet series was married to that of the book. As regards content, however, such a marriage could not be entirely successful. The repetitiousness appropriate to a pamphlet series became mere redundancy in a collected volume, and the obvious partisanship of the works likely rendered them suspect to scholarly readers who were accustomed to a tone of "scientific" detachment in the learned journals.

None of these structural weaknesses weighed upon two books written by Jean-Baptiste Dubos in the service of French propaganda. *Les Interêts de l'Angleterre malentendus dans la guerre présente* (1703) and *Histoire de la ligue de Cambray* (1709) were full-scale works whose erudition and imaginative powers were obvious to all contemporary commentators. Moreover, while both books reached conclusions entirely compatible with the theses of the *Lettres d'un suisse*, Dubos' works struck a tone of disinterested scholarship and employed sophisticated analytical techniques. They represent, then, Torcy's attempt to reach the very sophisticated with the message La Chapelle had delivered to a broader audience: that the war against France and Spain was counterproductive to the interests of the allied governments. Dubos was well suited to this task. We know him today as one of the most important writers of the early Enlightenment; he was a founder of relativist aesthetics and the accurate spokesman for a royalist interpretation of the medieval French constitution in his long debate with the historically wrong-headed, pro-Parlement Montesquieu.[1] This reputation, however, was completely unconstructed in 1701, when Dubos began composing works of propaganda for Torcy. The foreign minister had the insight to recognize the young writer's talent and to direct him toward the full-length, innovative works which became his forte.

Although he was past thirty when the War of the Spanish Succession began, Dubos' formation was still in progress. Born into a Beauvais merchant's family in 1670, he had left for Paris sixteen years later and completed studies that led to the *maître ès arts* and the *bachelier de théologie*. Dubos became an abbé, but whatever vocation he may once have felt for the ecclesiastical life soon disappeared. In Paris during the 1690's, the young man met the practitioners of French letters and their patrons; he wrote on archaeology, took an interest in opera, and cultivated correspondence with many foreign scholars who were willing to exchange news of the literary life in their localities for Dubos' Paris reports. The years between 1697 and 1701 found him embarked on a

---

[1] An excellent, comprehensive biography is A. Lombard, *L'Abbé Du Bos, un initiateur de la pensée moderne, 1670–1742* (Paris, 1913), from which are taken biographical data not otherwise attributed. On the significance of the Dubos-Montesquieu debate, see F. Meinecke, "Montesquieu, Boulainvilliers, Dubos, ein Beitrag zu Entstehungsgeschichte des Historismus," *Historische Zeitschrift*, 145 (1931), 53–68; and A. Mathiez, "La Place de Montesquieu dans l'histoire des doctrines politiques du XVIIIᵉ siècle," *Annales de la Révolution française*, 7 (1930), 99–104.

series of journeys to England, the Low Countries, and Italy. While in London, Dubos began to study English and soon declared himself fluent in reading the works of thinkers to whom he had been introduced by Huguenot scholars exiled across the channel; and in Holland Dubos visited Pierre Bayle, with whom he had begun an active correspondence in 1695.

Between 1692 and 1701, then, Dubos lived the life described by Paul Hazard in the opening passages of his brilliant study of Dubos' era, *La Crise de la conscience européenne*: "Men of learning added to their stores of erudition as they journeyed from city to city. . . . Philosophers went abroad, not to go and meditate in peace in some quiet retreat, but to see the wonders of the world." Hazard's description of the young European on the grand tour, "putting the finishing touch on his education," often "bent on self-improvement, conscientiously [examining] every cabinet of natural history specimens, every collection of antiques," might well have been written of the young French abbé.[2] This description reminds us that the moratorium enjoyed by Dubos in his twenties was typical of young men of letters at the end of the seventeenth century. When he began writing propaganda for Torcy, Dubos, though already in the fourth decade of his life, was embarking on his first attempt at a career. In 1707 Dangeau could still describe him with more accuracy than condescension as "a very capable boy."[3]

Dubos began writing for Torcy shortly after his return to Paris from Italy. Through the intermediary of Marshal d'Huxelles, the foreign minister asked the abbé to write a Latin treatise on *droit public* for use abroad. Dubos com-

[2] Paul Hazard, *La Crise de la conscience européenne* (Paris, 1935), trans. J. Lewis May as *The European Mind 1680–1720* (New Haven, 1952), pp. 6–8.

[3] Philippe de Courcillon, Marquis de Dangeau, *Journal*, 19 vols. (Paris, 1854–1860), XI, 397.

posed the first part of the work and outlined the second part, but this project went no further.[4] Instead, he turned to the work which became *Les Interêts de l'Angleterre malentendus dans la guerre présente*. Completed by January 1703, in the next two years the book ran through at least one Italian and six French editions published at Paris and Amsterdam.[5] Although the title page bore the words "traduit de l'anglois" and alleged that the author was a member of Parliament, and although Dubos was cited as merely the translator in a *Mémoires de Trévoux* notice, by late 1704 it had become common knowledge that the Frenchman was both author and translator. Inevitably readers in Holland dubbed the book "Les Interêts de l'Angleterre malentendus par l'abbé Dubos."[6] Still, the many editions and reviews of this book are indicators of its influence during the pre-Blenheim period when British withdrawal from the alliance remained a realistic goal of French diplomacy.

As *Les Interêts de l'Angleterre* was composed contemporaneously with those early *Lettres d'un suisse* which were directed at an English audience (and was even explicitly recommended by the Swiss in his nineteenth letter),[7] it is

[4] Dubos to Torcy, 18 July 1701, AAE, CP, Autriche 81, fols. 62–64; printed in A. Lombard, ed., *Correspondance de l'Abbé Du Bos* (Paris, 1913), p. 51.

[5] Jean-Baptiste Dubos, *Les Interêts de l'Angleterre malentendus dans la guerre présente. Traduit du livre anglois intitulé Englands interest mistaken in the present war* (Amsterdam, 1703 & 1704). Jean-Baptiste Dubos, *Gl'Interessi dell'Inghilterra male intesi nella Guerra presente. Dal libro Inglese, intitolato Englands interest mestaken* [sic] *en* [sic] *the present war, tradotto gia in Franzese, et ora dal Franzese in Italiano* (Amsterdam, 1704). The BN's ten French-language copies comprise at least six editions, of which the pagination followed here is that of Imp., Nc. 1728. F., dated "A Amsterdam, chez George Gallet, Imprimeur et Libraire, 1704." For reviews, see *Journal des savans*, May 1704; *Journal de Trévoux*, March 1704, pp. 417–428; October 1704, pp. 1682–1688.

[6] *Europäische Fama*, No. 31, 1705, p. 480; Jean Leclerc, *Bibliothèque choisie*, 28 vols. (Amsterdam, 1703–1718), VI, 316 ff. See Dubos to Bayle, 25 July 1705, in Gigas, *Correspondance*, p. 306; Lombard, *Du Bos*, p. 109.

[7] LS 19, IV:10.

not surprising to find that Dubos' work recapitulates many of La Chapelle's theses. Even more enlightening are the similarities between *Les Interêts* and the themes of Louis' correspondence with his English diplomats in 1701 on the arguments to be used against English involvement in the war. This correlation is particularly important, given the total absence of surviving letters describing the genesis of Dubos' book. The verbal parallels between *Les Interêts* and French diplomatic dispatches are good evidence that Dubos had access to Torcy's archives. Reproductions of this sort are particularly frequent in the second half of the book, where Dubos analyzed the origins of English involvement in the war. His treatment, for example, of Louis XIV's recognition of James II's son as the legitimate English sovereign closely followed Torcy's letters of 1701 to French diplomats. Both Torcy and Dubos claimed that the recognition in no sense overstepped the restrictions of the Treaty of Ryswick, by which Louis had promised not to trouble William in the possession of his states and to refrain from military support for any pretender to William's throne. Torcy permitted the envoys of 1701 to circulate assurances that the new Pretender would receive from Louis nothing more than his father had obtained since 1697: "only his subsistence and solace in his misfortune." Dubos confirmed that Louis' recognition would result in only "ceremonial treatment." Diplomatic dispatch and propaganda tract both emphasized the precedents for Louis' act of recognition. In this respect Dubos expanded upon Torcy's list and added what must be the ultimate instance, the traditional claim voiced by the monarchs of England in their title that they were also kings of France. No French king had taken this empty formalism for a threat to sovereignty; yet, Dubos noted, here were the English at war over a simple point of punctilio.[8] What we have in Dubos' book, then, is the continuation of Torcy's effort to soften the effects of Louis' act

[8] Torcy to Poussin, 18 September 1701, AAE, CP, Angleterre 211, fols. 274–275ᵛ. Cf. *Les Interêts de l'Angleterre*, pp. 120–138.

175

of recognition. *Les Interêts de l'Angleterre*, like the other works of propaganda Torcy commissioned, was an instance of diplomacy carried on, it being wartime, by other means. Yet *Les Interêts de l'Angleterre* is far more than a book assembled from materials supplied by Torcy. Dubos drew heavily on his knowledge of English letters in using sources that neither Torcy nor La Chapelle could read. The depth of his arguments betrayed an intimate acquaintance with the contemporary polemical literature of the English political scene, and this awareness brought a new dimension to French propaganda. Thus, when Dubos took up the question of how England was enticed into making war, he went beyond the conspiracy theory of William's machinations propounded by Tallard's dispatches and echoed by La Chapelle. *Les Interêts de l'Angleterre* broadens the explanatory framework to include the Dutch, the Huguenots, and some self-seeking ministers and members of Parliament. William is said to have had the interests of the Dutch closest to his heart, and the Dutch emerge in Dubos' book as the direct competitors of England. Dubos played on the lively suspicions of many Englishmen that the Dutch king and his ministers had been bent on destroying English trade. In light of England's interests, Dubos contended that Dutch insecurity regarding their barrier was beneficial, since fear of France made the United Provinces dependent on England.[9] Now these notions all had a respectable lineage in English pamphlet literature. The Dutch alliance remained a source of alarm for many Englishmen and a subject of fearful doubt for more, so much so that when St. John and Harley finally determined to extract England from the Grand Alliance in 1711, they needed to do little more in the propaganda tracts they commissioned than revive and update the apprehension of the Dutch that was one of Dubos' themes in *Les Interêts de l'Angleterre*.[10]

[9] *Les Interêts de l'Angleterre*, pp. 182–192; on William's role, see esp. pp. 260 ff.
[10] On these points, Coombs, *Conduct of the Dutch, passim*, provides extensive evidence. See also below, chap. 8, nn. 92–102.

The Huguenots were closely tied to the Dutch in Dubos' argument. While the Dutch are called parasites, their territory and their commerce dismissed as artifices gained by robbing nature and the workingmen of other countries, the *lardon*-composing Huguenot exiles in Holland emerge as parasites on the parasites. According to Dubos, these "noisy martyrs" turned England against France, convincing Englishmen that the reestablishment of the Edict of Nantes might be forced upon Louis XIV. As La Chapelle was to remind a Swiss audience three years later, Dubos emphasized that the exiled Huguenots were of a foreign religion and culture and hence residents in but not loyal citizens of the land that had granted them refuge. The ostensible member of Commons congratulated his countrymen on their wisdom in instituting Navigation Acts to exclude Dutch commerce; he hoped they would show equal perceptiveness in resisting the imprecations of the similarly predatory French refugees.[11]

King William, Dutchmen, and Huguenots could not have misled Englishmen so completely, in Dubos' analysis, without considerable domestic assistance. This was available in the form of ambitious and unscrupulous men who, as William's creatures, became powerful in English government and enriched themselves through the shady techniques of war profiteering. These individuals came to dominate the royal councils, and in this way there was created a dominant private interest in public warfare. The grafters, Dubos proclaimed, wished to prolong the war both to increase their gain and to forestall investigation of their malfeasance.[12]

For these arguments, Dubos was indebted above all to Charles Davenant, who, as we have seen, reasoned along similar lines in his pamphlets of 1701. The abbé acquired copies of several of Davenant's works in 1702, thanks to the diligence of his most eminent English correspondent, John Locke, in filling Dubos' book orders.[13] The Frenchman's

[11] *Les Interêts de l'Angleterre*, pp. 147–148, 174–181, 249–259.
[12] *Ibid.*, pp. 6, 27, 248.
[13] G. Bonno, "Une amitié franco-anglaise du XVIIᵉ siècle: John

reliance on Davenant was acknowledged in the numerous footnotes Dubos provided; for this contrived, polemical work is marked by a conscientiousness of annotation appropriate to its intended scholarly audience. Five of Davenant's works are cited in *Les Interêts de l'Angleterre*.[14] Dubos quoted the Englishman's *Essay upon the Balance of Power* (1701) to verify the contention that Louis did not violate the partition treaty in accepting the Spanish testament. When he sought to impress Englishmen with the power of the French monarchy, Dubos scarcely could have found a better text than the long passage he printed from Davenant's *Ways and Means of Supporting the War* (1695), in which the Englishman praised the efficiency of French government since Richelieu's day and urged upon his countrymen the thought that after two years of famine and six campaigns the French could still be expected to fight on, imbued with love of nation and monarch.[15]

These partisan positions, however, are only the superficial aspect of Davenant's influence on Dubos. The inspiration of the entire first, more innovative half of *Les Interêts de l'Angleterre* can be attributed with only slight exaggeration to Charles Davenant's works on politics. His polemical essays are not important here; instead, Dubos drew on the concepts that underlay Davenant's treatises on the new science of political arithmetic. Dubos' purpose was to show the damage done England's economy by the war of 1689–1697 and the dislocations her trade would undergo in con-

Locke et l'abbé Du Bos," *Revue de littérature comparée*, 24 (1950), 512.

[14] Davenant's works and the places they are cited in *Les Interêts de l'Angleterre* are as follows: "On the Uses of Political Arithmetic," Part 1 of *Discourses on the Public Revenues and On the Trade of England* (1695), pp. 5, 72, 179; *On Our Public Payments* (1698), p. 14; *Discourse on the East Indies Trade* (1696), pp. 90, 101; *Essay upon the Balance of Power* (1701), pp. 139, 173; *Ways and Means of Supporting the War* (1695), pp. 222, 233 ff.

[15] *Les Interêts de l'Angleterre*, pp. 139, 233 ff.

tinued war against France and Spain. To this end he presented a detailed analysis of England's financial resources, as expressed in debts, tax revenues, and international exchange in goods and specie. This mode of inquiry, pioneered in England by Sir William Petty and closely related to Gregory King's statistical data on English population, can be regarded as the quantitative aspect of the politics of interest which European statesmen were espousing.[16] If men were creatures acting each one in his own best interest as he perceived it, and if politicians were to manipulate these interests to the best advantage of their countries, a certain knowledge of the foundation of men's interests was essential. In an age of great trust in the efficacy of mathematical and mechanical analysis, and especially in a state dependent on foreign commerce, the invention of a systematic technique for investigating the volume and return of the national financial resources quickly found practical applications.[17] One of the most interesting features of *Les Interêts de l'Angleterre*, then, is its appropriation of the techniques of political arithmetic. Not only could this approach lend credence to Dubos' English mask, but it served to place the book in the mainstream of the debate about English policy.

Dubos' thesis was that war was disastrous to England's welfare because of its adverse effect upon her essential foreign trade. War brought increased taxation, unavoidable wastage of public funds, and the export of English money for the upkeep of troops abroad. Between 1689 and 1697 the English excise revenue diminished by twenty percent, according to statistics cited by Dubos. Davenant, who administered the excise until 1690, had attributed this drop to mismanagement by his successors, but Dubos argued that it reflected a drop in England's total population, an illustra-

[16] Dubos cites Petty's *Political Arithmetic* (London, 1687) in a note on p. 72 of *Les Interêts de l'Angleterre*; he quotes King's statistics on poverty, *ibid.*, p. 26.

[17] J.A.W. Gunn, " 'Interest Will Not Lie,' A Seventeenth-Century Political Maxim," *Journal of the History of Ideas*, 29 (1968), 563.

tion of the misery induced by war.[18] Comparing England's financial status in 1703 with the conditions of 1689, he found much deterioration and little prospect for the comfortable upkeep of an expensive war.[19]

Dubos perceived correctly that the English government was dependent on credit for the success of its military effort. Unlike La Chapelle, he was aware of the strength of the system of government bonds: as long as the governed retained confidence in the crown, the private resources of the realm could be tapped for public purposes. The confidence of investors was founded on their trust in the stability of the regime and their faith in the government's willingness to stand by the debts it incurred. Dubos attacked these twin pillars of the English financial system by suggesting that the Stuart pretender, whom he portrayed as more moderate on the religious issue than James II, stood a good chance of restoration before the bonds were to fall due; James Edward would likely then renounce the crown's debts, both to punish his enemies and clear his ledgers. The implicit conclusion of Dubos' presentation is that prospective bond purchasers would be well advised to invest their capital elsewhere.[20] An unfortunate side effect of this argument was the encouragement it gave to fear of a Jacobite succession on the part of men who had lent money to the government. Dubos and Torcy, however, were willing to accept this unavoidable handicap; they would rather have relieved France of the war against England than of the Stuart court at Saint-Germain.

Quite aside from public finance, the commercial consequences of the war would be disastrous, according to Dubos. England's Spanish wool trade, lost to Flanders and France for the duration of the war, would not be easily regained. In a formulation nearly identical to La Chapelle's, Dubos compared commerce to a flowing stream: "Once a people is in possession of a particular trade, it is not easy to remove

---

[18] *Les Interêts de l'Angleterre*, pp. 1–8, 105–106.
[19] *Ibid.*, pp. 17–26. [20] *Ibid.*, pp. 25, 31–38.

them from it. Commerce is like a river, easily contained in its bed if one takes some care to keep up the dikes that limit it. But it requires infinite pains, huge expenditures and much time to return it to its bed after it has cleared its limits and taken a new course."[21] Not only will England's Spanish trade wither, but the war will strike all the other branches of her overseas commerce, Dubos continued. The Beauvais merchant's son demonstrated by an elaborate discussion of the varieties of English commerce that the Spanish succession war was global in scope. One year before England gained Gibraltar, Dubos wrote that the Mediterranean would be closed to English ships by Spanish control of the straits. In America the war would severely reduce the ability of the British to prevent smuggling and would thus defeat the intent of the Navigation Acts. By reopening hostilities with France, there was the danger of permitting further French expansion in North America. Meanwhile, trade with Spanish America would also suffer a setback.[22]

Dubos warned his English readers not to hope for the acquisition of Spanish possessions in the New World. In a unique and impressive section toward the end of his book, he pointed out the unlikelihood of Habsburg agreement to such a transfer and went on to observe that in any case the residents of the Indies would have to be conquered in a long and bitter struggle. Were the area pacified, within a decade it would revolt against the totally alien English religion, culture, and legal system.[23] In this passage Dubos demonstrated his comprehension of the fact that men are not motivated exclusively by rationally perceived goals accountable by the rules of political arithmetic.

This last perception became the kernel of Dubos' second

[21] *Ibid.*, pp. 55–61 (quotation, p. 58).

[22] *Ibid.*, pp. 72–106. Dubos' mercantile family connections in Beauvais may well have contributed to the commercial sensitivity of his works. Cf. Pierre Goubert, *Familles marchandes sous l'ancien régime* (Paris, 1960), p. 96n.

[23] *Les Interêts de l'Angleterre*, pp. 189–218.

major work of the War of the Spanish Succession, the *Histoire de la ligue faite à Cambray*, first published at Paris early in 1709. In the years intervening between the appearance of the *Interêts* and the *Ligue*, Dubos had pursued a number of ventures connected with diplomacy. He penned the curious *Manifeste de l'Electeur de Bavière* of 1704, which we will consider below in a chapter on princely propaganda. This work and the *Interêts* brought him an ecclesiastical benefice by way of reward, but he received no further payments from Torcy. Meanwhile, Dubos became involved in the periphery of the Neuchâtel succession dispute as secretary to Matignon when the contestants converged on Switzerland in 1707.[24] Then, in the latter stages of the war, Dubos served as secretary to Marshal d'Huxelles during the negotiations of Gertruydenberg in 1710 and performed analogous tasks at the conferences of Utrecht, Rastadt, and Baden that tied up the many diplomatic loose ends of the Spanish succession conflict. At none of these negotiations, however, was he specifically working under Torcy in the royal service. Secretaries of Louis' external agents were generally maintained by the diplomat, not by the crown, and as a rule the staff of an embassy was replaced when the diplomat-patron left his post. Indeed, it was the chaotic nature of this system that Torcy sought to alter by establishing a permanent staff of salaried royal secretaries to accompany diplomats on their missions.[25] Dubos' career in these years offers an example of the workings of the old system: never on the royal payroll, he was paid by d'Huxelles for his service at Gertruydenberg and Utrecht. At the latter conference he supplemented his income by acting as spokesman for several aristocrats who wished to forward their varied claims to the innumerable tiny territories tucked among the interstices of the

[24] Dangeau, *Journal*, entry for 16 June 1707, XI, 397; Dubos to Abbé de Camps, Neuchâtel, 26 September 1707, BN, N.a. fr. 7409, fols. 228–229; Matignon to Chamillart, Pontarlier, 20 October 1707, AG, A1. 2036, pièce 49. Lombard, *Du Bos*, pp. 118–120.

[25] Klaits, "Men of Letters," pp. 581–582.

emerging great powers. The huge circle of acquaintances Dubos had cultivated all over Europe gave him an entrée among the dignitaries of the peace talks. But it is important to recognize that this was free-lance work: Dubos never held Torcy's patronage in the way La Chapelle did, and this fact helps explain the meagerness of the rewards he reaped. Compounding his problems was d'Huxelles' inability to be of much help during the Utrecht talks; himself bitterly at odds with Torcy, the marshal was rewarded by being made governor of Alsace only after Louis had passed him over for two previously vacant governorships.[26]

Yet if Dubos' efforts at propaganda were intermittent and relatively unrewarding despite his thoroughness of scholarship and originality of method, his work for Torcy nevertheless contributed in a significant way to the development of his mature historical scholarship. The overlapping transition from propaganda polemic to serious history can be illustrated in his *Histoire de la ligue de Cambray*. This is an important work, reprinted several times in the eighteenth century and noteworthy as a milestone in historiography; Voltaire commented that it made known "the customs and *moeurs* of the time; it is a model of its genre."[27] Criticizing earlier writers on the subject for providing "a Collection of Relations" rather than "Methodical History," Dubos set out "to account for the Motives of this War" and "the several

---

[26] Torcy to d'Huxelles, 9 January 1713 (copy), AAE, CP, Hollande 240, fol. 211. On Dubos' disappointment with his meager rewards, see Fénelon to Dubos, Cambrai, 20 November 1713 and 22 December 1713, in Denis, *Correspondance*, pp. 198–199; and Fénelon to Dubos, 4 January 1714 and 4 August 1714, in Lombard, *Correspondance*, pp. 62–63.

[27] Quoted in Lombard, *Du Bos*, p. 409. In these notes the page references to Dubos' *Histoire de la ligue faite à Cambray* are from the more widely available Paris edition of 1785, with the exception of citations from the preface (in Roman numerals); Dubos made substantive changes in the preface of later printings, so we will use the original preface as translated in the London edition of 1712.

Interests of the Princes who waged it," drawing his evidence only "out of true Manuscripts, and sufficient Vouchers."

The League of Cambrai of 1508 must have been an event pregnant in its implications to a scholar who had the flash of insight to recognize the analogy of his own day to the circumstances of precisely two centuries past. For the league was a vast alliance of all the princes of Europe against the merchant republic of Venice. Here was a consortium of princes who were more accustomed to mutual enmity than to confederation. Here was the result of a policy of balance of power, rigorously applied by the Venetian senate and pursued to the point that even the republic's friends turned against her. Dubos found many contemporary lessons in the League of Cambrai, among them an explanation of the origins of the Grand Alliance of 1701 and the mechanism of balance of power diplomacy. Like many of his successors among Enlightenment historians, Dubos wished to teach by example, and he habitually courted anachronism in what Friedrich Meinecke called "his irresistible inclination to modernize the past."[28] This trait, while a defect in the writing of history, could not fail to strengthen Dubos' work as propaganda.

There is no firm evidence connecting Dubos' *Ligue de Cambray* with Torcy. Although the book was published in Paris by Florentin Delaulne, preferred printer of French propaganda, it bore the royal privilege, which of course never appeared on anonymous tracts of crown propaganda. But reviewers were quick to point out the relevance of the events discussed to the contemporary scene.[29] Very obvious were the repeated references to the modern imperial claims on Italy, where "an inch of land is more precious to the Emperor than whole provinces in other countries," and where the Habsburgs claimed imperial fiefs and the right

[28] Meinecke, "Montesquieu," p. 62.

[29] See *Journal de Trévoux*, December 1709, pp. 2049–2079; and the Dutch *Nouvelles de la République des Lettres*, October 1709, pp. 445–469.

to levy war contributions without limit.[30] The German diet could always be relied upon to foolishly subsidize imperial expeditions to Italy, Dubos wrote.[31] He even claimed that Emperor Maximilian had "wanted to have himself recognized as head of the church in his quality of emperor and to reunite in his person the spiritual power and the temporal power, as did the emperors of pagan Rome." One of the sources quoted for this assertion was a tract by Baron Karg, "a writer [unnamed in the text] equally respectable for his erudition as for his eminent offices."[32] Dubos' work was written at the end of 1708, while Torcy was trying to convince Italians of the danger represented by the German presence in their homeland.

One of the major theses of the *Ligue de Cambray* is that all the members of the league, Maximilian excepted, had followed a mistaken policy: "Of all the sovereigns who signed the League of Cambray, Maximilian was the only one whom the Venetians should properly have distrusted. It suited him alone to sign this agreement, which would put him in position to gain much without risking any loss."[33] The other members of the league allowed their interests to be overcome by their passions, and Dubos saw in 1709 that this was not an unusual phenomenon: "Sovereign Princes suffer themselves so often to be led blindly by their Passions, that it cannot reasonably be supposed, that their Honour or Interest is always the Rule of their Conduct."[34] Thus did Dubos go beyond the politics of interest in his historical analysis. Nevertheless, he held that the rules of interest soon reasserted themselves when the League of Cambrai fell apart. Here is Dubos' verdict on the misled leaguers: " . . . the

---

[30] *Ligue de Cambray* (1785), I, 11–14, 20, 24; cf. 215–216.

[31] *Ibid.*, p. 222.

[32] *Ibid.*, pp. 289–291; see also pp. 333–360 for a full-scale digression on imperial claims in Italy. Karg's tract is *Additions au Manifeste de l'Electeur de Bavière* (1705), discussed below, chap. 7.

[33] *Ligue de Cambray* (1785), I, 20.

[34] *League of Cambray* (1712), p. iii.

Princes who Sign'd it, found cause oftner than once to repent that ever they entered into that Confederacy. Endeavouring to be too good Friends, they became Mortal Enemies to one another. The Alliance they then contracted against their Essential Interests; which obliged them never to endeavour the promoting of each others Greatness, gave occasion to those Quarrels and Wars which would never have happened, but for that close Union they so inconsiderately made. States and Kingdoms whose constant Interests are Diametrically opposite, can never enter into a Close Alliance for any Transient Advantage, without exposing themselves to Complaints, Divisions, and Wars."[35] As we know, for eight years past Torcy's propaganda had reiterated the proposition that the War of the Spanish Succession was in the interests of the emperor alone and that other princes and states, if they once realized their own true advantage, would withdraw from the house of Austria's private quarrel. In this light, the *Ligue de Cambray* can be interpreted as encouragement of French readers to persevere in the expectation of the collapse of the artificial alliance which had been constructed against them. In a strange twist, the Venice of two centuries past came to represent the France of 1709, and Dubos concluded his discussion with this suggestive sentence: "We may justly look upon the League of Cambray as a piece of modern History, abounding with proper and seasonable Lessons for all Governments; and therefore it ought to be set out in its true and full Light."[36]

Yet the author was still left with a historical problem: What had provoked so many rulers to blind themselves to the interests of their states and embark on an irrational alliance against Venice? Dubos described and resolved the enigma in his preface:

It is no extraordinary thing to see several States combine against one that is more powerful than any or all of them, either to set bounds to its Greatness or to bring

---

[35] *Ibid.*, p. v.   [36] *Ibid.*

down its Exorbitant Power; but it is what very rarely happens, that several Soveraigns should confederate against one State, less powerful, than any of them, with a design to destroy it. Alliances of this kind seem so contrary to all the establish'd Rules of Policy, that one would think such Events impossible, were there not Instances to prove them practicable.

. . . It deserves the utmost Curiosity to search into the Motives that induced so many Princes to agree in laying aside those Maxims of State by which they usually regulate their Conduct; and to enquire, by what Fatality it was, that all the Conjectures of Wise Men at that time about future Events, proved, by what followed, to be no other than so much false Reasoning. The History of such Events teaches all States and Kingdoms, not to be absolutely Secure, but to fear Accidents, even where the greatest Humane Prudence tells them that they cannot possibly happen. . . .

And yet, notwithstanding what has been said, upon further Reflection, I cannot think, that the League of Cambray was so miraculous, as at first Sight it seems to have been. The Ballance of Power, that darling Chimera of so many Politicians, which the Venetians endeavour'd to establish among their Neighbours, with so much Exactness and Evenness, without any Regard to the just Rights of Princes, or their own Alliances, did by a certain Counter-blow, really prove the necessary Cause of the League of Cambray. The Friends of the Republick, being weary of its Conduct, conceived a Disgust against them, as being Allies who little regarded any Ties or Obligations. The Haughtiness and Covetousness of the Venetians had exasperated their Enemies to such a Degree, as cut of[f] all Hopes of a sincere Reconciliation by any Treaty. And therefore it was, that both Friends and Enemies uniting in a perfect Aversion against them, and that producing a mutual Confidence, they all combin'd the Ruin of that Repub-

lick, whose Conduct and Practices had given so great
Disgust and Mortification to all the World.[37]

Dubos thus explained the irrationality of the league as the
result of Venice's assiduous devotion to balance of power
politics. He went on to generalize his findings: "The usual
chimera of flourishing republics is to establish a balance of
power among their neighboring princes, although the inclinations of peoples, the maxims of states, changes of reign
and internal revolutions render this point of equilibrium
impossible to recognize and often dangerous to seek."[38] Republics, then, are identified in Dubos' history with the illusory doctrine of the balance of power, a concept that can
only confuse rulers about their true interest. In this way the
Histoire de la Ligue de Cambray supplements and justifies
Les Interêts de l'Angleterre, arguing by implicit analogy
that the conclusions of the earlier work remain valid and
that England, like the other states of the Grand Alliance,
was being misled by the balance of power theories of the
Dutch.

The Holland of the early eighteenth century is never far
below the surface in Dubos' discussion of Venice in the
sixteenth, although to the credit of Dubos' scholarship he
refrained from drawing overfacile parallels between the
two commercial states; Dubos knew that Venice's enemies,
unlike Holland's, were not primarily motivated by an interest in controlling trade.[39] Hence there is in the history of the
League of Cambrai an important moral for the Dutch, a
warning to avoid rigid adherence to balance of power principles, lest Holland, though apparently at the height of her
power, find all Europe suddenly banded against her: "By
all the ordinary Rules of Politicks, the Republick of Venice
was in full Security, in the Year 1508. . . . Never had the
Republick of Venice been so Powerful, as it was at that

[37] *Ibid.*, pp. i–iii.
[38] *Ligue de Cambray* (1785), pp. 50–51.
[39] *League of Cambray* (1712), pp. iv–v.

Time; nor were ever their Neighbours, in all Appearance, less in a Condition to give them any Alarm or Disturbance than they were then."[40]

The original Paris printing of the *Ligue* was supplemented in 1710 by two editions published at The Hague and an English translation of 1712. The book's emphasis on the idea of the balance of power surely contributed to its popularity, for this was a prominent concept in anti-French polemic of Louis XIV's era, and at no time more so than during the War of the Spanish Succession. Much of the pamphlet controversy that swirled in England at either end of this war revolved around this subject, and it had become traditional for Louis XIV's apologists to argue against the validity of the balance of power concept.[41] What Dubos contributed to this debate was a large dose of skepticism about the optimistic assumption underlying balance of power diplomacy, that man had the ability to control his environment by reason. Dubos reminded his readers that any artificial effort to mechanically achieve equilibrium must sooner or later collapse against the weight of more solid, "natural" interests. At a time when the victorious allies began to extend their balance of power theses to the logical conclusion of dismembering France or reforming her government, Dubos called attention to the theoretical weaknesses of their position.[42] Other French propagandists whose works we shall examine below would soon respond to this threat on a less abstract level.

There is no need for recourse to conspiratorial hypotheses for an explanation of the contemporary analogies Dubos

[40] *Ibid.*, p. ii.
[41] See Herbert Butterfield, "The Balance of Power," in *Diplomatic Investigations, Essays in the Theory of International Politics*, ed. Herbert Butterfield (London, 1966), p. 139; and Meyer, *Flugschriften*, pp. 209–210.
[42] Cf. M. S. Anderson, "Eighteenth-Century Theories of the Balance of Power," in *Studies in Diplomatic History, Essays in Memory of David Bayne Horne*, ed. R. Hatton and M. S. Anderson (London, 1970), pp. 183–198.

drew in his *Ligue de Cambray*. It is most unlikely that he and Torcy plotted to deceive the public with a work of propaganda disguised as history. Instead, the lesson of the analogies lies in the close relationship they reveal between scholarly history and French war propaganda. In Torcy's view propaganda tracts were a means of enlightenment by which men's true interests were made known to them. This is very close to the eighteenth-century idea of history writing, a conception of which Dubos was an originator and practitioner. Further, the methods of doing history and the sort of propaganda Torcy favored were virtually identical. We have seen how much the tenets of French propaganda depended on an understanding of public law. It should be noted in this regard that Dubos considered his discussion of the sources of public law invoked in the League of Cambrai as the most original of his history's contributions.[43] There is a direct line from the investigations of the historical aspects of public law in his wartime books to his brilliant and exhaustive treatment of the same species of source material in Dubos' masterwork, the *Histoire critique de l'établissement de la Monarchie française* (1734). Dubos' foremost biographer remarked correctly that "his diplomatic efforts, far from having taught him the art of rapid improvisation and bold simplification, on the contrary augmented his scrupulousness in revealing to him the multiplicity of the sources and the immense richness of the historical literature."[44] In the *Ligue de Cambray* Dubos had accomplished a feat rare in the French historiography of Louis XIV's time: he successfully applied the fruits of erudition to a narrative and then derived general conclusions from the evidence. In bridging the gap between the textual analysis of the *érudit* and the didactic and literary concerns of general histories, Dubos was moving toward modern principles of historical writing.

Nor was the identification of history and propaganda a

[43] *League of Cambray* (1712), pp. v–ix.
[44] Lombard, *Du Bos*, p. 391.

trait peculiar to Dubos among Torcy's propagandists. As soon as the foreign minister saw La Chapelle's talent as a writer, he put him to work on a history of the partition treaties drawn from the original sources in the foreign ministry archives. La Chapelle, overwhelmed by what he called the "*mare magnum*" of the materials, soon abandoned this project, and so it is interesting to observe that when Torcy established the curriculum for his Académie politique in 1711 he made the historical analysis and summary of these dispatches one of the assignments of the students.[45] As for Joachim Legrand, a propagandist we will meet later, he was already a published historian and an experienced archivist when he came to work in Torcy's bureau. Clearly the foreign minister had a deep sense of the historical responsibilities of his office. This emerges in the reorganization he initiated of the archives of foreign affairs,[46] as well as in his careful attention to the need for historical veracity in his *Mémoires*, expressed in this prefatory remark: "Those who love truth would be sorry it lay buried in obscurity; . . . it is full time that those who have been let into the secret, should prepare and leave to their children such memoirs or papers, as shall one day inform posterity."[47]

In an important sense, then, Dubos' history-laden propaganda works can be regarded as Torcy's modernization of the crown's traditional use of official historiography to record, interpret and defend the actions of Louis XIV. History, in fact, had been underused in royal propaganda through most of the reign. Thus, the most notable omission from the list of royally sponsored academies under the Sun King was a body devoted to the study of history. To be sure, the Academy of Inscriptions and Medals often used historical materials in its research, but this body's concern with the past, as stated in its *règlement*, was principally limited to the hagiographical task of lauding "the memory of famous

[45] La Chapelle to Puyzieulx, Paris, 12 February 1703, AAE, CP, Suisse 143, fols. 117–118; Klaits, "Men of Letters," p. 592.

[46] Baschet, *Dépôt*, pp. 101–117.   [47] Torcy, *Memoirs*, 1, 2.

men and their good works."[48] History as such was not institutionalized in an academy patronized by the crown. Fontenelle tells us that in the 1660's there was a proposal to include historical studies in the planned Academy of Sciences, but that history was dropped because it involved too many sensitive issues, particularly matters of public law.[49] Academic debates on historical themes could easily acquire contemporary relevance, while academicians working with archival sources might publicize state secrets. Jean Chapelain, Colbert's literary adviser, had already counseled against hiring historians to recount the king's glory, even while he urged subsidies to composers of panegyrics and creators of various forms of visual display. These hesitations reflect the memory of the Fronde and the wars of religion, during both of which historians and jurists had drawn anti-monarchical conclusions from their sources. Such writers cast a long shadow, one that could not but look menacing to Louis XIV's ministers.

More fundamentally, critical historical analysis in itself was deemed potentially subversive of Louis XIV's absolutism. Divine-right monarchy under the Sun King was constructed upon principles which explicitly eliminated sovereignty from the realm of the rational and consigned it instead to the shadowy world of authority and tradition. For a subject to treat politics in a rationally analytical way smacked of subversion, since in the official view monarchy was at its heart a sacred mystery beyond the powers of mortal men to penetrate. Only a churchman like Bossuet might attempt to interpret these matters in light of scriptural revelation. Better to raise statecraft to the plane of mystery than to test the authority of the king in the crucible of historical disputation, reasoned the king's servants early in

[48] *Lettres patentes du Roy qui confirment l'établissement des Académies royales des inscriptions et des sciences, avec les règlements pour lesdites deux académies* (Paris, 1713), p. 5.
[49] Yates, *French Academies*, p. 304n. Cf. Charles Perrault's note to Colbert, in Clément, *Lettres . . . de Colbert*, v:512–513.

the reign. Thus, while Colbert did bestow *gratifications* on a number of Frenchmen to undertake historical works, nearly all the writers were innocuous: either *érudits* whose interests were entirely antiquarian or official royal historiographers, all of whom—except for Mézeray, who proves the point because he was dismissed for an excess of independence in publishing his views—produced little history printed during the Sun King's reign. These political biases against historical analysis seem to have exerted a stultifying influence on the development of the discipline through most of the Sun King's reign.[50] Torcy's biases, however, were clearly in favor of history as a medium of royal publicity and justification. The habitual use of documentary materials in the propaganda works he commissioned points to the foreign minister's conviction that the historical record could serve as an effective response to the accusations lodged against Louis XIV by his foreign enemies and domestic critics.

[50] Cf. William F. Church, "France," in Orest Ranum, ed., *National Consciousness, History and Political Culture in Early Modern Europe* (Baltimore, 1975), pp. 54–58; Roger Chartier, "Comment on écrivait l'histoire au temps des guerres de religion," *Annales-E.S.C.,* 29 (1974), 886–887.

CHAPTER SEVEN

Princely Propaganda and the Crisis
of 1709–1710

THE TRADITION

THIS investigation of French propaganda during the War of the Spanish Succession has emphasized up to now the government's sponsorship of anonymous works which camouflaged their connection with the crown. We have also considered the propaganda of Louis XIV's diplomats, hedged about as it was by the restrictions derived from their status as personal representatives of the monarch. Where in all this propaganda was the king himself? Was any propaganda written by or ascribed to Louis?

In fact, the dominant conceptions of royal dignity in seventeenth-century France traditionally prohibited the king from engaging in all but the most formal kinds of public address. Laconic edicts, ordinances, and letters to prelates were deemed appropriate, and the monarch often sent reserved memoirs via his diplomats to inform foreign governments of his will; but this was all. Official statements by the king or his representatives arguing a thesis, presenting a point of view for discussion, or requesting assistance were noticeably absent through most of the reign, a gap reflecting the prevailing popular image in France of the monarch as a sacred personage. Ritual and panegyric, which emphasized essentially mythic portrayals of the monarch as a priestly or military hero endowed with supernatural attributes, remained the preferred mode of royal representation before 1700.

To the extent that traditional assumptions about the nature of authority still characterized the European cultural universe, their force also made it unnecessary for Louis to explain his actions to non-French audiences. Plainly, the image of heroic absolute monarchy personified by the Grand Monarch evoked awe, esteem, and imitation all over Europe. But after 1680, when Louis' growing reputation for bellicosity reacted upon newly emerging patterns of political thought, the model of the Sun King began to tarnish rapidly. The communications revolution manifested in the growth of the printed news periodical and the proliferation of political pamphlets was one symptom of a European consciousness which was beginning to see rulers less in mythic terms drawn from religious and poetic imagery and more in a rigorous framework of contract and reciprocal obligation. But this mentality came relatively late to France, where the *Gazette* continued its role of Platonic edification in narratives evoking the grandeur of aristocratic achievement, and where Louis XIV continued to be portrayed and to address his subjects in time-honored formulas.

Until Torcy's arrival in the king's council, none of Louis XIV's later ministers exhibited any degree of sensitivity to the need for effective printed propaganda signed by the king. Before 1700 Louis XIV issued only one set of war manifestos presenting a logical argument. This occurred in 1688, when the government published two documents over the king's name: a letter to Pope Innocent XI and a declaration to the German princes.[1] Both these public letters accompanied aggressive actions by the king, in the latter case the attack that began the War of the League of Augsburg. Interpreted abroad as ultimata, the manifestos comprised a propaganda disaster that served, if at all, to unify foreign opposition to Louis. Their tone of hauteur, disdain, and intimidation reflected the utter incapacity of the royal government to respond effectively in the light of changing conditions of public opinion. As an anti-French publicist

[1] See above, chap. 4, n. 16.

summed it up: "It is hardly the custom in France . . . to publish manifestos and apologies. The thing has worked out so badly that they have practically abandoned that method, provided as they are with other, more certain means of attracting, if not approbation and praise, at least respect and fear from those who bear witness of doubt as to the justice of their cause."[2]

Even in the first years of the Spanish succession war there was no departure from the pattern of official royal silence. The absence of systematic publicity justifying Louis' acceptance of Charles II's testament indicated that in 1700 the policy of royal nonresponsiveness still remained intact. Although Torcy sent detailed explanations of the king's rationale to French agents for their use in private diplomacy,[3] Louis engaged in no public, signed attempts to explain his apparent rejection of the partition treaties. The king's legal case for accepting the testament was in fact quite solid, but it emerged only in scattered, incomplete form as an element of the published memoirs delivered early in 1701 by d'Avaux, the king's plenipotentiary to the Dutch.[4]

While Leopold and the imperial diet used their declarations of war against France as excuses for lengthy justificatory manifestos,[5] Louis' war ordinance of July 1702[6] is nothing more than a brief formula, fully half of which is taken up with the niceties of commencing wars: closing the bor-

---

[2] Casimir Freschot, *Réponce au manifeste qui court sous le nom de S.A. Electorale de Bavière ou Réflexions sur les raisons qui y sont déduites pour la justification de ses armes* (Pamplona, 1705), pp. 3-4.

[3] See Louis' letters to Blécourt and Dupré, in A. Legrelle, *La Diplomatie française et la succession d'Espagne*, 6 vols. (Paris, 1895-1899), IV, 183-187; also Louis to Briord, 14 November 1700 (minute), AAE, CP, Hollande 190, fols. 26-30ᵛ.

[4] These memoranda are reprinted in Lamberty, *Mémoires*, I, 221-227, 390, 391-395, 396-397, 483 ff.; II, 91.

[5] The declarations of war of the United Provinces, the emperor and the imperial diet are reprinted *ibid.*, II, 107-117, 213-216.

[6] *Ordonnance du Roy, portant déclaration de Guerre contre l'Empereur, l'Angleterre, les Etats-Généraux des Provinces-Unies et leurs alliez du 3. Juillet 1702*; reprinted *ibid.*, II, 208-209.

ders, revocation of passports, and so on. The king barely allowed himself an allusion to the justice of his cause before rushing on to the orders and the signature. The ordinance mentioned the manifestos of the allies, but only as examples of enemy treachery, not by way of rebuttal. This declaration simply expressed the royal will without attempting to justify it.

In the next eighteen months the allied governments issued several more signed manifestos on various aspects of the war,[7] and this fact did not fail to make an impression on Torcy. Very early in the *Lettres d'un suisse* La Chapelle began to rebut the manifestos of enemy leaders, a practice that became a regular feature of his pamphlets.[8] The minister and the propagandist knew that, in addition to substantive refutation, the *Lettres* needed to present some explanation for official Bourbon silence. Thus we find the Swiss of 1702 and 1703 labeling the declarations of Louis' enemies as scurrilous, libelous, and unworthy of response: "I am not surprised that neither the King of France nor the King of Spain has had issued any response to the latest manifesto addressed to the peoples of Spain under the Emperor's name."[9] "The edict of M. de Darmstadt is, strictly speaking, nothing more than the harangue of a seditious declaimer who exhorts peoples to destroy the legitimate authorities, to plunder the rich, to slaughter the grandees and to invade their estates; and who promises rebels immunity for their crimes. If those who speak and act this way are the fathers of their country, who are the ones we should regard as its enemies?"[10] Again, in reply to the archduke's manifesto of 1704, the Swiss wrote: "It is not surprising that this august house [of Bourbon] disdains to respond to such chimerical predictions and to coarse insults. Invective is the lot of those with a weak and

---

[7] See, for instance, the manifesto of August 1702 by Landgrave George of Hesse; reprinted in *LS* 2, 1:165–189, and as a supplement to *LS*, IV.

[8] *LS* 2, *LS* 5, *LS* 12, *LS* 22, *LS* 23.

[9] *LS* 2, 1:19. [10] *Ibid.*, pp. 28–29.

unjust cause. The Kings of France and Spain . . . content themselves with supporting the justice of their cause by the force of their arms."[11]

A change of policy would have served Torcy's purposes far better than the reiteration of excuses made lamely obsolete by the new circumstances of public opinion, and the change began to appear at the end of 1703. When the crown published Louis' declaration of war against Victor Amadeus of Savoy,[12] Frenchmen and foreigners read a document several times longer than the war declaration of 1702. The very first words of the Savoy order made clear that the king intended to answer "the manifesto distributed by the Duke of Savoy in his states for the purpose of engaging his subjects to take up arms for their preservation." Even though Victor's duplicity was well known, Louis' order continued, his manifestos "might have produced some effect upon people's minds" and consequently required refutation. Louis then proceeded to a sober narrative of his relations with the duke since 1696, the purpose of which was to demonstrate Victor's ingratitude and treachery in contrast to the French king's consistent spirit of compromise and reasonable approach to their differences.

One month later, in January 1704, the crown made public a long letter by Louis to Pope Clement XI, recounting in much greater detail the purported indignities he had suffered at the hands of Victor Amadeus.[13] The letter even included excerpts from diplomatic correspondence as corroboration of the royal thesis. In dispatches from Victor to Leopold I and William III the Savoyard double game was revealed in irrefutable detail. And, Louis told the pope, Victor had also plotted with the other Protestant allies to support the Huguenot "fanatics of Languedoc" and to arouse the Protestants of the Dauphiné against their king.

[11] *LS* 22, IV: 129–130.

[12] *Ordonnance du Roy, portant déclaration de guerre contre le Duc de Savoye, du 4. Decembre 1703* (Paris, 1703).

[13] *Lettre du Roy au Pape contenant les motifs de la guerre de Savoye* (Paris, 1704).

Torcy was the author of both the war ordinance and the papal letter. He was also the source of the pressure to make of these documents lengthy and public apologies.[14] Supported by Puyzieulx, who wrote from Switzerland that "if His Majesty would deign to have circulated a manifesto explaining why he had the Duke of Savoy's troops disarmed and his own troops enter that prince's territories, it would have a wonderful effect on the next diet," Torcy's response was the declaration of war ordinance.[15] Permission to print the letter to Clement with its excerpts from confidential dispatches and the concession that the king was troubled by domestic rebellion was more difficult to extract; only after it arrived in Rome was the decision taken, as Torcy told Puyzieulx, "to give it to the public."[16]

Both documents were widely circulated in print, particularly to a French audience. The ordinance went through three printings in Paris alone, while the letter to the pope was published by Florentin Delaulne in Paris and by provincial printers who had purchased the rights of republication. This letter also appeared in at least one Dutch and two Italian editions, and Puyzieulx saw to its reprinting in Switzerland.[17] Clearly, by 1704 there were influential members of the royal service who believed in the benefits of signed royal printed propaganda and had prevailed upon Louis to allow them to act in his name.

Consequently, in a *Lettre d'un suisse* published in June

[14] Baschet, *Archives*, p. 128.

[15] Puyzieulx to Torcy, Soleure, 20 November 1703, AAE, CP, Suisse 142, fols. 101v–102v.

[16] Torcy to Puyzieulx, Versailles, 30 January 1704, AAE, CP, Suisse 147, fol. 244.

[17] Italian: BN, Imp., 4° Lb37.5229; Dutch: BN, Imp., 4° Lb37.4237. bis. Both crown letters were reprinted in Dutch periodicals and appeared in *The Present State of Europe*, December 1703, pp. 482–484; March 1704, pp. 92–102. Provincial editions were Rouen: BN, Imp., 4° Lb37.4237B; Lyon: BN, Imp., 8° Lb37.4237C. Both these editions contain privileges revealing their links with Delaulne; see also the privilege in Delaulne's Paris edition, BN, Imp., 4° Lb37.4237.

1704, La Chapelle—who also had urged upon Torcy the printing of the papal letter—could gloat over the contrast between Louis' explicitly forthright declarations and an anonymous manifesto issued on behalf of the king of Portugal. Forgetting his excuses for Bourbon silence, the Swiss exulted:

> All these manifestos in which kings do not speak for themselves or do not instead have some estimable and well-known personage speak on their behalf fail to garner my respect and find no credence with me. I regard them as libels filled with falsehoods, not at all as sincere explications of royal rights. The declaration of war is the most important and the most lofty action of the ministry which God has conferred upon kings in this world. It is in this action that they resemble God most closely, speaking, like Him, amidst lightning and thunder. Why are they heard, in the awe that should accompany their thoughts, in an anonymous, indistinct voice, subject to disavowal, rather than in their own voices? Is it not because in this way they tacitly acknowledge that they have no grounds, or that their false, frivolous, and unworthy grounds would shame them if revealed?

The Swiss concluded that kings had a personal obligation "to inform their subjects of major resolutions whose consequences will be felt throughout the world."[18]

It is fascinating to find La Chapelle expressing his justification of Louis' printed, signed manifestos in the most old-fashioned terms imaginable. His evocation of the semidivine warrior-monarch can be understood as an attempt, perhaps an unconscious one, to find links between the traditional expression of royal authority in metaphorical imagery and a new mode of representation dependent upon docu-

---

[18] *LS* 23, IV:215–216. La Chapelle to Puyzieulx, 20 January 1704, AAE, CP, Suisse 151, fol. 32; La Chapelle to Puyzieulx, Paris, 13 February 1704, *ibid.*, fol. 45.

mentary evidence and historical debate. Louis' Savoy letters of 1703–1704 appeal to reason and to rational principles of political equity. Their rhetoric is that of the diplomatic dispatch or indeed the political pamphlet, and their foundation lies in the source materials of the historical record. Despite La Chapelle's claims, Louis spoke to Europeans not with the absolute monarchical trappings of "thunder and lightning" but in the same naturalistic framework of political logic shared by a pamphlet- and gazette-reading European public.

As 1704 began, the confidence of the French court ran high. Despite the defections of Savoy and Portugal and the check of the 1703 campaign in Germany, Louis and his ministers looked forward to military success on the Danube leading to a peace that would cap the Sun King's triumphs. The signed royal propaganda of this moment mirrored the crown's hopes. One more reflection of royal ambitions is provided by an additional crown-sponsored manifesto of 1704, written in the name of the French-allied Elector Max Emmanuel of Bavaria. Published first in French under the title *Manifeste de l'Electeur de Bavière*, this document was composed by Dubos with the help of Torcy and Monasterol, Max's minister at Versailles.[19] Its initial purpose was to support the anticipated military successes of French and Bavarian forces in Germany; accordingly, the manifesto adopted the technique of Louis' Savoy letters, explicitly rebutting the emperor's proclamations against Max by a review of events between 1698 and 1703. This account was meant to show that "His Imperial Majesty declar'd War against me, only because I refus'd to make War to assist him to Dethrone the King of Spain my Nephew; and because I would not take up Arms against France, and without cause break the Solemn treaty that I sign'd at Reswick with the most Christian King."[20] After

[19] On Dubos' authorship, see Lombard, *Du Bos*, pp. 111–115.
[20] *The Manifesto of the Elector of Bavaria* (London, 1704), p. 4 (in the Special Collections, Columbia University Library).

taking the public into his confidence, the elector drew the lesson of the narrative:

> My Cause is that of my Country. The House of Austria, after many Infractions upon the Constitutions of the Empire, wanted but one step more to turn it into a Monarchy, and that was to be in a condition to oblige the Empire to make Peace and War at their Pleasures. This they attempted, and many submitted for want of sufficient Force to oppose; others wanted Courage, some were reduc'd; and in short, all of them show'd a Patience that was formerly unknown to Germany. Mine happen'd to be the only Family that had both the necessary Valour and Forces to oppose the Torrent. If it had once bore me down, nothing else could have stopp'd its Current. After having examined my Conduct, if any one carefully weigh that of the Emperor, since the Peace of Reswick, it will be easie to know who is the Author of the Troubles in Germany.[21]

More broadly, the electoral manifesto also insisted on the menace of Habsburg ambitions to other European states. When Philip succeeded to the Spanish crown, for example, the emperor immediately decided upon war; "he took no notice of the Unanimous Consent of the Spaniards to submit themselves to this Prince, without remembering that 12 years before, he made so great account of the Consent of the English, to raise to their throne William III whom for that reason he own'd to be King of England without hesitation."[22] As for the empire, Max's manifesto held up the prospect of universal ruin:

> The Grandeur and Power to which the House of Austria is arrived, does already threaten too much the Liberty of Germany, without such an Augmentation

[21] *Ibid.*, p. 16.   [22] *Ibid.*, p. 7.

of Credit as to have a King of Spain Brother to the Emperor. . . .

Besides the Empire's form of Government stands in need of Peace to maintain it. That alone assures the Liberty of the publick, and the Rights of particular Persons. War puts the Weak in the Mercy of the Strong, whose Usurpations are pass'd over, because their assistance is necessary, and then both one and t'other are exposed to the Capricio's and Views of an Emperor, armed at the Expence of the Empire. For he has the sole Right during the War to put in Execution the Resolves of the Empire, with an Absolute power which exempts him from taking the advice of the Diet, as to his Conduct, or to account to them for it. He has an opportunity to enlarge his Authority, to mortifie those who dare quote Laws contrary to his Will, to Levy the Roman Months as he pleases, to make himself Master of Elections, and to put Garison where he thinks fit, under the Specious pretext of curbing those who are disaffected.

An Emperor has 1,000 other occasions, in War, to enrich by Arbitrary Winter quarters, the Princes and Generals of the Circles that devote themselves to his Interests; and in short every day to commit new Violences, under the specious pretext of the necessity of the Times and the publick Good, which will not allow him to act conformable to the Rules prescribed by the Constitutions of the Empire.[23]

The *Manifeste de l'Electeur de Bavière* appropriated the main theses of Torcy's pamphlet propaganda and planted them in the context of a historical narrative above a princely signature. But this document met with mixed success in the Europe of late 1704 and 1705. It was composed in the full expectation of an imminent military tri-

[23] *Ibid.*, pp. 8–9.

umph, but Torcy's order to d'Argenson for printing the manifesto went out only two days before the news of Blenheim reached Versailles.[24] After some hesitation, Torcy released it anyway,[25] and within a year the tract had appeared in many reprintings and at least three translations,[26] as well as several new editions augmented by the supplements of Baron Karg.[27] Unfortunately for Max, the

[24] D'Argenson to Torcy, Paris, 22 August 1704, AAE, CP, Bavière 50, fol. 74: "Je n'ay receu que ce matin la lettre que vous m'avez fait l'honneur de m'escrire le 19° de ce mois pour permettre l'impression du Manifeste de Mr. l'Electeur de Baviere et je vous supplie de me faire scavoir si les nouvelles circonstances ne changent rien à l'ordre qu'il vous a plu de me donner."

[25] Abbé de Pomponne to Dubos, Fontainebleau, 14 October 1704, in Denis, *Lettres*, pp. 183–184: "Je n'ay point ouy rien dire icy sur la publication du Manifeste de l'Electeur." Karg to Torcy, Lille, 7 November 1704, AAE, CP, Bavière 49, fol. 93: "Monseigneur le Marechal de Boufflers souhaitant d'avoir encore quelques exemplaires du petit Imprimé qui paroit depuis peu sous le titre du Manifeste de l'Electeur de Baviere." According to Léonard's notes, AN, K. 1305, No. 33, Dubos' *Manifeste* appeared in Lyon at the beginning of October 1704.

[26] Three French editions are in BN, Imp.: (1) M. 29419; (2) Mp. 845; (3) Mz. 4024, Mz. 4676, Mz. 4939. These editions have slight verbal variations but are substantially identical. Copies of two other editions, both dated Brussels, 1704, are AN, K. 1305, Nos. 30¹, 30². Italian: *Manifeste de l'Electeur de Bavière. Manifesto dell'Elettor di Baveria* (French-Italian versions in parallel columns), BN, Imp., M. 11476; German: *Europäische Fama*, No. 30 (1704), pp. 388–425; English: *Manifesto of the Elector of Bavaria*. For a review of the variants in some of these editions, see F. Feldmeier, "Das angebliche kurbayerische Manifest von 1704," *Oberbayerisches Archiv für vaterländische Geschichte*, 61 (1918), 198–208.

[27] The augmented version is *Manifeste de l'Electeur de Bavière* (n.p., 1705), BN, Imp., M. 14612, M. 15199, M. 29417. The new section follows the original text under the heading "Additions de ce qui est le plus essentiel dans le Manifeste de l'Electeur de Cologne." On Karg's editions, see Karg to Torcy, Lille, 6 December 1704, AAE, CP, Bavière 49, fol. 150: "Voici une apologie pour mon Ser^me Maitre, faite en forme d'addition au manifest de SAE de Baviere pour en mieux cacher l'Auteur." Karg sent virtually identical announcements to Rouillé (AAE, CP, Cologne 56, fol. 158) and Chamillart (AG, A1. 1739, pièce 150). Also see Karg to Torcy, Lille, 16 March 1705, AAE,

self-assured tone of the manifesto no longer conformed to his reduced condition. Exiled to the Spanish Netherlands, the elector felt compelled to disown his manifesto in letters to various German princes and even to his wife, a daughter of the Habsburgs. In these letters Max protested that he had known nothing of the work until he found it on public sale, and he blamed "the zeal of a man in France who produced it," as well as Karg, "who furnished the substance and had it printed."[28] Well might the elector deny a manifesto written before the debacle of August 1704, for the immediate repercussion of its publication was an increased sentiment on the part of his enemies to place Max under imperial ban.[29] Indeed, the text seems to foresee this:

CP, Cologne 57, fol. 46 (in Feldmeier, "Manifest," pp. 215–216); Torcy to Karg, Versailles, 18 March 1705, AAE, CP, Cologne 57, fol. 47 (in *ibid.*, p. 215); Rouillé to Karg, 23 March 1705, AAE, CP, Cologne 56, fol. 140ᵛ (in Ennen, *Erbfolgekrieg*, p. xlii). On the circulation of the *Manifeste*, see Karg to Torcy, Lille, 7 November 1704, AAE, CP, Bavière 49, fol. 93; Karg to Torcy, Lille, 6 December 1704, AAE, CP, Bavière 49, fol. 150, asking permission "d'envoyer quelques centaines d'exemplaires à Paris, pour qu'on les y puisse vendre publiquement"; and a memorandum by La Chapelle, AG, A1. 1739, pièce 151, arguing against allowing the circulation of Karg's expanded edition in Paris primarily because of its barbarous style, but additionally on the grounds that the *Lettres d'un suisse* had presented Karg's theses long before and thus the "Additions" were superfluous. In *LS* 28, v:131–133, published in December 1704, La Chapelle praised the *Manifeste* and its "Additions" but attributed the following sentiment to a Swabian correspondent: "On n'avoit besoin ny du Manifeste, ny des additions pour estre persuadé, que la guerre presente estoit une guerre de la Maison d'Autriche."

[28] Max to Marie Casimir, Brussels, 23 December 1704; Max to Therese Kunegunde, Brussels, 19 January 1705; both quoted in Feldmeier, "Manifest," p. 213.

[29] Therese Kunegunde to Max, Munich, 7 January 1705: "On dit, qu'à Ratisbonne ils en sont fort irrités." Bequet to Malknecht, Munich, 10 January 1705: "Le Manifest francois de S.A.E. y [at Ratisbon] faisoit grant bruit, et qu'il paroissoit fort sensible aux Imperiaux, et que Sa dite Altesse E. etoit menacé d'etre mis en bann de l'Empire." Both letters are quoted in Feldmeier, "Manifest," pp. 213 ff.

as explanation for the delay in answering the long-standing imperial charges against Max, the author wrote that he "was not ignorant that it would have heightened their Resentments more against me, to have discovered their Weakness and Breach of Faith, than to have taken their towns, or defeated their Armies."[30]

Here then was the negative side of signed princely propaganda. Unshielded by the camouflage of anonymous writers, the sovereign who published in his own name risked standing naked before his enemies; only a ruler confident of his strength could successfully run the risk. Torcy's brother-in-law and diplomatic colleague, the abbé de Pomponne, remarked that although the arguments of the *Manifeste de l'Electeur de Bavière* were well supported the only truly adequate buttress would be an army of fifty thousand men to replace the one lost at Blenheim.[31] Without military might to back them up, signed propaganda pieces seemed useless, even harmful. In those days of personal politics, every printed attack upon the enemy had to be weighed carefully against the measure of rancor it might provoke. Signed propaganda was powerful medicine, apt to poison the diplomacy of exposed princes. More, for a ruler, and especially the ruler of France, to adopt the style of an anonymous pamphleteer implied the abandonment of his traditional suprahuman status. Only a French king very confident of his political situation at home and his military

---

[30] *Manifesto of the Elector of Bavaria*, p. 4.

[31] Pomponne to Dubos, Fontainebleau, 14 October 1704, in Denis, *Lettres*, pp. 183–184. This sentiment helps explain Dubos' unwillingness to compose a rebuttal of Freschot's *Réponce* to the electoral manifesto. See Dubos to Bayle, 25 July 1705, in Gigas, *Choix*, pp. 306–307; and Bayle to Dubos, Rotterdam, 6 August 1705, in Bayle, *Oeuvres diverses*, IV, 857–858. Dubos may also have written the *Mémoire en forme du manifeste des raisons alléguées par les Mécontens de Hongrie* (1705), attached to the sixth volume of the *Lettres d'un suisse* (Lombard, *Du Bos*, p. 549); according to Köpeczi, *La France et la Hongrie*, pp. 377, 383–385, this tract did not come from Rákóczi's supporters but probably had a French origin.

strength abroad—as was Louis XIV early in 1704—would dare to tamper with the ideological foundations of his own authority by publicly engaging in naturalistic political argumentation. Thus, while it is often said that Louis XIV's government resorted to propaganda only in moments of military insufficiency,[32] the lesson of the documents we have examined is precisely the opposite. The printed words of the rulers were intended to herald their triumph, not excuse their defeat. To reinforce this conclusion, we need only observe that as the French military situation continued to decline from 1704 to 1709, signed royal propaganda reverted to its traditional formulas and narrow channels of brief edicts and letters to prelates.

1709

To move from the archival correspondence of the pre-Blenheim period to that of 1709 and 1710 is to experience the effects of a dizzying succession of French disasters. The arrogant confidence of the early war years was replaced by the famine year of 1709 with a dominant mood of helpless despair, from which none of Louis XIV's councillors was entirely immune. Vacillation, contradiction, and sudden shifts became normal in this time of crisis; they are superficial indications of the depths of panic actuating the court. Any description of French "policy" in these years runs the risk of mistaking almost day-to-day improvisation for coherent, strategic planning. The months of greatest chaos stretched from the collapse of the peace negotiations of The Hague in June 1709 to the beginning of productive contacts with the English Tories in the fall of 1710. In these fifteen months or so, factions in the king's council formed, disintegrated, and reformed with breathtaking rapidity over the central issues of peace and the price to be paid for it. Torcy was no exception to the rule of disorder,

[32] Picavet, *Diplomatie*, p. 217; Zeller, "French Diplomacy," p. 208.

sometimes erratically discarding his general thesis of the necessity of a negotiated settlement in favor of diehard warfare and Bourbon unity in the defense of Philip. Yet throughout this dark period Torcy retained consistent convictions on the need for printed propaganda to place the French case before European public opinion, and especially before the king's own subjects. In the next chapter we shall examine the anonymous pamphlet propaganda of 1709 and 1710; here our concern is the signed propaganda of the king and his diplomatic representatives.

The most famous propaganda document of Louis XIV's reign is doubtless his June 1709 public letter to the royal governors. This missive represented the king's unprecedented effort to explain the demise of the peace talks in Holland and to rally his exhausted subjects for continued warfare. Its appearance was a measure of royal desperation, for never before had Louis bothered to justify an aborted negotiation in public. Indeed, Torcy's unvarying position before 1709, one that reflected the conventional wisdom of Louis XIV's diplomacy, was that public discussion of secret negotiations was nearly always counterproductive. Thus, the foreign minister told Rouillé after the evaporation of peace feelers in 1706: "I do not see what we can make public on the subject of the conference proposals. If such knowledge might produce a good effect on the one hand [i.e., in France], it could produce a bad one in Spain, and in general it would provide a new occasion to say that the need for peace is extreme and that the regret at having missed the occasion to treat is proportionate to the necessity of finishing the war."[33] Even in 1709 the French gov-

[33] Torcy to Rouillé, Versailles, 2 December 1706, AAE, CP, Bavière 51, fol. 419. See also Torcy to Basnage, Marly, 1 July 1711 (copy): "Il semble que ce soit abandonner tout veüe de renouer une Negotiation d'imprimer avant que la paix soit faite les details qui ont precedé un traitté qui n'est pas encore conclu. Cet ouvrage ne sera pas apparemment si conforme à la verité qu'on ne puisse en refuter plusieurs circonstances et les reponses en ces matieres mettent toujours une aigreur qu'il seroit bon de calmer au lieu de la reveiller."

ernment maintained complete silence in public on the subject of the developing conferences of The Hague. No mention of the talks appeared in the official *Gazette*, for example. The Dutch gazettes, on the other hand, started reporting the progress of the talks even before they began. They discovered Rouillé, Louis' plenipotentiary, as he was traveling through the Spanish Netherlands in March, and by the time he reached The Hague every literate in Holland must have known that the Sun King had deigned to talk of peace. Petkum, the envoy of the duke of Holstein-Gottorp to the United Provinces and the intermediary between Dutch and French in arranging the peace talks, reflected allied suspicion when he accused Torcy of intentionally leaking the news of Rouillé's journey in order to sabotage the talks.[34] But Torcy wanted to preserve the secrecy of the negotiations even more than the Dutch did, and he impressed on Rouillé, a career diplomat with many connections from previous missions to the Low Countries, that discretion was essential, even with members of his own family.[35] Torcy foresaw, and events bore him out, that the negotiations would become highly complicated once they became public. New factors would enter the diplomatic mix, and should the talks break down the negotiators would have to move carefully to make it appear that the other side was to blame for their collapse. Furthermore, Torcy knew that French resources were near the breaking point: a lengthy negotiation followed by stalemate and renewed fighting would severely strain the collective psyche of the

[34] Petkum to Torcy, 28 February 1709, AAE, CP, Hollande 217, fol. 78; Torcy to Petkum, Versailles, 21 March 1709, *ibid.*, fol. 173; Torcy to Petkum (minute), 4 April 1709, *ibid.*, fol. 242; Torcy to Hennequin, Versailles, 22 April 1709, Hollande 218, fol. 90ᵛ. Cf. Heinsius to Marlborough, The Hague, 26 March 1709, in B. van 'T Hoff, *The Correspondence of John Churchill and Antonie Heinsius* (The Hague, 1951), p. 432.

[35] Torcy to Rouillé, Versailles, 14 March 1709, AAE, CP, Hollande 217, fol. 170ᵛ.

nation and run the risk of destroying morale entirely. On the one hand, publicity in itself might be a force contributing to the failure of the peace talks, for the Dutch were predisposed to believe in Louis' insincerity at the bargaining table and construed any public mention of the talks as evidence of the king's desire to stall for time and win a good press. On the other hand, so broad and deep was the popular desire for peace within France that public pressure might well propel the French government into an agreement on unfavorable terms. For all these reasons, Torcy wished to maintain a profound silence on the progress and prospects of the peace talks.[36]

Meanwhile, Europe followed the unfolding negotiations through April and May 1709. The Dutch and English newspapers reported on Louis' decision to send Torcy himself as French emissary in the climactic phase of the talks, and they reflected the convictions of allied leaders that this step reinforced the certainty of an imminent settlement. Sure that the shattered condition of France had led Louis to accept peace no matter what the price,[37] the allies set forth ever increasing demands which culminated with their insistence that Philip vacate the Spanish throne as a prerequisite to the peace treaty. Two secret articles of the proposed peace preliminaries granted a sixty-day armistice while Philip was to vacate Spanish territories, re-

[36] Torcy, *Mémoires*, pp. 584-585.

[37] Marlborough to Heinsius, London, 12/23 March 1709, in van 'T Hoff, *Correspondence of John Churchill*, p. 431: "We have certain intelligence from France that the King is advised by his ministers to give any conditions rather than venture the next campaign; so that you may insist boldly on such conditions as you think good for the common cause." Bleak characterizations of the condition of France appeared repeatedly in London periodicals during these months: see *Daily Courant*, January 26, 1709; *The Present State of Europe*, April 1709, p. 137; *Review*, May 10, 1709, p. 62; *ibid.*, June 4, 1709, pp. 106-107. A. D. MacLachlan, "The Road to Peace 1710-1713," in *Britain After the Glorious Revolution*, ed. G. Holmes (London, 1969), p. 201, quotes St. John on England's contemporaneous misery. See also above, ch. 2, n. 26.

quired Louis to turn over certain frontier forts to the allies as security, and spoke of "suitable measures to be taken in concert" by Louis and the allies should Philip refuse to revert to the status of duke of Anjou. This last clause raised the possibility of armed action by the leader of the Bourbon dynasty against his grandson, and it was this implication that Louis XIV found unacceptable. His resistance led the allied leaders to break off talking and resume the war early in June.[38]

Now the crown's problem was how to win new sacrifices from Frenchmen who, together with other Europeans, had been led by the Dutch press to believe that the war was at an end. A host of remarkably radical measures were suggested to Louis XIV. Already since 1706 at the latest, as influential a leader as the duke of Vendôme had recommended convening the Estates General to authorize new taxes and mobilize public support.[39] Louis' illegitimate son, the duke of Maine, now counseled the king to go before the Parlement of Paris, have the chancellor read out the allied peace terms, and await the benefits of popular indignation against France's enemies which he was certain would follow forthwith.[40]

For the Sun King to turn in his distress to the bygone prestige of the parlements or the Estates General would have been to acknowledge symbolically the defeat of everything Louis had stood for as absolute monarch of France. Yet these options apparently were the subject of the king's careful, personal consideration. A draft address dating from this period and written in Louis' shaky hand attests to his readiness for unprecedented steps to rally

[38] An able summary of these negotiations may be found in C.-F. Lévy, *Capitalistes et pouvoir au siècle des lumières* (Paris & The Hague, 1969), pp. 322-330.

[39] See E. Lavisse, *Histoire de France*, Vol. 8, Part 1: A. de Saint-Léger, *Louis XIV: La Fin du règne (1685-1715)* (Paris, 1911), p. 115.

[40] Maine to Maintenon, Versailles, 3 June 1709, in Boislisle, *Mémoires de Saint-Simon*, xvii, 598-600.

public support.[41] Appealing to a proposed assembly which most likely was meant to have included members of all three estates,[42] Louis wrote: "Up to now I have employed those extraordinary means which have been used on similar occasions to raise sums proportionate to essential expenses. Now that all these sources are nearly exhausted I come to you in order to ask your counsel and your aid in this meeting, which will assure our salvation. By our united efforts our enemies will know that we are not in the state they wish to have believed, and we can by means of the indispensable aid I ask of you oblige them to make a peace at once honorable for us, durable for our tranquility and acceptable to all the princes of Europe." Calling on his subjects' patriotic pride, Louis' draft spoke of showing the enemies "that a fully united France is stronger than all the powers assembled with such painstaking force and artifice to crush her."

The radical plan of a royal appeal to the estates was not put into effect. Yet some communication by Louis with his subjects was essential, if only because already the allied press was carrying distorted accounts that gave no hint of the exorbitant demands made of France at the peace talks. It was at this point that Torcy proposed the issuance of a full-scale manifesto detailing the course of the conferences. The foreign minister knew that the disproportionate demands of the allies had made the king's case quite strong, and in the royal dispatch to Rouillé dated 2 June Torcy wrote that "the public will easily judge that they [the allies] do not want peace."[43] Now that the outcome of the talks was common knowledge, he continued, it could easily

[41] "Projet de Harangue," BN, Mss. fr. 10331, fols. 135–137, printed by Jean Longnon, ed., *Mémoires de Louis XIV* (Paris, 1927), pp. 287–288.

[42] "C'est par la valeur de ma noblesse et le zèle de mes sujets que j'ai réussi dans les entreprises que j'ai faites pour le bien de l'Etat." *Ibid.*

[43] Quoted by Torcy in his *Mémoires*, pp. 628–629.

be shown that Louis had "given incontestable proofs of his sincere desire to sacrifice his *gloire* and his interests to the general pacification of Europe."[44] As late as 20 June the foreign minister would still promise Petkum a full public vindication of royal actions.[45] During this three-week period, Eusèbe Renaudot, a long-time intimate of Torcy, continually predicted the imminent appearance of a lengthy manifesto.[46] The unique and desperate circumstances of crisis clearly had prompted Torcy to revise his deep convictions about the inviolable nature of private diplomacy.

No such document appeared, however; instead, the king issued two public letters, one to the episcopacy of France and the other the celebrated message to the royal governors. Their purpose, as Torcy recorded in his memoirs, was to instruct Frenchmen "about the offers the King had made to purchase the repose of his subjects; to have made known to them the full extent of the passion of the enemies of the French nation; their bad faith in negotiations; to expose to the faithful people, zealous for their master's *gloire* and for their *patrie*, what had happened in the talks, and, further, of what it had been possible to learn with certitude of the plans of the powers leagued against France."[47] While to the duke of Maine these letters seemed quite insufficient—he reported that it had been decided to remain silent and not publish any manifesto—and while Renaudot expressed disappointment that no manifesto but "only two letters" had been issued,[48] their publication al-

[44] *Ibid.*, p. 589.
[45] Torcy to Petkum, Marly, 20 June 1709 (minute), AAE, CP, Hollande 219, fol. 65.
[46] See Renaudot's Paris newsletter, in Duffo, *Correspondance*, III, 197–199.
[47] Torcy, *Mémoires*, pp. 584–585.
[48] Maine to Harcourt, Marly, 25 June 1709, in Boislisle, *Mémoires de Saint-Simon*, XVII, 601–602; Renaudot's Paris newsletter for 24 June 1709, in Duffo, *Correspondance*, III, 202. See also [Donneau de Visé], *Recueil de diverses pièces*, p. 95, where Louis' letter to the governors is described as something "qui peut passer pour un manifeste."

lowed the crown to communicate the heart of its message in a format that seemed traditional enough to avoid the appearance of radical measures born of desperation.

Despite its length, Louis' letter to the provincial governors of 12 June 1709, which we know was written by Torcy,[49] is so important that it should be quoted[50] in its entirety:

> The expectation of a speedy peace was so generally diffused throughout my kingdom, that I think it my duty, in return for the fidelity which my people have shewn me, during the course of my reign, to give them the satisfaction of being acquainted with the reasons, which still hinder them from enjoying that repose, which I intended to procure them.
>
> In order to re-establish a general peace, I should have accepted terms very much opposite to the security of my frontier provinces; but the more I have shewn myself ready and disposed to remove all suspicions, which the enemy affect to entertain of my power and designs, the more they have multiplied their pretensions, insomuch, that by gradually adding new demands to the former, and making use of the duke of Savoy's name, or pretending the interest of the princes of the empire, they have equally shewed, that their intention was only to enlarge, at the expense of my crown, the states which border upon France, and to open an easy way for themselves, to penetrate into the heart of my kingdom,

---

[49] Renaudot commented that the two royal letters were "très bien faites, comme toutes celles qui sortent des mains de M. de Torcy" (letter of 24 June 1709, in Duffo, *Correspondance*, III, 202). See also drafts of the letter to the governors and bishops, with changes in Torcy's hand, in AAE, MD, France 1163, fols. 264–266 and 267, respectively. See also covering letter to La Vrillière, Versailles, 12 June 1703, *ibid.*, fol. 268; and "Eloge de Torcy," BN, Mss. fr. 10668, fol. 88.

[50] In the translation accompanying the London edition of Torcy's *Memoirs*, I, 404–407.

whenever it should be agreeable to their interests to commence a new war. Even that which I now maintain, and was desirous to finish, would not be at an end, were I to consent to the proposals they have made me: for they limited to two months, the time, wherein I was on my part to execute the treaty; and during that interval, they pretended to oblige me to deliver up the strong towns which they demanded of me in the Netherlands and in Alsace, and to demolish the fortifications of others. They refused on their side, to enter into any other engagement, than to suspend all acts of hostility till the first of August, reserving to themselves the liberty of renewing then the operations of war, if my grandson the king of Spain persisted in the resolution to defend the crown which God hath given him, and to perish rather than forsake a faithful people, who these nine years have acknowledged him for their lawful sovereign. Such a suspension of arms, more dangerous than the war itself, retarded peace rather than forwarded the conclusion of it; for I was not only obliged to continue the same expense for maintaining my armies, but my enemies, after the expiration of the term of suspension, would have attacked me with new advantages, by reason of the strong holds, which I was to deliver into their hands, at the same time that I demolished those, which serve as a barrier to some of my frontier provinces. I shall take no notice of the insinuations they have made to me, to join my forces to those of the confederacy, and to compel the king my grandson to descend the throne, unless he voluntarily consented to live henceforward without any dominions, and to reduce himself to a private condition. It is shocking to humanity, to believe that they could entertain any thoughts of engaging me to enter into any such alliance with them. But though my affection for my people is as sensible as that which I have for my own children; though I share with them all the calamities which war draws on such faithful subjects; and though I have manifested to all Europe, that I was sincerely desirous of procuring a peace for them, yet I am persuaded that they themselves would be against receiving it, upon conditions equally opposite to justice and the honour of the French name.

It is therefore my intention, that all those who for such a series of years have given me proofs of their zeal, in contributing by their labour, their property, and their blood, to support so burdensome a war, should be informed, that the only return the enemy pretended to make to my offers, was a suspension of arms; which being limited to the space of two months, would have procured them much greater advantages, than they can expect from the confidence they put in their troops. As I put mine in the protection of the Almighty, and as I hope that the purity of my intentions will draw down the Divine Blessing upon my arms, I am willing that my people within your jurisdiction should know from you, that they should already enjoy peace, had it depended merely on my will to procure them a blessing which they wish for with reason; but which must be obtained by new efforts, since the immense concessions I was ready to make, are of no effect for restoring the public tranquillity.

This royal letter convincingly linked Louis' duty as *bon père* to Philip with the interests of the king of France and those of the French nation. No damage was done to Louis' reputation as an upholder of monarchical legitimacy; yet the Sun King also appeared as the benefactor of his subjects. To be sure, Torcy struck the traditional royal tone of paternalistic majesty, but the role of the monarchical father is here transformed from a search for personal *gloire* into a benevolent devotion to state, nation and people. It is worth noting in this regard that some printings of the royal letter set the words "nom François" in capital letters, as if to emphasize typographically the king's identification of his cause with that of the nation.[51] The Sun King's plea for public support invoked the images of mythic symbolism that had long characterized the mystique of French royalty. Louis appeared as the personification of courage in the face of adversity, the exemplar of justice and pious trust in God—in short as a composite of the good king depicted in a historiographical tradition that stretched back to medieval chronicles and forward to the general histories of the seventeenth century.[52] The royal letter joined Louis XIV to his subjects through rhetorical imagery which lay at the very heart of their national identity.

What was novel was not the content but the format and massive dissemination in print which the royal letter received. For despite the disappointment of Maine and Renaudot at the brevity of the king's propaganda, this document received enormous circulation. Most of the governors realized at once that Louis meant his message to have the widest possible audience and gave it a proper send-off with cover letters like this one from the Marquis d'Antin to the municipal officials of Blois: "I believe there is no better way to execute the King's orders than by sending you a copy of his letter to me. There you will find the just reasons the King had to refuse the scandalous peace propositions of the enemies, shameful for the entire nation and so inappropriate for procuring public repose. I have no doubt that you will be appropriately indignant and that you will bend all your efforts to place His Majesty in the position of procuring for his subjects a more reliable and more honorable peace."[53] The royal letter, often with in-

[51] See, for instance, BN, Imp., LB[37].4346, *Lettre du Roy à Mr. le Marquis Dantin du 12 Juin 1709.*

[52] See Tyvaert, "L'Image du Roi," pp. 531–535.

[53] BN, Imp., Lb[37].4346, *Lettre du Roy à Mr. le Marquis Dantin du 12 Juin 1709.* See also the letter of the over-cautious L. A. de Bourbon

troductory orders from the governors, was printed under local auspices throughout France, and often in multiple editions. At the same time, the French episcopacy joined in an appeal for support of the war effort. Archbishop Cardinal de Noailles of Paris, for example, echoed the king's words[54] in ordering public prayers:

> His Majesty, being more sensibly concern'd for the Quiet and Happiness of his People, than for his own Glory and particular Interest with that of his Royal Family, has omitted nothing to procure for his Kingdom and for all Europe the Peace it so much wants. He would have sacrific'd All for so great a Good; and refus'd nothing but what was against Justice,

---

to Torcy, in which the prince sought explicit instructions on the printing of Louis' letter (AAE, CP, Hollande 226, fol. 204).

[54] The king's letter to the prelates, as it appears in *Lettre du Roy à Monseigneur l'Evesque Comte de Chaalons, Pair de France* (Châlons-sur-Marne, 1709), BN, Imp., Lb[37].4349, follows: "Mon Cousin, J'ai regardé comme un de mes premiers devoirs, d'emploier tous mes soins pour procurer le repos à mes peuples, dans un tems où les maux de la guerre ne sont pas les seuls, dont il a plû à Dieu d'affliger mon Roiaume; mais quelques offres que j'aye faites à mes ennemis pour le retablissement de la tranquillité publique, j'ai vû par leurs reponses que, confiant en leurs forces, ils ont encore des veües bien opposées à celles de travailler à la Paix de l'Europe. Comme les évenemens de cette campagne doivent en décider, qu'ils sont absolument entre les mains de Dieu, et qu'il s'agit de sa Cause, puisque nôtre Sainte Religion est attaquée par mes ennemis et que ses interêts sont abandonnés de ceux mêmes qui devroient les soûtenir avec le plus d'ardeur, j'ai lieu d'esperer qu'il lui plaira de me donner de nouvelles marques de sa protection divine, connoissant la pureté de mes intentions, et les Sacrifices que j'avois résolu de faire pour le repos de tant de peuples. Il faut cependant implorer, avec autant de confiance que d'humilité, ses misericordes, pour en obtenir l'effet: Ainsi mon intention est que vous excitiez encore la ferveur des peuples, en indiquant de nouvelles prieres pour la prosperité de mes armes et pour une heureuse conclusion de la Paix. Et ne doutant pas que vous ne continuiez à donner en cette occasion des marques de vôtre zele, et de vôtre Pieté ordinaire. Je prie Dieu qu'il vous ait, mon Cousin, en sa sainte et digne garde."

Probity, and even natural Right. . . . Let us assist with all our Power his Majesty, in a War which he did not undertake but for Reasons the most just, the most natural, and the most lawful; which he continues against his Will; and which he will be glad to end, as soon as he can do it with Honour, Justice, and Safety: Let us assist him, I say, in a War wherein the Interest of private Persons is no less concern'd than that of the State, every ones Possessions being equally expos'd; . . .[55]

Donneau de Visé, the publisher of the *Mercure galant*, left us a vivid account of the reception of the king's letter in Paris. The governor of Paris, like his fellows all over the kingdom, had ordered the printing of the royal appeal. The public demand was immense, wrote Visé, and after the first printing was sold out in a day, new editions were run off that night, while a large crowd waited impatiently outside the printer's door. Then, "when everyone had been provided a copy, and when the letter had been read and reread, enthusiasm for the war was rekindled. Everyone was aroused, and each man resolved to aid the King according to his talents, even to the point of shedding his own blood if it were necessary."[56] As for the letter's effect upon Louis' troops, Marlborough's spy reported that Villars was "delighted" with it: "He read it to the whole army, and asked the soldiers and officers if they did not wish to avenge the honour of the King which his enemies were insulting. So saying, he called for cheers from them all, and when they threw their hats in the air, he threw his up, too."[57]

Of equal importance was the credence with which such accounts of renewed French fervor were received abroad. Gaultier, Torcy's agent in London, put himself in an En-

[55] *The Present State of Europe*, June 1709, pp. 217–219.
[56] [Donneau de Visé], *Recueil de diverses pièces*, pp. 95–98.
[57] Quoted in Churchill, *Marlborough*, vi, 98.

glishman's boots in this description of London's reaction to the news: "I cannot begin to tell you of our astonishment since we heard that the king of France has resolved not to sign the peace preliminaries and to continue the war. . . . Our astonishment is all the greater since we flattered ourselves into believing that France could do no more, that she was reduced to the last extremity, that it was impossible for her to support any longer the burden of war and that she absolutely had to make as shameful and disadvantageous a peace as we would like." "But what surprises us even more is that we hear from all over France that the people are infuriated at the extraordinary demands we have made and that despite their great misery they are entirely disposed to assist the king with everything remaining to them."[58] Significantly, Gaultier's report emphasized English incomprehension of the latent power stored in the symbols of the French monarchy, a power which Torcy knew how to unleash and channel when the king addressed his subjects. There is an overwhelming contrast between the other propaganda pieces sponsored by Torcy and the royal letter of 1709. Whereas in the anonymous pamphlets and even in the king's Savoy letters the writers almost always employed a modernized rhetoric emphasizing concepts of interest and utility, the 1709 letter returned to the most ancient symbolism of French history. To explain the difference we need only observe that, unlike the letter of 1709, most of Torcy's propaganda was primarily directed abroad. The main intended audience in 1709 was French; it comprised that group which could participate in the public myth of the monarch as a being who personified the state and gave form to the nation. In the guise of the good king of French tradition, even Louis XIV might take his subjects into his confidence. But could he do more and, as Torcy would urge him a few months later, publicly argue a case in the language of law and diplomacy?

[58] Gaultier to Torcy, London, 14 June 1709, AAE, CP, Angleterre 228, fol. 39; and 18 June 1709, *ibid.*, fol. 41.

1710

For this was only half the story. In the next year Louis again sent plenipotentiaries to Holland to engage in peace parleys. These talks bear many resemblances to the negotiations of 1709, but in several crucial particulars they were altogether different. For one, there was no attempt by Torcy to draw a curtain of secrecy over these conferences. Concluding from his experience of the previous year that all efforts at silence were fruitless in the face of the freedom of the allied periodicals, the foreign minister regarded the conferences of 1710 as a confrontation in which the public was an invisible but ever-present participant.[59] Another significant difference in these new talks was that Louis and his government were far less optimistic about the possibilities of negotiated settlement than they had been early in 1709. Whereas the king seemed genuinely surprised by the hard enemy terms presented at The Hague, he was understandably less scandalized when he heard roughly the same demands eleven months later.

These two changes together worked a fundamental reorientation of the royal government's view of propaganda and the negotiations. The public nature of the talks and the pessimism about their outcome made Torcy consider from the start the manner in which the king might best present his version of the peace talks to his subjects and to all Europe should the talks fail. Hence we find in the diplomatic dispatches of 1710, as well as in Torcy's unique and highly valuable private diary, regular attention to public opinion of the discussions, a topic almost entirely absent from the dispatches of 1709.

Polignac and d'Huxelles, the two negotiators sent to Holland late in January 1710, were well aware of what was at stake. Villars' holding actions of the previous campaign

[59] Torcy, *Journal*, p. 128; Torcy, *Mémoires*, p. 638. Torcy to Petkum, Versailles, 29 January 1710 (minute), AAE, CP, Hollande 222, fol. 61ᵛ.

had delayed a military decision, but France's condition was still desperate. In February there were strong doubts that the king would even be able to find subsistence for his armies in a new campaign. Everyone in the council wanted a settlement,[60] and in this they were not alone. The abbé de Polignac, one of Torcy's close confidants, reported that as his entourage made its way from Paris to the Flemish border, people gathered along the road shouting "Peace! Peace!"[61] Yet there was a problem, and d'Huxelles put his finger on it just before departing. The marshal begged the king to resolve once and for all either to undertake a war on Philip or give up as doomed a peace negotiation whose failure would make the whole nation despair. Louis said nothing, awaiting word of the allied position in the opening session of the new talks.[62]

By mid-March the king had his answer. The envoys reported from Gertruydenberg, the tiny, isolated fishing hamlet to which they were confined by the allies, that the Dutch deputies had rejected all the French expedients for evading the allied insistence that Louis participate in Philip's removal from the Spanish throne. In effect, they replaced the negotiations squarely in the position they had occupied in June 1709. Torcy read the dispatch of the plenipotentiaries to Louis' council meeting of 14 March,

[60] Torcy, *Journal*, p. 135. The shifting sentiments of the royal councillors during this period are analyzed by John C. Rule, "France and the Preliminaries to the Gertruydenberg Conference, September 1709 to March 1710," in *Studies in Diplomatic History, Essays in Memory of David Bayne Horn*, ed. R. Hatton and M. S. Anderson (London, 1970), pp. 99–115.

[61] Polignac to Torcy, Mons, 12 January 1712, AAE, CP, Hollande 232, fol. 34ᵛ, where Polignac contrasts this experience with the absence of such demonstrations on his way to Utrecht. Cf. Torcy, *Mémoires*, p. 568: "Le nom de paix présente l'idée d'un état si heureux, qui quiconque s'y oppose directement est regardé comme ennemi du bonheur et de la tranquillité publique: ceux qui se plaisent le plus aux horreurs de la guerre dissimulent leurs sentimens et veulent qu'on les croie pacifiques."

[62] Torcy, *Journal*, pp. 142–143.

and at the session of 15 March the council concluded unanimously that France must prepare for another season of war.[63] That day Torcy wrote these lines to d'Huxelles and Polignac: "I beseech both of you to be good enough to consider from now on how to prepare the materials that would compose an account of your conferences. It seems to me that it will become necessary to inform the public of the hardships you are suffering, so that some day it may be seen that peace still would have been very uncertain or rather that it would not have been concluded even if the King had been able to consent to make war on the king of Spain."[64] Torcy's suggestion met a receptive audience in Holland. D'Huxelles and Polignac immediately replied that they were preparing the suggested account and added that they wanted it enlarged to include the events of the previous year, "it being impossible to inform the public too much of the advances the King has made for peace and of the insurmountable obstacles which he has encountered."[65] The envoys immediately entrusted the task of drafting this *relation* to La Blinière, a celebrated lawyer in the Parlement of Paris whom Torcy and d'Huxelles had recruited to serve as secretary to the negotiators. Within a week after the council's decision to fight on, the projected account of the peace negotiations was begun in Holland.[66] This quick work, together with the precaution of bringing along a man of La Blinière's powers of persuasion, argues that the *relation* of March 1710 was a reincarnation of the manifesto of June 1709, the document left unpublished when Louis' letters to the governors and bishops were issued.

[63] *Ibid.*, pp. 149–150.

[64] Torcy to d'Huxelles and Polignac, Versailles, 15 March 1710, AAE, CP, Hollande 223, fol. 77.

[65] D'Huxelles and Polignac to Torcy, Gertruydenberg, 19 March 1710, *ibid.*, fol. 110ᵛ.

[66] La Blinière to Torcy, Gertruydenberg, 23 March 1710, *ibid.*, fol. 126; Torcy to La Blinière, Versailles, 3 April 1710 (minute), *ibid.*, fol. 199.

Nothing that happened at the Gertruydenberg talks during the month of April made Louis any more confident of the good will of the allies. Indeed, by the middle of the month it was the consensus of the council that negotiations would soon break down, and it was further agreed that Torcy's suggestion of putting the blame on the allies for demanding unreasonable terms concerning Spain was the right tack to follow.[67] Here is an excerpt from the royal dispatch to d'Huxelles and Polignac of 15 April 1710 which Torcy wrote and had submitted to the council meeting the preceding day:

I now consider the rupture of your conference to be very near. . . . I am confirming all the orders I have given you, including the one to wait for my enemies to break off the conferences first. For it is essential to my service that the truth appear, that everyone know how, after all the advances and all the offers I have made for peace, my enemies have consented only to a truce of whose continuation they have constantly refused to assure me. That, having maintained an improper silence about certain "further demands," they in effect are reserving to themselves pretexts for resuming the war whenever they might find it in their interest to attack me. That despite all their injustice . . . I proposed all the expedients which I believed capable of advancing the negotiation, consenting to receive as mediators even the princes whose intentions seemed to me the most suspect. . . . It is scarcely to be believed that people who pride themselves on good faith and who wish to appear zealous for the public repose should refuse the securities and the necessary explications I asked of them for the conservation of the public tranquility. It is this which it will be well to make known to all Europe if you return here without

[67] Torcy, *Journal*, p. 166.

having concluded peace, as I cannot but expect will happen.[68]

In most of the diplomatic dispatches composed by the Sun King's foreign ministers, we find outlined every conceivable argument that might be of service to an envoy in his dealings with heads of foreign governments. This dispatch of mid-April 1710 presented some of the arguments that might be made in the written account of the peace talks then being prepared under the aegis of the plenipotentiaries. That Louis himself was now entirely won over to this campaign for public support is clear from Torcy's account of the council meeting of 21 April, where the king declared that "when the conferences were finished, it would be absolutely necessary to inform the public of what had happened and of the unjust conditions and refusals of the enemies."[69]

In the succeeding two weeks the foreign minister spurred La Blinière and the plenipotentiaries to attend to the work of a narrative of the peace talks. Torcy and the envoys agreed that La Blinière should write not in Louis' name but as if he were rendering "an account to the King of which His Majesty permits the public to be instructed."[70] Soon, however, a major obstacle arose which the plenipotentiaries described to Torcy:

Up to now we have found two difficulties in doing a good job [on the *relation*]. One is that when we get to the request we made for a partition [of the Spanish empire], what it would be suitable to tell Frenchmen would perhaps not suit the Spanish. The other is that

[68] Louis to d'Huxelles and Polignac, Versailles, 15 April 1710, AAE, CP, Hollande 224, fols. 51, 55–55ᵛ.

[69] Torcy, *Journal*, p. 167.

[70] Polignac to Torcy, Gertruydenberg, 27 April 1710, AAE, CP, Hollande 224, fol. 147; Torcy to d'Huxelles and Polignac, 30 April 1710, *ibid.*, fol. 142ᵛ (the quotation is from this letter); Torcy to Polignac, Versailles, 4 May 1710, *ibid.*, fol. 153.

were we to avoid a positive statement on our acceptance of the idea of partition, the allies would not fail to respond that without this all our propositions were illusory and in bad faith. . . . As this is the principal point that has caused the failure of our negotiations, it will also make our account more difficult. For as to the rest, that is, the refusal of a mediator, the refusal of a guarantee [of the extension of the armistice] and the matter of the "further demands," nothing would be easier than putting the Dutch in the wrong. . . . One can touch the people of France [with these arguments], not displease the Spanish and even rouse those Dutchmen who yearn for peace.[71]

Here was the problem of 1709, the recurrent problem that stemmed from Louis' divided loyalties. A choice could not be evaded. The *relation* must decide between Louis' interests as king of France and his attachment to his dynasty. To Torcy no account could succeed without reference to Louis' offers of partition, but for the time being the question was not to be resolved, and Torcy's reply betrays no hint of his intentions: "Whatever honor there might be for me, Messieurs, to think as you do, I am very disappointed to see by your letter of the 30th of last month that you found in the work which M. de la Blinière is to compose the same difficulties which up to now have seemed to me impossible to surmount. I was reproaching myself for being unable to imagine the solution of this embarrassment, and I hoped that others more able than I would succeed. I still hope so, and I cannot believe that with justice and reason on our side we still lack, together with so many other resources, the means of making them known."[72] For the moment, this dif-

---

[71] D'Huxelles and Polignac to Torcy, Gertruydenberg, 30 April 1710, *ibid.*, fols. 166–167ᵛ.

[72] Torcy to d'Huxelles and Polignac, 8 May 1710, *ibid.*, fol. 172. Polignac, who eventually wrote one version of the planned *relation*, had succeeded Bossuet to membership in the Académie française in 1704. On his literary career, see L. C. Rosenfield, *From Beast-Machine*

ficulty was pushed aside, and the plenipotentiaries reported that La Blinière was ready at any time to draw up his notes in the prescribed form.[73]

Here things stood in early May. The Gertruydenberg peace talks were in imminent danger of collapse. Louis had instructed his envoys on the manner of their leave-taking, and both Frenchmen and Dutchmen were poised to resume their war of words together with that of armies.[74] That the peace conferences of 1710 continued for another two months beyond this point was primarily the work of Marshal Villars. The commander had a private conference with the king on the evening of 7 May. Villars minced no words in his description of the miserable condition of the troops and the necessity of fighting a battle during the month of May, before the enemies succeeded in establishing their siege positions. Both king and soldier knew that this was, in Torcy's paraphrase, "to gamble the State on the luck of a single day." Villars left Louis with the good subject's honest counsel: "to make peace under hard terms, even by declaring war on the King of Spain, rather than lose all." The king was left profoundly shaken by this interview; Villars was, after all, the most daring and self-confident of the Sun King's military men.[75] Louis approved Torcy's suggestion of drawing up new letters to the plenipotentiaries offering secret French subsidies to the allies for the upkeep of a war against Philip.[76]

In the double game that Torcy was playing, fighting for peace while preparing for the possibility of war, the success of one-half of his policy meant the eclipse of the other.

to Man-Machine, The Theme of Animal Soul in French Letters from Descartes to La Mettrie (New York, 1940), pp. 50–51.

[73] D'Huxelles and Polignac to Torcy, Gertruydenberg, 11 May 1710, AAE, CP, Hollande 224, fol. 218ᵛ.

[74] D'Huxelles and Polignac to Torcy, ibid.: "les gens cy se disposent de leur costé à escrire, et ils dissimuleront autant qu'ils pourront l'article essentiel de la seureté."

[75] Torcy, Journal, p. 177.   [76] Ibid., pp. 177–179.

Thus we do not hear of the proposed *relation* for two months while Torcy tried to steer the peace negotiations to a successful conclusion. He was not to succeed, for many reasons. One was that Marshal d'Huxelles had lost faith in the talks by early May. Convinced that the parleys were futile and his personal position shameful, he was fully prepared to leave Holland when Louis' orders arrived calling for an offer of subsidies. It required an explicit command from the king to keep the marshal from deserting his post. Torcy knew that to instigate a rupture by the French would have served the Dutch cause admirably. Even Polignac, who in general bore his tribulations with a diplomat's stoicism far exceeding the patience of his colleague, had to be lectured by Torcy. "In truth," wrote the foreign minister, "one must sometimes sacrifice himself to the public weal and understand that there is a significant service to perform in preventing the people from despairing utterly of peace and being misled by the declarations of the enemies so that they will not reproach the king for having let slip the occasion to negotiate, as too many voices are already publicizing."[77]

[77] *Ibid.*, pp. 181 ff.; Torcy to Polignac, Versailles, 18 May 1710, AAE, CP, Hollande, Suppl. 9, fol. 64. D'Huxelles was not Louis' first choice for negotiator; had d'Harcourt's health permitted, he would have had d'Huxelles' place (Torcy, *Journal*, p. 131). D'Huxelles complained loudly of the misery of his task; see Torcy to Polignac, Versailles, 4 May 1710, AAE, CP, Hollande 224, fol. 153. La Blinière reflected the marshal's dissatisfaction with Torcy, whom he blamed for mishandling the talks; see La Blinière's "Journal des conferences de Gertruydenberg," AAE, MD, France 1874, fols. 55ᵛ, 61ᵛ, 73. It is in light of this impatience of the negotiators that we should interpret the following response of Polignac to Torcy: "Nous serons des moutons, et nous ferons toute notre possible de tirer des choses en longueur" (quoted in J. G. Stork-Penning, "The Ordeal of the States—Some Remarks on Dutch Politics During the War of the Spanish Succession," *Acta Historiae Neerlandica II* [Leiden, 1967], pp. 218–219). Stork-Penning adduces this remark as evidence for the conclusion that France's real aims at Gertruydenberg were to gain time. However, the meaning of *moutons* in this sentence can only be the one illustrated in the *Dictionnaire de l'Academie françoise*

It was, however, left to the allies to reap the lion's share of the responsibility for the failure of the talks of 1710. In mid-June they reacted to Louis' offer of subsidies with a demand of four cities along the Flemish border as security. They began to unveil their mysterious "further demands" with talk of Alsace and Lorraine. To Torcy this appeared not a bad bargain, all things considered. Louis, however, was doubtful. At this point the foreign minister played one of his last cards. New word from the army once again emphasized the shortage of money and food, the high desertion rate, and deteriorating morale. Torcy argued in a private talk with the king that the welfare of his subjects must have the highest priority, "that the cessions made in making peace would not prevent France from remaining the most powerful kingdom in Europe." The foreign minister contended that after a few years "France would find the happy circumstances to avenge herself of a forced treaty, the obligation of which appears to me very like that of a promise a man makes to robbers who are threatening to murder him in the woods." Louis, however, "implied to me in a few words, and I saw it even more clearly in his eyes," that his advanced age made such talk of future vengeance very dubious. Torcy wrote in his diary that other courtiers might have shed crocodile tears at this suggestion, but that he made an effort to hide his own genuine tears, finishing his presentation with the recommendation that Louis forsake Alsace, even to the

---

(Paris, 1694), II, 97: "On dit fig. d'un homme qui est d'humeur douce et traitable, que c'est un *mouton*, qu'il *est doux comme un mouton*." The usage connotes anything but deceptiveness; it represents Polignac's and d'Huxelles' resolution to make a new attempt at patience in the face of adversity. Surely Torcy wished to prolong the conferences, and this was partly to demonstrate to France and Europe the Sun King's sincerity. But it is a gross misrepresentation to write that the talks were a calculated French hoax. The story is really more complex and more interesting than that. Since I do not read Dutch, it should be added that I am unable to comment on Stork-Penning's detailed study of the peace talks, *Het Grote Werk* (Groningen, 1958).

duke of Lorraine, give up Valenciennes to the Dutch and subsidize a war against Philip to the tune of one million livres per month.[78] It would be difficult to produce a confrontation better symbolizing the different perspectives of the king and his minister. Torcy here argued for France and the institution of the French monarchy, while Louis upheld his family obligations and personal *gloire*.

Before the king had time to digest Torcy's most recent proposal, it was outrun by events. Without waiting for a response to their offer of the previous week, the Dutch delegates informed d'Huxelles and Polignac that the allies were withdrawing all previous offers. They were now prepared unofficially to offer Philip Sicily and Sardinia as compensation, but if he refused they would require that Louis *alone* assume the full burden of expelling his grandson from the Spanish empire. The council was so astounded by this turn of events that Louis asked for a clarification. It came back two weeks later, on 16 July: the Dutch deputies had declared explicitly that there was no peace to be had if the king did not promise to use his own forces exclusively to oblige his grandson to cede Spain and the Indies within a term of two months. After sixty days the allies reserved the right to resume the war against Louis on all fronts if the cession had not been accomplished, even were the French king to execute all the other articles of the preliminaries. The allies left Louis' representatives fifteen days to respond.[79]

When the council heard this ultimatum there was general indignation, but composure was regained quickly. Everyone agreed that the plenipotentiaries should leave Holland, but the royal councillors wanted to be certain that the full opprobrium of breaking up the negotiations fell on the Dutch. Thus Voysin expressed the consensus by suggesting that d'Huxelles and Polignac write to Heinsius recapitulating the events of the last conference, demonstrating that "the request of impossible conditions constituted a rupture of the talks, and that since those in power wanted to break off, the

[78] Torcy, *Journal*, pp. 206–207.   [79] *Ibid.*, pp. 214, 222–223.

conferences could serve no purpose and the deputies could only return to France."[80]

Between the close of the morning council meeting and the evening of the sixteenth, Torcy had time to reconsider. He must have realized that the allied terms in themselves represented his defeat because their issuance indicated how little he had succeeded in convincing the enemy leaders of France's ability and Louis' willingness to fight on. Still, he could not bring himself to accept the new, absurd terms at their face value. The foreign minister was determined to make one final try for peace through negotiations with the Dutch. When he brought back the drafted letter to d'Huxelles and Polignac for approval, Torcy spoke with the king alone and secured Louis' agreement to an additional order, namely, that the plenipotentiaries make their letter to Heinsius public in "all the provinces of Holland."[81] This addendum completely changed the character of the royal orders. In the morning the king had decided to lay the groundwork for the recall of his envoys, but in the evening Louis was appealing for peace over the heads of the Dutch leaders to the Dutch and English public. Torcy explained his reasoning in his own letter to the plenipotentiaries: "While it appears by the latest response of the Dutch deputies that you will soon be delivered of this disagreeable commerce, I can scarcely believe that those who ought to fear the reproaches of the public will let you depart. I would not be surprised if the unjust proposition they made to you was a feeler [*tentative*] to prompt you to reveal the most extreme powers which they believed you had [and were withholding]. If this is not so, it seems to me they are risking quite a lot in appearing to be the authors of the continuation of the war, for so they will appear when their last declaration to you becomes public."[82] The foreign minister elaborated his thoughts in this entry in his diary:

[80] *Ibid.*, p. 223.   [81] *Ibid.*

[82] Torcy to d'Huxelles and Polignac, Marly, 16 July 1710 (minute), AAE, CP, Hollande 226, fol. 86.

> It appeared . . . that those who were conducting affairs in England and in Holland were running a great personal risk in delaying peace. Their peoples desired it. They were already attributing the continuation of the war to the selfish ambition of private individuals. To reject the King's reasonable propositions and to insist on an impossible demand was to confirm this opinion of the public.
>
> The enemies could not desire a better war situation than they had at the moment. . . . [But] the domestic affairs of the enemies were not as favorable to them as the external ones. Money was beginning to run short in Holland, and most particularly the confusions of the English kingdom were increasing. Marlborough's reputation was under attack, his nephew Sunderland deprived of his office of secretary of state, the duchess of Marlborough disgraced. . . . This was a favorable situation for stirring up passions in England and obliging the English nation to occupy herself with domestic affairs exclusively.[83]

This, then, was the immediate background to Louis' instructions to the plenipotentiaries "to send copies [of their letter] to Amsterdam, and to forget nothing in seeing that it is made public throughout the provinces of Holland. The truth must get out. The people of those provinces must understand the conduct of those who are sacrificing the public weal to their private interests."[84] For months d'Huxelles and Polignac had tried to present the French case to the Dutch, but they were hampered by a lack of contacts and by the proposition, constantly reiterated in the Dutch gazettes, that Louis was insincere, wanted continued war, and could not be trusted.[85] Now they openly played for the favor of the

---

[83] Torcy, *Journal*, pp. 223 ff. Cf. Torcy, *Mémoires*, p. 655, on the reaction in France to the events in England.

[84] Louis to d'Huxelles and Polignac, 16 July 1710, in Legrelle, *La Diplomatie française*, v, 559–560.

[85] D'Huxelles and Polignac to Torcy, Gertruydenberg, 13 April

allied peoples in their public letter to Heinsius, dated Gertruydenberg, 20 July 1710.

The plenipotentiaries opened their letter[86] with a review of the conditions presented by the Dutch deputies at the last session of the conferences. The first item in this résumé was "That the Resolution of their Masters and their Allies, was to reject absolutely all Offers of Money on the Part of the King to assist them to maintain the War in Spain, whatever the same might be, and whatever Security his Majesty would give for the Payment." Thus it was admitted by the king's representatives that Louis had been ready to subsidize a war against his grandson. The plenipotentiaries went on to summarize the other allied demands: Louis must take sole responsibility for removing Philip from Spain and the Indies within two months; the armistice granted by the allies having expired and Philip remaining in Spain, the allies would be free to resume the war against Louis. The envoys recounted that they had pointed out to the deputies the utter novelty of this proposition: "We Replied to this, with an unanswerable Argument; by demanding of them, whether in all our Conferences a Partition had not been the Matter in Question? And whether upon that Foundation they had ever requir'd any thing else of us, than the taking of Measures in Concert, and the Union of Forces?" Thus did Louis'

1710, AAE, CP, Hollande 224, fol. 78ᵛ; Torcy to d'Huxelles and Polignac, Versailles, 24 April 1710 (minute), *ibid.*, fol. 107. In this connection, note these two passages from Torcy's *Mémoires*: "Ils [the allied leaders] ne cesserent de répandre qu'il falloit se défier continuellement de ses artifices [France's] et n'oublièrent rien pour empêcher que la sincerité des intentions du Roi ne fût connue et ne fût sur les peuples une impression trop vive" (p. 642). "Les discours rebattus depuis longtemps en Hollande étoient que la France avoit proposé et renoué les conferences à dessein seulement de gagner du temps, de suspendre s'il étoit possible les hostilités, d'arrêter par ce moyen les progrès des alliés, enfin de les tromper" (p. 650).

[86] Manuscript in AAE, CP, Hollande 226, fol. 1358. Printed, BN, Imp., Lg⁶. 380, *Missive van de Heeren Fransche Ministers* (text in French). Quoted from translation in *The Present State of Europe*, July 1710, pp. 263-265.

envoys reveal that their king had been negotiating for months on the basis of a partition of his grandson's empire. They went on to accuse the allies of plotting to break up the talks by shifting the basis of discussions so radically. "His Majesty has long since intimated, That for the Sake of a definitive and secure Peace, he would yield to such Conditions as he himself could execute; but he will never promise what he knows impossible for him to perform. If by the Injustice and Obstinacy of his Enemies, he be depriv'd of all Hope of obtaining Peace; then, trusting in the Protection of God, who is able when he pleases to humble those whom unhop'd for Prosperity elevates, and who make no Account of the publick Calamities, and the Effusion of Christian Blood, he will leave it to the Judgment of all Europe, even to the Judgment of the People of England and Holland, to distinguish who are the true Authors of the Continuance of so bloody a War." Now the envoys' letter has slipped into the future tense, implying that this missive would not be Louis' last word of self-justification. "On one Hand they will see the Advances which the King our Master has made, the Consent he has given to the hardest Proposals, and the Engagements into which his Majesty yielded to enter, for removing all Diffidence, and forwarding the Peace. On the other Hand they may observe a continual Affectation to speak obscurely, that there might be always room to form Pretensions beyond the Condicions agreed; insomuch that we had no sooner yielded to one Demand, and such as seem'd to be the utmost that could be ask'd, but it was receded from, to substitute another more Exorbitant in its place." Then the plenipotentiaries launched their peroration: "Last Year the Dutch and their Allies look'd upon it as an Injury, that Men shou'd think them capable of demanding of the King to unite his Forces to those of the Confederacy, to oblige the King his Grandson to quit his Crown. They appeal'd even to the Preliminaries, which speak only of taking Measures by Concert."

They would now have his Majesty undertake it singly; and they have the Assurance to say, That if they would have formerly contented themselves with less, their Interest, which they now better understand, induces them not to be content with it any longer. Such a Declaration, Sir, is a formal Rupture of all Negociation; and 'tis what the Chief of the Allies wish for.

Should we continue longer at Gertruydenbergh, should we spend whole Years in Holland, our Stay would be to no purpose, seeing those who govern the Republick are persuaded, that 'tis their Interest to make the Peace depend upon an impossible Condition. We do not offer to persuade them to prolong a Negociation, which they have a Mind to break; and in short, whatever Desire the King our Master has to procure Quiet to his People, it will be less grievous to them to support the War, an End of which they know his Majesty would purchase by so great Sacrifices, against the same Enemies with whom he has been fighting these Ten Years; than to have him add the King his Grandson to those Enemies, and imprudently undertake to conquer Spain and the Indies in Two Months, in a certain Assurance, when that Term is expir'd, to find his Enemies strengthned by the Places he must yield to them; and by Consequence, in a Condition to turn against himself the new Arms he should put into their Hands.

Finally, the plenipotentiaries could not resist adding a public note on the personal mistreatment they had received during the negotiations: "We pass over in Silence the Proceedings towards us in Contempt of our Character. We say nothing to you of the injurious Libels full of Falshood and Calumny, which have been suffer'd to be printed and dispers'd during our Stay, with Design to inflame the Minds of those whom we were labouring to Reconcile. . . . None can reproach us with having attempted any of the least Practices contrary to the Laws of Nations, which were violated towards us. And 'tis palpable, that by hindring any from making Visits to us in our kind of Prison, the thing most fear'd was, our discovering such Truths as were industriously kept conceal'd."

The reply of the Dutch Estates General to this French letter was immediate. The estates declared the opinion of all the allied delegates at The Hague that, since the French had rejected their propositions, they had "no choice but to acquiesce in this breakdown" and not to continue the conferences while the enemies maintained their current attitude.[87] Even Torcy now saw that the rupture of the conferences was irreparable.[88] The envoys left Holland on 25 July and four days later reported to Louis at Versailles.

The peace talks had failed, but when Torcy secured Louis' approval for public dissemination of the plenipotentiaries' letter to Heinsius he scored a success in his campaign to convince Europe of allied responsibility for continued war. This letter, moreover, was meant as only the first salvo in a barrage of French propaganda statements conceived and commissioned by Torcy. The government-controlled *Gazette* soon reported the breakdown of negotiations and summarized the final allied conditions.[89] The *Journal de Verdun*, a publication strongly influenced by Torcy's wishes, reprinted the plenipotentiaries' public letter in its September issue.[90] Most important, the plan to publish a full-scale account of the negotiations was now revived. The connection between the failure of the talks and the proposed *relation* is neatly illustrated by the exchange of letters between the court and the envoys when the final Dutch terms were presented. D'Huxelles and Polignac declared that "now is the time to write everywhere and to reveal the secret of this negotiation, so genuine on our side and on theirs so

[87] Torcy, *Journal*, p. 230.   [88] Torcy, *Mémoires*, p. 659.
[89] *Gazette*, 2 August 1710. Cf. draft of this item with changes in Torcy's hand, in AAE, CP, Hollande 226, fol. 179.
[90] *Journal de Verdun*, XIII, 200–206.

fraudulent." In his reply Louis confirmed that he was convinced of "the necessity of instructing the public about the injustice of my enemies and for that end to inform them of what has happened in your conferences with the Dutch deputies. I know that you have included its principal events in a *relation* which must be printed immediately after your return."[91] But the projected *relation* was never printed, nor was any other manifesto, letter or royal proclamation substituted for it. In August there arose strong and decisive resistance in the council to the idea of further royal propaganda concerning the recent diplomatic episodes.

Let us examine why this was so.[92] It is clear that one of Torcy's first actions after the return of the envoys and their secretaries was to send for La Blinière and urge upon him the importance of completing the account of the negotiations envisioned in the diplomatic correspondence of March and April. We know that Torcy also asked Polignac to submit such an account. The two versions were written independently of each other. La Blinière locked himself in d'Huxelles' Paris residence and, working from the marshal's papers, supplemented by others from Torcy's files, completed his manuscript in five days, probably around 15 August. Unfortunately, no copy of La Blinière's work has come down to us, but we do have Polignac's draft. From this document and from La Blinière's letters, it can be learned that the *relations* were now intended not only to present a narrative of the French version of the negotiations, but also

---

[91] Louis to d'Huxelles and Polignac, Versailles, 16 July 1710, in Legrelle, *La Diplomatie française*, v, 559–560.

[92] The following account is drawn from these sources: La Blinière to Pecquet(?), Paris, 5 August 1710, AAE, CP Hollande 228, fol. 258; *mémoire* by La Blinière, January 1713, AAE, MD, France 1874, fols. 32–33; "Journal des conferences de Gertruydenberg" by La Blinière, *ibid.*, fol. 92; Torcy, *Mémoires*, p. 659; Torcy, *Journal*, p. 243; Polignac, "Relation des conferences de Gertruydenberg," AAE, CP, Hollande 227, fols. 114–130. The justificatory manifesto of the Estates General of the United Provinces was issued on 27 July 1710 and is in Lamberty, *Mémoires*, vi, 65 ff.

to rebut the statement already rushed into print by the Dutch Estates General describing the peace talks from the perspective of the allies. Thus Polignac said at the outset of his *relation*: "They [Louis' enemies] have even had the deceit to prejudice the hearts of their people at home by dishonest accounts. . . . In order to illuminate the truth which these governors have taken such care to disguise, we are going to simply report the facts of the most recent negotiation. Then we will refute their manifesto, which is nothing more than a tissue of equivocations and lies."

Marshal d'Huxelles, however, took exception to the view that this was the proper format for the planned publication. Fearing that a narrative written up as a report to the king would involve him and his secretary, La Blinière, in a war of words that the marshal heartily wished to avoid, d'Huxelles argued that the king ought to write a manifesto in his own name if the *relation* were to be a true response to the official, justificatory statement which the Dutch Estates General had made public when the talks collapsed. The marshal further urged that Louis send this manifesto to his parlements and, as the king had done one year before, write to the provincial governors; thus would the monarch encourage his subjects. Polignac and Torcy, on the other hand, were in agreement on the desirability of the less personal style of response. Louis' dignity surely would not allow him—as the king no doubt conceived it—to dirty his hands in a printed debate with a republican assembly. And the foreign minister, ever conscious of the connection between diplomacy and public opinion, wanted a more universally applicable account than Louis had written to the French nation in June 1709. In Torcy's view it was necessary not only to revive French patriotism, but also and especially to strengthen the hand of those citizens of enemy lands who were working for a settlement.[93]

[93] Torcy's *Mémoires* confirm this: "On ne pouvoit aussi se proposer d'autre utilité . . . que l'avantage de faire connoître à toutes les nations amies et ennemies que le Roi n'oublieroit rien pour pacifier

Polignac's account of the negotiations, comprising over thirty written folio sides, is a remarkably faithful account of the conferences of Gertruydenberg. Indeed, its defect, from the point of view of those opposing its publication, was precisely its strict adherence to the record of Louis' proposals to the allies. Polignac recounted that Louis proposed partition of the Spanish empire to Philip's great disadvantage.[94] The envoy told how Louis had offered to subsidize an allied campaign against Philip.[95] When he came to his refutation of the recent Dutch manifesto, Polignac denied the allegation that Louis had promised in 1709 to help the allies expel his grandson from Spain; but he also admitted that the French king was willing to stand aside while his enemies made war on Philip.[96] Although the *relation* argued the lack of realism in the allied insistence on partition and emphasized that it would be impossible for Louis to convince Philip to abandon Spain, it is all too obvious that earlier in the negotiation Louis had been dealing with his enemies on the basis of such a partition.[97] Polignac's *relation*, like the public letter he and d'Huxelles dispatched to Heinsius, would prove to doubting Frenchmen and to well-disposed people abroad that Louis had travelled very far down the road to peace.

---

l'Europe et terminer une guerre sanglante et onéreuse à tant de peuples" (p. 648). "Toute apparence de paix disparoissant, il étoit de l'interêt du Roi que la verité fût connue; que les Provinces-Unies, aussi bien que les nations engagées dans la guerre, apprissent de quel côté formoit tant d'obstacles à la conclusion de la paix. C'étoit une des principes raisons qui avoient porté le Roi a renouveler souvent à ses plénipotentiaries l'ordre de prolonger leur séjour en Hollande le plus qu'il seroit possible. Sa Majesté étoit persuadée qu'il convenoit mieux d'entretenir une négotiation languissante, de supporter la hauteur, l'injustice, la mauvaise foi des négotiations et de leurs maîtres, que de rompre tout reste de négotiation, comme le désiroient les partisans de la guerre" (p. 656).

[94] "Relation des conferences de Gertruydenberg," AAE, CP, Hollande 227, fols. 120-121.

[95] *Ibid.*, fol. 123. [96] *Ibid.*, fol. 125^{v}.

[97] *Ibid.*, fol. 128.

On 20 August Torcy introduced the two accounts by Polignac and La Blinière at the meeting of the king's council. They were discussed as possible "responses to the Dutch manifesto on the rupture of the Gertruydenberg conferences." Torcy judged both works "very strong and very well-written." He read them both to the king. The foreign minister entered this laconic summary of the discussion in his diary: "After differing opinions, that of the chancellor [Pontchartrain], the one that was followed, was not to write, because it was not suitable to acknowlege in an authorized work all the steps that had been taken against the Spanish."[98]

The chronic problem of French propaganda in these years, the conflict of Louis' roles as king and dynast, once again silenced Torcy's propaganda. In 1709 Louis XIV had garbed himself in the imagery of the just, pious and brave king espousing his grandson's cause and thus redeeming his own honor which was also the honor of France. That imagery echoed centuries of French monarchical idealization and inspired a ready response among the Sun King's subjects, in this way fulfilling the immediate need of giving heart to a defeated and hungry nation. The diplomatic needs of 1710 were much different, however. Torcy no longer had to fear domestic collapse. Instead, he could take the offensive in driving a wedge between the king's enemies. Thus the propaganda he required was to be directed outside France primarily, and a patriotic tone was inappropriate. What was called for was a carefully reasoned account of the peace talks, if not signed by the king then at least bearing clear royal authorization. But this account would inevitably show Louis in a guise wholly out of keeping with the idealized French monarch of godliness, courage and justice. The role of the conciliatory diplomat-king, striking pragmatic bargains and negotiating in an amoral universe of political discourse, was precisely the one required by cir-

[98] Torcy, *Journal*, p. 243.

cumstance, but this was a role the Sun King could not play in print without betraying his own and his subjects' sense of what a monarch should be.

In this way, the royal letter of 1709 and the aborted *relation* of 1710 illustrate the tremendous strength as well as the severe limitations of princely propaganda. The awesome majesty of kingship was a pattern of imagery so firmly rooted in the French national consciousness that Torcy and Louis needed only to place the king rhetorically within this tradition in order to tap deep wells of sympathy and identification. Yet the ancient monarchical myth did not at all conform to the realities of diplomatic action. In his public statements to his enemies the king needed to prove that he saw himself not as a mythicized embodiment of divine principles but as a reasonable and very human practitioner of modern politics. The weight of these opposed demands proved too great to allow the king a regular, continuing place in printed propaganda.

The second half of 1710, meanwhile, saw a gradual but definite revival of confidence among Louis' councillors. Indeed, there is evidence that the foreign minister himself was flirting momentarily in August 1710 with the strategy of Bourbon unity as the vehicle of peace, and perhaps it was partly for this reason too that he acquiesced in the nonpublication of an account of the peace talks.[99] In the fall of 1710 the idea of French-initiated peace negotiations became most unpopular in the French court, and the royal government devoted all its efforts to mobilizing for continued war. The consensus at Versailles was that any renewed offers of negotiation by Louis would only delay a settlement. To resuscitate the peace preliminaries, Torcy wrote, would threaten Spanish unity behind Philip, slow war preparations in France while damaging troop morale, and, above all, confirm the claims of the allied warhawks that France would shortly sue for peace. The foreign minister reasoned that the leaders

[99] *Ibid.*, pp. 240–243.

of the anti-French league again would make it appear that Louis was throwing himself upon the mercy of his enemies; thus, the king's peace offers would be used by his opponents as evidence of French weakness and might well push the Dutch and English citizenry toward further exertions for war. On the other hand, Torcy was able to conclude, "France's silence had aroused public impatience" for peace in Holland and England.[100] Torcy knew that effective propaganda sometimes meant verbal restraint.

The impression Torcy wished to foster of a revival of French power was heightened by the institution of a new war tax, the *dixième*, in October 1710. In his printed edict enacting the tax the king assured his subjects that the new revenues would "put us in a position to provide for the extraordinary expenses which the continuation of this war forces upon us, and to pay punctually the *rentes* established on our revenues, the salaries and other charges whose funds depend on our royal treasury." Given the resolve of the government implied by this new tax, in the preface to his edict Louis could risk telling his subjects something of his negotiating policies earlier in the year:

> The sincere Desire we have to make a Peace that might accommodate all Europe, inclined us to take such Steps, as might shew that we had nothing more at Heart, than to procure the Repose of so many Nations who require it. We sent our Plenipotentiaries to Holland; and the Offers we made for so desirable a Blessing having been publish'd by our Enemies, have made known the Uprightness of our Intentions. But the Interest of such as would perpetuate the War, and make Peace impracticable, has prevail'd in the Councils of the Princes and States, who are our Enemies: So that perceiving no Hopes of agreeing upon the Articles that would have conduc'd to a general Negociation, we were oblig'd to recall our Plenipotentiaries. In this Posture of Affairs,

[100] *Ibid.*, pp. 349–350.

we could no longer doubt that all our Care to procure a Peace serv'd only to put it further off, and that we have no other way to bring our Enemies to it, than by making War in good Earnest: But we thought before we came to this last Resolution it would be for the Good of our Subjects to inquire into, and to have laid before us all the Methods, to which we might have Recourse: And after the Advices of Persons, who have the most perfect Knowledge of the State of our Finances, and of the true Condition of the People of our Kingdom, had been consider'd, we found none of them more just and proper, than to demand of our Subjects the Tenth of the Revenues of their Estates.[101]

The sacrifices implied by the *dixième* and the loss of the profitable Dutch trade made clear to France's enemies that king and people were far from beaten. This was Torcy's intention, and his summation of affairs at the end of 1710 reflects his optimism. "The silence kept by the King for the last six months with regard to [peace talks with] the Dutch," he wrote in his journal, "the banning of commerce with them, and the sources of revenue which we seem to have found served everywhere to give a better opinion of French affairs, demonstrations of weakness being a bad way of moving enemies to pity and of acquiring friends."[102]

Ripening factional strife in England also contributed to Torcy's hopeful mood, and he was heartened above all by the news of Philip's decisive victory over Archduke Charles's army at Brihuega. Word of this victory reached Versailles just before Christmas 1710, and the French foreign minister realized at once that "this one day undoubtedly changed the face of affairs in Spain and in all Europe."[103] The Habsburg cause in Spain was now hopeless, and it was to be expected that if Louis only held firm he could gain for his

---

[101] This edict of 14 October 1710 is reprinted in Lamberty, *Mémoires*, VI, 86.

[102] Torcy, *Journal*, p. 327.   [103] *Ibid.*, p. 322.

house and his state a settlement far more favorable than the allies had deigned to offer at The Hague and Gertruydenberg. It was clear to Torcy that the heavy weight of the entanglement in Spain had suddenly been lifted from Louis XIV's shoulders, and that with it had disappeared the conflict of royal interest between dynasty and state. The council decided to order the singing of Te Deum throughout France for Philip's victory;[104] and in the letter Torcy wrote over Louis' name to French ecclesiastics the triumph was portrayed as a gain for France as well as for Spain: "I have all the more reason to render thanks to God for the benedictions which it pleased Him to bestow upon the arms of the King of Spain, my grandson, since my enemies, who are the same as his, have sufficiently made known their intention to employ their utmost efforts to accomplish the complete destruction of my kingdom, under the pretext of forcing me to accord them with regard to Spain peace conditions whose execution was entirely beyond my power."[105] To emphasize that Philip's triumph really belonged to all Frenchmen, Louis simultaneously ordered the provincial governors to "have fireworks set off in the streets, shoot cannon and give all the other signs and demonstrations of public rejoicing."[106] The king's Te Deum order, dated 4 January 1711, marks the end of the long years of defeat endured by Louis XIV in the War of the Spanish Succession. As the writer of an anonymous French propaganda pamphlet published soon afterward remarked, "God has at last declared Himself for the just cause."[107]

Throughout the crisis years of 1709–1710 Torcy had

---

[104] *Ibid.*, p. 321.

[105] *Lettre du Roy écrite à Monseigneur l'Evêque Comte de Chaalons* (Châlons-sur-Marne, 1711), BN, Imp., 4° Lb³⁷.4383.

[106] AAE, CP, Espagne 203, fol. 554ᵛ.

[107] [J. Legrand], *Mémoire touchant la succession à la couronne d'Espagne, traduit de l'espagnol. Réflexions sur la Lettre à Mylord, sur la necessité et la justice de l'entière restitution de la monarchie d'Espagne*, 2nd ed. (n.p., 1711), printer's note.

shown himself consistently aware of the importance of public opinion. In his view the extraordinary psychological circumstances required equally extraordinary responses in the area of signed crown propaganda. At the same time, he marshaled ambitious campaigns of unsigned propaganda to express ideas that restrictions of dignity and diplomacy denied to the king and his ambassadors. To round out our discussion of French propaganda we now turn to these anonymously published works.

CHAPTER EIGHT

Joachim Legrand and the Climax of Torcy's Propaganda

LEGITIMACY AND CONSTITUTIONALISM

THE crisis of 1709–1710 led Torcy to promote radical departures in the form and substance of Louis XIV's communication with the European public. At the same time, the foreign minister sponsored a series of anonymous pamphlets; their purpose was to complement royal pronouncements by amplifying themes which could only be suggested in Louis' signed statements. Most important among these themes were Philip V's legitimacy as ruler of Spain and the defense of French territorial unity and constitutional traditions. These issues were at the center of allied diplomacy and propaganda during the crisis years, and it is a measure of the desperate condition of the Bourbon cause that Torcy felt the need to commission works comprising direct rebuttals of the enemy arguments. The careful coordination that characterized French responses to allied propaganda reached its peak during the Gertruydenberg talks, when d'Huxelles and Polignac, finding the theses presented by allied diplomats identical to those appearing in enemy propaganda literature, sought to conform their planned royal *relation* of the conferences with pamphlet drafts sent by Torcy for their approval.[1] In this way the anonymous French tracts of 1709–

---

[1] See La Blinière's memorandum of January 1713 on this point, AAE, MD, France 1874, fol. 32, as well as the dispatches of d'Huxelles and Polignac to Louis and Torcy for March and April 1710, AAE, CP, Hollande 223 and 224, esp. the plenipotentiaries' letter to Torcy of 26 April 1710, AAE, CP, Hollande 224, fol. 136.

1710 were intended as a diplomatic weapon of even greater immediacy than the pamphlets of the early war years. Of the half-dozen pamphlets published under Torcy's auspices during this period, at least four were composed by Joachim Legrand. Legrand in fact became the most important French propagandist during the last years of the war, adding three more works in 1711 to his list of anonymous publications. A paid member of Torcy's staff since 1705, Legrand had earlier served as diplomatic secretary to members of his patron family, the d'Estrées, in embassies to Lisbon and Madrid. The skills he brought to diplomatic administration were drawn from long training in historical erudition, for in 1676, as a twenty-three-year-old Oratorian first arrived in Paris from his native Saint-Lô, Legrand had attached himself to Thévenot and Le Cointe in the Bibliothèque du Roy. This apprenticeship made him expert in the new science of textual analysis whose rules Mabillon was systematizing, and he soon applied his proficiency in archival research on the English reformation and the reign of Louis XI. To the linguistic skills which were the hallmark of the seventeenth-century *érudit*, Legrand gave witness in translations of two proto-anthropological travel accounts by Portuguese explorers.[2]

[2] On Legrand's early career, the main sources are: Legrand's letters to Léonard from Portugal, 1692–1697, BN, Clairambault 1023, *passim*; BN, Clairambault 174, fols. 127 ff.; AN, M. 769, No. 4$^{1-3}$; Legrand's letters to Léonard and Bulteau from Madrid, 1703–1704, AN, M. 769, No. 4$^{4-16}$; Abbé d'Estrées to Torcy, Madrid, 22 September 1703, AAE, CP, Espagne 117, fols. 346^v–347; memorandum by Legrand, AAE, MD, Espagne 368, fols. 167–172; and BN, Clairambault 1024, fols. 158–170; Legrand's letters to Clairambault, 1702–1704, BN, Clairambault 452, fols. 7–170, 185–222; notes by Léonard, BN, Ms. fr. 22585, fols. 85–88. See also "Eloge historique de Monsieur l'Abbé Le Grand," in Jean-Pierre Nicéron, *Mémoires pour servir à l'histoire des hommes illustres dans la république des lettres*, 43 vols. (Paris, 1727–1745), vol. 26; and Neveu, "La vie érudite," pp. 451–453. The works translated by Legrand are J. Ribeyro, *Histoire de l'Isle de Ceylan* (Amsterdam, 1701); and J. Lobo, *Voyage historique d'Abissinie* (Amsterdam, 1728). Lobo's work was widely read in the eighteenth century; Samuel John-

In Torcy's employ during the last decade of Louis' reign,[3] Legrand used his knowledge of European diplomacy to compose many policy memoranda. He also directed his erudition and first-hand experience in the embassies toward the organization of the ministerial archives and the aspiring diplomats in the Académie politique. Like many of his Oratorian brothers, Legrand was much interested in education; his influence in organizing and defining the purposes of the academy was very great. In his view the institution was meant to serve, among other things, as the vehicle for an archive-based historical justification of Louis XIV's actions. As Legrand told Torcy in a planning memorandum on the academy: "It is not enough that the actions of kings be always accompanied by justice and reason. Their subjects [*peuples*] must also be convinced of it, particularly when wars are undertaken which, although just and necessary, nearly always bring on much misery in their wake. Now how can kings and their ministers communicate the necessity of declaring war if they lack the means by which to prove that they have arrived at that extremity only after uselessly employing all other means and that the arms they are obliged to take up are truly *ratio ultima*?"[4] For Legrand, the means of making these points to Frenchmen lay in the his-

---

son praised it for its accuracy and judgment (Gay, *Enlightenment*, II, 320).

[3] Legrand's activities in this decade can be reconstructed from his papers, the bulk of which are in BN, Clairambault, esp. vols. 515, 518–521, and also vols. 284, 295, 549, 560, 1024; on the summons to Versailles in 1705, see Legrand to Gaignières, Paris, 4 March 1705, BN, Ms. fr. 24988, fol. 109; Torcy's payments to Legrand in the amount of three thousand livres annually after 1705 are recorded in AAE, MD, France 307, fols. 164 ff., fols. 254 ff., fols. 349 ff.; France 308, fols. 29 ff.; France 309, fols. 60 ff.; France 310, fols. 328 ff. Also see Legrand to Robert, Versailles, 29 July 1709, AN, K. 569, No. 104. Baschet, *Archives*, esp. pp. 102–106, uses some of these sources.

[4] Quoted by Baschet, *Archives*, p. 111. See *ibid.*, pp. 112–131, for other memoranda by Legrand on the Académie politique and the archives.

torical sources, the papers of Torcy's archive. The manuscripts could be organized to prove the need for war to Frenchmen who no longer were certain of their monarch's wisdom and authority. The archives were to be the source, and the research of the academicians one channel for the elaboration of a new propaganda based on history; that is to say, on the records of the past as filtered through the precepts of rational analysis. Where royal historiographers and panegyrists had failed or become outmoded, Legrand hoped a new method would succeed. Condemned by influential critics for his continual warfare, Louis XIV might yet win the approval of his subjects once they were instructed in the historical record.[5]

A similar impulse inspired Legrand's anonymous pamphlets. Convinced that his monarch's cause was suffering unjustly before the court of European public opinion, Legrand undertook to redress the balance. His intended audience was by no means limited to fellow-scholars. Instead, as he wrote to Torcy, "before rendering public a tract, people of great intelligence and ability should be consulted so as to see if it persuades them, and ordinary people of middling wit should be consulted to see if they are moved by it." In this way, Legrand believed Torcy might best reach "a sort of sample [abrégé] of the public" representing the varied groups to which French propaganda was meant to appeal.[6]

In all of Legrand's propaganda works the argument is structured by themes drawn from history and from history's close consort, the law. Appropriately, Legrand's first venture into pamphleteering stemmed from a long-standing historian's debate with Gilbert Burnet about the English reformation.[7] When Burnet spoke out on the war in a

---

[5] Klaits, "Men of Letters," pp. 580–581, 589–596.

[6] Memorandum in Legrand's hand, BN, Clairambault 518, p. 753.

[7] The debate began in 1685, five years after the publication of Burnet's *The History of the Reformation of the Church of England.* Burnet was visiting Paris and, since Legrand was conducting research

widely circulated sermon of 1706, Legrand set about composing a response. La Chapelle had already published a refutation of the clerical doctor in a *Lettre d'un suisse*, but, as Torcy wrote, there was nothing wrong with "attacking the imposter on several fronts," especially as "an old friend of Doctor Burnet, someone who knows him personally and who is familiar with the falsities which the spirit of untruth has inspired in him, has asked to take up the cudgels against him once again."[8] But Legrand's acquaintance with the bishop made his "Réflexions sur le sermon presché par le Docteur Burnet" a bit too personal for the foreign minister's taste. Legrand could not resist including a challenge to the bishop's scholarly qualifications and personal character in his substantive criticisms of the prelate's views. The bitterness of the *ad hominem* attack with which he opened the piece, citing the bishop of Salisbury as a hypocrite who was

on the same topic, Thévenot, the royal librarian who was Legrand's mentor, took the opportunity to arrange public discussion by the two scholars. At this session, Legrand offered certain criticisms of Burnet's methods and use of sources, which in no way prevented the Englishman from implying in the preface to a new edition of his history that Legrand had applauded Burnet's work. When Legrand's own history of Henry VIII's divorce appeared, it pointedly refuted Burnet's interpretation. There ensued an exchange of published letters to Thévenot, first from Burnet rebutting Legrand, then from Legrand concluding his attack on Burnet ("Eloge historique," BN, Clairambault 1024). The relevant works are G. Burnet, *The History of the Reformation of the Church of England*, 2nd ed., 2 vols. (London, 1681); J. Legrand, *Histoire du divorce de Henry VIII . . . avec . . . la refutation des deux premiers livres de l'"Histoire de la Reformation" de M. Burnes*, 3 vols. (Paris, 1688); *A Letter to Mr. Thévenot containing a censure of Mr. Le Grand's "History of King Henry the Eighth's Divorce" . . . together with some further Reflections on Mr. Le Grand, both written by Gilbert Burnet* (London, 1689); *Lettre de Mr. Burnet à Mr. Thévenot . . . Nouvelle édition augmentée d'un avertissement et des remarques de M. L. G. [Legrand] qui servent de réponse à cette lettre* (Paris, 1688); *Lettre de M. Le Grand à M. Burnet* (Paris, 1691).

[8] *LS* 41. Torcy to La Chapelle, Marly 1 June 1707 (minute), AAE, CP, Suisse 179, fol. 71.

sometimes a Presbyterian, sometimes an Anglican, but always a dangerous traitor, probably accounts for Torcy's decision to leave the tract unpublished.[9] Not until the second half of 1709 did Legrand resume the role of propagandist. His first published efforts were two brief pamphlets masquerading as letters of a Genevan to an Amsterdam burgomaster.[10] This format was clearly in the mold of the *Lettres d'un suisse*, which had stopped appearing a few months earlier. But by inventing two Protestant correspondents in place of La Chapelle's Catholics, Legrand and Torcy were able to plausibly court a Dutch audience. Thus the first and the second *Lettre d'un Conseiller de Genève à un Bourgemaistre d'Amsterdam* reflect Torcy's opinion that the road to peace ran through Holland. After the disappointment of the failed Hague negotiations the foreign minister attempted to place his views before potentially sympathetic Dutch and English via Legrand's pamphlets. The tracts were part of the French effort to soften up allied opinion in preparation for new peace talks which Torcy correctly anticipated would begin early in 1710.

As Louis' public letters sought to dispel allied convictions about the hopelessly desperate plight of France, Legrand's short pamphlets emphasized the still untapped French reserves available for the war effort. In the Genevan councillor's first letter, published in July 1709, the writer observed that although the allies had experienced unbroken military success for five years, the Dutch were reaping no benefits from these victories; for France still had great armies in the field, her provinces had not wavered in their support of the war, her soldiers were more devoted than ever and her people had resolved to make extraordinary sacrifices. Furthermore, the Dutch had succeeded only in strengthening their allies while they exhausted themselves. The house of Austria, already master of Italy, was anxious to turn the empire into

[9] The manuscript is in BN, Clairambault 295, pp. 421-461.
[10] See appendix.

an absolute monarchy; England was using the war to build up her maritime strength, while Portugal, Hamburg, and Lübeck would be happy to see Holland ruined. Turning the tables on his enemies, Legrand's Genevan wrote that the peace preliminaries would severely threaten Dutch safety by strengthening the emperor and the English. And in conclusion he advised Dutchmen to support Philip V as their chief bulwark against imminent domination by their over-mighty allies.

The *Lettre d'un Conseiller de Genève* soon provoked a rebuttal, so Legrand made this his pretext for publishing a sequel in December 1709. Similar to its predecessor in thematic content, the new tract struck a tone of bitter irony as it summarized the position of those who supported the league: that England would never desert Holland, that the emperor was the steadfast friend of the Dutch, "that as the most just party is always the happiest, the Queen who at present occupies the throne of Great Britain must have accomplished an action agreeable to God in contributing . . . to the deposition of the King her father, in persecuting her brother, in retaining the throne." The writer observed "that on the other hand, the Most Christian King reversed the laws of God and of man in approving the testament of the King his brother-in-law, in permitting his grandson to accept a crown to which he was called by the rights of blood, by the consent of all the estates. . . . Your friend proves all this to us so clearly that there can be no reply."[11] Gaultier saw to

---

[11] *Seconde Lettre d'un Conseiller du Grand Conseil de Genève à un Bourgemaistre d'Amsterdam* (n.p., n.d.), pp. 5–6. According to Bourgeois and André, *Sources*, IV, 347, Legrand also wrote an anonymous tract published in 1709 as *Traduction d'un écrit intitulé Réflexions sur l'état de l'Europe, avec la réponse à ces réflexions.* The bibliographical entry is very confused; it ties this tract to the Gertruydenberg talks which postdated it by a year. Further, as one may deduce from the title, this is not one tract but two; the second is a violent attack on France and certainly was not Legrand's work. The first piece, though more favorable to the French cause, expresses ideas not to be found in works commissioned by Torcy. Neither is

it that copies of these pamphlets came to the attention of Englishmen opposed to the Whig government. We have his testimony that the Genevan pamphlets "caused a great stir in Holland and inspired judgments reflecting badly on those opposed to peace." English warhawks, on the other hand, feared that "it would make an impression on the minds of the Dutch and would open their eyes."[12] The hurried publication of an answering pamphlet by the allies is good evidence that Gaultier's analysis was accurate.

Unraveling Torcy's propaganda during this period is a task complicated by the existence of still another anonymous tract with the title *Seconde Lettre d'un Conseiller du Grand Conseil de Genève à un Bourguemaître d'Amsterdam*. Although we cannot be certain of its authorship, this pamphlet of late 1709 is in the rhetorical style of the *Lettres d'un suisse* and, like several of La Chapelle's tracts, it refers its readers to the "proofs" of Dubos' *Les Interêts d'Angleterre malentendus*. Striking the same chords as did Legrand's Geneva tracts, this *Seconde Lettre* emphasizes that France was far from exhausted and adduced as evidence the results of Malplaquet, the gold and silver melted for coin, and Louis' inspiring open letter of June 1709. The propagandist warned the Dutch that they would never be able to dictate peace terms at Versailles or to overthrow Philip; he advised them

---

there any external evidence connecting this tract with Legrand. The confusion seems to have resulted from a hasty reading of the anti-French rebuttal to this tract. Its author likens the work under his review to the recently published *Lettre d'un Conseiller de Genève à un Conseiller d'Amsterdam*, calling them pieces "of the same genre," but in no way implying a common authorship. Jean Dumont, writing in 1713 (*Les Soupirs de l'Europe . . . or the Groans of Europe* [London], pp. 87–88), identified the author of the *Lettre d'un Conseiller de Genève* as the man who wrote the *Réflexions sur l'état de l'Europe*. The error has been perpetuated ever since. Legrand did not compose (or translate) the *Réflexions*, and the tract has no connection with Torcy.

[12] Gaultier to Torcy, 8 June 1709, AAE, CP, Angleterre 228, fol. 86; Gaultier to Torcy, 3 January 1710, AAE, CP, Angleterre 230, fol. 24.

not to trust the exaggerations of their own gazettes about the lack of food and money in France. Finally, in a reference to Philip V's disputed title, the author appealed to the Dutch to follow Grotius' rule that the law of nature and the *droit des gens* be observed with regard to succession and possession of states, especially when confirmed by the constituted bodies of the countries involved. His analogy, in a typical La Chapellian touch, was "the recent example of Neuchâtel, which you [the Dutch] affirm legitimate."[13]

Very soon this question of Philip's legitimacy became a leading theme of Torcy's propaganda. The problem of Charles II's inheritance was by no means the only staple in the polemicist's warehouse during the War of the Spanish Succession, a point amply documented by the diverse literature of controversy we have examined. But in 1710 the shopworn subject of Philip's legitimacy was polished up once more for marketing under the Whig slogan "No peace without Spain." The Marlborough-Godolphin government made this a virtually non-negotiable demand at Gertruydenberg, and their intransigent position is reflected in a series of allied pamphlets of 1709–1710. Most outstanding among these works was the *Lettre à Mylord sur la necessité et la justice de l'entière restitution de la monarchie d'Espagne*, published in Holland in February 1710.[14] This tract, Torcy soon realized, not only summarized the position of Marlborough and his associates on a crucial phase of the peace talks but was also providing a near-verbatim outline of the allied delegates' arguments at the early sessions of the Gertruydenberg conferences.[15] The French foreign minister im-

---

[13] *Seconde Lettre d'un Conseiller du Grand Conseil de Genève à un Bourguemaître d'Amsterdam* (n.p., n.d.), BN, Imp., Lb⁸⁷.4373, p. 8.

[14] This tract is attributed to Jean Dumont. The French plenipotentiaries sent Torcy a copy from Valenciennes; see Torcy to d'Huxelles and Polignac, Versailles, 3 April 1710 (minute), AAE, CP, Hollande 223, fols. 197ᵛ–198. Lamberty, *Mémoires*, printed the *Lettre à Mylord* in VI, 17–36. An annotated edition is in AAE, CP, Espagne 203, fols. 89–100ᵛ.

[15] Memorandum by La Blinière, AAE, MD, France 1874, fol. 32.

mediately set Legrand to work on an answer to the *Lettre à Mylord* and soon was able to dispatch a draft to d'Huxelles and Polignac for their comments. Encouraged by the pleni-potentiaries' praise of the work and their urgings that the pamphlet be published as a preliminary that would prepare people for the anticipated royal *relation* of the conferences, Torcy authorized Legrand to print twin treatises on Philip's legitimacy in May 1710.[16] That Legrand's propaganda up-held Philip's rights while the account would reveal Louis bargaining away Philip's title was not paradoxical to d'Huxelles, Polignac and Torcy. The French diplomats knew that "no peace without Spain" was a recipe for no peace at all. Hence in their anonymous propaganda works they tried to undermine the rationale for the English insis-tence on Philip's removal, while in their account of the con-ferences they hoped to show Louis' willingness to meet even unreasonable demands.

What were the arguments Legrand set out to rebut? The *Lettre à Mylord* stated that Philip could justify his claims to the Spanish crown neither by rights of blood nor by the grant of Charles II's testament. Whatever precedence Philip might have had in the line of succession, the writer explained, was signed away by his grandmother, Maria Theresa, when she married Louis XIV and renounced her rights to the Spanish throne. As for the testament, the author called it a forgery extorted from the dying Charles; even if it were genuine, the testament would be illegal, since it willed away the Spanish empire to a foreigner and thus violated the fundamental law of Spain that declared the monarchy in-alienable. Throughout the *Lettre à Mylord* there is heavy emphasis on the Whig doctrine of constitutional monarchy: "[It is] a fundamental maxim that kings do not hold their kingdoms *in dominio*, and that consequently they have no right to dispose of them. . . . Everyone knows that kingship is an office, an administration, giving kings no proprietary

[16] D'Huxelles and Polignac to Torcy, Gertruydenberg, 26 April 1710, AAE, CP, Hollande 224, fols. 135–136ᵛ.

255

possession. Kings exist for the people, not the people for them. They hold their original authority from the people. . . . A prince who cedes his kingdom or who submits it to another without the consent of the people or the estates which he represents, is held to have accomplished nothing, for such an act is contrary to the nature of government."[17] To flesh out this theory the writer painted the affecting portrait of a Spain ground down by the imported despotism of Louis XIV and yearning for liberation from the yoke of oppression through the victory of Archduke Charles.

The necessary conclusion was that Louis, who, among his many other ostensible crimes, had violated international law by overturning the renunciations of the Treaty of the Pyrenees, should be made to join with the allies in achieving the complete restitution of Charles's rightful inheritance. The allied writer listed the so-called French accessions and aggressions since 1648, holding that only by the complete removal of the Spanish empire from French influence could Europe be saved from Bourbon domination: to grant even Naples and Sicily to Philip "would be to render France mistress of all Mediterranean commerce and put her in the position of ruining our trade there and that of Holland, . . . [so that] after they rested for a few years it would be easy for the French to renew the war with great advantage over Spain on land and sea, before anyone could form a league capable of saving her [Spain]."[18]

Now during the preceding decade the Bourbon defense of Philip's rights first formulated when Louis accepted the Spanish testament had been reiterated without significant variation by Torcy's propagandists. From the *Gazette*'s account of the recognition ceremony of November 1700, through the compilations of Obrecht and the arguments rehearsed in the *Lettres d'un suisse*, and down through Louis' 1709 manifesto and Legrand's own *Seconde Lettre d'un conseiller de Genève*, the theme had remained constant: Philip's

---

[17] *Lettre à Mylord*, p. 14.   [18] *Ibid.*, p. 23.

claim rested upon the triple foundation of his rights of blood, the testament of his predecessor and the consent of the Spanish people. But in his *Mémoire touchant la succession d'Espagne* and *Réflexions sur la lettre à Mylord*,[19] Legrand chose the unusual strategy of building his case on the fundamental laws of the Spanish monarchy. Without disregarding earlier French reasoning based on rights of birth, the testament, and popular approval, he moved the argument to a new level by subsuming these three under a more inclusive schema that generalized and systematized them. Legrand wrote that the true foundation of Philip's rights was to be found in immutable, fundamental laws which overrode the actions of any king. In short, he made a constitutional argument, holding that "each state has its fundamental laws in accordance with which it is governed. No one is permitted to disturb them. Whatever authority the magistrates have in a state, they are only the ministers or the interpreters of the laws."[20]

By choosing these grounds for his battle with the *Lettre à Mylord*, Legrand undercut one of his adversary's strongest points, the claim that Philip's succession represented a victory for absolutist despotism over limited constitutional monarchy. Legrand also was shrewd in delimiting the area

[19] *Mémoire touchant la succession à la couronne d'Espagne, traduit de l'espagnol. Réflexions sur la lettre à Mylord, sur la nécessité et la justice de l'entière restitution de la monarchie d'Espagne* (n.p., 1710), BN, Imp., Lb[37].4368; a second edition, published in 1711, is nearly identical (BN, Imp., Lb[37].4889). A draft of the *Mémoire touchant la succession d'Espagne*, in Legrand's hand and with many changes in Torcy's hand, is in BN, Clairambault 518, pp. 355–385. One can follow the development of the *Réflexions sur la lettre à Mylord* through the following drafts in Legrand's hand: (a) BN, Clairambault 518, pp. 387 ff.; (b) BN, Clairambault 295, pp. 381 ff.; (c) BN, Clairambault 518, pp. 681 ff. Marginal comments in Torcy's hand appear in drafts (a) and (b).

[20] *Mémoire touchant la succession d'Espagne*, pp. 11–12. Argument for the Bourbon succession derived from Spanish fundamental law was not original with Legrand; cf. Wolf, *Louis XIV*, p. 655.

of the restrictive fundamental laws to matters of succession and inalienability. His argument required him to go no further in discussing limitations on kings, and this carefully chosen position gave the propagandist an opportunity to cast aspersions on a supposed English writer whose nation, he wrote, was so capricious that it could not have the slightest comprehension of what was meant by inviolable laws of succession as understood in France and Spain.[21]

Demonstrating the ludicrousness of the position that Philip could not rule Spain because he was a foreigner, Legrand showed that nearly all Spain's monarchs had descended from "foreign" stock, and that in fact the majority of them had had French antecedents. Next he noted that Spanish succession law neither excluded women nor deprived them of the right of passing on rights of succession to their offspring. Then the prior rights of Anne of Austria's descendants over those of the male Habsburg line were discussed. As for Maria Theresa's renunciation, as ordained by Philip IV, Legrand contended with irrefutable logic that if it were conceded that Philip had the right to alter the succession law by excluding his daughter's descendants, no one could deny Charles II the same right to further alter the succession by reinstating them. Still, Legrand was reluctant to rest his case squarely on the testament; he carefully added that, in any event, Philip's alteration of the succession was a departure from tradition, while Charles's testament restored the succession to its constitutional lines.

All these arguments were decked out with a great display of scholarly apparatus. Spanish sources, including the testaments of Emperor Charles V and of Philip II, were quoted in the original; the opinions of French and Spanish jurists, historians, and ecclesiastics were cited at length. In these pieces Legrand struck a tone of erudition far removed from the light rhetorical style of his Geneva pamphlets. Much more substantial than the *Lettres* in length, scholar-

---

[21] *Réflexions sur la lettre à Mylord*, pp. 77, 107.

ship, and intensity of analysis, the *Mémoire* and the *Ré-flexions* show Legrand aiming at an audience that was relatively sophisticated in matters of public law. The diverse character of the works he produced during 1709–1710 indicates that Legrand designed his writing to appeal to different cultural groups. If "people of great intelligence and ability" and "ordinary people of middling wit" might not share the same tastes in political pamphlets, it was at least possible to reach audiences at different levels of the cultural scale with a variety of pamphlet styles.

The heaviest salvo in Legrand's argument from authorities was his discussion of the propositions of Grotius on the rights of succession: first, that a king cannot renounce for or disinherit his offspring in a monarchy such as Spain's, whose fundamental law was lineal, cognate succession; and second, that a king has no jurisdiction over his successor. Legrand admitted that Grotius' commentators were divided in their interpretation of the latter proposition; but he showed, in an ingenious argument, that in any case Philip had to be the lawful heir. For if a king could bind his descendants, Philip III and Philip IV could not have legally excluded their daughters' offspring from the succession, as this had been expressly forbidden in the testaments of earlier Spanish kings. But if a king were not bound by his ancestors, Charles II had the full right to annul the acts of his father and grandfather and restore Philip to the line of succession.[22] Thus did Legrand seek to show Europe that Philip's succession stemmed not from any desire by Louis XIV to gather the Spanish crown into the French monarchy,[23] but from the invariable laws of Spain.

The application of *érudit* research techniques to propagandistic exposition was an important methodological feature of Legrand's *Mémoire* and *Réflexions*. The Oratorian's

[22] *Mémoire touchant la succession d'Espagne*, pp. 50–64. In the analogous passage of *Réflexions sur la lettre à Mylord*, pp. 72–75, Legrand also invokes the authority of Pufendorf.

[23] *Mémoire touchant la succession d'Espagne*, p. 39.

training, particularly his familiarity with Spanish scholarship, enabled him to draw freely upon documentary sources
and public law literature, while his writing skill transformed
the methods of antiquarian erudition into powerful tools of
propaganda. The tradition of royal patronage for *érudits*
that descended from Richelieu and Colbert thus was continued in Torcy's relationship with Legrand. Expertise in
historical scholarship proved equally valuable to Legrand
when he confronted the second major thesis of the *Lettre à
Mylord* which in Torcy's opinion required immediate and
decisive rebuttal: the need for the allies to impose constitutional reform in France.

For the author of the *Lettre*, the French monarchy's power to menace Europe would remain intact even were the
allies to impose the ultimate in territorial exactions upon
Philip V: "Whatever measures we might take, we will never
be fully secure against the enterprises of a powerful and
despotic [French] king."[24] Here, then, is the remedy proposed: "The essential thing is to profit from the present
state of affairs by putting the government of France on its
former footing, by reestablishing the Estates, so that the
king will no longer be able to undertake a war or levy any
taxes without their consent. Thus neighbors and subjects
will finally enjoy some peace. Although Frenchmen of today
appear born for slavery, although they seem to have become
used to it during Louis XIV's long reign, it is impossible to
believe that there are not to be found among them enlightened people zealous for their country who secretly lament
the loss of their privileges."[25] After proceeding to a description of the loss of influence suffered under Louis XIV by
clergy, nobility, third estate, and parlements, the propagandist ended his tract with these lines: "It is the interest
of France's neighbors to thus reduce her to the happy necessity of no longer beginning unjust wars. It is the interest of
all good Frenchmen [*bons français*] to cooperate in what-

[24] *Lettre à Mylord*, p. 23.   [25] *Ibid.*, p. 24.

ever we undertake to restore them to the possession of their former privileges, and it will be the summit of the *gloire* of our august Queen to avenge herself on her enemies only by bestowing upon them the enjoyment of all that is most precious and most worthy among men."[26] The *Lettre à Mylord*, then, not only called for the full rigor of the preliminaries of 1709 but added as an immense further condition the reform of France's system of government along whatever lines might suit her victorious enemies.

This extreme thesis was put with even greater emphasis in a highly condensed pamphlet that appeared simultaneously with the *Lettre à Mylord*, the *Lettre d'un ami de Londres à son ami de La Haye*. After a brief review of France's terrorizing policies under Louis XIII and Louis XIV, the work moved quickly to the point:

> As long as we allow despotic power to subsist in the heart of that kingdom [France] . . . our hopes for the repose of Europe are vain, even were France to renounce the entire Spanish monarchy for the moment. For what this despotic power has caused, reason and experience tell us she will continue to cause in the future. This power is the source of the ambition, and the ambition that of all the evils. . . . What to do, you will say, to abolish this despotic power within France? It is a domestic affair in which we have no right to meddle. Pardon me, Monsieur, but when a madman abuses his sword all men have a natural and acquired right to rip his sword from his hands. This is why I believe that we ought to roundly *declare* to France that along with the restitution of Spain and its dependencies she must reestablish her Estates as they were during the reign of the present king's grandfather and under all his predecessors, without the consent of which kings would not be able to raise troops and money or make peace and war.

[26] *Ibid.*

The pamphleteer exhorted the allies to make war for only two more years so as to be able to impose this law on France, "seconded and favored by all those in that great state—princes, *grands*, clergy, parlements, nobility and people—who are lamenting their hard servitude to this enormous power."[27]

By 1710 internal reform of France imposed from abroad had become a major issue of debate in the English and Dutch press. Writers argued the relative merits of resuscitating the estates and partitioning the country as devices by which to adjust the European balance of power.[28] Such discussion did not in itself seem threatening to Torcy; as he told d'Huxelles and Polignac, "This type of writing is not worthy of much attention in a country like Holland where everyone has the liberty to print and publish his visions." But these two pamphlets were special, the foreign minister continued, for he had learned that "this ridiculous project was spread through the Dutch provinces by the people who are most closely attached to the duke of Marlborough."[29] Torcy's apprehension that the military leader of the allies believed in overhauling the French government and was using his influence to foist this idea upon his colleagues was no invention of French paranoia. The foreign minister's intelligence service was remarkably accurate on this point, as Marlborough's letter to Godolphin of 7 June 1709 demonstrates: "[Should] God Almighty as hetherto bless with Success the Armes of the Allyes, I think the Queen should then have the honour of insisting upon putting the ffrench Government upon their being againe govern'd by the three Estates which I think is

---

[27] *Lettre d'un ami de Londres à son ami de La Haye* (n.p., n.d.), bound in BN, Clairambault 515, pp. 209–211.

[28] See, for instance, Defoe's *Review*, 5 April 1709, pp. 2–3; 19 April 1709, p. 26; 9 June 1709, pp. 114–115. See also Gillot, *L'Opinion publique*, pp. 300–303.

[29] Torcy to d'Huxelles and Polignac, Versailles, 20 March 1710, AAE, CP, Hollande 223, fol. 88.

more likely to give quiet to Christendom, than the taring provences from them for the inriching of others."[30]

A second, equally important reason for Torcy's apprehension was that, in his words to the plenipotentiaries, "these tracts do not fail to make an impression in France, perhaps even more so than in foreign countries."[31] A series of Huguenot writings published since 1685 had advocated the reconstitution of the French estates by Louis' foreign enemies as a brake to internal Bourbon tyranny. Even more ominous were the Catholic writers within France—of whom Fénelon was only the most celebrated—who urged similar constitutional reforms. Fénelon's "Tables de Chaulnes" of 1711 included provision for a permanent, elective Estates General, dominated by the old nobility and vested with power of the purse and an advisory role in foreign affairs. In the wake of the 1709 crisis, when calls for a meeting of the estates reached a crescendo, Torcy had every reason to be wary when the issue was raised in allied propaganda.[32]

Thus, the foreign minister hastily commissioned an answering tract which was already in print, although not released for distribution, when he dispatched an advance copy to d'Huxelles and Polignac. Unfortunately, no copy of this first edition appears to have survived, but we can guess its

[30] Quoted in Churchill, *Marlborough*, VI, 85. See also Trevelyan, *Queen Anne*, II, 127n, where Marlborough's plans for helping the Huguenot rebels of the Cévennes in 1706 are paired with his desire to convoke the Estates General. Many Englishmen advocated throughout the war that the reestablishment of the Edict of Nantes be made an allied war aim (cf. Trevelyan, *Queen Anne*, III, 36).

[31] Torcy to d'Huxelles and Polignac, Versailles, 3 April 1710 (minute), AAE, CP, Hollande 223, fol. 197ᵛ.

[32] F. Puaux, *Les Défenseurs de la souveraineté du peuple sous le règne de Louis XIV* (Paris, 1917), p. 64; Kleyser, *Flugschriftenkampf*, pp. 33, 110–111, 115–124, 144–145; G. H. Dodge, *The Political Theory of the Huguenots of the Dispersion* (New York, 1947), pp. 151–156; Mousnier, "Fénelon," pp. 198–202. Mousnier describes Fénelon's writings of this period as "un écho de la propagande ennemie." Cf. Anderson, "Balance of Power," p. 191. See also above, chap. 7, at n. 39.

tone from the plenipotentiaries' comment that "the portrait of Monsieur de Marlborough is too *au naturel* . . . and it seems to us that the horror the court would have at the idea of the Estates General of the kingdom is overemphasized; it can well be said that the estates are useless, but not that we dread them."[33] Accordingly, Torcy ordered the suggested changes and reprinted a new edition for public distribution under the title *Response d'un amy de La Haye, à son amy de Londres*.[34] Without a manuscript copy and in the absence of archival evidence we cannot be certain of this pamphlet's authorship, although its heavy reliance on historical sources and its arguments paralleling the *Réflexions sur la lettre à Mylord* point to Legrand.

Whoever wrote it, this tract is a powerful, effective document, one that touches on several important themes of Torcy's propaganda. The writer began by describing his rival as a man "blinded by passion or a man who wishes to blind others."[35] He focused on the English writer's assertion that "despotic power is the source of ambition, and ambition the source of wars," and in a series of rhetorical questions suggested that ambition is equally characteristic of republics and even of parliaments, not excluding England's. Moreover, "authority, no matter how absolute, will never drive peoples to the same efforts to which the art of winning them over [*séduire leur inclination*] can carry them; and this art is more common because it is more necessary in mixed governments than in absolute monarchies. Force gives out in the end, finding obstacles it cannot overcome. Passion alone has infinite resources which are never exhausted."[36] Why then, asked the writer, should the allies

---

[33] Torcy to d'Huxelles and Polignac, Versailles, 3 April 1710, AAE, CP, Hollande 223, fol. 197^v; d'Huxelles and Polignac to Torcy, Gertruydenberg, 13 April 1710, AAE, CP, Hollande 224, fols. 81^v–82.

[34] *Response d'un amy de La Haye, à son amy de Londres* (n.p., n.d.), BN, Imp., Lb^{37}.4364.

[35] *Ibid.*, p. 1.   [36] *Ibid.*, p. 2.

erect this illusory and unjust demand as a further obstacle to a peace already so difficult to achieve?

Torcy's propagandist went on to stress the utter novelty of this proposition. Should the principle of foreign intervention in domestic matters be once established, a new anarchy would threaten Europe. Frenchmen, he continued, had willingly yielded their private authority to the king for the sake of preserving order, and they were not ready to revoke their gift: "The French sometimes complain of those who reign, but they still love the throne; and this love of sovereignty always serves to reconcile them with the sovereign. . . . This affection is without limits, above all when the kings suffer misfortune. Such is the spirit of Frenchmen: always capable of murmuring against their princes in time of prosperity, inviolably attached to them when they fear losing them, and always ready to return to their duty when they perceive that the foreigner is going to profit from their fault."[37] Thus the demonstration of support for Louis in 1709 was typical of the French, and, in this connection, the writer pointed to the absence of dissident factions within France: "Where are the princes of the blood, the famous men led by blind ambition who would oppose the wishes of the king in an Estates General? . . . Whatever our Englishman says, and he is not as well informed of French affairs as he would have it appear, it is clear that 'princes, *grands*, clergy, parlements, nobility and people' all concur unanimously in giving vent to their zeal for the king."[38] If the English hoped for a rebirth of the Estates General of the sixteenth-century civil wars, the French writer continued, they were sadly misled, because forty years of obedience to the king had produced a new attitude. "Almost all private wealth depends on royal authority. Wages, pensions, huge loans, and arrears in *rentes* are attached to the king. Should the monarchy totter, all this wealth would be endangered; as it amounts to more than three-quarters of that of private

[37] *Ibid.*, p. 4.   [38] *Ibid.*

individuals, its ruin would necessarily cause the ruin of all other property. The French know this better than we. . . . They have forgotten that there once was an Estates General in their monarchy, and it would be imprudent of us to remind them of it."[39] The imprudence stemmed from the fact that, in the pamphleteer's view, kings of the fourteenth and fifteenth centuries had used meetings of the Estates General to "reestablish the *gloire* and fortune of the *patrie*," to awaken "the French spirit," "love of the *patrie*," and "the courage of the Nation" in the face of a common danger. Then "the enemies of France had time to comprehend that nothing is more dangerous for the victors than to push their unexpected victories too far."[40] As for the present, "the assembled French would understand the danger to their monarchy. . . . They love that monarchy, and the name and the blood of their kings. Do we hope to destroy such sentiments, strong as nature? The French will be instructed of our peace conditions. Let us not flatter ourselves. They will find them harsh and hateful, and they will perhaps dispute what their king has already accorded. Such an example would not be unprecedented. . . . Moreover, who does not know that a people's prejudices are invincible? Even their errors are dear to them. One would sooner deprive them of life than of certain usages they have received, of an old constitution, or of a long-standing custom."[41] Here is the unifying theme of Torcy's propaganda in 1710. Legrand's *Mémoire touchant la succession d'Espagne* and *Réflexions sur la lettre à Mylord* held that the fundamental laws of Spain would be upheld by Spaniards loyal to Philip V's succession. The *Response d'un amy de La Haye à son amy de Londres* disputed the Whig contention that internal reform in France was a practical war aim, holding that Frenchmen, like Spaniards, would defend their tradition of monarchy against all foreign interference.

The imposition of internal political reform by victorious

[39] *Ibid.*, p. 5.   [40] *Ibid.*, p. 6.   [41] *Ibid.*

enemies was a novel but logically inescapable extension of balance of power strategy propounded by allied theorists and statesmen. Thus Torcy's extreme sensitivity to any mention of the Estates General reflected the crown's real fear that the price of military defeat or a dictated peace might be the destruction of Louis XIV's absolute monarchy. Although Louis' enemies never formally embraced this position in their negotiating proposals, the French crown's vigorous response plainly indicates that the king and his ministers believed allied ambitions to comprise, as Louis put it in a Te Deum order, "the complete destruction of my kingdom."[42]

That this perception was not the product of momentary panic can be shown by a glance at Torcy's desperate reaction two years later to Henry St. John's offhand and apparently unintentional introduction of the estates into the secret discussions of an Anglo-French armistice. At issue in 1712 was the form of Philip V's renunciation of the French throne, and the English secretary of state asked that Philip's renunciation "be accepted by the Most Christian King and ratified in the most solemn manner by the estates of the kingdom of France."[43] This latter requirement shocked Torcy; St. John had never mentioned the French estates during the fruitful months of negotiation on the succession problem. Now the foreign minister's fears of allied designs upon the French constitution, nurtured through a decade of war and propaganda, were suddenly reawakened. In a long, repetitious and impassioned reply to St. John's draft, Torcy argued desperately for the elimination from the armistice agreement of all reference to the French estates.

> His Majesty declares that to insist on the clause . . .
> which holds that the king of Spain's renunciation of the

---

[42] *Lettre du Roy écrite à Monseigneur l'Evêque Comte de Chaalons, Pair de France* (Châlons-sur-Marne, 1711), BN, Imp., Lb[37].4383.

[43] The articles, signed by St. John, are in AAE, CP, Angleterre, Suppl. 4, fol. 154[v], and are printed in St. John, *Letters*, II, 366.

French crown for himself and for his descendants is to be ratified by the estates of the kingdom would be to bring about the collapse of a negotiation happily conducted to the point of conclusion. The estates in France do not concern themselves with the succession, and they have no power to either make or abolish these laws. . . . The examples of past centuries have shown that these have almost always led to troubles in the kingdom and the most recent estates [general], that of 1614, ended in civil war. . . . It suffices to find a method more in conformity with our customs, one which will not be subject to the inconveniences of an assembly of estates not convoked for nearly one hundred years and thus abolished in the kingdom.[44]

Torcy went on to suggest that no more ironclad and official method existed than simply registering the renunciations in all the French parlements. After commenting on the other points of the armistice agreement, the foreign minister closed his letter by returning to the subject of the estates: "Permit me to say," Torcy's draft reads, "that by accepting this proposition, subject as it is to a thousand inconveniences, we would be acting in contravention of the king's authority, of the peace of the kingdom and even of the general peace under discussion." The draft then concluded with these words: "Whatever desire His Majesty may have to immediately conclude the peace, one can say that the continuation of the war would be a lesser evil than assembling the estates." Torcy, or perhaps Louis himself, deleted this last revealing sentence from the final version, and the substitute shows that the crown was beginning to see the matter more clearly. "There is room to believe," concluded the amended dispatch, "that when the assembly of the estates was requested neither the uselessness of this precaution nor the

[44] Torcy to St. John, Marly, 22 June 1712 (draft), AAE, CP, Angleterre 241, fols. 163–165.

harm their convocation might produce were known."[45] Nevertheless, lingering suspicion prompted Torcy to fire off a private note to St. John on the subject of the estates and others to the Earl of Oxford and Matthew Prior striking the same chords.[46]

When St. John answered Torcy, he did not so much as mention the French estates. Overjoyed at Louis' general agreement to his proposals, the English secretary simply accepted the French substitute of ratification by the parlements in place of ratification by the estates.[47] Torcy's memoirs reduce the exchange to this laconic allusion: "The authority attributed by foreigners to the estates being unknown in France, the king changed this clause."[48] This is certainly the proper diagnosis; St. John clearly had no intention of creating obstacles to peace, much less of reforming the French government. His introduction of the Estates General was probably nothing more than a slip of the pen by which the Cortes of Spain, which were to ratify Philip's renunciation in accord with Spanish law, were equated with the French assembly.[49] That Torcy immediately placed the worst possible construction on St. John's demands was one symptom of the anxiety felt by Louis'

[45] Final text is in St. John, *Letters*, II, 390.

[46] Torcy to St. John, 22 June 1712, AAE, CP, Angleterre 241, fols. 167–168 (printed in St. John, *Letters*, II, 392–393); Torcy to Oxford, 22 June 1712, *ibid.*, fol. 169; Torcy to Prior, 22 June 1712, *ibid.*, fol. 170.

[47] St. John to Torcy, Whitehall, 20 June/1 July 1712, *ibid.*, fols. 209–212ᵛ.

[48] Torcy, *Mémoires*, p. 718.

[49] See St. John's memorandum of 4/15 March 1712, AAE, CP, Angleterre 237, fols. 97–99, as printed in St. John, *Letters*, II, 208n. The ratification of the renunciations was not concluded for a full year, but Bolingbroke and his supporters never doubted the sincerity of French intentions on this point. See Prior to Bolingbroke, 17/28 September 1712, in St. John, *Letters*, III, 95: ". . . in the main, you and I know, that these people [the French leaders] mean the renunciation should be as strong as we can ask it."

government at the mere mention of the Estates General. This fear was reflected in the propaganda of 1710 quite as much as in the negotiations of 1712.

While Torcy oversaw the creation of pamphlet propaganda at Versailles, as the Gertruydenberg talks continued he also urged d'Huxelles and Polignac to set their assistants to work on other anonymous tracts. The foreign minister recognized that the Sacheverell affair provided an ideal opportunity for Dubos, who was acting as d'Huxelles' secretary, to "exercise his talents." At the end of April Dubos responded with an essay, favorably received by Torcy, which asserted that the interests of the Church of England were menaced far more by Calvinists like the Dutch than by Roman Catholics.[50] Meanwhile La Blinière, the *robin* whose primary task was the crown *relation*, was asked to write still another response to the *Lettre à Mylord*. Because of illness or overwork La Blinière submitted only a rough draft and this project went no further.[51] Neither did Dubos' Sacheverell essay see the light of day, because Colonel Hooke, the Scottish Catholic who was about to translate it for an English audience, was suddenly dispatched on a mission of higher priority as Torcy's informant in Villars' army. A similar fate befell another pamphlet draft that Dubos submitted during the summer of 1710.[52]

After the end of the peace conferences the same forces that killed the royal *relation* also doomed anonymous propaganda works. Three pamphlets composed by Legrand as a continuation of the Genevan letter series also remained unpublished. The "Troisième lettre d'un conseiller de Genève" was a direct refutation of the Dutch resolution of 27 July 1710 that chastised Louis for allegedly sabotaging the peace

[50] Torcy to d'Huxelles, Versailles, 31 March 1710 (minute), AAE, CP, Hollande 223, fol. 169. See Lombard, *Du Bos*, pp. 126-127.

[51] D'Huxelles and Polignac to Torcy, Gertruydenberg, 26 April 1710, AAE, CP, Hollande 224, fol. 135; La Blinière to Torcy, Gertruydenberg, 26 April 1710, *ibid.*, fol. 145.

[52] See Lombard, *Du Bos*, pp. 127-128.

talks. A "Quatrième lettre" reverted to the theme of Philip's legitimacy and argued that the partition treaties were invalid, a thesis which presupposed the publication of still another Legrand work written several months earlier on this subject.[53]

This succession of unpublished and aborted propaganda efforts signaled the end of the French military and diplomatic crisis. Between the fall of 1710 and the following spring no propaganda pamphlets were printed under Torcy's auspices. While his secret contacts with the English Tories slowly ripened, the foreign minister could afford to put aside the pen as a diplomatic weapon. As always, Torcy was aware of the explosive potential of the printed word and no longer needed to risk antagonizing potential negotiating partners by public disputation. The lines Torcy's propagandist injected into the *Response d'un amy de La Haye* nicely illustrate the foreign minister's frame of mind: "In truth, . . . it is unworthy of us to allow all sorts of obscure and unacknowledged people this unbridled license to write injuriously against Frenchmen and against their king at the very time that we are working to reconcile ourselves with him. . . . Do we permit this because we fear peace? Or do we rather think that the French will not know how to respond? Do we want to provoke them into publishing some tract offensive to us, or which will so irritate some of our allies that all our efforts for peace and all our good intentions will be useless in the face of irreconcilable hatred?"[54] In the open diplo-

---

[53] "Troisième lettre d'un conseiller du grand conseil de Genève à un bourgemaître d'Amsterdam," manuscript in BN, Clairambault 515, fols. 221–258; authorship established by Legrand to Torcy, 23 August 1710, *ibid.*, fol. 257bis. "Quatrième lettre d'un conseiller du grand conseil de Genève à un bourgemaître d'Amsterdam," manuscript in Legrand's hand, BN, Clairambault 515, fols. 263–296. Legrand's letter to Torcy of 23 August 1710 identified the additional tract as a "translation" of "Papel tocante al tratado de la Repartition." This is the same tract whose imminent publication was predicted at the end of *Réflexions sur la lettre à Mylord*, p. 107.

[54] *Response d'un amy de La Haye*, p. 7.

macy forced upon Torcy during 1709 and 1710 the foreign minister was compelled to gamble with dramatic appeals to public opinion. But the steadily improving military and diplomatic circumstances of the war's last years allowed him to follow the safer course, that of eschewing printed propaganda which might well "embitter the hearts of those we are trying to reconcile"[55] via private diplomacy.

Meanwhile, the group of tracts appearing in 1709 and 1710 demonstrate that Torcy had molded his propaganda campaign into a coordinated effort. The expert platoon of writers he had developed during a decade of war included Legrand, La Chapelle, Dubos, d'Huxelles and Polignac, Hooke and La Blinière. Each contributed specialized talents and knowledge to the common endeavor of persuasion, and Torcy molded their separate projects into an organized, patterned series.

IMPERIAL INTERREGNUM

Only once between the summer of 1710 and the final cessation of hostilities in 1714 did Torcy think it necessary to launch a campaign of propaganda. The occasion was the interregnum created by the unexpected death of Emperor Joseph I in April 1711. The French government rapidly improvised a military and diplomatic strategy whose purpose was to delay a new imperial election indefinitely; propaganda writings were to be one arm of this delaying campaign. Torcy knew that a long interregnum might have many advantages for France, including a possible reduction of Vienna's influence over the German princes and the consequent weakening of anti-French military coordination. Ultimately, Torcy hoped to deadlock the imperial college, tie the issue of the imperial succession to a general peace conference and perhaps break the tradition of Habsburg em-

[55] Torcy to Basnage, 14 January 1712 (copy), AAE, CP, Hollande 242, fol. 10.

perors.[56] This grand design did not progress beyond an embryonic stage, however, for on 12 October 1711 the electoral college met at Frankfurt and elected as emperor Joseph's younger brother and Philip V's rival, Archduke Charles.

It was a rump electoral college that installed the new emperor. The two Wittelsbach brothers and French allies, Max Emmanuel of Bavaria and Joseph Clement of Cologne, were barred from attending under Emperor Joseph's ban of 1706,[57] and the archbishop of Mainz, president of the electoral college, failed to invite them to participate in the vote at Frankfurt.[58] This omission provided Torcy and the pro-French electors with the grievance they publicly advertised in the summer of 1711. At that time Torcy was sending envoys to the electors of Saxony and Brandenburg—the latter was still not recognized by Louis as king in Prussia—with the hope of spurring them to stand against the candidacy of Archduke Charles or of detaching them from the anti-French alliance.[59] The main thrust of Torcy's diplomacy in Germany, however, concerned the Wittelsbach electors. Baron Karg shuttled between Versailles and the pitiful electoral courts-in-exile at Valenciennes and Compiègne to help Torcy coordinate the French strategy.[60]

[56] See the instructions given to Hooke, Louis' envoy to Augustus of Saxony-Poland, dated 6 May 1711, in *Recueil des instructions données aux ambassadeurs de France*, vol. 4: *Pologne*, ed. I.-L. Farges (Paris, 1888), 267 ff.

[57] The texts of the bans, dated 23 and 29 April 1706, appear in Lamberty, *Mémoires*, IV, 43–51.

[58] He refused to accept any communications from the Wittelsbachs. See Joseph Clement to Torcy, Namur, 9 July 1711, AAE, CP, Cologne 59, fol. 165.

[59] For Brandenburg, see instructions to de la Marck, dated 12 July 1711, in *Recueil des instructions données aux ambassadeurs de France*, vol. 7: *Bavière, Palatinat, Deux-Ponts*, ed. A. Lebon (Paris 1889), 136 ff.

[60] Torcy to Karg, Marly, 26 April 1711 (minute), AAE, CP, Cologne 59, fols. 108–109, and Karg's letters of May and June, *ibid.*;

This was a military strategy above all. Torcy and Karg agreed at the end of April that the electors should at once write privately to the archbishop of Mainz and to the other electors asserting their rights, asking that they be invited to participate in electoral deliberations, and disclaiming responsibility for the potential consequences of any refusal to grant them their just due.[61] Karg and the electors realized that this implied threat would remain empty without armed force to back it up, and Torcy was not unsympathetic to the notion of providing the required troops.[62] Ever since 1708 the foreign minister had favored the opening of a second front to draw off allied troops from Flanders, thus relieving pressure on Louis' armies in the Low Countries.[63] For three years past, he had been told that it was impossible to spare a single soldier from the Flanders theater, but in May 1711 his growing influence in the royal council helped Torcy secure Louis' approval for moving a detachment of Villars' army to the Rhine. Just as Torcy had foreseen, Prince Eugene marched off with a large contingent of allied troops to counter the French move. The foreign minister took satisfaction from the decision to "finally . . . move the theater of war to the Rhine, instead of having it at the gates of Paris."[64] Marlborough was left with a severely reduced force, and, though he broke through Villars' *ne plus ultra*

Torcy, *Journal*, 27 April 1711, pp. 428–429; Torcy's memorandum on his interview with Max Emmanuel, *ibid.*, pp. 430–434.

[61] Max Emmanuel to his wife, Compiègne, 2 May 1711, printed in A. Rosenlehner, *Die Stellung der Kurfürsten Max-Emmanuel von Bayern und Joseph Klement von Köln zur Kaiserwahl Karls VI (1711)* (Munich, 1900), p. 131; Karg's memorandum to Torcy of 29 April 1711, printed in Ennen, *Erbfolgekrieg*, pp. lxix–lxxi. Joseph Clement's letters to the archbishop of Mainz, dated 7 May 1711 and 20 June 1711, and his letter to the pope of 30 June 1711, were printed as appendices to his *Protestation* of July. See printed copy in BN, Clairambault 284, fols. 32–43.

[62] Ennen, *Erbfolgekrieg*, pp. lxix–lxxi; Karg to Torcy, Paris, 6 May 1711, AAE, CP, Cologne 59, fol. 129; Karg to Torcy, Paris, 8 May 1711, *ibid.*, fol. 132.

[63] Torcy, *Journal*, pp. 4–6.   [64] *Ibid.*, p. 437.

lines in a brilliant tactical maneuver, the sole substantive loss to the French in the Flanders campaign of 1711 was the fall of Bouchain.

Only with this background in mind can we understand the printed propaganda of 1711. This comprised two distinct though related elements: manifestos in the names of Joseph Clement and Max Emmanuel, and anonymous tracts by Legrand and La Chapelle. The manifestos, or *Protestations*, were not published until the beginning of July, to coincide with the opening of the Rhine campaign. Torcy's correspondence makes it clear that he intended the protests of Louis' allies to pave the way for the arrival of French armies in Germany. Thus he arranged for their publication in French, Italian, Latin and German editions and urged the royal intendant in Alsace, Louis' ambassador to Switzerland and the French military commanders to spread copies throughout central Europe.[65] Evidently the *Protestations* were to serve as a sort of declaration of war.

[65] Karg began drawing up manifestos in early May (Karg to Torcy, Paris, 11 May 1711, AAE, CP, Cologne 59, fols. 134–135; cf. Max Emmanuel's memorandum of 26 May 1711, Rosenlehner, *Stellung*, pp. 141–143), but the *Protestations* were issued only at the beginning of July. On the distribution of the *Protestations*, see the following dispatches: Joseph Clement to Karg, Valenciennes, 28 June 1711, AAE, CP, Cologne 59, fol. 164; Joseph Clement to Torcy, Namur, 9 July 1711, *ibid.*, fol. 165; Karg to Torcy, Valenciennes, 9 July 1711, *ibid.*, fol. 168; Karg to Torcy, Valenciennes, 23 July 1711, *ibid.*, fol. 175. Karg to Torcy, Valenciennes, 30 July 1711, *ibid.*, fol. 180; de la Marck to Torcy, Luxembourg, 30 July 1711, *ibid.*, fol. 184; Joseph Clement to Torcy, Valenciennes, 23 August 1711, *ibid.*, fol. 203; Torcy to de la Houssaye, Fontainebleau, 27 August 1711, *ibid.*, fol. 207; Torcy to Joseph Clement, Fontainebleau, 27 August 1711, *ibid.*, fol. 211; Joseph Clement to Torcy, Valenciennes, 31 August 1711, *ibid.*, fol. 212; de la Houssaye to Marolot (?), Strasbourg, 31 July 1710, AAE, CP, Allemagne 351, fol. 178; du Luc to Torcy, Soleure, 17 August 1711, AAE, CP, Suisse 227, fol. 150. In Paris the *Protestations* were printed by Delaulne, the printer of most of Torcy's propaganda tracts; see Torcy to d'Argenson, Fontainebleau, 31 August 1711, AAE, CP, Cologne, 59, fol. 208; d'Argenson to Torcy, Paris, 6 August 1711, AAE, CP, Bavière 63, fol. 216; Emery to d'Argenson, 6 August 1711, *ibid.*, fol. 221.

The substance of these manifestos provides no novelty. Baron Karg, their author, recapitulated the account of imperial mistreatment that we know from his tracts of 1702, and he brought the publications up to date with arguments refuting the constitutionality of the imperial ban.[66] These latter points had appeared in print before, but always anonymously. In the atmosphere favorable to propaganda that prevailed at Versailles just after the collapse of the Hague conferences in 1709, Karg had received Torcy's approval of two anonymous tracts protesting against the imperial ban.[67] But the point was not pressed thereafter; neither had Torcy earlier seen any purpose in having La Chapelle write against the ban in his Swiss disguise, since without force of arms propaganda might boomerang in its effects. In July 1711 there was room to hope for French military success in Germany, and for this reason the *Protestations* were published. By September, however, it was clear that the Rhine campaign would end in stalemate and that Charles soon would be elected emperor. Torcy now turned down Karg's projects for new propaganda tracts, on the grounds that such literature was no longer useful.[68]

[66] *Protestation de M. l'Electeur de Bavière* (Namur, 1711), BN, Imp., Mp. 961; *La Protestation de S.A.S. Electorale de Cologne*, BN, Imp., Mz. 3666.

[67] *Lettre écrite de Ratisbonne à un curieux demeurant à La Haye, sur le procédé irregulier, qu'on a tenu contre S.A.E. de Cologne*, dated 18 July 1709, BN, Imp., Mp. 1160; *On demande si l'Empereur peut soûmettre au ban de l'Empire quelqu'un des Electeurs, ou Princes de l'Allemagne, du consentement du College Electoral seul, sans la participation des autres Princes du S. Empire?*, BN, Imp., Mz. 3667. See Karg to Torcy, Valenciennes, 25 September 1709, AAE, CP, Cologne 58, fol. 214. The latter tract was reprinted in *Journal de Trévoux*, September 1709, pp. 1524–1536, and in *Clef du cabinet*, August 1709, pp. 137–144.

[68] Karg to Torcy, Valenciennes, 25 September 1711, AAE, CP, Cologne 59, fol. 217. Karg to Torcy, 28 September 1711, *ibid.*, fol. 219; Karg to Torcy, Valenciennes, 30 September 1711, *ibid.*, fol. 221; Karg to Torcy, Valenciennes, 25 October 1711, *ibid.*, fol. 226; Karg to Torcy, Valenciennes, 9 November 1711, *ibid.*, fol. 228; Karg to

Even before the publication of the electors' manifestos, Torcy had supervised the publication of several anonymous works. To Basnage, the Huguenot leader in Holland, the foreign minister wrote with mock innocence that "various works" on the election of a new emperor would certainly appear. "Savants and ignorant men both speak on such occasions, the former to make known their erudition, the others to instruct themselves by raising questions. And as one tract gives rise to responses and rejoinders, I hope the public will profit from these disputes."[69] Accordingly, Torcy let down the bars of censorship in Paris and the tracts proliferated. Among them was an anonymous pamphlet called *Considerations politiques sur la prochaine élection d'un nouvel Empereur*. Dated May 1711, this tract was La Chapelle's contribution to Torcy's final propaganda campaign. It argued that the imperial diet should seize the occasion of the interregnum to "enact all that public utility requires" before the consistory of electors convened to choose Joseph's successor.[70] Through the following summary of European affairs we can hear Torcy's thoughts on the political situation early in 1711: "The allies let slip through their fingers a peace so advantageous that they will perhaps never again find its like; the interests of the king of Sweden may be on the point of drawing Ottoman arms into Germany; the princes and states of the empire are all equally

---

Torcy, 12 November 1711, *ibid.*, fol. 240; Karg to Torcy, Valenciennes, 15 November 1711, *ibid.*, fol. 244; Torcy to Karg, 22 November 1711 (minute), *ibid.*, fol. 245.

[69] Torcy to Basnage, Marly, 24 May 1711 (copy), AAE, CP, Hollande 231, fol. 94.

[70] P. 6; in BN, Clairambault 1024, fols. 186–193. This tract is attributed to La Chapelle by a manuscript note at the head of the printed BN copy. See also Karg's undated letter to Torcy, AAE, CP, Cologne 59, fol. 193, where La Chapelle is mentioned as translator of the Wittelsbach *Protestations*, presumably from Latin to French. For other works published in France during 1711 on the subject of the imperial succession, see above, chap. 2, at n. 43.

exhausted and without resources, while France seems to have found new resources with which to resist and support herself for some time."[71] The writer suggested that a general diet convene to reform the constitution of the empire. He maintained, just as had the *Lettres d'un suisse*, that the empire was properly a republic with a *chef* (the emperor) who had been attempting to transform it into an absolute monarchy under Habsburg domination. All the princes of the empire should therefore bend their efforts toward "searching for and devising what could reestablish Germanic *gloire* and the old Germanic liberty." This would take only a few months, La Chapelle wrote, and meanwhile the electors might consider their choice of emperor. A leisurely approach would permit other princes to come forward as candidates for the imperial dignity. The tract alludes often to a certain *Testament politique d'un ministre de Leopold I* —written, as we know, by La Chapelle in 1706—as the classic text for a statement of Habsburg plans on the subject of the empire.[72] Thus, while Torcy expressed shock in his propaganda about allied projects for constitutional reform in France, this in no way prevented him from arguing for changes in the nature of the empire.

La Chapelle found time in his short tract to put in a good word for the electoral rights of Max Emmanuel, but on the question of the composition of the electoral college he emphasized especially the desirability of restoring the kingship of Bohemia to its original elective status.[73] This seemed to the writer of the *Considerations politiques* a suitable task for the imperial diet, since Emperor Ferdinand II had illegally annulled the Bohemian constitution ninety years before. To prove the originally elective nature of the Bohemian crown, Torcy had Legrand publish a brief compilation of the relevant historical sources stretching back to the thirteenth century. In this anonymous pamphlet Legrand won-

---

[71] *Considerations politiques*, p. 1.
[72] *Ibid.*, pp. 7–11.　　　　[73] *Ibid.*, p. 12.

dered how Archduke Charles could participate in the imperial election as king of Bohemia without first being formally invested with this kingship,[74] a complexity that represented another of Torcy's efforts to keep the political pot boiling and trouble the election.

Legrand's pamphlet on the Bohemian kingship was in its turn only a footnote to his two major works of 1711. These closely related tracts were published together as *Discours politique sur ce qui s'est passé dans l'Empire au sujet de la succession d'Espagne*,[75] and *L'Allemagne menacée d'estre bien-tost reduite en monarchie absolue, si elle ne profite de la conjoncture présente pour asseurer sa liberté*.[76] For mere titles, these are a fine statement of Torcy's program. Although the tracts discuss themes elaborated in detail by Karg and La Chapelle, Legrand brought his own distinctive treatment to a rather hackneyed subject. Not that the author's skill stemmed from any special expertise in the field of German constitutional practice; in fact, when Torcy gave him the assignment, Legrand reported that he was "encountering great difficulties, due to my limited knowledge of the German language and the individual constitutions" of the various German states. But Legrand added, "I am not lacking in courage," as he bravely plunged on.[77] The first result of his efforts was the *Discours politique*. This essay had two

[74] *Lettre de Monsieur D*** à Monsieur le Docteur W****, touchant le Royaume de Bohême* (1711). A printed copy is in BN, Clairambault 518, pp. 659–667; a manuscript draft in Legrand's hand is *ibid.*, pp. 213–217.

[75] The word *politique* is omitted on the title page of the BN's printed copies, but appears in the titles at the head of the two sections of the work. Pagination follows that of BN, Imp., M. 4057. A draft of the first part, with the title in Legrand's hand, is in BN, Clairambault 518, pp. 403–481; a draft of the second part, in Legrand's hand, is *ibid.*, pp. 193–203.

[76] BN, Imp., M. 4057. A manuscript draft is in BN, Clairambault 518, pp. 265–272.

[77] Legrand to Torcy, "lundi matin," BN, Clairambault 518, pp. 187–189.

chief purposes: first, to show that emperors Leopold and Joseph had violated the constitution of the empire in persecuting and banning the Wittelsbach electors; second, that these imperial transgressions were no more than the most recent examples of the house of Austria's chronically illegal tactics. The tract cites Grotius and Pufendorf to show the mixed nature of the imperial constitution, for, according to these jurists, the electors were not "subjects" but "associates" in the government of the empire.[78] But Legrand was prepared to concede the point, and he argued that even given the premise of imperial absolutism Leopold and Joseph had violated the fundamental laws they were sworn to uphold. The major documents comprising the imperial constitution —the Golden Bull, the Treaty of Westphalia, the capitulation signed by each emperor at his accession—were quoted at length;[79] and these texts reveal that the emperor was legally bound to consult all three estates of the empire, not merely the other electors, before banning the Wittelsbach brothers. On more general grounds, the author argued that the entire imperial war effort was misplaced, for the quarrel between Archduke Charles and Philip V was a domestic affair stemming from the house of Austria's efforts to incorporate the full legacy of the Spanish crown. Thus, like all of Torcy's propagandists, Legrand found that the empire had no interest in fighting the War of the Spanish Succession.

Legrand's analysis of the reaction of the princes to the imperial violations is summarized in this vigorous passage: "Emperors Leopold and Joseph, profiting from the circumstances of the moment, raised themselves above the law. Never has there been a more despotic government than theirs in any country. Everyone believes he can give a good account of himself by suffering the yoke and hastens to make humble submission. Electors, princes, all are concerned exclusively with their interest and remain oblivious to the interest of the empire. They allow themselves to be dazzled by the clatter of the chains that bind and strangle them. In bartering away their rights and their privileges, they pretend not to notice that they and the empire are falling into a shameful slavery." In short, the emperor had "won over all Germany for his party."[80] But this diagnosis did not dissuade Legrand from arguing that emperors like Leopold and Joseph who had so blatantly trampled on the fundamental laws of the empire were still subject to deposition by those who originally elevated them:

> Being chief and administrator of the empire does not make the emperor its master. He is a principal member, as are the electors. The empire is above them, and it is to the empire that the sovereign right of investigation, of judgment and of sentence belongs. States that receive a prince on certain conditions, imposing certain laws for him to swear to, always reserve sovereign authority to themselves. This oath concludes a sort of contract. . . . Kings and emperors whose authority is limited in this way are nothing more than the first vassals of the state. Should they violate their oaths, should they undertake something prejudicial to the state, they fall into the crime of felony and can be punished like other vassals by the loss of their states. Those who elevated them to the supreme dignity are obliged by their own oaths to resist.[81]

Since the office of emperor was vacant at the time, Legrand continued, these drastic measures were superfluous. It was necessary, however, to guard against continued dilution of the imperial constitution under the new emperor.

This was the theme developed at length in Legrand's *L'Allemagne menacée*. The tract ranged back to the Thirty Years' War to elucidate the house of Austria's ambitions. Within Germany, the Habsburg purpose was said to have

[80] *Ibid.*, p. 7.   [81] *Ibid.*, p. 36.

been first the reduction of the imperial diet's college of cities, and now the reduction of the college of princes. The bans of 1706 appeared to Legrand as a maneuver in the campaign against the final college, that of the electors, a campaign that began when the king of Bohemia secured his admission to the deliberations of the electors and continued with the creation of an electorate for that Habsburg creature, the duke of Hanover. (The inconvenient precedent of Ferdinand II's elevation of the duke of Bavaria to electoral status is omitted.) Meanwhile the emperors succeeded in reducing the imperial circles to obedience by installing as directors of the circles relatives and other creatures of the Habsburgs.[82] Legrand explicitly rejected Pufendorf's recommendation that the princes should concern themselves with their own domains exclusively and not involve themselves with the affairs of the empire, a suggestion deemed impracticable because of the house of Austria's policy of encroachment on princely privileges. Instead, Legrand argued, the estates of the empire should insist on certain promises at the upcoming imperial election, and then they must see that these commitments would be carried out.[83]

The distinctive contribution of these works by Legrand was not so much their substance as their sources. The writer used Torcy's notes and the correspondence of the French diplomatic archives to construct his narrative of the partition treaties and the early years of the war. He also leaned heavily on the works of public-law theorists, especially Pufendorf, a writer whose techniques of juristic history, although highly influential in Germany, remained almost completely unknown in France. These were the sources Legrand hoped would help offset the bitterness left in the empire by the resounding "clinc-clanc"[84] of Louis XIV's invading armies.

While these tracts were being published, Torcy's initially vague and inconclusive contacts with the new British gov-

---

[82] *L'Allemagne menacée*, pp. 13–15.
[83] *Ibid.*, pp. 21–26.
[84] The phrase comes from *Europäische Fama*, No. 31 (1705), p. 480.

ernment rapidly approached fruition. In August 1711 Torcy dispatched to London Nicolas Mesnager, a member of the royal council of commerce, for hard bargaining with Henry St. John, and in the next six weeks the two put on paper the heart of what would become the Treaty of Utrecht. Thanks to an inadvertent news leak, all Europe discovered that England and France were conferring immediately after Mesnager and St. John signed the Preliminary Articles on 8 October 1711. Soon the foreign minister was rejecting Karg's draft of a new tract upholding Elector Joseph Clement's rights. "Although there is nothing to desire for the perfection of this piece," wrote Torcy, "you know the reasons we now have to make no protests; hence it will not be used."[85] To the end of the war Torcy commissioned no more pamphlet propaganda.

ENGLISH EPILOGUE

Diplomacy via public opinion became superfluous once the leaders of enemy governments were converted to the French foreign minister's point of view. Henry St. John, later Viscount Bolingbroke, was the first of these convert leaders; so close were his views to Torcy's that he hardly needed proselytizing. The English secretary of state steered his country away from the continental alliances which he, no less than Torcy, viewed as entanglements contrary to Britain's best interests. However, once the success of the Anglo-French talks became public knowledge, the British war-hawks and their allies abroad organized a campaign to sabotage the agreement. St. John and the other Tory ministers had to wage a hard fight in the last months of 1711 to retain

---

[85] Joseph Clement to Torcy, Valenciennes, 25 October 1711, AAE, CP, Cologne 59, fol. 227; Torcy to Karg, 22 November 1711 (copy), *ibid.*, fol. 245. Cf. Torcy's refusal in 1712 to allow the publication of a pro-Rákóczi pamphlet lest it interfere with the Utrecht talks; Torcy to d'Argenson, 26 December 1712, quoted in Köpeczi, *La France et la Hongrie*, pp. 380–381, and cited as AAE, CP, Hongrie 16, fol. 353.

their peace policy, their offices and ultimately their heads. In the process they coordinated a massive and successful propaganda effort to sway British opinion.[86] If Queen Anne's reign was a great age of English political pamphleteering, the few months between the signing of the October preliminaries and the convening of the Utrecht congress were its most splendid moments. Jonathan Swift, Daniel Defoe and a number of lesser-known writers argued with heart and mind for the Tory peace. In the process, they did Torcy's work for him. The French foreign minister confined himself to ordering the Paris publication of Swift's most important tract, *The Conduct of the Allies*, in a French translation.[87] For the rest, he watched while, as Polignac put it from Utrecht, the English Parliament "executed to the letter" the recommendations of Swift's book.[88]

This is not the place to review the battle for English public opinion during the last stage of the Spanish succession

[86] St. John to Watkins, Whitehall, 18 January 1712 (O.S.), in St. John, *Letters*, II, 160: "We have struggled this winter through inconceivable difficulties . . . ; and, I may say, we have combatted an habit of thinking falsely, which men have been used to for twenty years."

[87] Torcy to d'Argenson, 2 February 1712, AAE, CP, Angleterre 237, fol. 47. This publication order was issued only six weeks after the first printing of *The Conduct of the Allies* in England. (See Jonathan Swift, *Journal to Stella*, ed. Harold Williams, 2 vols. [Oxford, 1948], I, 422.) D'Argenson carried out Torcy's order immediately; d'Argenson to Torcy, Paris, 8 February 1712, AAE, CP, Angleterre 237, fol. 62. Cf. Sybil Goulding, *Swift en France* (Paris, 1924), pp. 64 ff. Torcy also had other English tracts translated into French, but the record does not show him ordering them printed; see AAE, CP, Angleterre 238, fols. 82–97ᵛ, 126–154. According to P. Dottin, "Daniel De Foe mystificateur, ou les faux mémoires de Mesnager," *Revue germanique*, 14 (1923), 271, Mesnager attempted to recruit Defoe as a propagandist late in 1711. Earlier in the war the French foreign minister oversaw the publication of translated documents supporting the Rákóczi rebellion in Hungary (Köpeczi, *La France et la Hongrie*, pp. 379–380).

[88] Polignac to Gaultier, Utrecht, 28 February 1712, AAE, MD, Angleterre 138ᵇⁱˢ, fol. 36.

war.[89] Torcy played no direct role in the Tory campaign to turn British sentiment away from the allies and toward peace, at least no direct role that the available evidence reveals. Nor need we recapitulate the well-known story of Swift's recruitment by St. John and the closeness of their collaboration on a series of pamphlets in 1711 and 1712. St. John, like Torcy, enjoyed the company of writers; more important, both ministers saw that if writers of political propaganda were elevated in status from treatment as hacks to a position of dignity great use could be made of their talents. Swift was not merely St. John's hireling; like La Chapelle, Dean Swift had cause to believe himself the friend and boon companion of the minister he served.[90] Not least among the explanations for the relatively smooth course of the Torcy-St. John negotiations in 1712 and 1713 we may count the presence of the poet Matthew Prior as intermediary. The "Matthieu" of Torcy's correspondence personified the image of the diplomat-man-of-letters cultivated both by the French foreign minister and the English secretary of state.[91]

It is clear beyond doubt that Swift's political pamphlets reflected St. John's political opinions.[92] Even more interesting, at many points Swift's propaganda matched the arguments Torcy had propounded over the preceding decade. Let us briefly examine, with this point of comparison in mind, Swift's *The Conduct of the Allies and the Late Ministry in Beginning and Carrying on the Present War*. The major theme of this famous pamphlet is that, while Britain's interest in the war was inconsequential compared to the in-

[89] On this subject, see Coombs, *Conduct of the Dutch*, chaps. 9–11, and the references cited therein.

[90] See Swift, *Journal to Stella*, esp. I, 339 to end; Trevelyan, *Queen Anne*, III, 98.

[91] See L. G. Wickham Legg's fine *Matthew Prior: A Study of His Public Career and Correspondence* (Cambridge, 1921), esp. pp. 168–169.

[92] St. John to Lord Raby, 6 May 1711 (O.S.), in St. John, *Letters*, I, 192–195, is virtually a précis of *The Conduct of the Allies*.

terests of the Dutch and of the emperor, England had been called upon to shoulder the major part of the war's financial burden. The Whig members of the "late ministry" were said to have gone very far toward bankrupting the country in their desperate efforts to raise war subsidies. As a result of a war policy dating back to 1689, a new "monied interest" had wrested control of the country from the landed classes; "by this Method one Part of the Nation is pawned to the other, with hardly a Possibility left of being ever redeemed."[93] Nor will this investment bring any return to England: "I have known some People such ill Computers, as to Imagine the many Millions in Stocks and Annuities, are so much real Wealth in the Nation; whereas every Farthing of it is entirely lost to us, scattered in Holland, Germany, and Spain; and the Landed-Men, who now pay the Interest, must at last pay the Principal."[94] England's involvement in the war, Swift continued, had never been of more than dubious value: "Without offering at any other Remedy, without taking time to consider the Consequences, or to reflect on our own Conditions, we hastily engaged in a War which hath cost us sixty Millions; and after repeated, as well as unexpected success in Arms, hath put us and our Posterity in a worse Condition, not only than any of our Allies, but even our conquered Enemies themselves."[95]

What good had come of all the battlefield victories, asked Swift? "It will, no doubt, be a mighty comfort to our Grandchildren, when they see a few Rags hung up in Westminster Hall, which cost an hundred Millions, whereof they are paying the Arrears, and boasting, as Beggars do, that their Grandfathers were Rich and Great."[96] Last year's campaign resulting in "a Town taken for the Dutch, is [this] a sufficient Recompense to us for six Millions of Money? Which is of so little Consequence to the determining the

[93] Jonathan Swift, *Political Tracts, 1711–1713*, ed. Herbert Davis (Oxford, 1951), p. 18.

[94] *Ibid.*, p. 59.   [95] *Ibid*, p. 15.

[96] *Ibid.*, pp. 55–56.

War, that the French may yet hold out a dozen Years more, and afford a Town every Campaign at the same Price."[97] Indeed, Swift strongly doubted, "as the Advocates of War would have it, that the French were so impoverished": [98]

> It must be confessed, that after the Battle of Ramillies the French were so discouraged with their frequent Losses and so impatient for a Peace, that their King was resolved to comply on any reasonable Terms. But when his Subjects were informed of our exorbitant Demands, they grew jealous of his Honour, and were unanimous to assist him in continuing the War at any hazard, rather than submit. This fully restored his Authority. . . . And he hath since waged War in the most thrifty manner, by acting on the Defensive. . . . All this considered, with the Circumstances of that Government, where the Prince is Master of the Lives and Fortunes of so mighty a Kingdom, shews that Monarch to be not so sunk in his Affairs, as we have imagined, and have long flattered ourselves with the Hopes of. For an absolute Government may endure a long War, but it hath generally been ruinous to Free Countries.[99]

In reviewing the terms of the Gertruydenberg preliminaries, Swift found it not credible that the authors of such impossible terms—"one of them was inconsistent with common Reason"—sincerely intended peace: "Give me leave to suppose the continuance of the War was the Thing at Heart, among Those in Power, both Abroad and at Home, and then I can easily shew the Consistency of the Proceeding; otherwise they are wholly unaccountable and absurd."[100] In short, wrote Swift by way of epitome, "we have been fighting for the Ruin of the Publick Interest, and the Advance-

[97] *Ibid.*, p. 20. [98] *Ibid.*, p. 23.
[99] *Ibid.*, p. 60. At this point Swift apparently confused the 1706 battle of Ramillies with the battle of Oudenarde two years later.
[100] *Ibid.*, pp. 49–50.

ment of a Private. . . . We have been fighting to raise the Wealth and Grandeur of a particular Family; to enrich Usurers and Stock-jobbers; and to cultivate the pernicious Designs of a Faction, by destroying the Landed Interest."[101]

If the reader has detected the similarity of much of this argument with Sir Charles Davenant's pamphlets of 1701, he will not have been the first to notice the resemblance. That distinction belonged to certain Dutchmen residing in London when *The Conduct of the Allies* was first published. In fact, these individuals were certain that Davenant was the author of this tract, and they inflicted upon the unfortunate doctor the same sort of ostracism he had experienced ten years earlier for publishing roughly identical sentiments.[102] Although wrong in their conclusion, the Dutch were right in their reasoning, for the arguments of *The Conduct of the Allies* closely resembled and updated those of the onetime "Poussineer." Like Davenant in 1701, like Dubos in 1703, like much of Torcy's propaganda throughout the war, Swift's argument could lead nowhere but to the verdict that England should withdraw from Europe's war. But Swift and St. John added an important ingredient to the reasonings adopted by Torcy's propagandist: a heavy measure of emotional patriotism. As only English natives could, they played on the widespread war-weariness and isolationist sentiments of their countrymen. *The Conduct of the Allies* is a propagandistic *tour de force* such that no foreigners could have produced.

While the private negotiations with St. John ran their course and relieved Torcy of the need for publishing his own propaganda tracts, the French foreign minister did not

---

[101] *Ibid.*, p. 59.

[102] Swift, *Journal to Stella*, 4 December 1711 (O.S.), I, 429. After a number of shifts of patron and opinion during the war, Davenant had published in 1710 a tract so similar in argument to Swift's work of 1711–1712 that St. John called it "one of the best pamphlets which the season has produced" (St. John to Drummond, Whitehall, 27 October 1710 [O.S.], in St. John, *Letters*, I, 9). On Davenant during the war, see Coombs, *Conduct of the Dutch*, pp. 6, 237–238.

ignore the necessity of communicating the king's desires to his subjects. In previous years, Louis had ordered the French episcopacy to arrange public prayers for the success of the coming military campaign. Now, as the congress of Utrecht opened, we find Torcy writing to the other French secretaries of state to point out that "the king has deemed it apropos to have public prayers said for the happy result of the peace conferences." Torcy enclosed a royal letter to the bishops and archbishops for this purpose. At last in 1712 there was good reason to order a Te Deum for the victory of French arms at Denain. One month later, in August, the king's government printed Louis' orders for a four-month armistice with the forces of "Princess Anne, Queen of Great Britain." When the armistice was renewed, a few days before Christmas, it was published with the same ceremonies and celebrations as marked the conclusion of formal peace treaties.[103]

Finally in April 1713, Louis' plenipotentiaries at Utrecht officially ended the war with Great Britain and the United Provinces. A few weeks earlier the Sun King issued letters patent barring Philip and his descendants from the French succession. Like all the other important royal orders of the war years, this one was printed, together with Philip's renunciation and the complementary renunciations of the Spanish inheritance by the dukes of Berry and Orléans. Louis' letters patent revoked his edict of December 1700, which had explicitly affirmed Philip's retention of his rights in the French line of succession. This new edict, the final instance of royal propaganda during the War of the Spanish Succession, raised once more a familiar theme in Louis' messages to his subjects, namely the relative priority of the king's responsibilities to his state and to his dynasty:

[103] Torcy to secretaries of state, Marly, 21 January 1712 (copy), AAE, MD, France 1186, fol. 42; *Traité de suspension d'armes entre la France et l'Angleterre*, BN, Clairambault 284, fol. 44 (see ms. note); *Ordonnance du Roy pour la publication du traité de suspension d'armes entre la France et l'Angleterre* (Paris, 1712), BN, Imp., F. 23620 (312).

We feel, both as king and as father, how desirable it would have been for the general peace to be concluded without a renunciation which causes so great a change in our royal house and in the order of succession to our crown. But we are even more sensible of our duty to promptly assure our subjects so necessary a peace. We will never forget the efforts they made for our sake over the long years of a war which we would have been unable to continue had not their zeal exceeded their strength. The welfare of so loyal a people is for us a supreme law, one which should prevail over all other considerations. To this law we sacrifice today the rights of a grandson who is so dear to us; and by the price that a general peace will cost our tenderness we will at least have the consolation of bearing witness to our subjects that, even at the expense of our very blood, they will always hold the first rank in our heart.[104]

Thus did the conflict between the king's private, dynastic interest and the public interest of the French nation receive its rhetorical resolution. Louis XIV, after fulfilling his duty as *bon père* of the house of Bourbon, now turned at long last to his duties as *bon père* of his subjects. As the Sun King made his peace with Europe, he also sought reconciliation with his people.

[104] Two original copies of the letters patent of March 1713 are AN, K. 122–135, No. 20⁴, 20⁷. For the printed version, see *ibid.*, No. 20⁸: *Renonciation du Roy d'Espagne à la couronne de France, de Monseigneur le Duc de Berry et le Duc d'Orléans, à la couronne d'Espagne avec les lettres patentes du Roy du mois de Decembre 1700. Et les lettres patentes de Sa Majesté du mois de Mars 1713 qui admettent les Renonciations cy-dessus, et revoquent les lettres patentes du mois de Decembre 1700* (Paris, 1713), pp. 49–50.

CONCLUSION

*Do I dare follow you, Monsieur, in speaking of that
incomparable Monarch whom I was permitted to ad-
mire only from afar while his august confidences were
often bestowed upon you? I would not allow myself to
be carried beyond my powers by an indiscreet zeal if,
in the course of those extraordinary events which have
held all Europe transfixed since the beginning of this
century, there had not occurred certain singular circumstances, even in my own obscure life, which authorize me to break the silence I had wished to impose upon
myself. . . . May I not conclude that it is an arrange-
ment of Providence, which wanted to teach men that
the heroic actions of Louis* le Grand, *somewhat similar
to God's marvels, needed nothing more than the simplest
mouths to publicize them? . . . The* [treaties of the]
*Pyrenees and of Westphalia, of Aix-la-Chapelle, Nym-
wegen and Ryswick saw Louis give peace to beaten and
disheartened peoples. Utrecht and Rastadt he made acceptable to enemies who were almost triumphant, with
their full force and threatening courage intact and who
only breathed for conquests and combat. In the other
treaties arbiter of the terms, in these last two he was also
arbiter of men's wills.*

—Jean de la Chapelle, oration delivered upon the reception of
Marshal Villars into the Académie française, 23 June 1714.[1]

*What advantages do those charged with negotiation
abroad not derive from letters? Letters give them a perspective far superior to that of men limited to their own*

[1] Jean de la Chapelle, *Discours prononcez dans l'Académie françoise le samedy vingt-troisième de Juin MDCCXIV à la réception
de Monsieur le Mareschal Duc de Villars* (Paris, 1714), pp. 13–14.

> *time. They are provided thereby with innumerable means of acquitting themselves of their commissions to the accompaniment of praise which can only honor a minister, enhance the reputation of the prince who chose him and augment the fame and renown which are as useful as troops and fortresses to the preservation of states. . . . What aid the man of letters lends to the man of state!*
>
> —Jean-Baptiste Dubos, acceptance speech delivered upon his admission to the Académie française, 3 February 1720.[2]

WITH phrases made conventional by a century of royal patronage, two of Torcy's propagandists sounded the most ancient theme of French academicians: men of letters enhance the power and prestige of men of state, the force of the pen augments and redoubles that of the sword. But behind the hackneyed rhetoric we have found a notable shift of emphasis. After 1700 the rhetorical and visual imagery of sacred, heroic monarchy which was at the core of the traditions of French royalty was reinforced by a kind of printed propaganda expressed in historical analysis, legal reasoning, and scientific calculation. No longer merely reaffirming the mythic attributes of the divine warrior-king, the works Torcy commissioned stressed the naturalistic themes of late seventeenth-century political discourse. Drawing on the precedents of Richelieu and Colbert, Torcy found writers who could modernize the advertising of the French monarchy in the face of theoretical challenges to its legitimacy and physical threats to its continued existence. These intellectual and political pressures from abroad mandated the primacy of foreign affairs in the considerations of crown servants, provided a structural basis for the leading influence of the foreign minister in the king's council, and conditioned a French propaganda response that was appropriate to the

[2] Jean-Baptiste Dubos, *Discours prononcez dans l'Académie françoise le samedy troisième Fevrier MDCCXX à la réception de Monsieur l'Abbé Du Bos* (Paris, 1720), pp. 5–6.

challenge from abroad. Torcy's propaganda, which soon took on systematic qualities, reflected his search for a new formulation of absolutist maxims founded upon the existence of an informed and growing public responsive to reasoned presentations.

The creation of this public was one result of the communications revolution of the seventeenth century, whose elements included the invention and proliferation of the printed periodical, as well as the publication of greatly increasing numbers of political pamphlets. The resultant new conditions presented a problem to French ministers whose ideology of authoritative government dictated a preoccupation with censorship. The measures taken by Colbert and Pontchartrain to control book production and distribution reflect their concern, as does Torcy's vigilance in this area. But while the other later ministers of Louis XIV did little more than adjust the floodgates of the censorship apparatus, Torcy embarked on an impressive series of more positive steps. As his was the first generation accustomed to the habitual diffusion of information in large numbers of serially published news periodicals, the foreign minister's control of the French periodical press and his commissioned pamphlets published in sequential "letter" form indicate a rapid adjustment to the novel circumstances of political culture. These innovations served continually and regularly to present the message of the crown to a European audience. Like the editors of the recently invented learned journal who assumed that intellectual progress could best be attained through the widespread dispersal of scientific information, Torcy's propagandists placed before their audience rational justifications of crown action, accepting as axiomatic the necessity for rulers to engage in regular communication if the state was to prosper.[3]

[3] On these points, see the excellent article by Howard M. Solomon, "The *Gazette* and Antistatist Propaganda: The Medium of Print in the First Half of the Seventeenth Century," *Canadian Journal of History* (April 1974), pp. 1–17.

In the emerging cultural context we call the Enlightenment, the role of public opinion became ever more explicit. The environmentalism which was perhaps the single most consistent unifying idea in eighteenth-century thought created a new sense of the immense latitude of human potential; Locke's rejection of innate ideas opened the way for far-reaching speculation on the controlling importance of experience, speculation that ultimately produced the modern propagandist's view of human beings as collections of prejudices and passions determined entirely by psychological and sociological forces. One practical effect of environmentalist axioms was an unprecedentedly powerful rationale for propaganda: it was the way to manipulate the responses of an otherwise inchoate public consciousness.[4] Thus, when Legrand wrote of the influence upon him of Locke's *Thoughts on Education* he was illustrating the crucial role that men of letters could play in service to statesmen newly aware of their vast capacity to shape opinion.[5] In this way intellectual changes combined with social and cultural developments to redefine the nature of propaganda and to enhance its importance. Torcy's encouragement of a diversity

[4] On propaganda in France after 1715, see Gay, *Enlightenment*, II, 487, 496, 511 ff.; Franklin Ford, *Robe and Sword: The Regrouping of the French Aristocracy after Louis XIV* (Cambridge, Mass., 1953), p. 101; Denise Aimé Azam, "Le Ministère des Affaires étrangères et la presse à la fin de l'Ancien Régime," *Cahiers de la presse*, No. 3 (1938), pp. 428–438; Madeleine Cerf, "La Censure royale à la fin du XVIIIᵉ siècle," *Communications*, No. 9 (1967), pp. 2–27; Darnton, "Reading, Writing and Publishing," pp. 240–254; A. Cobban, "The Political Ideas of Maximilien Robespierre during the Period of the Convention," in *Aspects of the French Revolution* (New York, 1968), pp. 172–184; Robert B. Holtman, *Napoleonic Propaganda* (Baton Rouge, 1950); David I. Kulstein, *Napoleon III and the Working Class: A Study of Government Propaganda Under the Second Empire* (Los Angeles, 1969).

[5] See Legrand's "Projet de l'estude" for the Académie politique, BN, Clairambault 519, p. 321, quoted by J.-J. Jusserand, "Grotius étudié par les secrétaires d'ambassade français en 1711," *Bibliotheca Visseriana*, VIII (1929), 3.

of propaganda treatments underscores his perception of the existence of a variety of publics for political controversy. Hence we find him continuing the tradition of publishing extended scholarly treatises justifying dynastic claims in terms of legal precedent, while accompanying these works with pamphlets for the less erudite as well as books employing fashionable kinds of modern scientific and historical methodology.

The foreign minister's ability to assess precisely the nature of an intended public and to target his message accurately is illustrated in the pieces Torcy wrote for Louis XIV's signature. Adopting the modern format of the narrative account when the primary audience was foreign and the king's armies were victorious, the minister had his ruler speak to his own subjects in the symbol-strewn patriotic style of the French monarchical tradition during a year of military and agricultural disaster. Yet a fundamental problem remained, only faintly perceived in Torcy's day: how to create a meaningful vocabulary by which the king could communicate with subjects who were already beginning to show signs of skepticism about the traditional ideology of sacred kingship. Later in the century, as rejection of the ancient symbols of monarchy became the dominant cultural style, this problem of finding new theoretical bases and modes of expression for kingship was to grow in intensity throughout western Europe. In France it never would be solved.

Perhaps the most generalized summation of Torcy's achievement, then, is that he attempted to adjust the practice of absolute monarchy to newly emergent patterns of political culture. Without abandoning the maxims of Richelieu and Colbert, which remained the foundation of his councillor's creed, the foreign minister sought to adapt Louis XIV's system of government to a European consciousness suddenly uncongenial to old-fashioned absolutist principles. Viewed in this light, Torcy's propaganda emerges as an attempt by the first of a series of imaginative but ultimately unsuccessful eighteenth-century royal ministers to recast the traditions of the French monarchy in response to pressures of overwhelming societal change—change the character and direction of which were strongly conditioned by the force of the printed word.

Attribution and Editions of Anonymous Works

INCLUDED in this appendix are only those works discussed above which do not appear in the Bibliothèque Nationale's *Catalogue des Auteurs* and for which definite attribution can now be established.

[Jean de la Chapelle]. *Testament politique ou derniers conseils d'un ministre de l'Empereur Léopold I.*

I. EIGHTEENTH-CENTURY EDITIONS

A. FRENCH

1. *Testament politique ou derniers conseils d'un ministre de l'Empereur Léopold I. Traduit de l'Italien en François.* A Roterdam, 1707. 12°. Title page + 63 pp. BN, Imp., M. 34341.

2. *Testament politique ou derniers conseils d'un ministre de l'Empereur Léopold I. Traduit de l'Italien en François.* A Roterdam, MDCCVII. 8°. Pp. 5–46. Bound with BN, Imp., Lb³⁷. 4341, *Lettres d'un suisse*, vol. 7.

3. *Derniers conseils ou testament politique d'un ministre de l'Empereur Léopold I.* A Roterdam, 1706. In Casimir Freschot, *Mémoires de la Cour de Vienne* (1706).

B. LATIN

Ultima Consilia sive Testamentum politicum Quod Comes *** moriens misit Leopoldo Imperatori augusto.

Hamburg: Apud Gotfridum Liebernickel. Anno Domini 1705. 8°. Pp. 3–56. Bound with BN, Imp., Lb³⁷ .4341, *Lettres d'un suisse*, vol. 8.

C. ITALIAN

No copies found, but see La Chapelle to Torcy, Soleure, 16 June 1706, AAE, CP, Suisse 170, fol. 150ᵛ: "Les Jesuites d'Italie ne sont pas si scrupuleux que ceux de France. Un des plus beaux Esprits de la société d'Italie a traduit en Italien le Testament politique. On l'a envoyé à M. le Pᶜᵉ de Vaudemont." La Chapelle to Torcy, 9 July 1706, AAE, CP, Suisse 170, fol. 213ᵛ, reports that the Italian translation was printed under Vaudemont's supervision.

D. GERMAN

No copies found and no references in manuscript correspondence. According to *Clef du cabinet*, March 1709, p. 171, a German edition was published.

II. MANUSCRIPT COPY

"Derniers Conseils ou Testament Politique d'un Ministre de l'Empereur Léopold en 1705." AAE, MD, Autriche 12, fols. 23–64ᵛ.

III. AUTHORSHIP

1. Torcy to La Chapelle, Versailles, 26 February 1706 (minute), AAE, CP, Suisse 173, fol. 145. Offers suggestions about a work which La Chapelle left with Torcy before his departure for Soleure; Torcy says it should be printed as it is very good and will be well received by the public, but he recommends some changes.

2. La Chapelle to Torcy, Soleure, 10 March 1706, AAE, CP, Suisse 169, fols. 85ᵛ–88: "Touttes celles que vous avez bien voulu faire sur le Testament m'ont ouvert les yeux et m'ont fait trouver fort laid, ce qui m'avoit paru beau. Je croy avoir mis l'ouvrage dans

l'Estat que vous desirés qu'il soit et j'ay pris avec M. l'Ambassadeur [Puyzieulx] de si bonnes mesures pour l'impression, que de longtemps on ne pourra deviner d'où part cet escrit. Vous en recevrez des exemplaires, et en mesme temps il en sera envoyé une grande quantité en Italie et en Allemagne sans que tout cela passe par icy. Si vous jugés apropos que j'en envoye à quelques gens en France, mesme à la Cour, et à M. les Ministres, je le puis faire, et ils ne soupçonneront pas que le pacquet leur vienne de moy. Ils ne le scauront que quand vous voudrés."

3. Torcy to La Chapelle, Versailles, 23 March 1706 (minute), AAE, CP, Suisse 169, fols. 111–111ᵛ: "J'attends avec beaucoup d'impatience les paquets que vous me promettez d'envoyer en quelque temps. . . . Je garderai le secret sur le nom d'autheur. Je crois cependant qu'il est necessaire de l'observer et que ce sera donner encore plus de force à l'ouvrage." He goes on to say that he is having a Latin translation made.

4. La Chapelle to Torcy, Soleure, 12 May 1706, AAE, CP, Suisse 170, fols. 63–64: "Permettés moy, Monseigneur, de vous parler à present des testamens nous en avons jetté de touts les costés en Italie et icy, et nous n'avons encor esté ny descouverts, ny soupçonnés. Il ne nous est rien revenu de l'effait que a pû faire la lecture. M. l'Ambassadeur d'Espagne a mandé seulement que M. le Nonce luy avoit dit qu'il avoit un livre très curieux: et comme M. l'Ambassadeur joüa très bien l'ignorant. M. le Nonce luy presta le livre à condition de le rendre fidellement. Le Nonce luy dit qu'il croyoit connoistre l'autheur, qu'il falloit que ce fust un Jesuite de Vienne qu'il luy nomma, ou un hongrois qu'il avoit vu à Rome, que sans doutte ce livre avoit esté fait en Latin, et traduit en Hollande par quelque françois refugié. Voylà tout le retour que nous avons de nos marchandises. Nous sommes occupés à en debiter dans touttes les cours d'Allemagne et surtout à Vienne. Je vous en envoye encor aujourdhuy un paquet de deux douzaines ne

scachant si vous en avés assés. J'ignore absolument quelle est en France la fortune de cet enfant exposé et abandonné de ses parents."

[Joachim Legrand]. *Lettre d'un Conseiller du Grand Conseil de Genève à un Bourgemaistre d'Amsterdam.* Manuscript copy in Legrand's hand: BN, Clairambault 515, pp. 299–312. I have found no printed copy; however, that there were printed copies is clear from the pro-allied response to this tract, *Lettre où l'on répond à celle du prétendu Conseiller de Genève à un Bourgemaître d'Amsterdam* (n.p., n.d.), BN, Imp., Lb^{37}.4372, whose author outlined the essay he was rebutting. This outline matches the Legrand manuscript.

[Joachim Legrand]. *Seconde Lettre d'un Conseiller du Grand Conseil de Genève à un Bourgemaistre d'Amsterdam* (n.p., n.d.). 8°. 7 pp. Printed copy: BN, Lb^{37}.4374. Manuscript copy in Legrand's hand: BN, Clairambault 515, pp. 343–348.

[Louis Rousseau de Chamoy], *Lettre de M***** escrite à M*** Envoyé Extraordinaire de *** à La Haye contenant diverses réflexions sur le traitté conclu entre l'Empereur, le Roy d'Angleterre et les Estats-Généraux des Provinces Unies le 7 septembre 1701.* A Frankfort, chez Pierre Olhenslagher. 1701. 12°. Title page + 3–33.

I. PRINTED COPY

AAE, CP, Hollande 196, fols. 140–156.

II. MANUSCRIPT COPIES

1. First draft: AAE, CP, Allemagne 342, fols. 286–293. "Envoyé avec la depesche de M. de Chamoy du 12 decembre 1701."

2. Second draft: AAE, CP, Hollande 196, fols. 258–270. "Receu avec la depesche de M. de Chamoy du 12 Jan.ʳ 1702."

III. AUTHORSHIP

1. Rousseau to Torcy, 12 December 1701, AAE, CP, Allemagne 342, fol. 294: "J'ay fait fort à la haste l'escrit que j'ay l'honneur d'envoyer aujourd'huy au Roy, et je n'ose esperer que vous le trouviez assez bon que je le souhaite. . . . Ces remarques previennent de bonne heure des esprits indifférents et desabusent quelque fois les préoccupés. Enfin en Allemagne ces sortes d'escrits font souvent un bon effet quand ils sont repandus assez tost et à propos et en cas que vous l'approuvassiez Monseigneur je me servirois quelque fois de ces moyens qui peuvent estre utile et qui n'engagent à rien par la precaution qu'on prend de ne les employer que sous des noms supposés."

2. Rousseau to Torcy, 12 January 1702, Ratisbon, AAE, CP, Allemagne 344, fol. 35: "J'ay appris avec une très grande joye par la lettre dont vous m'avez honoré le 29 du mois passé que vous estes content du memoire, en maniere de lettre, contenant diverses remarques sur le traitté de l'Empereur avec le Roy d'Angleterre et les Estats Generaux des Provinces unies, et vous m'ordonnez seulement d'y changer l'endroit où il estoit dit, en general, que l'Empereur a tenu ce traitté secret. . . . Ainsy j'ay changé cet endroit, comme vous l'avez trouvé à propos, Monseigneur, et je n'ay qu'à souhaitter que vous approuviez la maniere dont je l'ay fait. Au reste je vois que vous trouvez bon de respandre cet escrit. J'auray de la peine à le faire icy de maniere qu'il ne paroisse pas qu'il vienne de moy. Par cette raison je crois qu'il seroit bon de le faire imprimer à Bruxelles plutost qu'en aucun autre lieu, et que non seulement on en envoyast de là divers exemplaires aux envoyez du Roy

dans toutes les cours de l'Empire et autres, mais encore qu'on en addressast quelques uns icy par la poste ordinaire, tant à moy, tant à tous les Ministres des Electeurs, et à la pluspart de ceux Princes, en mettant seulement sur les paquets à M. N . . . Ministre de M. l'Electeur de . . . et M. le Duc de . . . à la Diette de Ratisbonne. C'est ainsy que la lettre du gentilhomme Italien sur l'affaire de M. le Duc de Mantoue a esté rendue publique. Et d'ailleurs je respandray celle cy de mon costé le mieux que je pouvray aussytost que je scauray que vous me l'aurey permis et que vous en aurez approuvé les changements que j'ay barrez au dessous pour vous les faire remarquer plus aisement dans la copie cy jointe."

[Louis Rousseau de Chamoy], *Réponse de Mr. de . . . Envoyé de Mr. le Duc . . . à Mr. de . . . aussi Envoyé du mesme Prince à . . . contenant diverses réflexions sur les mandements de l'Empereur contre Mr. l'Electeur de Cologne*. A Francfort, chez Pierre Olhenslagher. M.D. CCII, 12°. 40 pp.

I. PRINTED COPIES

1. AAE, CP, Allemagne 345, fols. 317–336^v.
2. AAE, CP, Cologne 51, fols. 146–177.

II. MANUSCRIPT COPY

AAE, CP, Cologne 51, fols. 160–171^v.

III. AUTHORSHIP

1. Rousseau to Torcy, Ratisbon, 13 March 1702, AAE, CP, Allemagne 344, fol. 134^v: "Au reste, Monseigneur, j'ay satisfait le plus promptement qu'il m'a esté possible à l'ordre que vous m'avey donné d'escrire aussy quelque chose sur l'affaire de M. l'Electeur de Cologne. J'espere de vous l'envoyer demain par Strasbourg."

2. Rousseau to Torcy, Ratisbon, 16 March 1702, *ibid.*, fol. 147. Reports that he sent off the *écrit* via Strasbourg on 14 March.

3. Louis to Rousseau, Marly, 30 March 1702 (minute), *ibid.*, fol. 151. On *écrit* concerning Cologne: "Comme il est remply de solides raisons j'ay cru qu'il estoit à propos de le rendre public et il est certain que quoyque ces memoires ne detruisent pas l'effet de la passion et des interests particuliers il est bon cependant de les repandre quand il ne se serviroient qu'à persuader ceux qui ne sont pas préjugés."

4. Rousseau to Louis, Ratisbon, 17 April 1702, *ibid.*, fol. 189ᵛ. Acknowledges receipt of Louis' permission to make public the *écrit* on Cologne: "L'envoyé de Vostre Majesté à Bonn [Des Alleurs] m'en a presque en mesme temps addressé exemplaires imprimez et ils ont esté aussitost distribuez icy d'une manière que je crois qu'ils auront depuis passé de main en main à la plus part des Ministres de la Diette. Quand dans les visites que je leur ay renduës je leur ay raporté à peu près les mesmes raisons, j'ay tousjours trouvé qu'ils y répondent mal, et je me suis assez apperçeu que quelques uns mesme conviennent de ces principes. Mais leur devoüement personnel appuyé de celuy de leurs maistres mesmes et la necessité imaginaire de s'unir contre les forces de Vostre Majesté jointes à celles d'Espagne qu'ils regardent comme une seule et mesme puissance, l'emportent sur toutes les conséquences de tant d'entreprises de la cour de Vienne. Et c'est de cette crainte qu'il s'agit de guérir les esprits en Allemagne, aussy bien qu'en Hollande, avant d'espérer que tant de raisons fassent dans le public l'impression qu'elles méritent."

[Louis Rousseau de Chamoy], *Traduction de la réponse d'un gentilhomme italien à une lettre d'un de ses amis sur la prétendue proscription du Duc de Mantoue* (n.p., n.d.). 4°. 8 pp.

APPENDIX

I. EDITIONS

1. In AN, K. 1304, No. 9.
2. In Lamberty, *Mémoires*, 1, 539–546.

II. MANUSCRIPT DRAFTS

1. Rousseau's first draft, with changes in Torcy's hand: AAE, CP, Allemagne 342, fols. 56–60ᵛ.
2. Rousseau's revised draft, identical with the printed version: AAE, CP, Mantoue 32, fols. 226–231.

III. AUTHORSHIP

1. Rousseau to Louis, Ratisbon, 1 August 1701, AAE, CP, Allemagne 342, fol. 61. Encloses the *écrit* Louis ordered him to compose: "Elle [Louis] y verra que j'y suppose que c'est la réponse d'un gentilhomme Italien à un de ses amis qui luy a demandé son sentiment sur cette affaire. C'est une maniere qui est assez d'usage en Allemagne en pareil cas et je crois y avoir mis les choses dans un ordre clair [et] naturel. . . . Si Votre Majesté l'approuve elle verra de quelle maniere elle trouvera a propos que l'escrit soit distribuée, et si ce devra seulement en respandant des copies, ou en le faisant imprimer."

2. Louis to Rousseau, Marly, 17 August 1701 (minute), *ibid.*, fol. 66. Acknowledges receipt of Rousseau's dispatch and the *écrit* he composed: "J'ai seulement fait marquer au commencement du memoire un article qu'il est necessaire que vous changiez. Vous en fist repandre quelques copies écrits à la main et puisqu'on ne peut imprimer à Ratisbonne sans permission vous pouvez l'envoyer en Hollande pour en faire faire l'impression."

3. Rousseau to Torcy, Ratisbon, 1 September 1701, *ibid.*, fol. 116. Acknowledges receipt of Louis' order of 17 August and notes that he changed the passage "sui-

vant que vous me l'avez ordonné." Encloses full revised copy. Reports that he is having manuscript copies made immediately; also that he is sending one copy to Holland to be printed "comme vous me permettez, et je l'adresse à M. Barré [French resident at The Hague] avec une lettre par laquelle je luy laisse entendre que je le fais avec ordre."

4. Rousseau to Torcy, Ratisbon, 5 September 1701, *ibid.*, fol. 120. Reports that he has distributed only three manuscript copies at Ratisbon so as not to make it appear that he is the pamphlet's source: "Une de ces trois produira d'autres qui se repandront, et il sera bon que M. Barré à La Haye en fasse mettre plusieurs exemplaires à la poste de ces quartiers sous les couverts que je luy marqueray."

5. See above [Louis Rousseau de Chamoy], *Lettre de M***** escrite à M*** Envoyé Extraordinaire de *** à La Haye*, III: 2.

BIBLIOGRAPHY

I. MANUSCRIPT SOURCES

Archives du Ministère des Affaires étrangères

1. Correspondance Politique
   Allemagne: 335, 341–345, 351
   Angleterre: 190, 210–216, 228, 230, 234, 237, 239–242, 248, Supplément 4
   Autriche: 81
   Bavière: 47, 49–51, 63
   Cologne: 11, 12, 50–52, 54, 56, 57, 59, 60
   Espagne: 117, 203
   Gênes: 46, 47
   Genève: 23
   Hollande: 90, 190, 193, 194, 196, 198, 217–228, 231, 232, 242, Supplément 9
   Hongrie: 16
   Lorraine: 55
   Mantoue: 31, 32
   Munster: 3
   Prusse: 9–11
   Suisse: 128–132, 133, 135, 137, 139, 140, 142–144, 147, 151, 152, 158, 160–163, 166, 168–175, 179, 181, 185, 193
   Toscane: 43
   Venise: 155
2. Mémoires et Documents
   Allemagne: 49 (Obrecht papers)
   Angleterre: 138bis (Gaultier papers)
   Espagne: 368 (Legrand)
   France: 221 (Académie politique); 307–310 (financial records and d'Argenson corr.); 1106, 1118, 1129, 1137, 1145, 1160, 1163, 1173, 1186, 1187

(d'Argenson corr. and reports); 1166 (postal service); 1580, 1581 (intendants' corr.); 1874 (La Blinière memoranda)

Archives du Ministère de Guerre
Series Al: 1560 (Cologne, 1702); 1739 (Allemagne, 1704); 2036 (Neuchâtel, 1707)

Archives Nationales
K. 122–135 (carton des rois); K. 569 (Condé papers); K. 1304, M. 757, M. 758, M. 766, M. 767, MM. 824 (Léonard papers); M. 769 (Léonard-Legrand corr.); Minutier Central, Donneau de Visé

Bibliothèque de l'Arsenal
MS. 6516 (Obrecht papers), 10571 (nouvellistes)

Bibliothèque Nationale, Cabinet des Manuscrits
1. Manuscrits Français: 10668 (Torcy); 21741, 21743, 21745, 21949 (prohibited books); 22585 (Léonard papers); 23209 (Te Deum); 24477 (nouvelles à la main); 24988 (Legrand); 32585 (Delaulne)
2. Nouvelles Acquisitions Françaises: 7409 (Dubos corr.); 7488, 7492 (Renaudot papers)
3. Collection Clairambault: 174, 295, 452, 515, 518, 519, 521, 1023, 1024 (Legrand papers and corr.); 284, 492 (pamphlets)
4. Collection Lorraine: 269 (*Journal littéraire de Soleure*)
5. Dossiers bleus: 168 (La Chapelle)

II. PRINTED SOURCES

This list does not comprise a recapitulation of material provided in the notes and appendix on multiple editions, reprints, translations, and library catalogue numbers of propaganda pamphlets and royal letters. In general, only a single edition of such works is cited here, and documents reprinted in Lamberty, *Mémoires*, are not separately listed. The reader is referred to the annotative apparatus above for complete documentation.

Animadversions on a Late Factious Book. London, 1701.

[Aubery, A.]. *Des justes prétentions du Roi sur l'Empire.* Paris, 1666.

———. *Histoire du Cardinal de Richelieu.* Paris, 1660.

Bayle, Pierre. *Oeuvres diverses.* 4 vols. The Hague, 1727–1730.

———. *Réponse aux questions d'un provincial.* 5 vols. Rotterdam, 1705–1707.

[Bilain, A. (?)]. *Traité des droits de la reine très-chrétienne sur les divers états de la monarchie d'Espagne.* Paris, 1667.

Bolingbroke, Henry St. John, Viscount. *Letters and Correspondence Public and Private of the Right Honourable Henry St. John, Lord Viscount Bolingbroke,* ed. G. Parke. 4 vols. London, 1798.

[Chemnitz, B. von]. *Dissertatio de ratione status in imperium romano-germanico* (1647), trans. [H. Bourgeois du Chastenet] as *Interêts des Princes d'Allemagne.* 2 vols. Paris, 1712.

La Clef du cabinet des Princes de l'Europe, ed. Claude Jordan. Luxembourg & Verdun, 1704–1713.

Clément, Pierre, ed. *Lettres, instructions et mémoires de Colbert.* 8 vols. Paris, 1862–1882.

Daily Courant. London, 1709.

Dangeau, Philippe de Courcillon, Marquis de. *Journal.* 19 vols. Paris, 1854–1860.

Davenant, Charles. *Political and Commercial Works,* ed. Sir Charles Whitworth. 5 vols. London, 1771.

Defoe, Daniel. *Review.* London, 1709.

Denis, Paul, ed. *Lettres autographes de la collection de Troussures.* Beauvais, 1912.

Depping, G.-B., ed. *Correspondance administrative sous Louis XIV.* 4 vols. Paris, 1850–1855.

Description de feu de joie dressé devant l'Hostel de Ville pour la prise de la ville de Namur. n.p., 1692.

Dictionnaire de l'Académie françoise. 2 vols. Paris, 1694.

[Donneau de Visé, Jean]. *A History of the Siege of Toulon.* London, 1708.

————. *Diary of the Siege of Luxembourg by the French King's Forces Under the Command of the Marshal de Créqui.* London, 1684.

————. *Recueil de diverses pièces touchant les préliminaires de paix proposez par les Alliez, et rejettez par le Roy.* Paris, 1709.

Dubois, Alexandre. *Journal d'un curé de campagne au XVIIe siècle,* ed. Henri Platelle. Paris, 1965.

Dubos, Jean-Baptiste. *Discours prononcez dans l'Académie françoise le samedy troisième Fevrier MDCCXX à la réception de Monsieur l'Abbé Du Bos.* Paris, 1720.

————. *Histoire de la ligue faite à Cambray.* Paris, 1709. Translated as *History of the League of Cambray.* London, 1712.

————. *Les Interêts de l'Angleterre malentendus dans la guerre présente.* Amsterdam, 1703.

————. *Manifeste de l'Electeur de Bavière.* n.p., 1704–1705. Translated as *The Manifesto of the Elector of Bavaria.* London, 1704.

Duffo, F.-A., ed. *Correspondance inédite d'Eusèbe Renaudot avec le Cardinal François-Marie de Médicis, 1703–1712.* 3 vols. Paris, 1915–1927.

[Dumont, Jean]. *Les Soupirs de l'Europe . . . or The Groans of Europe.* London, 1713.

L'Esprit des cours de l'Europe, ed. N. de Gueudeville. The Hague and Amsterdam, 1701, 1705.

Europäische Fama. Leipzig, 1704, 1705.

Feu de joie tiré à Dijon le dimanche 28. Novembre 1688 pour la prise de Philisbourg. Dijon, 1688.

[Freschot, Casimir]. *Réponse au manifeste qui court sous le nom de S.A. Electorale de Bavière ou Réflexions sur les raisons qui y sont déduites pour la justification de ses armes.* Pamplona, 1705.

La Gazette. Paris, 1700–1712.

Gigas, E., ed. *Choix de la correspondance inédite de Pierre Bayle.* Copenhagen & Paris, 1890.

Journal de Trévoux. See *Mémoires de Trévoux.*

Journal de Verdun. See *Clef du cabinet des Princes de l'Europe.*

Journal des Savans. Paris & Amsterdam, 1701–1711.

Journal historique sur les matières du tems. See *Clef du cabinet des Princes de l'Europe.*

Journal littéraire de Soleure, ed. C.-L. Hugo. Nancy, 1705.

[Karg von Bebenburg, J. F. I.]. *Additions au Manifeste de l'Electeur de Bavière.* n.p., 1705.

————. *Lettre écrite de Ratisbonne à un curieux demeurant à La Haye, sur le procédé irregulier, qu'on a tenu contre S.A.E. de Cologne.* n.p., n.d.

————. *Manifeste en forme de lettre pour S.A.S.E. de Cologne, dont les moyens sont tirés de la lettre latine qu'Elle a écrite à l'Empereur le 19 mars 1702.* Paris, 1702.

————. *On demande si l'Empereur peut soumettre au ban de l'Empire quelqu'un des Electeurs, ou Princes d'Allemagne, du consentement du Collège Electoral seul, sans la participation des autres Princes du S. Empire?* n.p., n.d.

————. *Protestation de M. l'Electeur de Bavière.* Namur, 1711.

————. *La Protestation de S.A.S. Electorale de Cologne.* n.p., n.d.

————(?). *Réflections sur les mandemens impériaux contre M. l'Electeur de Cologne.* Frankfurt, 1702.

[La Chapelle, Jean de]. *Considerations politiques sur la prochaine élection d'un nouvel Empereur.* n.p., 1711.

————. *Discours prononcez dans l'Académie françoise le samedy vingt-troisième de Juin MDCCXIV à la réception de Monsieur le Mareschal Duc de Villars.* Paris, 1714.

————. *Lettres d'un suisse à un françois.* 8 vols. [Paris] "Basel," 1703–1709.

————(?). *Seconde Lettre d'un Conseiller du Grand Conseil de Genève à un Bourguemaître d'Amsterdam.* n.p., n.d.

[La Chapelle, Jean de]. *Testament politique ou derniers conseils d'un ministre de l'Empereur Léopold I.* "Rotterdam," 1707.

Lamberty, Guillaume de. *Mémoires pour servir à l'histoire du XVIIIe siècle.* 14 vols. Amsterdam, 1735–1740.

Lanchey, L., and E. Mabille, eds. *Notes de René d'Argenson.* Paris, 1866.

Leclerc, Jean. *Bibliothèque choisie.* 28 vols. Amsterdam, 1703–1718.

[Legrand, Joachim]. *L'Allemagne menacée d'estre bien-tost reduite en monarchie absolue, si elle ne profite de la conjoncture présente pour asseurer sa liberté.* n.p., 1711.

————. *Discours politique sur ce qui s'est passé dans l'Empire au sujet de la succesion d'Espagne.* n.p., 1711.

————. *Lettre de Monsieur D^{xxx} à Monsieur le Docteur W^{xxx}, touchant le Royaume de Bohème.* n.p., 1711.

————. *Mémoire touchant la succession à la couronne d'Espagne, traduit de l'Espagnol. Réflexions sur la Lettre à Mylord, sur la nécessité et la justice de l'entière restitution de la monarchie d'Espagne.* n.p., 1710; 2nd ed., n.p., 1711.

————(?). *Response d'un amy de La Haye, à son amy de Londres.* n.p., n.d.

————. *Seconde Lettre d'un Conseiller du Grand Conseil de Genève à un Bourgemaistre d'Amsterdam.* n.p., n.d.

Lettre d'un ami de Londres à son ami de La Haye. n.p., n.d.

Lettre où l'on répond à celle du prétendu Conseiller de Genève à un Bourgemaître d'Amsterdam. n.p., n.d.

Lombard, A., ed. *Correspondance de l'Abbé Du Bos.* Paris, 1913.

Longon, Jean, ed. *Mémoires de Louis XIV.* Paris, 1927.

Louis XIV. *Lettre du Roy à Monseigneur l'Evesque Comte de Chaalons, Pair de France.* Châlons-sur-Marne, 1709.

————. *Lettre du Roy à Mr. le Marquis Dantin du 12 Juin 1709.* Paris, 1709.

————. *Lettre du Roy au Pape contenant les motifs de la guerre de Savoye.* Paris, 1704.

BIBLIOGRAPHY

————. *Lettre du Roi écrite à Monseigneur l'Archévêque de Paris, pour faire chanter Te Deum en l'Eglise de Nôtre Dame, afin de remercier Dieu de la Prise de la Ville de Philisbourg par l'armée du Roy, commandée par Msgr. le Dauphin.* Paris, 1688.

————. *Lettre du Roy, écrite à Msgr. l'Archévêque de Paris, pour faire chanter le Te Deum en l'Eglise Nôtre-Dame, en action de grâces de la Paix.* Paris, 1697.

————. *Lettre du Roy, écrite à Msgr. l'Archévêque de Paris pour faire chanter le Te Deum en l'Eglise Nôtre Dame, en action de grâces de la prise de Barcelonne par l'armée de Sa Majesté en Catalogne.* Paris, 1697.

————. *Lettre du Roy écrite à Monseigneur l'Evêque Comte de Chaalons.* Châlons-sur-Marne, 1711.

————. *Lettre du Roy envoyée à Messieurs les Prevost des Marchands et Echevins de la Ville de Paris, pour assister au Te Deum, et faire faire des feux de joye, et autres réjouissances publiques, pour la prise de la Ville de Maëstrick.* Paris, 1679.

————. *Lettre du Roy, envoyée à Monseigneur l'Archévêque de Paris, sur la prise de la Ville de Douay et Fort Descarpel.* Paris, 1667.

————. *Lettre du Roy, envoyée à Monseigneur l'Archévêque de Paris, sur le sujet de la prise de la ville et Château de Tournay.* Paris, 1667.

————. *Lettres du Roy écrites à Monseigneur l'Evêque Comte de Châlons, Pair de France, pour faire chanter Te Deum dans l'Eglise Cathédrale, et dans toutes celles de son Diocese, en action de grâces de la Prise de la Ville de Suze par l'Armée du Roy, commandée par Monsieur le Duc de la Feuillade; Et de la naissance de Monseigneur le Duc de Bretagne. Avec le Mandement de Mondit-Seigneur.* Châlons, 1704.

————. *Memoirs for the Instruction of the Dauphin*, trans. and ed. Paul Sonnino. New York, 1970.

————. *Ordonnance du Roy, portant déclaration de guerre contre le Duc de Savoye, du 4. Decembre 1703.* Paris, 1703.

313

Louis XIV. *Ordonnance du Roy, pour la publication du traité de suspension d'armes entre la France et l'Angleterre.* Paris, 1712.

————, *et al. Renonciation du Roy d'Espagne à la couronne de France, de Monseigneur le Duc de Berry et le Duc d'Orléans, à la couronne d'Espagne avec les lettres patentes du Roy du mois de Decembre 1700. Et les lettres patentes du Roy du mois de Mars 1713 qui admettent les Renonciations cy-dessus, et revoquent les lettres patentes du mois de Decembre 1700.* Paris, 1713.

Marcel, G., ed. *Journal d'un bourgeois de Caen, 1652–1733.* Paris, 1848.

Mémoires de Trévoux. Trévoux, 1701–1712, 1744.

Mémoires pour servir à l'histoire des sciences, et des beaux arts. See *Mémoires de Trévoux.*

Mercure galant, ed. Jean Donneau de Visé. Paris, 1672, 1684, 1704–1709.

Mercure historique et politique. The Hague, 1704.

Nouvelles de la République des Lettres. Amsterdam, 1709.

[Obrecht, Ulrich]. *Excerpta historica et juridica de natura successionis in monarchiam Hispaniae.* n.p., 1701.

Payne, William L., ed. *The Best of Defoe's Review.* New York, 1951.

The Present State of Europe. London, 1692, 1697, 1703, 1706, 1709.

Ravaisson-Mollien, F. *Archives de la Bastille.* 19 vols. Paris, 1866–1904.

Recueil des instructions données aux ambassadeurs français depuis la paix de Westphalie jusqu'à la Révolution française. Vol. 4: *Pologne,* ed. I.-L. Farges. Paris, 1888. Vol. 7: *Bavière, Palatinat, Deux-Ponts,* ed. A. Lebon. Paris, 1889. Vol. 17: *Rome-2,* ed. G. Hanotaux. Paris, 1911. Vol. 18: *Diète germanique,* ed. B. Auerbach. Paris, 1912. Vol. 25, part 2: *Angleterre-3 (1698–1791),* ed. P. Vaucher. Paris, 1965. Vol. 28, part 2: *Etats allemands—Cologne,* ed. G. Livet. Paris, 1963.

Recueil des Testaments politiques. 4 vols. Amsterdam & Paris, 1749.

Relation de ce qui s'est fait à Lyon, au passage de Monseigneur le Duc de Bourgogne et de Monseigneur le Duc de Berry. Lyon, 1701.

Relation de ce qui s'est passé à Châlon sur Saone à l'entrée de Msgr. le Duc de Bourgogne, le 14 Avril 1701. Lyon, 1701.

Relation des réjouissances faites à Caen par Monsieur Foucault, . . . Intendant de Basse-Normandie, pour la naissance de Monseigneur le Duc de Bretagne. Caen [1704].

Relation sommaire de ce qui a été fait à Toulon pendant le séjour que Nosseigneurs les Ducs de Bourgogne et de Berry y ont fait. Paris, 1701.

Rochas d'Aiglun, A. de, ed. *Vauban, ses oisivités et sa correspondance.* 2 vols. Paris, 1910.

[Rousseau de Chamoy, Louis]. *Lettre de M.***** escrite à M.**** Envoyé Extraordinaire de *** à la Haye contenant diverses reflexions sur le traitté conclu entre l'Empereur, le Roy d'Angleterre et les Estats-Généraux des Provinces-Unies le 7 septembre MDCCI.* Frankfurt, 1701.

———. *Réponse de Mr. de . . . Envoyé de Mr. le Duc . . . à Mr. de . . . aussi Envoyé du mesme Prince à . . . contenant diverses reflexions sur les mandements de l'Empereur contre Mr. l'Electeur de Cologne.* Frankfurt, 1702.

———. *Traduction de la réponse d'un gentilhomme italien à une lettre d'un de ses amis sur la prétendue proscription du duc de Mantoue.* n.p., n.d. [1701].

Saint-Simon, Louis de Rouvroy, duc de. *Mémoires,* ed. A. de Boislisle. 41 vols. Paris, 1879–1928.

Swift, Jonathan. *Journal to Stella,* ed. Harold Williams. 2 vols. Oxford, 1948.

———. *Political Tracts, 1711–1713,* ed. Herbert Davis. Oxford, 1951.

Tamizey de Larroque, P., ed. *Lettres de Jean Chapelain.* 2 vols. Paris, 1883.

Torcy, Jean-Baptiste Colbert, Marquis de. *Journal inédit de Jean-Baptiste Colbert, Marquis de Torcy*, ed. F. Masson. Paris, 1884.

———. *Mémoires du Marquis de Torcy*. In *Nouvelle collection des mémoires pour servir à l'histoire de France*, ed. J. F. Michaud and J.J.F. Poujoulat. Ser. 3, vol. 8. Paris, 1839.

———. *The Memoirs of Jean-Baptiste Colbert, Marquis de Torcy*. 2 vols. London, 1757.

The Tories Great Doubts and Difficulties Fully Resolv'd, by More Important Doubts and Difficulties. With Some Queries about Monsieur Poussin Paying his Foy to three Members of the H——— of C———s. London, 1701.

Troullai, R. de, ed. *Mémoires et Lettres du Maréchal de Tessé.* 2 vols. Paris, 1886.

Vanhuffel, M., ed. *Documents inédits concernant l'histoire de France et particulièrement l'Alsace et son gouvernement sous Louis XIV*. Paris, 1840.

van 'T Hoff, B., ed. *The Correspondence of John Churchill and Antonie Heinsius.* The Hague, 1951.

Vauban, Sébastien Le Prestre, Maréchal de. *Projet d'un dixme royale*, ed. E. Coornaert. Paris, 1933.

A Vindication of Dr. Charles Davenant. London, 1702.

III. SECONDARY WORKS

d'Alembert, J. le R. *Histoire des membres de l'Académie françoise*. 6 vols. Paris, 1785–1787.

Anderson, M. S. "Eighteenth-Century Theories of the Balance of Power." In *Studies in Diplomatic History: Essays in Memory of David Bayne Horn*, ed. R. Hatton and M. S. Anderson. London, 1970.

Auerbach, B. *La France et le Saint Empire Germanique depuis la paix de Westphalie jusqu'à la Révolution française*. Paris, 1912.

Azam, Denise Aimé. "Le Ministère des Affaires étrangères

et la presse à la fin de l'Ancien Régime." *Cahiers de la presse*, No. 3 (1938), 428–438.

Barbier, A. *Dictionnaire des ouvrages anonymes.* 4 vols. Paris, 1872–1879.

Baschet, A. *Histoire du dépôt des Archives des Affaires étrangères.* Paris, 1875.

Baxter, S. B. *William III.* London, 1966.

Bellanger, Claude, *et al. Histoire générale de la presse française.* 2 vols. Paris, 1969.

Birn, Raymond. "The Profits of Ideas: *Privilèges en librairie* in Eighteenth-Century France." *Eighteenth-Century Studies*, 4:2 (Winter 1970), 131–168.

————. "Le Journal des Savants sous l'Ancien Régime." *Journal des Savants*, No. 1 (1965), 15–29.

Blanc-Roquette, Marie-Thérèse. *La Presse et l'information à Toulouse des origines à 1789.* Toulouse, 1967.

Bloch, Marc. *Les Rois thaumaturges. Etude sur le caractère surnaturel attribué à la puissance royale particulièrement en France et en Angleterre.* Strasbourg, 1924. Translated by J. E. Anderson as *The Royal Touch. Sacred Monarchy and Scrofula in France and England.* London, 1973.

Boislisle, A. de. "Le Grand Hiver et la disette de 1709." *Revue des questions historiques*, 73 (1903), 486–542; 74 (1904), 442–509.

————. *Les Suisses et le Marquis de Puyzieulx.* Paris, 1906.

Bollème, Geneviève. *Les Almanachs populaires aux XVIIᵉ et XVIIIᵉ siècles.* Paris, 1969.

————, *et al. Livre et société dans la France du XVIIIᵉ siècle.* Paris, 1965.

Bonno, Gabriel. "Liste chronologique des périodiques de langue française du XVIIIᵉ siècle." *Modern Language Quarterly*, 5 (1944), 3–25.

————. "Une amitié franco-anglaise du XVIIᵉ siècle: John Locke et l'abbé Du Bos." *Revue de littérature comparée*, 24 (1950), 481–520.

Bossuat, André. "La Littérature de propagande au XVᵉ siècle." *Cahiers d'histoire*, 1 (1956), 131–145.

Bourgeois, E. "La Collaboration de Saint-Simon et Torcy." *Revue historique* (1905), 251–277.

———. *Neuchâtel et la politique prussienne en Franche-Comté, 1702–1713*. Paris, 1887.

———, and L. André. *Les Sources de l'histoire de France: le XVIIᵉ siècle*. 8 vols. Paris, 1913–1935.

Braubach, M. *Geschichte und Abenteuer, Gestalten um den Prinzen Eugen*. Munich, 1950.

———. *Kurköln, Gestalten und Ereignissen aus zwei Jahrhunderten rheinischen Geschichte*. Münster, 1948.

Brown, Harcourt. "History and the Learned Journal." *Journal of the History of Ideas*, 33 (1972), 365–378.

Butterfield, Herbert, ed. *Diplomatic Investigations*. London, 1966.

Camusat, D.-F. *Histoire critique des journaux*. 2 vols. Amsterdam, 1734.

Candaux, Jean-Daniel. "Inventaire provisoire des périodiques littéraires et scientifiques de langue française publiés en Suisse de 1693 à 1795." In M. Couperus, *L'Etude des périodiques anciens*. Utrecht, 1970.

Céleste, Raymond. "Bordeaux au XVIIIᵉ siècle, le roi d'Espagne à Blaye, Bordeaux et Bazas (1700–1701)." *Revue historique de Bordeaux*, 1 (1908), 49–61, 134–149.

Cerf, Madeleine. "La Censure royale à la fin du XVIIIᵉ siècle." *Communications*, No. 9 (1967), pp. 2–27.

Chartier, Roger. "Comment on écrivait l'histoire au temps des guerres de religion." *Annales-E.S.C.*, 29 (1974), 880–887.

Chauvet, Paul. *Les Ouvriers du livre en France des origines à la Révolution de 1789*. Paris, 1959.

Church, William F. "Louis XIV and Reason of State." In *Louis XIV and the Craft of Kingship*, ed. John C. Rule. Columbus, 1969.

———. *Richelieu and Reason of State*. Princeton, 1972.

———, ed. *The Impact of Absolutism in France*. New York, 1969.

Churchill, W. S. *Marlborough, His Life and Times*. 6 vols. New York, 1933–1938.

Clark, G. N. *English Commercial Statistics, 1696–1782*. London, 1938.

Cobban, A. *Aspects of the French Revolution*. New York, 1968.

Collas, George. *Jean Chapelain*. Paris, 1912.

Coombs, Douglas. *The Conduct of the Dutch, British Opinion and the Dutch Alliance during the War of the Spanish Succession*. The Hague, 1958.

Couperus, M. *L'Etude des périodiques anciens: Colloque d'Utrecht*. Utrecht, 1970.

Cranfield, G. A. *The Development of the Provincial Newspaper, 1700–1760*. Oxford, 1962.

Darnton, Robert. "Reading, Writing and Publishing in Eighteenth-Century France: A Case Study in the Sociology of Literature." *Daedalus*, 100:1 (Winter 1971), 214–256.

Davis, Natalie Zemon. *Society and Culture in Early Modern France*. Stanford, 1975.

de Beer, E. S. "The English Newspaper from 1695 to 1702." In *William III and Louis XIV: Essays 1680–1720 by and for Mark A. Thomson*, ed. R. Hatton and J. S. Bromley. Liverpool, 1968.

Delavaud, L. "L'Education d'un ministre." *Revue de Paris*, 15 March 1910, pp. 331–368.

———. "Une grande dame au XVIIIe siècle: Marguerite-Thérèse Colbert de Croissy, Duchesse de Saint-Pierre." *Revue du XVIIIe siècle*, 1 (1913), 95–103.

———. "Scènes de la vie diplomatique au XVIIIe siècle." *Revue du XVIIIe siècle*, 2 (1913), 141–160, 258–274.

Desautels, Alfred R. *Les Mémoires de Trévoux et le mouvement des idées au XVIIIe siècle, 1701–1734*. Rome, 1956.

Desgraves, Louis. "Les 'Bulletins d'Information' imprimés à Bordeaux au XVIIe siècle." *Bulletin de la Société des bibliophiles de Guyenne*, No. 79 (1964), pp. 15–54.

Dodge, G. H. *The Political Theory of the Huguenots of the Dispersion.* New York, 1947.

Dottin, P. "Daniel De Foe mystificateur, ou les faux mémoires de Mesnager." *Revue germanique,* 14 (1923), 269–282.

Droysen, J. G. *Geschichte der preussischen Politik.* 14 vols. Berlin, 1855–1886.

Duchêne, Roger. "Lettres et gazettes du XVIIIe siècle." *Revue d'histoire moderne et contemporaine,* 18 (1971), 489–502.

Duffo, F.-A. *Un Abbé diplomate.* Paris, 1928.

Dupont-Ferrier, G. "Le Sens des mots 'patria' et 'patrie' en France au moyen âge et jusqu'au début du XVIIe siècle." *Revue historique,* 188 (1940), 89–104.

Ehrard, J., and J. Roger. "Deux périodiques français au XVIIIe siècle: le 'Journal des Savants' et les 'Mémoires de Trévoux.'" In G. Bollème *et al., Livre et société dans la France du XVIIIe siècle.* Paris, 1965.

Eisenstein, Elizabeth L. "L'Avènement de l'imprimerie et la Réforme. Une nouvelle approche au problème du démembrement de la chrétienté occidentale." *Annales-E.S.C.,* 26:6 (1971), 1355–1381.

———. "Some Conjectures about the Impact of Printing on Western Society and Thought: A Preliminary Report." *Journal of Modern History,* 40:1 (1968), 1–56.

Ellul, Jacques. *Propaganda, the Formation of Men's Attitudes.* New York, 1965.

Elton, G. R. *Policy and Police: The Enforcement of the Reformation in the Time of Cromwell.* Cambridge, 1972.

Ennen, L. *Der spanische Erbfolgekrieg und der Kurfürst Joseph Clemens von Köln.* Jena, 1854.

Feldmeier, F. "Das angebliche kurbayerische Manifest von 1704." *Oberbayerisches Archiv für vaterländische Geschichte,* 61 (1918), 193–225.

Feller, Richard. "Die Schweiz des 17. Jahrhunderts in den Berichter des Auslandes." *Schweizer Beiträge zur allgemeinen Geschichte,* 1 (1943), 55–117.

————. *Die Schweiz und das Ausland im spanischen Erbfolgekrieg.* Bern, 1912.

Fleury, Michel, and Pierre Valmary. "Les Progrès de l'instruction élémentaire de Louis XIV à Napoléon III." *Population*, 12 (1957), 71–92.

Ford, Franklin. *Robe and Sword: The Regrouping of the French Aristocracy After Louis XIV.* Cambridge, Mass., 1953.

————. *Strasbourg in Transition, 1648–1789.* Cambridge, Mass., 1958.

Fraser, Peter. *The Intelligence of Secretaries of State and Their Monopoly of Licensed News, 1660–1688.* Cambridge, 1956.

Funck-Brentano, F. *Figaro et ses devanciers.* Paris, 1909.

————. *Les Nouvellistes.* Paris, 1905.

Furet, F. "La 'Librairie' du royaume de France au 18e siècle." In G. Bollème *et al.*, *Livre et société dans la France du XVIIIe siècle.* Paris, 1965.

————, and W. Sachs. "La Croissance de l'alphabétisation en France XVIIIe–XIXe siècle." *Annales-E.S.C.*, 29 (1974), 714–737.

Gay, Peter. *The Enlightenment: An Interpretation.* 2 vols. New York, 1967–1969.

Gembruch, Werner. "Reformforderungen in Frankreich um die Wende von 17. zum 18. Jahrhunderts." *Historische Zeitschrift*, 209 (October 1969), 265–317.

Gillot, H. *Le Règne de Louis XIV et l'opinion publique en Allemagne.* Paris, 1913.

Gilot, Michel. "Quelques sortes de lettres de lecteurs." In M. Couperus, *L'Etude des périodiques anciens.* Utrecht, 1970.

Godechot, Jacques. "Nation, patrie, nationalisme et patriotisme en France au XVIIIe siècle." *Annales historiques de la Révolution française*, 43 (1971), 483–501.

Goubert, Pierre. *Familles marchandes sous l'ancien régime.* Paris, 1960.

Goulding, Sybil. *Swift en France.* Paris, 1924.

Grand-Mesnil, M.-N. *Mazarin, la Fronde et la presse, 1647–1649*. Paris, 1967.

Gross, Hanns. *Empire and Sovereignty. A History of Public Law Literature in the Holy Roman Empire, 1559–1804*. Chicago, 1973.

Gunn, J.A.W. " 'Interest Will Not Lie,' A Seventeenth-Century Political Maxim." *Journal of the History of Ideas*, 29 (1968), 551–564.

———. *Politics and the Public Interest in the Seventeenth Century*. Toronto, 1969.

Hahn, Roger. *The Anatomy of a Scientific Institution: The Paris Academy of the Sciences, 1666–1803*. Berkeley, 1971.

Haller, Johannes. *Die deutsche Publizistik in den Jahren 1668–1674*. Heidelberg, 1892.

Hanson, Lawrence. *Government and the Press, 1695–1763*. Oxford, 1936.

Hatin, Eugène. *Les Gazettes de Hollande et la presse clandestine du XVIIe et XVIIIe siècles*. Paris, 1865.

———. *Histoire politique et littéraire de la presse en France*. 8 vols. Paris, 1859–1861.

Hatton, Ragnhild M. "Louis XIV: Recent Gains in Historical Knowledge." *Journal of Modern History*, 45:2 (June 1973), 277–291.

Hatton, R., and M. S. Anderson, eds. *Studies in Diplomatic History: Essays in Memory of David Bayne Horn*. London, 1970.

———, and J. S. Bromley, eds. *William III and Louis XIV: Essays 1680–1720 by and for Mark A. Thomson*. Liverpool, 1968.

Hazard, Paul. *La Crise de la conscience européenne 1680–1720*. Paris, 1935. Translated by J. Lewis May as *The European Mind 1680–1720*. New Haven, 1952.

Henriet, Maurice. "Discours de M. de la Chapelle sur Racine à l'Académie française (1699)." *Annales de la Société historique et archéologique de Château-Thierry* (1902), pp. 53–67.

Hippeau, C. *L'Avènement des Bourbons au trône d'Espagne.* 2 vols. Paris, 1875.

Holmes, G., ed. *Britain After the Glorious Revolution.* London, 1969.

Holtman, Robert B. *Napoleonic Propaganda.* Baton Rouge, 1950.

Isherwood, Robert M. *Music in the Service of the King: France in the Seventeenth Century.* Ithaca, 1973.

Jusserand, J.-J. "Grotius étudié par les secrétaires de l'ambassade français en 1711." *Bibliotheca Visseriana*, 8 (1929), 1–4.

Keens-Soper, Maurice. "The French Political Academy, 1712: A School for Ambassadors." *European Studies Review*, 2 (October 1972), 329–355.

Klaits, Joseph. "Men of Letters and Political Reform in France at the End of the Reign of Louis XIV: The Founding of the Académie Politique." *Journal of Modern History*, 43:4 (December 1971), 577–597.

Kleyser, Friedrich. *Der Flugschriftenkampf gegen Ludwig XIV. zur Zeit des pfälzischen Krieges.* Berlin, 1935.

Knachel, Philip A. *England and the Fronde.* Ithaca, 1967.

Köpeczi, B. *La France et la Hongrie au début du XVIIIᵉ siècle.* Budapest, 1971.

Koser, R. "Das Politische Testament Karls V. von Lothringen von 1687." *Historische Zeitschrift*, 48 (1882), 45–94.

Kramnick, I. *Bolingbroke and His Circle: The Politics of Nostalgia in the Age of Walpole.* Cambridge, Mass., 1968.

Kulstein, David I. *Napoleon III and the Working Class: A Study of Government Propaganda under the Second Empire.* Los Angeles, 1969.

Lanette-Claverie, Claude. "La Librairie française en 1700." *Revue française d'histoire du livre*, N.S., 2:3 (1972), 3–31.

Ledré, Charles. *Histoire de la presse.* Paris, 1958.

Legrelle, A. *La Diplomatie française et la succession d'Espagne.* 6 vols. Paris, 1895–1899.

Lévy, Claude-Frédéric. *Capitalistes et pouvoir au siècle des lumières.* Paris & The Hague, 1969.

Lewis, P. S. *Late Medieval France: The Polity.* London, 1968.

Livet, Georges. *L'Intendance d'Alsace sous Louis XIV.* Paris, 1956.

―――. "Louis XIV et l'Allemagne." *XVIIe Siècle,* Nos. 46–47 (1960), pp. 29–53.

―――. "Problèmes rhénanes du XVIIe siècle. Libelles et pamphlets à la fin du XVIIe siècle. Strasbourg entre la France et l'Empire." *Cahiers de l'Association interuniversitaire de l'Est* (Strasbourg), No. 6 (1964), pp. 23–31.

Lombard, A. *L'Abbé Du Bos, un initiateur de la pensée moderne, 1670–1742.* Paris, 1913.

Longin, E. *François de Lisola.* Dôle, 1900.

Lottin, A. *Vie et mentalité d'un lillois sous Louis XIV.* Lille, 1968.

McInnes, Angus. *Robert Harley.* London, 1970.

MacLachlan, A. D. "The Road to Peace, 1710–1713." In *Britain After the Glorious Revolution,* ed. G. Holmes. London, 1969.

Major, J. Russell. *Representative Institutions in Renaissance France.* Madison, 1960.

Malssen, P.J.W. *Louis XIV d'après les pamphlets répandus en Hollande.* Amsterdam, 1936.

Mandrou, Robert. *Louis XIV en son temps, 1661–1715.* Paris, 1973.

Marchand, J. *La Mission extraordinaire du Marquis de Torcy et son voyage en Danemark-Norvège et en Suède, 1685.* Paris, 1951.

―――. "La Vie du Marquis de Torcy." *Revue d'histoire diplomatique,* 46 (1932), 310–343; 47 (1933), 51–76, 189–214.

Martin, Henri-Jean. *Livre, pouvoirs et société à Paris au XVIIe siècle, 1598–1701.* 2 vols. Geneva, 1969.

―――. "Un polemiste sous Louis XIV: Eustache Le Noble

(1643–1711)." *Positions des thèses de l'Ecole des Chartes* (1947), pp. 85–91.

Mathiez, A. "La Place de Montesquieu dans l'histoire des doctrines politiques du XVIIIᵉ siècle. *Annales de la Révolution française*, 7 (1930), 97–112.

Meinecke, Friedrich. "Montesquieu, Boulainvilliers, Dubos. Ein Beitrag zu Entstehungsgeschichte des Historismus." *Historische Zeitschrift*, 145 (1931), 53–68.

Mélèse, Pierre. *Un homme de lettres au temps du Grand Roi, Donneau de Visé, fondateur du Mercure galant.* Paris, 1936.

―――. *Répertoire analytique des documents contemporains d'information et de critique concernant le théâtre à Paris sous Louis XIV, 1659–1715.* Paris, 1934.

―――. *Le Théâtre et le public à Paris sous Louis XIV.* Paris, 1934.

Merland, M.-A. "Tirage et vente de livres à la fin du XVIIIᵉ siècle: des documents chiffrés." *Revue française d'histoire du livre*, N.S., 3:5 (1973), 87–112.

Meyer, R. *Die Flugschriften der Epoche Ludwigs XIV. Eine Untersuchung der in schweizerischen Bibliotheken enthaltenen Broschüren, 1661–1679.* Basel, 1955.

Michaud, L. G. *Biographie universelle.* 85 vols. Paris, 1811–1862.

Moulinas, René. "Les Journaux publiés à Avignon et leur diffusion en France jusqu'en 1768." *Provence historique*, 18 (1968), 121–138.

Mousnier, Roland. *L'Assassinat d'Henri IV, 14 Mai 1610.* Paris, 1964. Translated by Joan Spencer as *The Assassination of Henry IV.* London, 1973.

―――. "Les Idées politiques de Fénelon." *XVIIᵉ Siècle*, Nos. 12–14 (1951–1952), 190–206.

Neveu, Bruno. "La Vie érudite à la fin du XVIIᵉ siècle d'après les papiers du P. Léonard de Sainte-Catherine (1695–1706)." *Bibliothèque de l'Ecole des Chartes*, 124 (1966), 432–511.

New Cambridge Modern History. Vol. 5: *The Ascendancy of France, 1648–1688*, ed. F. L. Carsten. Cambridge, 1961.

Nicéron, Jean-Pierre. *Mémoires pour servir à l'histoire des hommes illustres dans la république des lettres*. 43 vols. Paris, 1727–1745.

Orcibal, Jean. *Louis XIV contre Innocent XI*. Paris, 1949.

Palmer, R. R. "The National Idea in France Before the Revolution." *Journal of the History of Ideas*, 1 (1940), 95–111.

Pappas, John N. *Berthier's Journal de Trévoux and the Philosophes*. Geneva, 1957.

Parguez, G. "Essai sur l'origine lyonnaise d'éditions clandestines de la fin du XVIIe siècle." In *Nouvelles études lyonnaises*. Geneva, 1969.

Picavet, C.-G. *La Diplomatie française au temps de Louis XIV (1661–1715)*. Paris, 1930.

Place, Richard. "The Self-Deception of the Strong: France on the Eve of the War of the League of Augsburg." *French Historical Studies*, 6:4 (1970), 459–473.

Pocock, J.G.A. "Machiavelli, Harrington and English Political Ideologies in the 18th Century." *William and Mary Quarterly*, ser. 3, 22:4 (1965), 549–583.

Pottinger, David T. *The French Book Trade in the Ancien Régime, 1500–1791*. Cambridge, Mass., 1958.

Pribram, Alfred F. *Franz Paul, Freiherr von Lisola, 1613–1674, und die Politik seiner Zeit*. Leipzig, 1894.

Price, J. M. "A Note on the Circulation of the London Press, 1704–1714." *Bulletin of the Institute of Historical Research*, 31 (1958), 215–224.

Prutz, Hans. *Aus den Grossen Kurfürsten letzten Jahren*. Berlin, 1897.

Puaux, F. *Les Défenseurs de la souveraineté du peuple sous le règne de Louis XIV*. Paris, 1917.

Quéniart, Jean. *L'Imprimerie et la librairie à Rouen au XVIIIe siècle*. Paris, 1970.

Ranum, Orest. *Paris in the Age of Absolutism: An Essay*. New York, 1968.

————, ed. *National Consciousness, History and Political Culture in Early Modern Europe.* Baltimore, 1975.

Redlich, Oswald. "Das angebliche Politische Testament eines Ministers Kaiser Leopolds I." In *Aus Politik und Geschichte. Gedächtnisschriften für Georg von Below.* Berlin, 1928.

Richards, James O. *Party Propaganda under Queen Anne: The General Elections of 1702–1713.* Athens, Ga., 1972.

Ringhoffer, Carl. *Die Flugschriften-Literatur zu Beginn des spanisches Erbfolgekrieges.* Berlin, 1881.

Rosenfield, Leonora Cohen. *From Beast-Machine to Man-Machine. The Theme of Animal Soul in French Letters from Descartes to La Mettrie.* New York, 1940.

Rosenlehner, A. *Die Stellung der Kurfürstern Max-Emmanuel von Bayern und Joseph Klement von Köln zur Kaiserwahl Karls VI (1711).* Munich, 1900.

Roth, William. "Jean-Baptiste Colbert, Marquis de Torcy." In Roland Mousnier, *Le Conseil du roi de Louis XIII à la Révolution.* Paris, 1970.

Rothkrug, Lionel. *Opposition to Louis XIV: The Political and Social Origins of the French Enlightenment.* Princeton, 1965.

Rousset, C. *Histoire de Louvois et de son administration politique et militaire.* 4 vols. Paris, 1861–1863.

Roux, René. "Les Missions politiques de Jean de la Chapelle, de l'Académie française (1655–1723)." *Revue d'histoire diplomatique,* 40 (1926), 239–281.

Rowen, Herbert H. *The Ambassador Prepares for War: The Dutch Embassy of Arnauld de Pomponne.* The Hague, 1957.

————. "Arnauld de Pomponne: Louis XIV's Moderate Minister." *American Historical Review,* 61:3 (1956), 531–549.

Rule, John C. "France and the Preliminaries to the Gertruydenberg Conference, September 1709 to March 1710." In *Studies in Diplomatic History: Essays in Memory of David Bayne Horn.* London, 1970.

Rule, John C. "King and Minister, Louis XIV and Colbert de Torcy." In *William III and Louis XIV*, ed. R. Hatton and J. S. Bromley. Liverpool, 1968.

———, ed. *Louis XIV and the Craft of Kingship*. Columbus, Ohio, 1969.

Salomon, F. *Geschichte des letzten Ministeriums Königin Annas von England (1710–1714)*. Gotha, 1894.

Sauvy, Anne. *Livres saisis à Paris entre 1678 et 1710*. The Hague, 1972.

Schmidt, Paul. "Deutsche Publizistik in den Jahren 1667–1671." *Mitteilungen der Institut für österreichischen Geschichte*, 28 (1907), 577–630.

Seguin, Jean-Pierre. *L'Information en France de Louis XII à Henri II*. Geneva, 1961.

Sgard, J. "Table chronologique des périodiques de langue française avant la Révolution." In M. Couperus, *L'Etude des périodiques anciens*. Utrecht, 1970.

Small, Melvin. "Historians Look at Public Opinion." In *Public Opinion and Historians: Interdisciplinary Perspectives*, ed. Melvin Small. Detroit, 1970.

Solomon, Howard M. *Public Welfare, Science and Propaganda in Seventeenth-Century France: The Innovations of Théophraste Renaudot*. Princeton, 1972.

———. "The *Gazette* and Antistatist Propaganda: The Medium of Print in the First Half of the Seventeenth Century." *Canadian Journal of History* (April 1974), pp. 1–17.

Soman, Alfred. "The Theatre, Diplomacy and Censorship in the Reign of Henri IV." *Bibliothèque d'Humanisme et Renaissance*, 25:2 (1973), 273–288.

Sprunck, A. "La première Gazette du Duché de Luxembourg." *Annales de l'Institut archéologique de Luxembourg* (Arlon), 92 (1961).

Stone, Lawrence. "Literacy and Education in England, 1640–1900." *Past and Present*, No. 42 (February 1969), 69–139.

Stork-Penning, J. G. "The Ordeal of the States—Some Remarks on Dutch Politics during the War of the Spanish Succession." *Acta Historiae Neerlandica II.* Leiden, 1967.

Tapié, V.-L. "Quelques aspects généraux de la politique étrangère de Louis XIV." *XVIIe Siècle*, Nos. 41–47 (1960), pp. 3–26.

Thuau, E. *Raison d'état et pensée politique à l'époque de Richelieu.* Paris, 1966.

Trevelyan, G. M. *England under Queen Anne.* 3 vols. London, 1930–1934.

Trout, Andrew P. "The Proclamation of the Peace of Nijmegen." *French Historical Studies*, 5:4 (Fall 1968), 477–481.

Tyvaert, Michel. "L'Image du Roi: Légitimité et moralité royales dans les histoires de France au XVIIe siècle." *Revue d'histoire moderne et contemporaine*, 21 (1974), 521–547.

Vaillé, E. *Le Cabinet noir.* Paris, 1950.

Vanel, J.-B. *Une Nouvelliste lyonnaise à la fin du règne de Louis XIV.* Lyon, 1903.

Ventre, Madeleine. *L'Imprimerie et la librairie en Languedoc au dernier siècle de l'Ancien Régime (1700–1789).* Paris, 1958.

Villiers, A. *L'Abbé Eusèbe Renaudot.* Paris, 1904.

Waddell, D. "The Writings of Charles Davenant (1665–1714)." *The Library*, ser. 5, 11:3 (1956), 206–212.

Weber, F. "Hippolithus à Lapide." *Historische Zeitschrift*, 29 (1873), 254–306.

Weill, G. "Les Nouvellistes." In *La Régence.* Paris, 1970.

Wentzcke, Paul. *Johann Frischmann, ein Publizist des 17. Jahrhunderts.* Strasbourg, 1904.

Wickham Legg, L. G. *Matthew Prior: A Study of His Public Career and Correspondence.* Cambridge, 1921.

Wieruszowski, Helene. *Von Imperium zum nationalen Königtum.* Munich, 1933.

Wolf, John B. *Louis XIV.* New York, 1968.

Woodbridge, B. M. *Gatien de Courtilz, Sieur du Verger.* Baltimore, 1925.

Yardeni, M. *La Conscience nationale en France pendant les guerres de religion (1559–1598).* Louvain, 1971.

———. "Gueudeville et Louis XIV, un précurseur du socialisme, critique des structures sociales louis-quatorziennes." *Revue d'histoire moderne et contemporaine,* 19 (1972), 598–620.

———. "Journalisme et histoire contemporaine à l'époque de Bayle." *History and Theory,* 12:2 (1973), 208–229.

Yates, Frances A. *The French Academies of the Sixteenth Century.* London, 1947.

Zipper, Hanns. *Jean de la Chapelle.* Weilburg-Lahn, 1920.

Zwiedineck-Südenhorst, Hans von. *Die öffentliche Meinung in Deutschland, 1650–1700.* Stuttgart, 1888.

INDEX

Library of Congress Cataloging in Publication Data

Klaits, Joseph.
    Printed propaganda under Louis XIV.

        Bibliography: p.
        Includes index.
        1. France—Politics and government—1643–1715.
2. Public opinion—France.   3. Propaganda, French.
I. Title.
DC128.5.K58   354'.44'00751   76-3268
ISBN 0-691-05238-7